Consortium Project

Knowledge Acquisition:
Principles and Guidelines

KAREN L. MCGRAW
COGNITIVE TECHNOLOGIES, ANNAPOLIS, MD

KARAN HARBISON-BRIGGS
UNIVERSITY OF TEXAS AT ARLINGTON

PRENTICE HALL, ENGLEWOOD CLIFFS, NEW JERSEY 07632

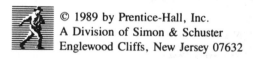 © 1989 by Prentice-Hall, Inc.
A Division of Simon & Schuster
Englewood Cliffs, New Jersey 07632

Printed in the United States of America

10 9 8 7 6 5 4 3 2 1

ISBN 0-13-516436-2

Prentice-Hall International (UK) Limited, *London*
Prentice-Hall of Australia Pty. Limited, *Sydney*
Prentice-Hall Canada Inc., *Toronto*
Prentice-Hall Hispanoamericana, S.A., *Mexico*
Prentice-Hall of India Private Limited, *New Delhi*
Prentice-Hall of Japan, Inc., *Tokyo*
Simon & Schuster Asia Pte. Ltd., *Singapore*
Editora Prentice-Hall do Brasil, Ltda., *Rio de Janeiro*

Contents

Preface

It is with considerable pleasure that I accepted the offer to write the preface for Knowledge Acquisition: Principles and Guidelines. At the same time, the task holds considerable trepidation for me. For just as its authors have taken the risk of exposing their professional beliefs for the first time, so too, am I--this is my first preface.

I believe the professional knowledge engineer, as well as those aspiring to become such, will find the hefty work of Knowledge Acquisition: Principles and Guidelines to be very useful. After reviewing various versions of it a total of three times, I still find several gems tucked away. The first section contains guidelines which have "long" been part of the expert system development methodology folklore. How refreshing it is to see them collected, codified, and backed up by the authors' considerable professional experience, as well an unparalleled bibliography. Of special interest to me is the work detailed regarding the difficulties of garnering expertise from multiple experts, *and* some solutions.

The later chapter on tools is an excellent place to begin research, so long as the reader understands that this is an extremely rapidly changing arena. But the authors look beyond transitory features and trends and concentrate on the underlying issues and characteristics of a wide variety of tools available for the professional. I am particularly encouraged to see such attention paid to software tools. Just because we are "professionals" hardly means we are forced to rely solely on pencil, paper, and those "high-tech" tools of audio and video recorders! As a practicing software professional for 25+ years, it has always pained me how we consistently build very powerful and useful tools for others, yet persist in using paper and pencil when trying to do the critical work of needs assessment, requirements analysis, and specification. Only in the last few years has the concept of applying powerful software tools to the front-end of the software life cycle begun to make its appearance in the guise of Computer-Aided Software Engineering (CASE). This was possible only after some common methodologies were increasingly widespread (i.e., Yourdon/DeMarco and Gane/Sarson).

By the same token, I can see that the methodology espoused in Knowledge Acquisition: Principles and Guidelines may well begin to lay substantial groundwork for the field of knowledge engineering. Others will take up the challenge of building the automated tools to support the methods presented. So it is exciting to think that this work may have such an influence.

The initial primary audience for this work will probably be those in the software engineering world. Hence, these individuals will find the chapters on the subject to be a good introduction to the world of knowledge engineering. The analogies to software engineering are manifold, with considerable contributions from the field. By the same token, software engineers (and others) who take the time to read, understand, and discuss the material presented here will find their set of skills expanded considerably. More importantly, I believe, is that the reader will be able to formulate solutions for problem domains once considered intractable. That, perhaps, is the essence of expert knowledge-based systems and the associated critical component of knowledge acquisition: that we will now be able to attack an increasingly complex set of problems which confront the world.

In summary, this book will be a key addition to the library of a professional. It is not intended to be an introductory text for the field of expert systems. There are many such excellent works. Nor is it simply a cataloguing of several papers on knowledge acquisition. It is a comprehensive, detailed, and first-hand account of an unusually literate professional on a very timely topic. I am sure the reader will agree!

Kenneth L. Modesitt
Chatsworth, California
May 20, 1988

Acknowledgments

Developing a book that reflects an integration of research and current development efforts requires the assistance of many professionals. Initially, we wish to thank the many knowledge engineers and domain experts who have worked with us on both small and large expert system development projects. We have taught each other much--and many of our shared "lessons learned" lie between the covers of this book.

In finalizing the contents of this book, we gratefully acknowledge assistance from colleagues in both university and corporate environments. In particular, we appreciate the suggestions and/or helpful reviews that the following individuals contributed:

Dr. Ken Modesitt, Rocketdyne, a Division of Rockwell International
Major Steve LeClair, Air Force Wright Aeronautical Laboratories
Dr. Robert Hoffman, Adelphi University
Dr. Nancy Martin, SoftPert Systems
Mr. John Boose, Boeing Computer Services
Dr. Bill Derr, Arizona State University
Ms. Kathy Palko, Texas Instruments
Mr. Stephen Kennedy, Grimes Insurance
Ms. Mary Seale, Texas Instruments and North Texas State University
Ms. Barbara Brown, Texas Instruments
Mr. Vince Waldron, Ohio State University and Waldron Communications
Ms. Kathy Waldron, Waldron Communications
Mr. Bruce McGraw, Falcon Microsystems
Mr. Artie Briggs, the H-B Group

Additionally, we salute the members of our families and the people with whom we currently work--both groups have displayed extraordinary patience and support, without which we could not have finished this project. Finally, we have benefitted from the editorial expertise of Ms. Valerie Ashton, Ms. Lisa Garboski, and Ms. Joyce Turner, our editors at Prentice-Hall, and Mr. E. David Zwiegl and Cognitive Technologies, who prepared the text for publication using Macintosh™ computers and Quark XPress™.

About This Book

The fascination with expert systems applications is evidenced by the appearance of expert system-related articles not only in academic journals but, more recently, in the business press. Some researchers (Partridge, 1986) claim that in the very near future, operational expert systems will be able to offer advice ranging from assistance in planning a complex business trip to sophisticated medical diagnosis.

Perhaps the prevailing enthusiastic view is based on the increasing number of successful expert systems. Expert systems are helping maintenance personnel diagnose specific types of system failures, offering financial planning advice, assisting with resource management problems, and even configuring complex computer hardware. In addition, the enhanced memory and speed of personal computers (PCs) and the concurrent development of PC-based expert system shells have propelled expert system technology out of the labs and into the marketplace.

However, problems in the development, maintenance, and enhancement of expert systems may severely restrict their integration into operational settings. While some of these problems relate to hardware deficiencies, such as the need for "real-time" processing, we believe that many others involve faulty knowledge-base development methodologies. In fact, the developmental area most often cited as the "bottleneck" in expert system development is knowledge acquisition, the process of extracting and translating expert-level knowledge into rules that become the heart of an expert system.

In this book we propose an organized approach to knowledge acquisition. This approach is based on experiences building both large and small expert systems in research and industrial settings. Within it we detail a set of techniques to help the knowledge engineer structure the knowledge acquisition process, integrating it into the expert system development paradigm. To increase the usefulness of this methodology, we offer guidelines, procedures, and a set of techniques for knowledge acquisition. Finally, we address the problem of evaluating the effectiveness of both the knowledge acquisition session or process itself and the resulting knowledge base.

Purpose and Content

This book presents a practical view of the knowledge acquisition process, its methodologies, and its techniques, in order to enable readers to develop expert system knowledge bases more effectively. It is intended to strike a balance between presenting (1) summaries of research in the field of knowledge acquisition and (2) methodologies and techniques that have been applied and tested on numerous programs in various contexts.

Intended Audience

This book is written for novice knowledge engineers or others tasked with acquiring knowledge for the systematic development of expert systems. Since knowledge engineers tend to come from diverse backgrounds, the presentation of the material does not presume a background in either computer science or artificial intelligence.

Project managers for expert system development projects may also be interested in this book, as it suggests a methodological approach to knowledge acquisition and presents chapters on guidelines and techniques that knowledge engineers can use to accomplish their tasks more effectively.

Structure

This text is structured in two parts. Part One includes Chapters 1 through 3 and presents background information to help the reader develop a successful knowledge acquisition methodology and program. Part Two, consisting of Chapters 4 through 11, describes suggested knowledge acquisition techniques, together with guidelines and considerations for their use.

Advance Organizers

Techniques to increase a reader's readiness for a chapter's content include the use of a Contents Page, Introduction, Objectives, and Key Terms.

Contents Page. Each chapter begins with a structure resembling a table of contents. Its purpose is to provide the reader at a glance with the contents and major focus of the chapter. Scanning the contents page provides the reader with a mindset for the material that will be presented. In addition, readers who are interested in specific sections may skim through the chapter to access them directly.

Introduction. The Introduction provides a context for the topics that will be covered in the chapter, a brief summary of the primary issues that will be discussed, and a general overview of the topics that will be presented.

Objectives. Each chapter was written with a specific set of purposes in mind. These purposes are enumerated in the Objectives section at the beginning of each chapter. Readers may wish to review the objectives prior to reading a chapter in order to select those chapters that best meet their needs. Reviewing the objectives upon completion of the chapter can help solidify the learning process.

Key Terms. The fields of expert systems and knowledge acquisition are laden with specialized terms. Terms that are critical to the comprehension of each chapter are presented at the beginning of each chapter. Each term is boldfaced when it is introduced in the text and it also appears in the Glossary at the end of the book.

Enrichment

The book is designed to encourage the reader to extend his or her understanding of the text through the presentation of Suggested Readings and opportunities for Application.

Suggested Readings. A brief bibliography of materials that provide more information on the topics presented in the chapter appears at the end of each chapter.

Opportunities for Application. Each chapter in Part Two (Chapters 4 through 11) concludes with an application activity. This activity provides an opportunity to extend the reader's understanding of the concepts presented in the chapter.

Chapter Contents

Chapter 1 presents background information on expert systems and the knowledge acquisition process. It concludes with a discussion of some major problems that affect knowledge acquisition to lay the groundwork for the philosophy and purpose of this text.

Chapter 2 reviews traditional software development methodologies and lessons that can be adapted for use in expert system development. It proposes a systems-oriented knowledge acquisition methodology that addresses some of the weaknesses that current literature ascribes to knowledge acquisition. This methodology provides the structure for the topics discussed in the remainder of the book.

Chapter 3 presents a practical, structured approach to knowledge acquisition, from using knowledge acquisition templates and building a knowledge acquisition database, to knowledge base review efforts. This approach includes tested guidelines and procedures that allow the knowledge acquisition process to be managed and controlled, enabling auditability and traceability of the developing knowledge base.

Chapter 4 acknowledges the crucial role played by the domain expert in the knowledge acquisition process and the importance of positive, effective knowledge engineer-domain expert working relationships. We suggest techniques for establishing and maintaining positive relationships, getting the most out of a knowledge acquisition session, and handling common problems.

Chapter 5 investigates the related problems of conceptualizing an expert's domain and analyzing the content of information garnered from knowledge acquisition sessions. It presents graphical, statistical, and other methods to portray domain information, either for use in structuring the knowledge base or as recording/feedback mechanisms.

Chapter 6 discusses the role of analysis techniques, such as task analysis, in a knowledge acquisition methodology. It describes a procedure for using analysis techniques to build a structure for the developing knowledge base and presents specific techniques knowledge engineers can use with different types of knowledge.

Chapter 7 examines the interview as a knowledge acquisition technique, explores how it can be made more efficient, and offers guidelines for planning and conducting knowledge acquisition interviews. It describes basic interview structures, various types of interview sequences, question types and levels, and techniques knowledge engineers can use in interviews to gather more usable knowledge.

Chapter 8 discusses process tracing and protocol analysis as techniques that can help knowledge engineers view and analyze a domain expert's decision-making strategies, priorities, and process. It provides some background on the use of these techniques in other fields, describe how to structure a knowledge acquisition session based on the use of these techniques, and explains how to use results from process tracing sessions.

Chapter 9 considers the rewards and problems associated with knowledge acquisition sessions with multiple experts. It presents guidelines for knowing when to use multiple experts, considerations for selecting multiple experts, techniques that are appropriate for use with multiple experts, and suggestions for using knowledge acquired from multiple sources.

Chapter 10 focuses on the possibilities, appropriateness, and considerations for using automated knowledge acquisition tools, prototypes, and simulations for knowledge acquisition. It discusses the continuum along which knowledge acquisition may be automated and presents examples of some of the current crop of tools.

Chapter 11 explores an area that presents a major challenge to expert system effectiveness, the evaluation of knowledge acquisition effectiveness. It considers the verification-and-validation problem and presents some ongoing methods that developers can use to monitor the effectiveness of both the delivery of knowledge acquisition sessions and the content of the knowledge base.

An **Appendix** is provided for readers who desire more background information on theories related to how humans process and store information (Appendix A) and on disadvantages of verbal reporting (Appendix B).

The **Glossary** presents definitions for key terms used throughout the text.

1

Knowledge Acquisition for Expert Systems

Expert Systems: An Overview

   Examining the Terminology
   Sampling Expert Systems

Knowledge Acquisition in Expert Systems Development

   Conceptualizing Knowledge Acquisition
   Knowledge Acquisition Modes and Approaches
   Knowledge Acquisition Process
   Knowledge Acquisition Stages

Identifying and Tapping Knowledge

   The Nature of Knowledge
   The Relationship Between Knowledge and Expertise

Impediments to Effective Knowledge Acquisition

   Lack of Management and Organization
   Incompletely Trained Knowledge Engineers
   Translating Knowledge from Session to Code
   Knowledge Base Flexibility
   Handling Conflicting or Uncertain Information
   Verification and Validation Procedures

INTRODUCTION

Knowledge acquisition is the most critical element in the development of expert systems. It is both people and time intensive. As expert system development finds its way out of research labs and into the business world, the cost of being people and time intensive will impact the success of a project. Current development methodologies stress the rapid prototyping approach, which provides few guidelines and procedures to help a knowledge engineer organize the knowledge acquisition process.

This chapter provides the reader with a foundation for the study of knowledge acquisition in expert systems development. This foundation helps one understand the "state of the art," typical problems, and critical issues. First, we provide an overview of expert systems, knowledge engineering, and knowledge acquisition, followed by a discussion of the various approaches or modes that have been used to acquire knowledge. Next, we present a historical view of knowledge acquisition stages. Subsequently, we provide information on the nature of knowledge, and we address problems associated with its identification and extraction. We discuss both the importance of knowledge and expertise in knowledge acquisition and the difficulties they present the knowledge engineer. In the final section we explore some of the impediments to expert systems development with which knowledge acquisition is associated.

OBJECTIVES

This chapter presents information on vocabulary, concepts, and problems related to knowledge acquisition. Specifically, it enables readers to accomplish the following:
- Understand basic terminology and concepts related to expert system development and knowledge acquisition
- Identify historical and current approaches to expert system development and knowledge acquisition
- Conceptualize the various categories of knowledge that must be acquired
- Identify difficulties in the acquisition of knowledge from domain experts
- Recognize impediments to the successful application of current approaches

Key Terms

knowledge engineering	expert systems	knowledge acquisition
rapid prototyping	knowledge engineer	domain expert
knowledge base	heuristics	declarative knowledge
semantic knowledge	procedural knowledge	episodic knowledge
concept	concept hierarchy	salient features
metaknowledge	model approach	team approach
brittle	chunking	knowledge elicitation
user interface	induction	inference engine

EXPERT SYSTEMS: AN OVERVIEW

Because the focus of this text is on the knowledge acquisition process, it is important to understand vocabulary that is related to knowledge acquisition. The following sections provide explanations and context for key terms and examples of existing expert systems.

Examining the Terminology

The terminology presented below, although not all-inclusive, provides a useful framework for understanding the process of knowledge acquisition and its role in expert system development.

Expert Systems

In an introductory handbook on Artificial Intelligence (AI), Mishkoff (1985) defines **expert systems** or "knowledge-based systems" as computer programs that contain both declarative knowledge (facts about objects, events, and situations) and procedural knowledge (information about courses of action) to emulate the reasoning processes of human experts in a particular domain or area of expertise. Harmon and King (1985) define expert systems as AI programs designed to represent human expertise in a specific domain. The more specialized and identifiable the domain or problem area, the more successful developers seem to be in acquiring, structuring, and representing domain knowledge in knowledge bases.

Typical expert system application areas include diagnosis, planning, instruction and management, monitoring, and design. Diagnosis, for example, has long been a popular expert system application area. Some of the first expert systems used a domain expert's **heuristics** ("rules of thumb") to advise on diagnosis within restricted fields (e.g., pulmonary, internal) of medicine (Shortliffe, Buchanan, & Feigenbaum, 1979). Such programs typically prompt for user input in response to questions about symptoms that may be present. The expert system uses this input in combination with rules in the knowledge base to suggest possible diagnoses with attached "certainties" or probabilities (i.e., a rating as to how probable this diagnosis is in light of the present symptoms and contents of the knowledge base). A key feature is that, when requested by the user, the system offers justifications or explanations for suggesting a specific diagnosis. The user is able to understand the reasoning process used to modify the diagnosis based on information the system might not have had. Thus, the human expert remains in control, using the expert system as a job aid.

Components. Expert systems are composed of at least three basic entities: the knowledge base, an inference engine, and a user interface. The **knowledge base** contains rules expressing an expert's heuristics for the domain. The **inference engine** is made up of rules that are used to control how the rules in the knowledge base are used or processed. The **user interface** allows communication or interaction between the expert system and an end user (Figure 1-1).

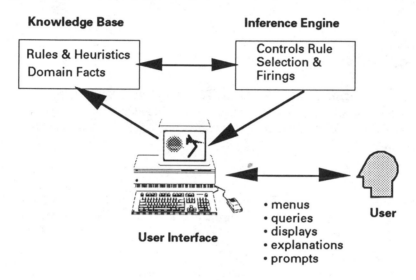

Figure 1-1. Components of an Expert System

A knowledge base contains facts about the domain and heuristics for using them. For example, a knowledge base for an expert system that troubleshoots automotive faults would contain facts that name the various systems (e.g., fuel, electrical), definitions of the relationships between these facts, and attributes that set normal and tolerance limits for the systems. An inference engine directs or controls the operation of the expert system. In other words, the inference engine "drives" the expert system, deciding which rules to fire, how they will be applied, when the process is complete, and when a possible solution can be suggested. In our automotive example, the inference engine would contain instructions for using the rules in the knowledge base about the car's various systems to diagnose the cause for a particular problem. Finally, the user interface allows the user to input questions or specific information to the expert system or to receive explanations and other responses from the expert system. Common techniques or devices that enable this communication include the keyboard, mouse, and touch screens. Response from the expert system may include screen-displayed recommendations, explanations, or requests for more information.

Knowledge Engineering

Knowledge engineering is the term used to describe the overall process of developing an expert system. The text, <u>Building Expert Systems</u> (Hayes-Roth, et al., 1983) defines it both as the discipline that addresses the task of building expert systems and as the tools and methods that support expert system development. The task of building an expert system involves information gathering, domain familiarization, analysis, and design efforts. In addition, accumulated knowledge must be translated into code, tested, and refined. The goal of the knowledge engineering process is to capture and incorporate a domain expert's fundamental domain knowledge, as well as his or her prediction and control processes. The end result of the knowledge engineering process should be strong, robust performance on the part of the expert system (Kahn, et al., 1985).

Knowledge engineering involves a variety of personnel. Expert system development team size depends on the complexity and breadth of the desired system, available domain expertise, and of course, funding. Key technical personnel involved in this development effort include knowledge engineers and domain experts.

Knowledge Engineer

A knowledge engineer is the individual responsible for structuring and/or constructing an expert system. A closer examination of this term reveals diverse perspectives on the qualifications and responsibilities of the knowledge engineer. In a 1986 survey of employment within the AI industry, various recruiting firms across the United States were asked basic questions about salary, training, and job qualifications for knowledge engineers. <u>Knowledge Engineering</u> reported that responses to the survey consistently questioned "just what a knowledge engineer is" (1986, p. 2). Figure 1-2 summarizes responses to this question and illustrates the variety of titles currently given to knowledge engineers.

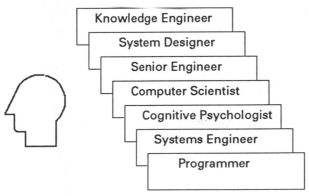

Figure 1-2. Titles Currently Given to Knowledge Engineers

One explanation of the diversity of titles is that it is not unusual for a knowledge engineer's job is to be defined on a program-by-program basis. For example, on one expert system development project, knowledge engineers may be responsible primarily for programming; on another they may be responsible for acquiring and structuring, but not coding, the domain knowledge. Often, the knowledge engineer assumes the tasks similar to those carried out by systems analysts on conventional information systems. These tasks include

- Analyzing information flow
- Determining program structure
- Working with experts to obtain information
- Performing design functions.

Whether or not responsibilities include programming expertise, knowledge engineers must be able to efficiently acquire necessary knowledge, suggest module structures, suggest representation mechanisms, and keep accurate records to enable knowledge traceability. To ask appropriate questions, the knowledge engineer should have some mastery of the domain and be able to identify the type of knowledge that is required. Other skills that seem to be linked to knowledge engineering success include the ability to conceptualize and analyze the domain, its concepts, and interrelationships, and the ability to communicate effectively with domain experts (Figure 1-3).

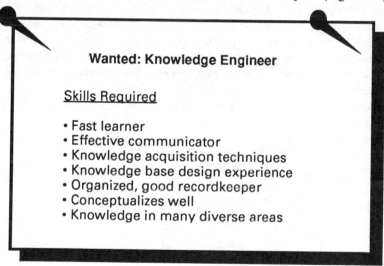

Wanted: Knowledge Engineer

<u>Skills Required</u>

- Fast learner
- Effective communicator
- Knowledge acquisition techniques
- Knowledge base design experience
- Organized, good recordkeeper
- Conceptualizes well
- Knowledge in many diverse areas

Figure 1-3. Knowledge Engineer Skills

Domain Expert

Knowledge is the key to expert system functionality. In most cases the source for this knowledge is the domain expert. A **domain expert** is an individual selected for expertise in a given field and for his or her ability to communicate that knowledge. Many variables determine the qualifications of a domain expert, including whether he or she is "practicing" (currently active in the domain) or "experienced" (not currently active in the domain). Domain experts are often retiring "sole sources" of information whose expertise companies wish to preserve. In other cases multiple domain experts may be called on to offer expertise that can be combined and shared among less expert workers. Whatever his or her initial *professional* role, a person's ability to serve as a domain expert will depend on characteristics such as the ability to

- Explain important knowledge or heuristics
- Be introspective
- Be patient
- Communicate effectively.

Chapter 4 provides more detail on the identification, selection, and use of domain experts.

Sampling Expert Systems

Many existing expert systems represent research or prototype efforts, while others are operational. Some of them serve as "front ends" or intelligent user interfaces to other systems (e.g., large databases), while others are self-contained and are used as decision or job aids. Figure 1-4 provides a tabular view of selected expert systems and the domains in which they operate. These differ in the domains in which they focus, the manner in which they reason, and their success as operational tools. In addition, some have been capable of performing as well as an average individual; others have been used primarily to provide suggestions or to complement human decision making.[1]

EXPERT SYSTEM	ACTIVITY AND DOMAIN
MYCIN (Shortliffe, 1976)	Diagnosing infectious diseases
R1/XCON (McDermott, 1982)	Configures DEC VAX system
PROSPECTOR (Duda, et.al.,1979)	Advises on mineral exploration
MACSYMA (MACSYMA, 1977)	Performs symbolic mathematical tasks
DENDRAL (Buchanan, et al.,1969)	Analyzes chemical experiment data to infer structures of unknown compounds
ISIS (Fox, 1983)	Job shop scheduling conflicts
PUFF (Kunz, et al.,1978)	Diagnoses pulmonary diseases
CADUCEUS (Pople, 1977)	Diagnoses within the realm of internal medicine
COOKER (Herrod & Smith, 1986)	Troubleshooting hydrostatic cookers
COMPASS (Goyal, et al.,1985)	Telephone Switching Maintenance

Figure 1-4. Typical Expert Systems and Their Domains

Knowledge acquisition is concurrently referred to as the most important aspect of expert system development and the most problematic. It alternately has been tagged "knowledge extraction," **"knowledge elicitation,"** and "knowledge acquisition." It refers to the "transfer and transformation of problem-solving expertise" from a knowledge source (e.g., human expert, documents) to a program (Hayes-Roth, 1983). This terminology adequately describes the dual process of extracting and translating expert-level knowledge or "heuristics" (rules of thumb) into rules.

Conceptualizing Knowledge Acquisition

To understand the knowledge acquisition process, one must have a general picture of its role in expert system development (Figure 1-5). Traditional knowledge acquisition can be best understood in the larger context of knowledge engineering, the process of acquiring knowledge and building an expert system (Feigenbaum, 1977). In fact, some authors (Buchanan, et al., 1983) suggest that the term "knowledge engineering" has become almost synonymous with the method by which an expert interacts with a knowledge engineer to build an expert system. The knowledge engineering process encompasses both (1) the task of reducing an exhaustive body of diverse domain knowledge into a precise, easily modifiable set of facts and rules and (2) the tools and methods that support expert system development.

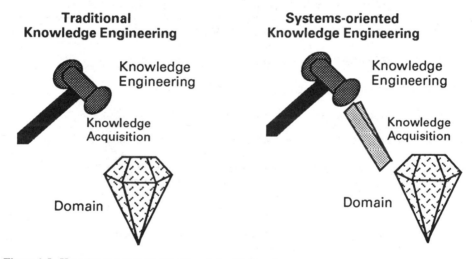

Figure 1-5. Knowledge Acquisition in Knowledge Engineering

The idea of acquiring knowledge from an expert in a given field for the purpose of designing a specific presentation of the acquired information is not new. Reporters, journalists, writers, announcers, and instructional designers have been practicing "knowledge acquisition" for years. In addition to these non-computer science personnel, systems analysts have functioned in a very similar role in the design and development of conventional software systems. The knowledge engineer's responsibilities and the tasks that are required to develop accurate knowledge bases parallel in many ways those of the systems analysts.

As Figure 1-5 illustrates, traditional knowledge engineering applies knowledge acquisition as a "brute force" mechanism to extract information from the domain. Within the systems approach to development that we describe in Chapter 2, knowledge acquisition is the "chisel" that allows knowledge engineers to extract domain information in a more structured fashion.

Knowledge Acquisition Modes and Approaches

There are a number of ways to approach knowledge acquisition for expert systems development. Parsaye (1985) visualizes three major approaches.
- Interviewing experts
- Learning by being told
- Learning by observation.

In reality, none is used to the total exclusion of the others. In some cases, a hybrid approach is adopted. In others, a single approach serves as primary for one phase of development, while additional approaches are adopted for use in later stages.

The first approach entails having the knowledge engineer meet with and extract domain knowledge from a human expert and program it into the knowledge base. It can be very tedious and requires that the knowledge engineer have a multitude of skills (e.g., communications, conceptualization, etc.). It also places great demands on the domain expert, who must be able not only to demonstrate expertise but also to express it. However, it requires little equipment, is highly flexible, portable, and can yield a considerable amount of information if the knowledge engineer is trained in its use.

The second approach, learning by being told, requires that the expert-system user interface be able to conduct a "dialogue" with the expert for the purpose of securing the necessary information. In this approach, the expert is responsible for expressing and refining his or her own knowledge, and the knowledge engineer handles design work and clarifies expert activity. A number of current knowledge acquisition tools are based on this approach and have been used successfully, especially in the domain conceptualization phase of knowledge acquisition. The success of this approach depends on the cooperation of the domain expert, his or her ability to respond to numerous prompts (ranging from binary responses and menus, to scale development techniques), on the premise on which the tool was built, and on the knowledge engineer's use of the information that is acquired.

The third approach, learning by observation, entails allowing the expert system to present the expert with sample problem scenarios or case studies (which the expert solves). A variation involves analyzing examples and previous case histories using a machine learning (Michie, 1982) algorithm. This approach is commonly referred to as **induction**.[2] Induction permits experts to concentrate on formulations of examples from which rules may be automatically derived instead of on how to express their knowledge as heuristics. While they may have difficulty explaining what they know, experts generally are adept at communicating expertise through the use of examples (Arbab &

Michie, 1985). The use of induction in rapid protoyping and incremental development (at both the module and complete system level) is growing rapidly (Modisett, 1988).

One can also investigate the *mode* that is used to acquire the knowledge. Traditionally, knowledge acquisition for expert systems has been approached from two major vantage points, manual and automated acquisition of expertise. Buchanan and others (1983) presented four different modes, each representing a variation of the manual and automated perspective. Figure 1-6 depicts five knowledge acquisition modes, each of which vary along a continuum from manual to automated, based on the knowledge source and the transfer mechanism.

KNOWLEDGE SOURCE   **KNOWLEDGE ACQUISITION MODE**

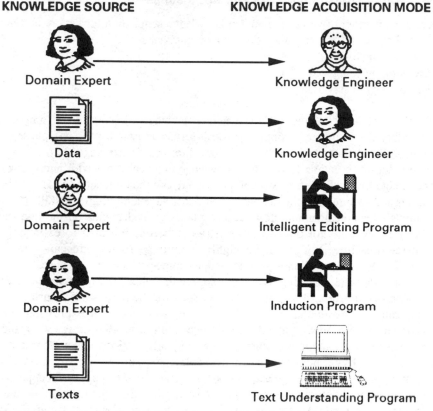

Figure 1-6. Variations in Possible Knowledge Acquisition Mode

The first two knowledge acquisition modes represented in Figure 1-6 are manual in nature and are representative of the majority of current development efforts, while the third, fourth, and fifth modes reflect varying degrees of automation. In the first mode, the knowledge engineer works personally with a domain expert to extract knowledge that is encoded into rules. The second mode depicts the source information residing in data, which could include hard-copy training manuals, videotapes, user manuals, other such material. The knowledge engineer studies the material to determine the rules that are encoded into the knowledge base. The third mode suggests that in some circumstances the domain expert can input his or her conceptual organization and basic heuristics directly into the knowledge base through the use of an intelligent editing program. The fourth mode represents knowledge acquisition through "machine learning," in which an induction program reviews actual scenarios and case studies to "infer" the rules needed in the knowledge base. The final mode represents a futuristic knowledge acquisition mode, in which a computerized text understanding program "reads" diagrams and text in a training manual in order to discern the rules that become a part of the knowledge base.

Technological advances are necessary before the final two modes depicted in Figure 1-6 can be implemented completely. Until these gains are made, knowledge acquisition will be handled manually, or with partial automation, as presented in the first three modes. Within these partially automated modes, differences in knowledge acquisition approaches exist. Two primary approaches are the model approach and the team approach. The **model approach** entails using an existing model that is well-suited to the new domain to develop a set of axioms and rules. The model approach was used to develop PUFF (Kunz, 1978). In the **team approach**, a domain expert and a knowledge engineer work closely together for an extended period and produce a model and computer program that is comparable in performance to human specialists. The team approach was used to develop PROSPECTOR (Duda, 1978), INTERNIST (Miller, Pople, & Myers, 1982), and R1/XCON (McDermott, 1981).

Knowledge Acquisition Process

Previous authors have identified various phases or stages of the knowledge acquisition process. In most depictions, expert system development takes place using a general methodology known as **rapid prototyping**. Rapid prototyping entails the selection and rapid development of a section of the expert system, testing on the partial system, iterative refinement, and further development.

This methodology is based on the belief that once initial design and knowledge-base decisions have been made, a subset of the total expert system (i.e., a prototype) should be developed very rapidly to allow developers to test their conceptions of design, knowledge representation, and processing. For example, as the small "slice" of the system is completed, developers learn whether or not the selected implementation tool is adequate to meet the processing requirements of the system (e.g., speed). Additionally, they can determine whether or not the initial design seems optimum. The prototype expert system may not be very "smart" and later development iterations may be required to expand the depth and breadth of coverage.

The use and benefits of rapid prototyping are exemplified by the expert system, COOKER, developed jointly by Texas Instruments and Campbell Soup (Herrod & Smith, 1986). One month after the first knowledge acquisition session between the TI knowledge engineer and Campbell Soup's domain expert, the developers returned to Campbell with a prototype system. Although the prototype contained only 32 rules and its knowledge did not have much depth, it "served as a catalyst for uncovering a vast wealth of cooker knowledge previously not thought relevant by the expert" (p. 17). Concurrently, it allowed management to receive some tangible evidence of what this expert system might be able to do, which helped control expectations and eventually led to an expansion of the system's capabilities.

Knowledge Acquisition Stages

In the most widely supported view of knowledge acquisition stages, Buchanan, Barstow, Bechtal, Bennett, and others (1983) subdivide knowledge acquisition activities throughout the life of an expert system development project into the following major tasks:

• Initially entering knowledge
• Reducing or avoiding erroneous knowledge
• Augmenting acquired knowledge.

To explain this view, these authors present a framework for knowledge acquisition that identifies the major stages as identification, conceptualization, formalization, implementation, and testing (Figure 1-7).

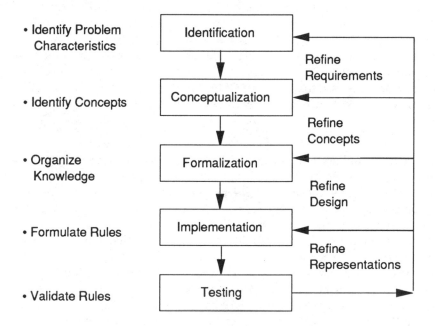

Figure 1-7. Knowledge Acquisition Stages
Adapted from <u>BUILDING EXPERT SYSTEMS.</u> © 1983, Addison-Wesley Publishing Co., Inc., Reading, Massachusetts. Adapted from Fig. 5.5 Reprinted with permission.

Identification refers to the process of characterizing key problem aspects, including "participants, characteristics, resources, and goals" (p.141). During this stage the knowledge engineer becomes familiar with the domain, sets initial development goals, and selects appropriate, available domain experts and other source materials.

Conceptualization involves specifying how the primary concepts and key relationships among the concepts in the domain are depicted and related by domain experts. This very difficult step may entail conceptually mapping the assumed organization of knowledge.

Formalization requires the knowledge engineer to "map" the recognized concepts, subtasks, relations, and other information into formal representation mechanisms. The identification of an underlying model of the process experts use to generate solutions in their domains is an important accomplishment during this stage.

Once formalized, the acquired knowledge is implemented. The *implementation* stage involves funnelling formalized knowledge into a representational framework for the selected expert system development tool. The primary goal of this stage is to develop a "prototype system," which allows developers to test out design and implementation decisions using only a small subset of the eventual knowledge base for an expert system. The knowledge engineer's primary tasks during this phase are to evaluate the selection of a representation scheme and to provide detailed documentation that will link the knowledge base content back to an original source.

The final stage, *testing*, requires that the prototype system be evaluated as to the efficacy of the system's formalization, basic assumptions, accuracy, and knowledge acquisition efficiency. To enable appropriate testing, developers must investigate and select an appropriate test scenario or problem set. Once the chosen scenario has been applied to test the system, results from testing are used to revise the prototype. Common revisions may include reformulating initial concepts, refining knowledge representation schemes and interrelationships, and modifying or reselecting knowledge acquisition methods.

IDENTIFYING AND TAPPING KNOWLEDGE

What we seek to acquire during knowledge acquisition is difficult to define, identify, and isolate. A primary task of the knowledge engineer is to conceptualize what a domain expert knows and uses to solve problems. Thus, before we can acquire knowledge from domain experts, knowledge engineers must have a basic understanding of what knowledge is, how it is stored, and how domain experts access it.

The Nature of Knowledge

Philosophers, writers, books, and entire courses have attempted to answer the question, "What is knowledge?". Feigenbaum (1983) suggests clarifying first that knowledge it is *not* synonymous with information. Rather, knowledge is information that has been interpreted, categorized, applied, and revised.

This refined information can exist in many forms. Waterman (1981) reports that knowledge can be exemplified by concepts, constraints, heuristic methods for using probabilistic data, and principles that govern domain-specific operations. Hayes-Roth (1983) contends that domain knowledge consists of descriptions, relationships, and procedures. More specifically, knowledge consists of (1) symbolic descriptions of definitions, (2) symbolic descriptions of relationships, and (3) procedures to manipulate both types of descriptions. To understand these symbolic descriptions we must investigate the building blocks of knowledge--concepts.

Concepts as Building Blocks

Much as a bricklayer uses individual bricks to build, layer upon layer, a strong structure, humans use individual concepts to create their symbolic understanding of the world. A **concept** is a symbol that stands for a common characteristic or relationship shared by objects or events that are otherwise different (Kagan, 1972). By the time we reach adulthood, we have developed a variety of concepts that enable us to deal more effectively with our world. Metaphorically, concepts of mature, intelligent individuals resemble a library cataloging system. Any single concept may have many "cards" filed beneath it. These cards, or entries, describe definitions, functions, attributes, historical or episodic information, and relationships with other cards (Figure 1-8).

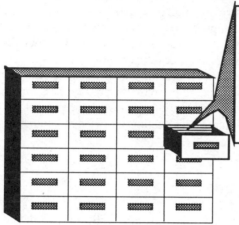

CONCEPT: Horse
DEFINITION: Solid-hoofed quadraped with mane & tail
ATTRIBUTES: large, mammal, mane, tail, hooves, domestic
RELATIONSHIP: Mammal
HISTORICAL: Had horse named "Traveller" at age 12

Figure 1-8. Cataloging Concepts

Salient Features of Concepts

Each of us has definitions for his or her own concepts. These definitions are determined by what *we* perceive to be the attributes and salient features of each concept (Figure 1-9). **Salient features** are those that distinguish the objects, events, or ideas that the concept represents from other concepts. Consider the salient feature(s) of two common, visually-similar substances--sugar and salt. Each of us has experienced and defined these concepts. If asked to describe them, we focus on *color*, *size*, *function*, and *taste*. Our background and current context would influence which features were the most salient. For example, if we were chemists, we might first consider salt as having chemical properties and initially ignore all other attributes. This mental technique allows us to more efficiently store and retrieve important information and indicates the use of concept hierarchies.

Concept Hierarchies. A **concept hierarchy** is a structural taxonomy or arrangement of the associations that make up a concept (Kagan, 1972). Concept hierarchies are usually formed such that the *strongest* associations are at the "top" (i.e., recalled immediately) and the weaker ones toward the "bottom." The concepts we have learned, the way we have structured them into hierarchies, and our system for interweaving them comprise our personal method of organizing our worlds. This organization influences what we choose to attend to, how we perceive inputs, and how we organize what we sense. Consequently, it influences the thinking patterns, judgment, and perception of the domain experts with whom knowledge engineers work.

FEATURES	SALT	SUGAR
COLOR	white	white
TEXTURE	granular	granular
SIZE	small	small
TASTE *	salty	sweet
FUNCTION *	seasoning	sweeten food
	curing	

* salient features

Figure 1-9. Differentiating Between Concepts Using Salient Features

The Relationship Between Knowledge and Expertise

Although we cannot directly observe someone's knowledge, we can observe and learn to identify expertise. There are at least two discernible types of expertise-- expertise that is skill or motor based (e.g., controlling a machine) and expertise that is primarily cognitive (e.g., making a medical diagnosis). In either case, expertise is a demonstration of the application of knowledge. We can actively observe the crane operator's skill in using levers, dials, and switches to maneuver the crane. Likewise, we can observe the effects of a diagnostician's decision processes to isolate the cause of an illness. But what if two individuals both possess similar knowledge? Can we predict that they will demonstrate the same *use* of that knowledge? The answer is no and the difference is the notion of expertise.

Novices and Experts

The nature of expertise has been investigated through research in problem solving. Bhaskar and Simon (1977) report that the differences between experts and novices in "semantically rich" domains of skilled problem solving are both qualitative and quantitative. Not only do experts perform better than novices on quantitative measures, but they also demonstrate qualitative differences in their use of representations and strategies (Adelson, 1984). These differences can be summarized as follows:
- Experts are more knowledgeable about their domain
- Experts can apply and use knowledge more effectively than novices.

The Role of Experience

Research indicates that experience, not innate capacity, is the major differentiator between novices and experts. It influences knowledge organization, storage, and retrieval, heavily contributing to the metamorphosis from novice to expert. To paraphrase Kolodner (1983), experience is the factor that changes unrelated facts into expert knowledge.

It is common for beginning knowledge engineers to focus on how *much* knowledge experts have and what rules they use. There is a tendency for this to result in the development of expert systems that function ineffectively. For even though these expert systems may have the same basic rules as an expert, they may have little of the *refined* knowledge that results from using and applying basic knowledge repeatedly, and in diverse instances or contexts.

Becoming an Expert

Kolodner (1983) contends that there is an "evolution of memory" of knowledge from novice to expert. Initially, knowledge is incrementally refined based on specific episodes in which it is applied and adapted. Facts that at first may have seemed discrete and unrelated later can be grouped based on concurrent use over a number of episodes. Experience using knowledge allows us to refine our reasoning processes and determine the usefulness and adaptability of our existing internal rules. As we monitor the failures and successes that result from rule application and skill performance, certain rules and skills are reinforced or altered.

Knowledge Organization and Expertise

Multiple research efforts suggest that experts and novices differ in their abilities to process large amounts of meaningful information. Enhanced information processing capabilities allow experts to collect, retrieve, and use information more effectively and quickly. This difference has been observed in many domains, including chess, Go, electronics, bridge, music, physics, and computer programming (Chase & Simon, 1973A, 1973b; Reitman, 1976; Sloboda, 1976; Egan & Schwartz, 1979; Engle & Bustel, 1978; Charness, 1976; Larkin, McDermott, Simon, & Simon, 1980; McKeithen, Reitman, Rueter, & Hirtle, 1981).

The organization of an expert's knowledge can be referred to as knowledge compilation. In much the same way a programmer compiles a computer program to enable more efficient processing, so too can an expert compile or store knowledge for efficient use. This technique is advantageous, as it enables experts to optimize their memory capacity, process relevant information quickly, and become less confused by extraneous information (Fisk & Dyer, 1983). An extensive body of research supports the *organization of knowledge* as a major differentiating factor between novices and experts. Chi, Glaser, and Rees (1981) suggest, for example, that the schema the novice uses represents surface features of a problem while the schema an expert uses represents the more abstract, semantic principles. Lewis (1981) observes that experts and novices solve algebra problems in a way that suggests that experts restructure the problem while novices do not. Experts in these target research domains tended to form abstract, conceptual representations of problems before attempting to solve them. Conversely, novices tended to form and use representations that retained the surface elements of the problem (Adelson, 1984).

Chunking. Superior organization of information (not merely more information) seems to be critical to expert performance. Not only do experts have more information, but they organize it into more meaningful "chunks." Chunks are groups of items that are stored and recalled together. Cohen (1966) theorizes that we most often recall all of the items of one chunk before processing subsequent chunks. Consequently, the efficiency of item storage and organization impacts our item recall proficiency. In fact, the organization of information that one seeks to remember is *central* to recall (Bousfield, 1953; Mandler, 1967; Tulving, 1962). Research by Bushke (1976) suggests that the more **chunking** an individual does, the better the recall. Instead of perceiving and recalling discrete pieces of "knowledge," experts process meaningful *groups* of information. The net result is that an expert's perception and recall performance is enhanced (McKeithen, Reitman, Ruete, & Hirtle, 1981).

Impact of Chunking on Knowledge Acquisition

Although chunking is useful to experts, it may inhibit their ability to be cognizant of their own knowledge and express it to others. Research by Fisk and Linville (1980) suggests that experts have somewhat rigid cognitive structures, which may optimize routine information processing, but negatively impact processing. Thus, an expert may be inclined to "see" only one solution path when other, equally effective ones may exist.

Additionally, experts may have difficulty describing their knowledge. As in the programming world, compiled programs are very difficult to interpret. It may be extraordinarily difficult for an expert to de-compile chunked knowledge and translate it from semantic to verbal code. Some researchers (Bruner, Oliver, & Greenfield, 1966; Neisser, 1967; Schiffrin & Schneider, 1977; Simon, 1979) theorize that performance over time becomes more automatic. Behavior that is automatic requires less cognitive awareness. Behavioral awareness hinders an expert's ability to verbally describe the knowledge or essential steps an action or solution requires. Thus, we can conclude that the very factors that assist experts in storing, processing, and retrieving knowledge (e.g., chunking, compiling) can be problematic in settings requiring flexibility and verbalization of knowledge (Figure 1-10).

CHARACTERISTICS OF EXPERTS	IMPACT ON KNOWLEDGE ACQUISITION TASKS
• More, better organized knowledge	• Difficult to de-compile knowledge
• More refined reasoning processes	• Difficult to express knowledge in basic form
• Can evaluate usefulness of heuristics from many diverse applications	• Tendency to express from a preconceived mindset
• Can process meaningful information quickly	• Compiled knowledge is hard to express

Figure 1-10. Characteristics of Experts and Their Impacts on Knowledge Acquisition

IMPEDIMENTS TO EFFECTIVE KNOWLEDGE ACQUISITION

We next examine issues that impede the effectiveness of knowledge acquisition, laying the groundwork for the knowledge acquisition methodology we suggest in Chapter 2.

Numerous researchers have identified knowledge acquisition as the key source of difficulty in expert system development efforts. For example, Buchanan and others (1983) describe knowledge acquisition as "the bottleneck" in expert system development. Cookson and others (1985) refer to knowledge acquisition as the "central problem" in the successful application of expert systems. Gammack and Young (1985) argue that the shortcomings of current knowledge acquisition are due to a mismatch of knowledge and representation schemes and inherent problems with the use of the interview as the primary elicitation method.

Lack of Management and Organization

Unstructured knowledge acquisition may not be fatal in the development of small expert systems projects that require input from only one domain expert and knowledge engineer. When building larger operational systems, however, lack of structure and organization can result in the following:
- Lack of traceability from knowledge source to code
- Redundancy of knowledge gathered
- Increased development time and cost
- Difficulties scoping the focus of knowledge acquisition
- Knowledge that is acquired at the wrong level (e.g., surface-level knowledge where semantic knowledge is needed) or abstraction
- Lack of appropriate documentation
- Wasted knowledge engineer time
- Disgruntled domain experts.

Lessons learned in software development efforts should not be lost on those developing expert systems. For example, in 1982, Kedzierski investigated the question, "What causes the most problems during the development and application of complex interactive software systems?" and discovered that the answer was communication. An informal study concluded that designers spent only one-fifth of their time working with the existing system and that most communication activity was handled by "word of mouth" instead of by the system, by on-line means, or by written project communication files (hard-copy). This led to inefficient or faulty communication. Kedzierski concluded that breakdowns in communication were the cause of major problems in software development or evolution, because communication plays a large part in the programming process. This conclusion parallels that proposed by Keider (1974), who investigated reasons for failure of software development projects in general. Most of the reasons involve communication breakdowns, which result in ineffective project management. Creating an expert system development methodology that provides a structured means of on-line or hard copy communication among team members can reduce project development difficulties and enhance productivity.

Another management-related issue is the time and cost involved in expert system development. Mishkoff (1985, p. 59) relates that, "expert system development is a time-consuming task." Although it may be possible for one or two people to develop a small expert system in a few months, the development of a sophisticated system may require a team of several people working together for more than a year. Much of the time required for development can be attributed to knowledge acquisition. Figure 1-11 illustrates how one development team's time was expended on the domain familiarization stage of a research project.

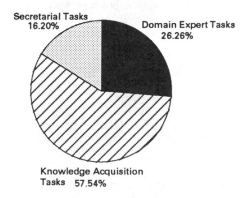

Figure 1-11. Time Expenditure on Domain Familiarization

While it is useful to view project-wide efforts, management must also realize how much time (in hours) and effort a single knowledge engineer expends during planning, conducting, and reviewing one session. Average responses to an informal knowledge acquisition survey taken during the domain-familiarization phase of knowledge acquisition are summarized in Figure 1-12.

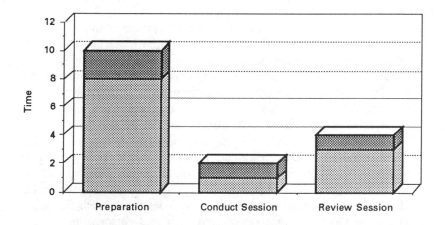

Figure 1-12. Individual Knowledge Engineer Time Spent in Domain Familiarization Phase of Knowledge Acquisition

Thus, a one-hour knowledge acquisition session during the initial phase of knowledge acquisition could take 12 to16 hours from planning to session review, write-up, and initial rule formulations. As the knowledge engineers on the project became more seasoned and familiar with the domain, the time required for preparation decreased dramatically. In later sessions, for example, the average time required to conduct and complete a knowledge acquisition session may be more in the range of 4 to 6 hours.

The anatomy of any single knowledge acquisition session would also yield interesting statistics. An informal TRW report examined the separate subtasks that comprise the knowledge acquisition task. Figure 1-13 shows a breakdown of the types and percentages of knowledge acquisition labor represented.

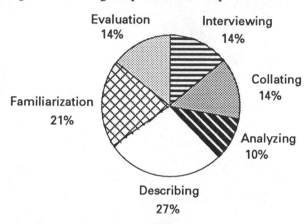

Figure 1-13. Decomposing the Knowledge Acquisition Task

Incompletely Trained Knowledge Engineers

Another major weakness of current knowledge acquisition disguises itself as poor selection and delivery of knowledge acquisition techniques. We argue that this weakness is actually due to incompletely trained knowledge engineers.

What makes a knowledge engineer "effective" depends primarily on the project with which he or she is associated. On small, one-man systems, in which the knowledge engineer, domain expert, and programmer are the same individual, programming skills are the critical element. However, an individual whose expertise is programming may not be as effective if he or she is also required to analyze types of knowledge within a domain, use interpersonal skills to extract knowledge from a domain expert and conceptualize and compartmentalize retrieved knowledge. In addition to the diversity in responsibilities, individuals who become knowledge engineers are often trained in the computer sciences and may not have been trained to use the interview and analysis techniques that are more often taught in the fields of communications and psychology. Yet these skills may be critical to a knowledge engineer's ability to handle the knowledge engineering tasks described above. Appropriate training in the use of various knowledge acquisition techniques, knowledge engineering methodology, and personal interaction and communication skills can lessen complaints of "poorly chosen and delivered techniques."

Translating Knowledge from Session to Code

Another weakness that limits expert system development success and directly impacts the knowledge acquisition process is the difficulty knowledge engineers have tapping, translating, and transferring knowledge from an expert to a knowledge base. For example, it is widely known that human experts solve many problems using "intuition." While most of us understand that intuition is not magical (it is generally based on previous episodes and analogical reasoning), it is nonetheless difficult to tap. How, for example, can a knowledge engineer observe an expert using visual imaging to solve a problem and effectively translate all of the constraints, steps, and considerations into a rule that will allow an expert system to reach a similar conclusion?

Mapping Human Knowledge to Computer Knowledge

A problem related to this question is the selection of knowledge acquisition techniques that enhance a knowledge engineer's ability to tap and extract at least portions of an expert's knowledge. Gammack and Young (1985) contend that part of the problem is our inclination to compare various techniques rather than investigating which techniques seem most *appropriate* for the knowledge within the domain. For example, they propose that knowledge types should be characterized and matched to appropriate knowledge acquisition techniques. They conclude that major knowledge engineering problems include the recognition and analysis of domain knowledge and the ability to select a knowledge acquisition technique that 'matches' the type and nature of the domain knowledge. Figure 1-14 presents one way to categorize knowledge.[3]

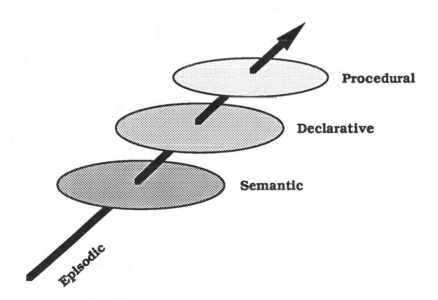

Figure 1-14. Categories of Knowledge

Procedural knowledge includes the skills an individual knows how to perform. It can be likened to "knowing how" to do something. Procedural knowledge involves an automatic response to a stimuli and may be reactionary in nature. Examples of procedural knowledge include learned psychomotor skills, such as executing a sharp turn while riding a bicycle. However, not all procedural knowledge is motor in nature. Knowledge of one's native language is procedural (Anderson, 1980) because while most people have this knowledge, they find it very difficult to state rules that describe precisely how to *use* the language.

The procedures for carrying out these kinds of skills are deeply embedded and linked sequentially. That is, completing one step in the procedure may serve as the mental trigger to complete the next step. Consequently, these "steps" may be so highly compiled that they are difficult for the expert to identify or discuss (McGraw & Riner, 1987). As Anderson (1980) describes, when the same knowledge is used over and over again in a procedure, we lose "access" to it and consequently, our ability to report it. The example he gives to illustrate this principle is our recalling a telephone number without glancing at the dial plate or moving our fingers in the dialing pattern. When the number is first learned, we can both report and dial it. Once we have dialed the number many times, however, some of us may lose the ability to verbally report it. The difficulty that experts may have in sharing procedural knowledge necessitates that knowledge engineers use special techniques to analyze this automatic, reactionary knowledge.

Declarative knowledge equates to "knowing that." It represents surface-level information that experts can verbalize. The primary distinction between procedural and declarative knowledge focuses on the ability to verbalize or express the knowledge. Consider how difficult it would be for most of us to verbally describe how to tie a shoe or ride a bicycle (examples of procedural knowledge) in an accurate manner!

It should be noted that declarative knowledge is useful in the initial stages of knowledge acquisition but is of less value in later stages. Declarative knowledge is an expression of what the expert is aware of knowing. As such, it may not accurately depict the expert's cognitive foundations and concepts that he or she uses to relate the information in a meaningful fashion (McGraw & Riner, 1987).

Semantic knowledge represents one of the two theoretical types of long-term memory. It reflects cognitive structure, organization, and representation. Tulving (1972, 1983) describes it as organized knowledge about the following:
- Words and other verbal symbols
- Word/symbol meanings and usage rules
- Word/symbol referents and interrelationships
- Algorithms for manipulating symbols, concepts, relations.

Because this type of knowledge includes memories for vocabulary, concepts, facts, definitions, and relationships among facts, it is of primary importance to the knowledge engineer (McGraw & Riner, 1987). In fact, it is semantic information that will determine whether or not the expert system actually emulates the work of an expert in the given domain.

Episodic knowledge is autobiographical, experiential information that the expert has grouped or chunked by episodes.[4] Episodic knowledge is theorized to reside in long-term memory. It contains information about "temporally dated episodes or events and temporal-spatial relations among these events" (Tulving, 1972, p. 385). It is believed to be organized by time and place of occurrence and often may be described in terms of perceptual characteristics (Best, 1986).

Wallace (1972) presents a detailed analysis of a type of episodic knowledge that most of use on a daily basis--that of driving to work. Although we use this knowledge daily, we may find it very difficult to abstract any discrete rules about driving a car, speed per stretch, choice of lane, etc. The information is ingrained and chunked episodically to the extent that we may often get to work only to realize that we cannot recall our behavior during certain portions of the trip! Because it is highly compiled and autobiographical, episodic knowledge is one of the most difficult to extract and dissect and may necessitate the use of task analysis techniques and special equipment such as simulators or videotaped task completion episodes (McGraw & Riner, 1987).

Figure 1-15 illustrates a suggested mapping of type of knowledge to knowledge acquisition techniques. Note, for example, that if the knowledge acquisition activity for a particular phase is to "identify general heuristics that are available on a conscious level," the knowledge engineer would be seeking knowledge that is primarily *declarative* in nature. Declarative knowledge is generally available in the short-term memory, which allows the domain expert to express it verbally. In this case, a structured interview might be an appropriate knowledge acquisition technique. However, if the knowledge engineer is seeking to identify "analogical problem solving heuristics," the interview would be far less appropriate because episodic knowledge is very difficult for an expert to relate verbally. In this case, techniques such as simulations and process tracing would be far more appropriate. (Note that the chapter in which each of these techniques is discussed appears to the right of the technique.)

KNOWLEDGE	ACTIVITY	SUGGESTED TECHNIQUE
Declarative Knowledge	Identifying general (conscious) heuristics	Interviews (7)
Procedural Knowledge	Identifying routine procedures/tasks	Structured Interview (7) Process Tracing (8) Simulations (Ch. 10)
Semantic Knowledge	Identifying major concepts/vocabulary	Repertory Grid (5) Concept Sorting (5)
Semantic Knowledge	Identifying decision making procedures and heuristics (unconscious)	Task Analysis (6) Process Tracing (8)
Episodic Knowledge	Identifying analogical problem solving heuristics	Simulations (10) Process Tracing (8)

Figure 1-15. Correlating Knowledge Type and Acquisition Technique

Not only is knowledge type important, but the knowledge acquisition procedures selected should vary depending on phase of development (McGraw & Seale, 1987a). In fact, the two issues are related. One failing of knowledge acquisition in which the interview is the primary technique throughout the development cycle is that this technique is most effective at the beginning of development (e.g., unstructured interviews or tutorials) or after basic knowledge has been acquired (e.g., structured interviews for clarification or content extension). For example, during the domain-familiarization or identification phase of development, knowledge engineers will be most concerned with identifying major concepts, vocabulary, and organizations of the domain. During this phase they may make use of unstructured interviews and content analysis, repertory grid analysis, and concept sorting techniques. Later, when knowledge engineers are most interested in isolating problem-solving heuristics and constraints, the primary technique may be process tracing and protocol analysis.

Expressing Metaknowledge

Metaknowledge can be described as a conscious awareness of what we know and how we use what we know. Individual differences among experts affect their ability to describe what they know. Knowledge engineers must be alert to experts' tendencies to infer "what they know" from what they can remember or describe. Compounding the problem is the fact that not only may experts not have *access* to metaknowledge, but they may not be willing to *admit* its inaccessibility. Experts appear to have a "meta rule" about the human mind that tells them they could retrieve important things if these things were important (Gentner & Collins, 1981). The more a domain expert knows about a topic area, the stronger this assumption.

Dealing with Inexactness

Human experts are not exact (and not necessarily accurate) in expressing their knowledge. They are prone to "guesstimate" based on particular episodes. Their expressions of factors such as distance (How far was it?), time (How long did it take?), sensory perceptions (How loud was it?), and regularity (How often did it happen?) tend to be hard to quantify. As explained in Chapter 4, verbal communication is inherently vague. We speak in generalities that reflect our individual perceptions and structures. Because of this, quantifiers or describers such as "average," "a lot," and "very close" may mean different things to each of us. A knowledge base that embodies certainty weightings based on such vague terms is doomed to fall short of its goal.

Dealing with Diversity

As long as the knowledge engineer develops an expert system based on the inputs of one "authorized" expert, diversity may not be an issue. More than likely, however, knowledge engineers will work with multiple experts when developing an expert system. When this is the case, differences in obtained knowledge, must be considered, evaluated, and represented. For example, if two experts respond differently to a critical question, how does the knowledge engineer resolve the difference (and keep both experts satisfied!)? If resolution can be managed effectively, diversity can enable knowledge engineers to observe different problem-solving approaches and considerations.[5]

Knowledge-Base Flexibility

Lenat and others (1986) point to "brittleness" as one of the major limitations in building complex software systems. McCarthy (1983, p. 129) describes a system as **brittle** if it is "difficult to expand beyond the scope originally contemplated by their designers." A common development approach is to acquire knowledge and build expert systems using a "breadth-first" philosophy. Once the structure is in place, developers can expand an area of the expert system in attempts to deepen the represented knowledge and enhance reasoning ability. Similarly, an expert system may well depend on knowledge that is not static, necessitating that rules be added, deleted, and modified during the course of the system's use. The problem of acquiring and structuring these rules in a manner which enables ease of modifiability must be considered.

Currently, modifying a knowledge base may require a knowledge engineer who is familiar with the design of the expert system and the structure of the knowledge base (Froscher & Jacob, 1985). In fact, the person best suited for this task is most often the knowledge engineer who originally constructed the knowledge base. This presents other problems. For example, the need for modifications may extend over a period of years, during which time turnover of development personnel is expected. Concurrently, an expanded understanding of the system's functionality occurs and may result in many suggestions for changes. A case in point is the R1/XCON system developed at Carnegie-Mellon University (McDermott, 1981; 1982). The purpose of R1/XCON was to configure the components that comprise a DEC VAX 11/780 computer. Since it was developed to be used in an operational setting, it was required to reflect all changes to the VAX computer line. This made it necessary to add more knowledge and expand XCON's capability. Over a period of 7 years, XCON grew to over 6,000 rules, of which 50% change each year (Soloway, Bachant, & Jensen, 1987).

As expert system technology moves from research settings to operational environments, the need for knowledge base flexibility and modifiability will grow because re-implementation will not be operationally feasible. Original programmers will not be available for program maintenance. Knowledge must be acquired, structured, and grouped in ways that allows developers to understand the source of the knowledge, the conditions under which it is valid, relevant rules or considerations, and the effect of modifications.

Partitioning for Modifiability

To date, researchers have proposed several methods for partitioning expert system knowledge bases to make them easier to maintain as well as more understandable and efficient. Selecting one of these approaches depends on the type of expert system that is being developed and the anticipated extent of required modifications. One approach is to develop the system made up of several separate knowledge bases, as is exemplified by PROSPECTOR (Duda, et al., 1978). Another approach (that used by LOOPS) is to use rule sets, that when called, return a single value that is used elsewhere in the knowledge base (Bobrow & Stefik, 1981). A third approach, used by Clancey (1983), is to separate the control strategies (termed meta rules) from the specific domain knowledge; this enables the developer to group rules that contribute to certain goals together in the knowledge base. Froscher and Jacob (1985) suggest subdividing the information in the knowledge base, thus reducing the amount of information that each single programmer must understand to make a change to the knowledge base. To accomplish this, they group rules together based on the principle "If a change is made to one rule, to what extent would the other rule be affected?" (p. 247). Thus, when rules in one group use facts generated by rules in other groups, these facts are flagged to let the knowledge engineer identify values that were set outside of the group. Soloway (et al., 1987) reports that the XCON-in-RIME language features a domain-specific, classification that is imposed on the rules to help ensure "one function, one rule." Modeling the Dewey Decimal system, in which each set of numbers carries with it a message pertaining to the topic area, each classification set makes the function that the rule is performing explicit.

Documenting for Modifiability

Knowledge engineers can also attack the problem of accommodating later changes during knowledge acquisition. Chapter 3 discusses general procedures for documenting knowledge acquisition efforts, in planning the knowledge acquisition session, extracting rules from the session, and continually adding to a knowledge acquisition database. One of these documentation techniques involves the use of a rule content form, similar to rule templates (Soloway, et al., 1987) that guide the development of rules. In either its electronic or hard-copy form, the rule content form contains a description of a rule that includes its basic content, source, and interdependency with other rules in the knowledge base. Additional rule documentation procedures include information as to when the rule would be applicable, why it is important (justification), explanation phrases for the user, and historical information. Such information can be embedded in the rule header and extracted from the program on a periodic basis to provide up-to-date, printed documentation of the knowledge and can become a valuable aid in later review and modification efforts.

Handling Conflicting or Uncertain Information

Expert systems that were developed for research purposes rarely needed a large development team and typically were restricted to well-defined domains. It was fairly common for the tasks of knowledge engineer, domain expert, and programmer to be handled by one individual. As developers began building expert systems for the operational workplace, however, selected domains were often represented by multiple subsets of knowledge. In addition, access to real "experts" in the field of choice was discovered to be problematic, due to workload or geography. In many instances developers had to use a set of domain experts who either had expertise in the subsets of knowledge the system was to represent or who could be accessed to acquire "cumulative" knowledge about the domain in general. While this solved the problem of access, it created problems that still plague developers. The use of multiple experts often results in the acquisition of diverse, even conflicting information. Not only is it difficult to acquire information from multiple experts, but it is also challenging to develop techniques to compare, evaluate, and code this information.

Even with a single expert a similar problem may arise, in that the confidence an expert displays about an event may be dependent on very detailed contextual information. Obtaining the explicit data that differentiates the confidences is a difficult task for the expert and the knowledge engineer. In addition to context-dependent uncertainties, expert system development problems may also be triggered by the dynamic nature of uncertainties in events. For example, during the course of an expert system development project, the domain expert may increase (or become more aware of) his or her expertise. Thus, values associated with related uncertainties may change, and must be reflected in the knowledge base.

Verification and Validation Procedures

Finally, expert system development suffers from a lack of stable, widely recognized verification and validation procedures. Currently, this set of techniques, whose purpose is to analyze whether or not (1) the information in the knowledge base is correct and (2) the system uses the information to perform as it should, is an art. Some of the approaches currently used to verify and validate knowledge include system tests, system review by experts, knowledge base documentation and review, and comparison to expert decisions. Most of these occur at the end of a development cycle. If problems are discovered with the knowledge at this point, much development time and money is wasted. The team may have to throw out design and coding efforts to date. However, developers can minimize this problem by making verification and validation of the knowledge base a part of the ongoing knowledge acquisition and review process. (Chapter 11 discusses this problem and some suggested solutions.)

ENDNOTES

[1] For a discussion of other expert systems, see Hayes-Roth (1983), Rauch-Hindin (1986) and others.

[2] Donald Michie of the Turing Institute in Scotland initiated much of the work on this approach.

[3] While cognitive psychologists generally theorize that each type of knowledge is a separate entity, the labels and the distinctions between some of the pairs are not absolute.

[4] Previous researchers sought specific distinctions between semantic and episodic memory or knowledge. While Tulving (1972) agreed that there was heavy interdependence between the two, he argued that they were distinct entities. Other researchers (Anderson & Ross, 1980; McClosky & Santee, 1981) contend that the distinction is not valid, concluding that both types of memories must affect performance on every task.

The basic distinction between the two is that semantic knowledge consists of facts that could be organized hierarchically. For example, most of us would group "chair" and "couch" together functionally as "things you sit on." In addition, we would realize that these items would also belong to a superordinate group known as "furniture." These examples of semantic memory have no attached temporal or spatial component, however, so they would be distinct from episodic knowledge. Episodic knowledge, on the other hand, is not organized or categorized by concepts or relations, but by temporal, spatial means. For example, instead of hierarchical concepts and attributes that can be applied globally, it may represent a specific experience we may have had in which we sat in an antique chair that then broke. Even though cognitive psychologists still disagree as to the exact divisions between these two types of knowledge, both are important when knowledge engineers attempt to extract target knowledge from an expert and translate that knowledge into an efficient organization.

[5] Chapter 9 addresses this problem and possible solutions in more depth.

SUGGESTED READINGS

Buchanan, B. "Expert Systems." Journal of Automated Reasoning 1 (Winter, 1985).

Davis, R. "Expert Systems." In The AI Business: Commercial Uses of Artificial Intelligence. Edited by P. Winston and K. Prendergast, Cambridge, MA: MIT Press, 1984.

Feigenbaum, E. "Knowledge engineering: The applied side of artificial intelligence." Annals of the New York Academy of Sciences 426 (1984), pp. 91-107.

Hayes-Roth, F., D. Waterman, and D. Lenat, eds. Building Expert Systems (Chapters 1, 2, and 3). Addison-Wesley Publishing Co., Reading, MA, 1983.

Michie, D. 'Mind-like' capabilities in computers: A note on computer induction, Cognition, 12, 1983, pp. 97-108.

2

A Systems Engineering Perspective on the Knowledge Acquisition Process

INTRODUCTION

A common heuristic among software engineers is that "on the third attempt you get the program right." These professionals are referring to "the pancake principle," a set of common experiences that programmers and project managers have had while attempting to solve complex problems by designing large-scale computer programs. After the first attempt at design and implementation, the problem itself becomes better understood. After the second attempt, developers generally are able to satisfy more of the problem requirements. After the third (or subsequent) attempt, the code is implemented and streamlined for modifiability and maintainability, most likely at 100% over budget. Some 25% of these systems are never delivered (Modesitt, 1988).

Unfortunately, cost and time factors seldom allow developers to complete three successive iterations toward the solution of any one problem. Ramifications of the cost limitation are that problem solvers usually have only one opportunity to find the solution. Software engineers have developed a number of methodologies for conventional software that assist developers in their attempt to get the program "right the first time."

The early researchers and programmers of AI approaches to solving problems were not limited to a single iteration. In early AI development, researchers' goals were focused more on the development of *approaches* to solutions than on an integrated solution to a large-scale problem. During these development efforts, AI researchers were successful with a method called rapid prototyping. This method worked well for the size and complexity of the problems solved during the research phase of AI, in which general methodologies were developed. The amount of knowledge acquired for the domains considered was sufficiently small that it could be managed with the rapid prototyping approach.

The limitations of rapid prototyping as a software engineering methodology in and of itself were revealed when nonconventional problem solvers undertook larger, more complex problems. They discovered that the problem-solving process, ranging from the acquisition of knowledge through its translation into programs, was unmanageable without some governing structure. As they progressed from small- to large-scale solution and development efforts, they confronted issues similar to those faced by conventional problem solvers.

As they move into more complex domains, AI problem solvers should not ignore the lessons learned by conventional programmers. Hopefully, many of the software and systems engineering methodologies can be adapted for problems that require the application of AI solutions. The merging of AI approaches to solutions with conventional programming approaches and the application of software engineering methodologies to the overall development process will allow problem solvers to attack larger, more complex problems with greater assurance of success.

This chapter presents an overview of systems and software engineering methodologies that can contribute to the success of AI approaches to solving problems. First, we present background on methodologies. Next, we investigate the same methodologies from the vantage point of knowledge-intensive problems. Then we present a description of the systems engineering approach to solving problems, with modifications for artificial intelligence techniques. Finally, we describe a paradigm for knowledge acquisition that embodies principles adapted from software and systems engineering.

Objectives

This chapter proposes a knowledge acquisition methodology for large-scale, knowledge-intensive problems that is based on adaptations of software/systems engineering methodologies. Specifically, it enables readers to accomplish the following:

- Comprehend similarities in the solution of conventional and knowledge-intensive problems
- Describe conventional software engineering models and approaches
- Recognize the role of knowledge acquisition in conventional and knowledge-intensive problem solving
- Adapt software engineering techniques and systems approaches to the solution of problems requiring AI
- Describe and/or implement a systems-oriented knowledge acquisition methodology.

Key Terms

software engineering	knowledge-intensive problems	waterfall model
systems approach	baseline	validation
configuration management	incremental development	verification

THE PROCESS OF SOLVING CONVENTIONAL PROBLEMS

Developing a computer program or procedure to meet customer requirements entails developing a systematic way in which to attack, represent, evaluate, and solve problems in the domain for which the system is intended. Years of experience in the development of conventional software yielded approaches and techniques that assist programmers both in developing a system that solves domain problems and in solving problems related to the development effort itself (e.g., analysis/design, configuration management).

Problems that prompt developers to use AI techniques are typically large-scale and knowledge-intensive in nature. These factors complicate the development process, which is, in large part, based on knowledge acquisition. To build a foundation on which a systems-oriented knowledge acquisition methodology can be proposed, the sections that follow detail the role and techniques of software engineering for conventional problem solving.

Software Engineering for Conventional Problem-Solving

Boehm (1981) describes **software engineering** as

The application of science and mathematics by which the capabilities of computer equipment are made useful to man via computer programs, procedures, and associated documentation.

Software engineering, when viewed from this perspective, covers the entire process--from identifying and encoding knowledge to program test and acceptance. From a second perspective, the definition must include cost and usability factors that promote human acceptance of the system. In summary, software engineering should satisfy the need for a more disciplined approach for developing software (Conte, 1986).

The management of the software development process through the application of good software engineering practices reduces the impact of the complexity and size of the problem, limitations imposed by the ability of the personnel involved, and the characteristics of the computer system used. It is important to understand the development process and its characteristics before discussing knowledge acquisition techniques.

Software Life Cycle

The process of developing and maintaining software is termed the software life cycle. It consists of several phases, each having a definite starting and ending point. Theoretically, all activities in the process are discrete and fall within a specific phase. In practice, the phases overlap and sometimes interweave. In any case, the activities must be well-defined, and some metrics must be available for confirming that the activities have been completed successfully.

The software life cycle model encompasses all the activities required to define, develop, test, deliver, operate, and maintain a software product. Different models emphasize different aspects of the life cycle and are appropriate for varying types of problems. An acceptable model improves project manageability, resource allocation, cost control, product quality, and correctness. Some possible life-cycle models include those that follow (Fairley, 1985):

- Phased model
- Prototype model
- Successive-versions model
- Cost model.

We discuss first the two models used by conventional software engineers that are most applicable to the development of knowledge-intensive software.

Waterfall Model

One of more commonly accepted phased models for the software life cycle is the phased **waterfall model** (Royce, 1970; Rosove,1967; Boehm, 1981).[1] Figure 2-1 depicts the model as it is used in conventional software engineering. A modified version for knowledge-intensive problems is described later in the chapter.

Analysis Phase	Design Phase	Implement Phase	System Test	Maintenance Phase
Planning Requirements	Definition			
Verify	Architecture Details			
	Verify	Code Debug Unit Test		
Verify		Verify	Integration Acceptance	
Verify				Enhance Adapt Fix

Figure 2-1. The Phased Waterfall Model
Barry W. Boehm, <u>Software Engineering Economics</u>, © 1981, p. 36. Adapted with permission of Prentice-Hall, Inc., Englewood Cliffs, NJ.

FEASIBILITY:

      The definition of an overall acceptable concept for the product, its feasibility over the life cycle, and its advantages and disadvantages related to other concepts.

REQUIREMENTS ANALYSIS:

      The complete specifications of the required functions, interfaces, and performance of the product; the validation of the specifications.

PRODUCT DESIGN:
>The complete specifications of control and data structures and overall hardware and software architectures of the product, plus the necessary manuals; the verification of these specifications.

DETAILED DESIGN:
>The control and data structures, the input/output parameters, the algorithms, the assumptions for each program component, and the verification of the specifications of these components.

PROGRAMMING:
>The expanded code of each program component and its verifications.

SYSTEM INTEGRATION:
>The functioning program composed of the program components.

IMPLEMENTATION:
>The fully functional software-hardware system with training, installation, and customer acceptance.

MAINTENANCE:
>The functional updates to the software-hardware system throughout its lifetime.

In theory, the phases in Figure 2-1 are sequential. In reality they are interdependent, since a change in one phase can significantly affect activities in another (either a predecessor, successor, or both). Ideally, work would progress forward through the phases, such that the work done in the current phase would affect future phases. The reality of system development is that, in many cases, work in the current phase will lead to the discovery of information that affects a previous stage. Modifications to previous stages, which are then carried forward once more, can significantly impact the cost of development.

Within each phase, developers should complete the following activities:
- Verification
- Validation
- Configuration management.

Verification is confirmation that the product is being built correctly, to meet the specifications at each phase, and to satisfy the requirements overall.

Validation is confirmation that the right product is being built for its operational objectives during that phase and to solve the problem overall.

Configuration management is a process pursued in parallel with each of the phases of the software life cycle that ensures that a definitive version of the product of that phase can be provided.

The completion of each phase should yield an intermediate product known as a **baseline**. A baseline product cannot be changed without the agreement of all parties. This restriction stabilizes the product at each stage and ensures that a definitive version of the product is available at all times. Baselines are established at the milestones of each phase. At this point in each phase the product supposedly has satisfied the requirements for that phase, signalling that development may proceed to the subsequent phase. This milestone-baseline progression unifies the management of the software process and the product (Boehm, 1981).

Systems Configuration Management. Currently, most conventional software projects include a systems configuration management technique similar to that presented by Bersoff (1984) within the waterfall model. This approach proposes that at each phase developers impose extensive verification and validation on the product. This technique ensures that the phase has accomplished its objectives, that the implementation to that point meets the specifications, and that the specifications continue to satisfy the initial requirements (Figure 2-2). This technique is a formalization of the two subphases proposed by Boehm (1973).

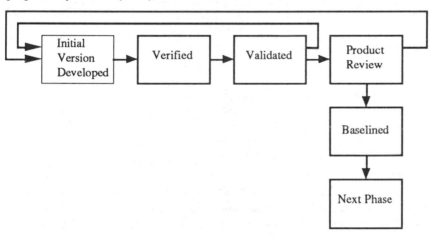

Figure 2-2. The Configuration Management Technique

For most small, simple problems, completing each phase in the waterfall model may seem unnecessary, especially if the developer understands the problem well and uses a method such as rapid prototyping. However, a less formal approach can and often does lead to unacceptable results. Following the model is a means of assuring success of the product. This has been confirmed in larger, more complex projects in which disasters have been recorded. Lack of compliance with the phases has resulted in serious problems with software in both the commercial and the defense markets (Boehm, 1973; Aviation Week, 1970).

Prototyping. Rapid prototyping is a technique in which a simplistic model of the system is devised to demonstrate some functionality, to experiment with different approaches, and to evoke user feedback (Figure 2-3). It inherently forces multiple iterations through the knowledge. Some projects have a tremendously high cost for acquiring and analyzing the knowledge that is needed to determine requirements. In others, the task of finalizing the requirements specifications entails minimal time, effort, and cost. For projects in which the cost for acquiring knowledge to determine requirements is *high*, developers may wish to build a prototype with which users interact instead of applying an approach that is entirely sequential. An initial prototype can be used to assist the developer and user ascertain quickly some specific preferences. The rapid prototyping approach may be even more advantageous in small, better-understood problems, where it can be used as the life cycle model itself.

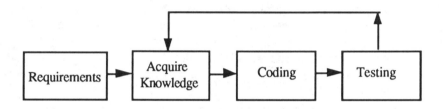

Figure 2-3. The Rapid Prototyping Approach

An initial criterion for this approach is the availability of a tool for rapid prototyping that is appropriate for the domain and the problem. In conventional software engineering a rapid prototype is a quick implementation of a part of the system to test its ability to meet the user's requirements or to explore technical issues in the proposed product. A prototype incorporates some of the actual components of the product.

A prototype normally includes the screens and reports that the user desires, plus the major operations that the system should accomplish in terms of messages, data formats, and interactive dialogues. For small, controllable components of the system, the prototype is the input/output for those components, along with drivers and stubs to other components. As the project increases in size and complexity, the ability to represent the system with a single "rapidly-developed prototype" decreases, even with available tools, because the ability to understand the interaction of data and processes degrades. At this point the rapid prototyping paradigm needs to be placed within the confines of a method such as the waterfall model.

Incremental Development. **Incremental development** represents a refinement to the waterfall model into which the rapid prototype paradigm fits well. This refinement entails an integration of prototyping and top-down, structured programming, in which the software is developed in increments of functional capability. In other words, developers first implement basic capabilities and operations of the current model to gain experience with the product. Then they may add simple algorithms and output reports. If needed, they may also test access methods and other functionalities (Figure 2-4).

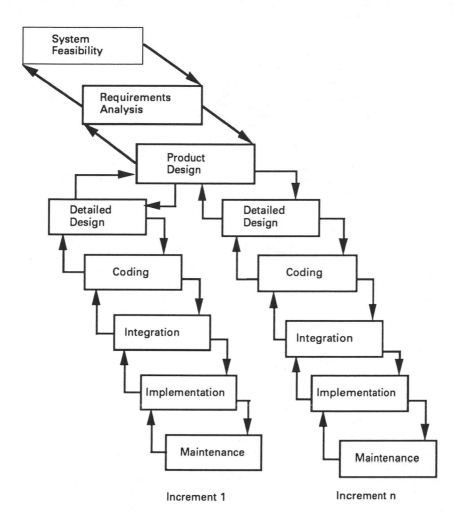

Figure 2-4. The Incremental Development Process

Incremental development of functionality is advantageous for numerous reasons. First, increments of functional capability are easier to test than the intermediate products sometimes created with top-down design for a specific phase. Second, in a project in which it is not feasible (e.g., due to costs, etc.) to build a large prototype, the process of incremental development enables programmers to continue to incorporate user experiences and requirements as the project develops (Boehm, 1981).

Knowledge Acquisition: Principles and Guidelines   **37**

Figure 2-5 illustrates the components of the waterfall model. The sections and the phases within the sections are similar to those in the IEEE Standard for Software Quality Assurance Plans (Fairley, 1985; Buckley, 1979).[2]

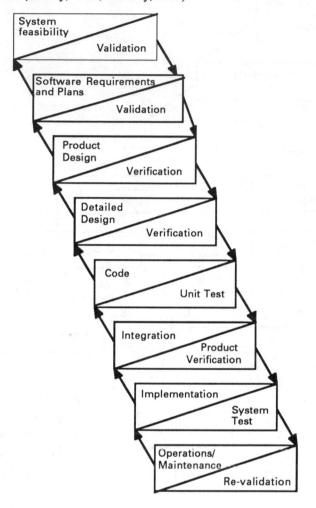

Figure 2-5. Waterfall Model Components
(From R.E. Fairley, Software Engineering Concepts, © 1985, McGraw-Hill Book Co. Reprinted with permission.)

Systems Approach

Analysis. In a discussion of paradigms for knowledge acquisition, the most relevant part of the software life cycle is the analysis component of the waterfall model. Analysis consists of planning the development process and determining the requirements, which together encompass both feasibility and requirements analysis. The products of this process include a system definition and a project plan. During analysis, developers must complete the following procedures:

A Systems Engineering Perspective

- Understand the customer's problem
- Perform a feasibility study
- Recommend a solution strategy
- Determine acceptance criteria
- Plan the development process.

At the end of the requirements analysis, developers produce a software requirements specification. This document identifies the basic functions of the software components with an emphasis on what the software should do and the constraints under which it performs its functions. The specification describes the processing environment, the required software functions, the constraints on size and speed, priorities, and the acceptance criteria.

A systematic approach to the analysis phase is often applied in the waterfall model. This approach consists of techniques for analyzing the possible consequences of alternate decisions within the context of a given system. It narrows the candidate systems to a small number, which can be analyzed in more detail. Reducing the number of candidate systems involves determining

- The objectives to be optimized or satisfied
- The decisions that can be controlled to meet the objectives
- What items dictate the constraints on the range of choices
- The criteria to be used to evaluate the remaining alternatives
- The sensitivity of the decisions to assumptions made during the analysis, based on the above criteria.

Upon completion of these considerations, designers should reconsider previous steps if the performance based on the decisions is unacceptable.

Quade (1968) describes the **systems approach** to analysis as one of formulation, search, evaluation, interpretation, and iteration. Formulation clarifies the objectives and limits the problem. Search then looks for the data and its dependencies, as well as the alternatives that could solve the problem. Evaluation involves building models and using them as predictive mechanisms for comparing alternatives. Interpretation compares the alternatives further to derive conclusions about them and decide upon an approach. Finally, developers iterate through the process until the desired performance levels are reached.

Design. In the waterfall model, software design follows analysis. During the design process, developers identify software functions, data streams, and data stores and specify relationships among the components and the software structure. This process provides a form for the implementation phase. Thus, design acts as the bridge between software requirements and implementation and includes the product design and detailed design phases of the waterfall model.

A systematic approach to design involves the following three major activities:
- Transitioning from requirements definition to a high-level system architecture
- Specifying a system structure that meets the constraints and the requirements from the analysis phase
- Specifying algorithmic processes and data representations.

There are numerous design notations and techniques that developers can utilize to complete the design phase. Design notations include data flow diagrams, structure charts, structured flowcharts, HIPO diagrams, pseudocode, and Jackson structure diagrams. Design techniques include structured design, integrated top-down programming, stepwise refinement, and Jackson structured programming. Developers may select different notations to work with a technique to solve a particular software design problem. These systematic methods and techniques are necessary for software design but as yet do not guarantee a perfect solution.[3]

Knowledge Acquisition in Conventional Problem-Solving

In conventional problem solving more emphasis has been placed on developing a test bed for verification and validation at the *end* of the cycle than on knowledge acquisition at the *beginning* of the project. The explicit knowledge acquisition that does occur in conventional programming is in the form of requirements determination. Interviewing, reporting forms, and algorithmic software analyzers are methods software analysts employ during requirements analysis to delineate the problem.

THE PROCESS OF SOLVING KNOWLEDGE-INTENSIVE PROBLEMS

In contrast to the well-understood processes of conventional problems, there is a class of complex problems for which the algorithms and data are not explicitly known. Many of these problems can be termed **knowledge-intensive**. The information content is the most critical aspect of software development for knowledge-intensive problems. The processes themselves may be information in the same sense that data is information. This treatment of processes and data results in a symbolic manipulation of the information, usually with some kind of reasoning involved.

The techniques developed for conventional software engineering cannot be applied directly to this more complex class of problems. For example, traditional dataflow diagrams and structured analysis procedures assume that the processes and data can be specified completely and in a deterministic manner. The best that can be done in this case is to leverage off of the established software engineering methodologies and modify them to meet the differing needs of knowledge-intensive problems.

Software specialists who have undertaken solving complex problems have found that there is no straightforward mapping of complex problems to current software engineering methodologies. Two factors impede the mappings. First, the current software engineering practices were developed with algorithmic solutions and constraints in mind. Second, the processing that is required by conventional programming is explicit and is directly tied to the data to be manipulated (rather than being implicit, as are complex reasoning tasks).

The software life-cycle process for AI problem solving must describe the problem and enable the knowledge engineer to select appropriate techniques for implementation. Constraints on this process include the fact that the problem may not be described completely at any phase and the domain knowledge must be acquired explicitly.

In the next section we describe the characteristics of problems for which AI solutions work well. These characteristics can then be matched to the appropriate solution technique. Since a number of textbooks are available to assist in applying the correct AI approach for a particular problem, this subject is not discussed further.[4] After describing AI problems, we present information pertaining to software engineering techniques for AI problems. Finally, we address the importance of knowledge acquisition to the software engineering process for knowledge-intensive problems and offer a knowledge acquisition methodology that embodies these principles.

Characteristics of Knowledge-Intensive Problems

Problems that require developers to implement "intelligent" solution approaches are normally knowledge-intensive (Figure 2-6). Intelligence requires knowledge; this fact has been confirmed throughout the last twenty years of research in AI. The knowledge may come in the form of data, information, or processes. Data and information are declarative forms of knowledge. Data is a primitive form of knowledge which is converted to information through some kind of processing. Processes are procedural forms of knowledge. All three of these forms of knowledge are usually present in problems that developers solve with AI approaches.

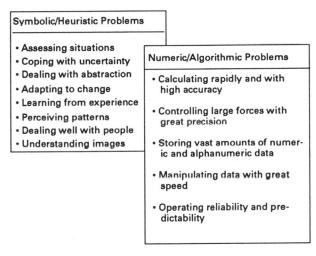

Figure 2-6. Conventional versus Knowledge-Intensive Problem Characteristics
McGraw, K. "Artificial intelligence: The competitive edge in expert systems development," <u>Texas Instruments Engineering Journal</u>, 3:1 (1986), Copyright © Texas Instruments. Reprinted with permission.

A second characteristic of knowledge-intensive problems is the symbolic manipulation of the knowledge. Conventional problems may be solved using numeric or algorithmic means, such as making rapid calculations, while problems in the AI domain require symbolic or heuristic manipulation as depicted Figure 2-6. In the AI domain, the manipulation is usually a reasoning process, such as an intelligent search activity. If the data from a data acquisition problem is assessed through a reasoning process, then an AI approach is suitable. If the data is processed through equations in a straightforward numerical manner, procedural approaches are more appropriate. If a reasoning system selects the appropriate procedure to be applied to the data, an AI approach is applicable. In the latter case, developers treat the procedures as symbols to be manipulated by the reasoner.

Often the knowledge contains less desirable properties that impede a simple solution. Such knowledge is usually voluminous, hard to define accurately, incomplete, and dynamic. To solve these types of problems, developers must be able to generalize and group similar objects, to represent knowledge in understandable forms, to reflect changes in the world state easily, and to adapt to any number of situations.

Software Engineering for Knowledge-Intensive Problems

The development of expert or knowledge-based systems to solve large, complex problems requires a disciplined approach that facilitates management of the project while continuing to be correct technically. These requirements follow those of conventional software, which uses software engineering methodologies for the same purpose. The process of building an expert or knowledge-based system using similar methodologies is referred to as knowledge engineering.[5]

For many projects in which the product is a knowledge-based system, the actual software life cycle could be described as iterations of interacting with the expert and the coding. This simple "acquire-and-code" process worked well in constrained domains with a single knowledge engineer. The documentation was minimal, and the code substituted for specifications and design. Unfortunately, operational systems that are in use continually expand and mutate. At some point the size of the problem outgrows the ability of a simple knowledge acquisition-coding cycle.

A number of elements of software engineering are lacking in the acquire-code cycle. Most of the absent components remind developers of the lessons that conventional programmers have learned over the last forty years. For example, during the analysis phase, developers determine the scope of the problem, investigate alternative views of the task, and produce a software requirements specification to which all personnel can work. For the project as a whole, personnel should construct planning and communication aids. Finally, to help ensure that the requirements are met, project personnel should establish a methodology to enable the production, validation, and verification of intermediate products.

Boehm (1983) has listed seven guidelines of software engineering for conventional problem solving that apply equally well to knowledge-intensive problems:
- Manage the project with a phased software life-cycle plan.
- Continuously validate and verify at each phase.
- Maintain product control through baselines and milestones.
- Use modern programming practices such as structured analysis and tools (e.g., CASE).
- Maintain clear accountability for results.
- Use better, more experienced, and fewer people.
- Commit to improve the process through adopting different methods and techniques as they apply.

Martin (1987, 1988) presents these points in lectures, advocating the use of these guidelines in AI software engineering methods. The acquire-and-code process utilizes only two of the guidelines in most cases--continuous validation, and the use of fewer people (Martin, 1987). Continuous validation is performed by expert review of the prototype during the acquire-and-code process. The process itself usually involves only two or three people, including the domain expert, the knowledge engineer, and possibly, a tool expert. The use of configuration management methods can help maintain product control and accountability of results as developers discover the necessity of delivering a usable product.

Rapid Prototyping

Rapid prototyping, when used as a methodology complete in and of itself, embodies some of the basic principles stated above but does not exhibit a phased life cycle. However, there are at least three conditions under which rapid prototyping can be successful in developing solutions to knowledge-intensive problems[6]

- The problem is sufficiently small that one person can understand and encode the problem directly;
- The system is experimental and will not require maintenance or modification;
- A tool is available for developing the prototype.

Owing to the availability of LISP machines, which serve as excellent prototyping workstations, rapid prototyping found more of a following as a methodology in the AI community than it had in conventional software. These workstations delayed somewhat the impact of neglecting good software engineering practices until solutions to larger, more complex problems were sought.

Since the use of rapid prototyping as an overall approach to system development is limited to the above three conditions, more extensive life cycles have been developed. A typical life cycle for an expert, or knowledge-based system, includes the stages shown in Figure 2-7. The life cycle used by Walters and Nielsen (1988) has two major phases: 1) design and 2) development, testing, and validation. Within these phases are stages, such as development of systems requirements, feasibility study, prototyping, pilot version, and maintenance.

Walters and Nielsen (1988) also mentioned three strategies that can be used to build prototypes within the development, testing, and validation phase

1. Building a single prototype for the entire application with testing and refining in successive versions.

2. Building a skeleton prototype that has the breadth of the overall application, with depth in some sections. Testing and enhancing of successive versions involves expending other sections.

3. Building a separate prototype for each part of the application, with testing of each part and then a final integration to the complete application.

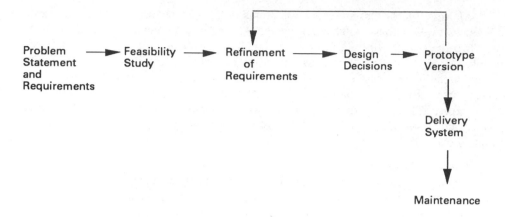

Figure 2-7. Typical Life Cycle for an Expert System

The three strategies have the same advantages and disadvantages as procedural development strategies in conventional software engineering. The first strategy is useful in small applications. The second and third strategy work better for larger applications. The second strategy has an advantage over the third strategy in that final integration difficulties and the lack of common knowledge representations are not issues (Walters and Nielsen, 1988).

Martin (1987) has developed an approach to software engineering AI projects that includes rapid prototyping as a stage in the software engineering process. The Expert System Controlled Iterative Enhancement (ESCIE) development methodology is modified from such models as Basili's Iterative Enhancement and Boehm's Incremental development. It addresses the failure of the acquire-and-code method for building expert systems. In the ESCIE model there is one feasibility stage and one rapid prototyping stage (Martin, 1988). During other stages there are parallel rapid prototyping stages. The model is a good example of modifying conventional software engineering models to fit AI problems and making use of the strengths of rapid prototyping.

Waterfall Model

When the problem space is larger than can be accommodated by a rapid prototyping approach, the waterfall model becomes applicable. As explained in the section on conventional software engineering methodologies, the model offers a set of abstract phases that can be instantiated for specific projects. It acts as a basis for negotiations with management and as a control for project performance. If the model is appropriate for the problem, it provides technical guidelines for the project team and specifies the documents to which they work.

In applying the waterfall model to the solution of problems that reflect AI approaches, developers discover that the process entails completing activities very much like those described by the conventional waterfall model software life cycle. For example, in each phase of the cycle, developers must specify decisions, products, documents, milestones, reporting mechanisms, tools, and verification and validation requirements. Developers who are using AI solution approaches can also follow the incremental development model, consisting of product specification and software development interwoven with intermediate products.

A major difference between the complex, less-understood problems and those solved with conventional approaches is that in conventional approaches the nature of requirements and specifications is static. In knowledge-based systems the requirements are not well-known, and in fact, the developers may uncover requirements during the design and implementation process. This deviation from the norm implies that developers will be required to revisit the analysis phase throughout the life-cycle process. As one can imagine, the added cycling complicates the life-cycle process considerably.

Developers managing AI approaches must also consider the fact that, when applied to complex problems and solutions, not all conventional phases are necessarily equal in importance. The developmental phase that increases dramatically in importance for the more complex problems is analysis and requirements specification. Most of the increase in focus and importance during this phase can be attributed to knowledge acquisition. A stage that in conventional models consists of diagramming and noting processes and data now requires specific elicitation and follow-up procedures. Buchanan and others (1983) have defined the global process for transferring knowledge to program structure, including the basic steps of Identification, Conceptualization, Formalization, Implementation, and Testing.[7] Most developers using AI approaches approximate these overall development "steps," yet to date most have interpreted the phases rather loosely and have not attempted to adapt systems engineering techniques to the knowledge acquisition process.

Solving Complex Problems with the Waterfall Model. Some questions that developers can ask when using the waterfall model with less-understood problems are listed below[8]

REQUIREMENTS ANALYSIS:
  What does the problem space look like?
  What does the solution space look like?
  Can the size be estimated?
  Can the knowledge and control structures be estimated?
  Can the level of reasoning be determined?
  What are some prototypical problems and scenarios?

PRODUCT AND DETAILED DESIGN SPECIFICATIONS:
  What language should we use?
  What definitions and abstractions are given?
  Can I build any needed abstractions and structure definitions?
  How do I express the problem?
  How do I express the solution?

ARCHITECTURAL DESIGN:
  What architecture should be chosen?

Can the processes be described as classification, diagnosis, etc?
What are the major components?
What are the interactions within the components?

IMPLEMENTATION:
How efficient is the resulting code?
Are pieces of the architecture available to give to programmers?

Is all information for a piece available to the programmers?
What are the context dependencies in the segments of code?

EVALUATION:
How close is the prototype to the requirements?
What should be attempted next in implementation?
What areas need further revision or elicitation?

As a result of the evaluation, developers may need to loop back to the detailed design phase, the architectural design phase, or the requirements analysis. Normally, the number of modifications that a developer must make is a function of the number of phases that must be reworked. Thus, knowledge-intensive reasoning problems are in a higher risk category and can become more costly than problems that are solved with more conventional means.

Systems Approach

The systems approach provides a body of techniques for analyzing the likely consequences of alternatives pursued during analysis. The techniques are used extensively during the feasibility and requirements phases, in which the primary goal is to make appropriate choices of what kind of system to develop. The systems approach assists a software developer in reducing myriad possibilities to a small number that can be analyzed in detail, allowing him or her to converge on the most appropriate selection from the remaining number. The systems approach also emphasizes the consideration of the subjective, unquantifiable factors that are prevalent in problems that are less well defined. Developers investigating the application of a systems approach should consider at least two reasons that seem to favor its use. First, the systems approach is one of constraint optimization versus mathematical optimization techniques (which are more suitable for computer networks and straightforward algorithms). Boehm (1981) notes that another reason to prefer this approach over one of mathematical optimization is its ability to settle for a feasible but nonoptimal solution in domains that may not be well bounded.

Analysis. A systematic approach to the analysis component in the solution of complex problems has the same general objectives as in conventional software engineering. Developers may follow any of three basic approaches
1. Extract the reasoning behavior of an expert by coding the intuitive and implicit problem-solving techniques found in manuals, systems, and the human expert.

2. Induce the rules that represent decisions and procedures by monitoring the human or machine during problem-solving behavior.

3. Instantiate a theoretical model by using an existing model or a prototypical model that has been developed into executable form.

These approaches answer the questions that the systems analysis process usually stimulates and allow developers to explore alternatives through use of the prototype that is produced.

The issues that developers need to determine during the analysis segment of the systematic approach are as follows:
- The incompletely specified problem description
- The feasibility of solving the problem through computerization
- The advisibility of having a product
- The project requirements.

The problem *description* or objectives should contain the problem statement, the problem classification, the contributing areas of AI, and the domain characteristics in terms of problem space, solutions space, and reasoning requirements. System characteristics in terms of enhancements, visibility, and interface requirements are important, since most developers base the evaluation of performance, reliability, and usability on these characteristics.

Feasibility should include estimates of the difficulty of the problem from a point on a continuum from straightforward, industrial applications to experimental research. Developers establish this point by assessing the risks of cost, time to availability, software/hardware resources, the expertise of the development team, and relevance to corporate goals.

Advisibility covers the cost to benefit ratio, the receptiveness of the user community to the product, and the impact on humans. These factors are sometimes probabilistic and may include hidden factors or adjustments.

Another major project requirement that developers should establish during analysis is the potential design approach. This decision is at least partially determined by the availability of experts and other knowledge sources. Developers also must have sufficient tools and development environments to carry out the analysis, plus a production and management methodology that supports the design segment described below.

Design. In the design phase of a systems approach, developers determine the processes and descriptions for selecting structures, components, and connections to structures. For knowledge-intensive problems, developers may model the domain by defining the problem space in terms of parts of speech, by formalizing concepts and relationships, or by specifying operations, entities, and actions.

MYCIN is an example of a problem in which developers used a solution-space model. Diagnosis was the operation that was selected for MYCIN; it was performed over the domain of bacteriology. The terms, in this case diseases and symptoms, were grouped and differentiated by connections to allow the classification to occur (Clancey,

1985). This same approach worked well in an aviation identification problem for friend-or-foe (Harbison, 1985).

In problems with more than one type of reasoning, developers have shown strong acceptance for the approach that formalizes conceptual relations. For example, in cardiac rehabilitation monitoring, there are a number of concurrent activities, such as classifying, predicting, planning, diagnosing, and assessing. The same information may be manipulated in different reasoning styles and for different purposes during execution of the system (Harbison, 1987). Developers can model the concepts and relationships of the domain by determining states (observable data), relations among the states, and the strengths of belief. These three factors then form the specification language for the domain model.

States of the data can be defined as follows:
- Circumstantial findings -- temporal, contextual, etc.
- Direct findings -- measured data, sensed data, specific data, globals
- Hypotheses -- partial descriptions abstracted during reasoning
- Assumptions -- guesses of predictions.

Relationships form different types of hierarchies and networks for the model. The relationships that a piece of information has with other data determine its role in the domain. Developers appropriately name the relationships to allow for specificity and comparison with other relationships.

The third method for defining a domain space applies to planning problems. The development of a plan involves selecting the sequence of operators whose actions will lead to accomplishing the goal. The operators act on entities in the domain and cause these entities to change state and new entities to be added. The definition of the operators, entities, and actions is a major part of the design process. Another part of the process is determining the strategy by which the operators are selected during the planning process. Manufacturing scheduling, process control, and mission planning are examples of problems for which this method is appropriate.

Documenting the Design Process

Developers can document the design process through techniques that have been adapted from conventional system design and modified to meet the requirements of the three approaches described previously. Developers have found dataflow diagrams, functional decomposition, and Petri nets, as well as others, useful for defining and formalizing the design. Each has some useful characteristics, depending upon the problem domain.

Dataflow Diagrams

Dataflow diagrams that programmers organize by levels of abstraction have been used in some hierarchical solution sets and can represent the flow of information in diagnostic problems. The development of Neomycin and other medical diagnostic problems are good examples of the application of this technique. A dataflow diagram shows the processes and the flow of data among those processes. At the higher level, dataflow diagrams can enable programmers to depict events and transactions. At the lower level they allow developers to depict programs, modules, rule sets, and the flow of data among the modules. A dataflow diagram is primarily a systems tool that software engineers use to draw the basic procedural components and the data that passes among them. The application of this tool is limited by the ratio of procedural information to declarative information. In knowledge-intensive problems that exhibit higher levels of abstraction, procedural information may consist entirely of a reasoning strategy that is applied to the declarative knowledge. In this case, developers may find the flow difficult to describe through dataflow diagrams. Figure 2-8 illustrates a simple dataflow diagram with its data flow, processes, sources, and links.

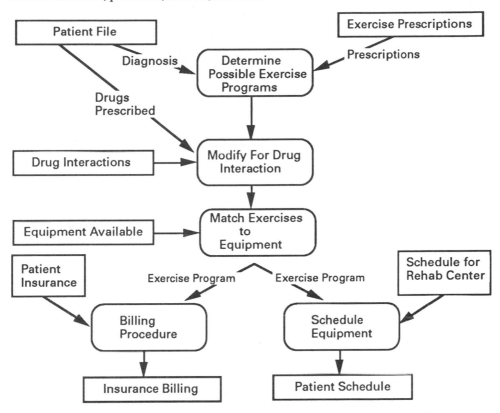

Figure 2-8. Dataflow Diagram Showing High-Level Reasoning Modules for a Cardiac Rehabilitation Prescription Program

Petri Nets

Petri nets are another tool that AI developers may wish to adapt to study and document systems development. Petri nets allow developers to mathematically represent the "system," which they can then analyze to reveal information about its structure and dynamic behavior. Developers apply Petri nets through modeling (Peterson, 1981). A model is a representation of the important features and behaviors of the system which can be manipulated to test for completeness and to acquire new knowledge without the presence of the system itself. Specifically, Petri nets are designed to model systems with interacting concurrent components, which promotes the maximum utilization of parallelism in the system.

Developing a Petri net representation of a system involves transitioning from higher levels of abstraction that describe processes to the finer levels of detail that describe rules or procedures (Figure 2-9). At each level, the input and output functions relate the transitions from state to state. While the theoretical work on Petri nets involves the bag-theory formalisms of Petri net structures, a graphical representation is more useful for modeling systems. The graph is a bipartite-directed multigraph, which has had widespread use in conventional software engineering methodologies.

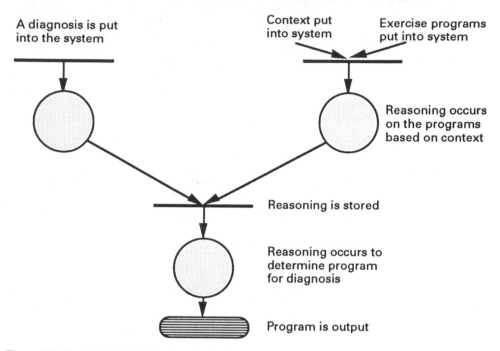

Figure 2-9. Cardiac Rehabilitation Program in Petri Net Format

The Petri net structure consists of places and transitions related by input and output functions. The corresponding graph has two types of nodes: a circle to represent a place and a bar to represent a transition. Directed arcs (arrows) connect the places and the transitions. An arc from a place to a transition defines the place to be an input of the transition. An arc from a transition to a place represents an output place. Multiple arcs for both input and output are indicated by multiple arrows. Since multiple arcs are allowed and the arcs have direction, the graph is a directed multigraph. More specifically, in that the nodes are members of one of two sets--places or transitions--such that an arc is directed from a member of one set to a member of the other set, the graph is actually a bipartite directed multigraph (Peterson, 1981).

The Petri net view of a system concentrates on the events and the conditions. *Events* are actions that take place in the system. The triggering of these events is controlled by the state of the system, which is composed of a set of *conditions*. The conditions that are required for an event to occur (e.g., preconditions of the event) are similar to rule antecedents. The conditions that result from the occurrence of an event (e.g., postconditions) are a result of the actions in the consequents of a rule. These concepts of events and conditions are relevant to knowledge-intensive problems, especially to those that are rule-based.

Two important features of Petri net representation are the ability to
• Represent the inherent parallel nature of problems and
• Represent the inherent asynchronous nature of problems.

Petri nets do not, however, represent either a measure or the flow of time. The Petri net model is a sequence of discrete events, such that the order of occurrence of these events is not specified uniquely. Thus, Petri net execution exhibits nondeterminism. These features fit many of the complex real-life problems being solved today and enable their use in design documentation. For example, most complex, real-life problems can be viewed as systems of separate, interacting components. Each component may be a system with its behavior described independently of other systems. (Exceptions include defined interactions with other components.) Each component has its own state of being, which is an abstraction of relevant information describing possible action. If the components exhibit concurrency or parallelism, then there will be some synchronization among the otherwise synchronous states. Petri net formalism was designed specifically to model these asynchronous/synchronous/concurrent states of components. Petri nets allow specification of the states and interactions without specifying artificial sequencing of states in a mathematical and graphical form, making them a useful means of documentation.

KNOWLEDGE ACQUISITION FOR KNOWLEDGE-INTENSIVE PROBLEMS

An obvious difference between conventional problem solving and knowledge-intensive problems is the degree to which the explicit acquisition of knowledge is important. In solving many of the conventional problems, programmers could rely on a fairly straightforward development approach and had access to materials that could be used during the requirements and analysis phases. The acquisition of knowledge during the development of knowledge-based systems is a more complex undertaking owing to the following tasks and issues:
• Comprehending domain-specific terminology and concepts
• Identifying, selecting, and accessing appropriate domain experts
• Conceptualizing an expert's organization of a domain
• The ephemeral, dynamic nature of knowledge
• Problems relating to the ability of experts to express their knowledge
• Difficulties inherent in planning an organized approach to knowledge acquisition
• The need to verify and validate knowledge-base content
• Requirements to provide audit trails for knowledge-base content
• Problems related to the need for and use of multiple domain experts
• Selecting appropriate, effective knowledge acquisition techniques

- Lack of standardization in the presentation and interpretation of existing knowledge acquisition techniques
- Lack of standard "knowledge engineering methodologies"
- Knowledge engineers unfamiliar with the use of a variety of knowledge acquisition techniques.

Recent emphasis has been on methodologies to (1) structure the knowledge acquisition process and (2) assure that the process meets the communication requirements of the application's organization (Grover, 1983). A concurrent focus is on refining the rapid prototyping methodology. De Greef and Breuker (1985) summarize the two basic approaches to knowledge engineering that characterize its historic application as follows:

- Skills/programming-based rapid prototype and test approach (Hayes-Roth & Waterman, 1983; Brownston, Farrell, Kant & Martin, 1985)
- Structured knowledge engineering, which guides and supports an initial knowledge acquisition phase while deferring implementation (Freiling, Alexander, Messick, et al., 1985; Kline & Dolins, 1986; DeGreef & Breuker, 1985).

Both these approaches to knowledge engineering in general and knowledge acquisition specifically have been effective in small-scale efforts. However, the lack of complexity of previous development efforts has enabled developers to cling to the notion that knowledge engineering is an art (Feigenbaum, 1977). Faced with the difficulties described above, developers of current, more complex expert systems have attempted to mold the art into a science. While no single knowledge acquisition standard has emerged, developers have experimented with a diverse set of knowledge acquisition techniques, from the unstructured interview to computer-based knowledge acquisition. We have found that the effectiveness of the knowledge acquisition technique depends on many factors, including the following:

- Knowledge engineer training and conceptual abilities
- Domain expert receptiveness and abilities
- Phase of knowledge acquisition
- Type of knowledge being accessed.

Based on these issues, we propose a systems-oriented approach to knowledge acquisition that represents a merging of the two approaches delineated by DeGreef and Breuker (1985).

A Systems-Oriented Knowledge Acquisition Methodology

The knowledge acquisition methodology that we suggest is founded in a systems approach to development and has been refined through its application on both small- and large-scale development efforts. Within this methodology the knowledge acquisition process emerges as the vehicle to propel development from requirements definition through to prototype development. As knowledge engineers work with domain experts, they do so in a specified framework of guidelines and procedures that serve to provide some degree of standardization over the selection and application of knowledge acquisition techniques. In addition, the knowledge engineering methodology that we suggest includes the use of a variety of templates or forms that structure and document the acquisition of knowledge from a knowledge source.[9] The end result is a knowledge base whose content may be traced to its original source and whose development is well documented to enable later maintenance and modification efforts.

An Adaptive Waterfall Model for Knowledge Acquisition

Figure 2-10 portrays a knowledge acquisition methodology that embodies elements of systems and software engineering, represents an adaptation of the waterfall model, and enables a "managed" rapid prototyping.

Within this model developers initially work through the feasibility and requirements phases, in which they analyze customer requirements to determine functional objectives. Using these objectives as guidelines, they begin to converge upon the overall software development plans that help ensure the desired functionality. At a finer level, software development plans yield a core set of goals which, when met, determines project completion.

Using the functionally derived goals, the developers begin traversing the model, selecting specific knowledge acquisition and implementation techniques to enable them to focus on specific needs, phase of development, and type or level of knowledge required. The nature of knowledge-intensive problems will mean that developers will be unable to identify knowledge requirements, data, and problem-solving approaches early-on in the project. Additionally, although analysis work can yield design guidelines, all design work cannot be completed prior to implementation efforts. Thus, this model is not sequential in nature, but more accurately reflects managed iteration and enhancement.

As the vertical evaluation line depicts, each stage in the development process enables the developer to stop and evaluate current development efforts to determine completion. Specific responses to the question of whether or not overall system goals are met include the following, which then help route the developer to an appropriate development stage and set of knowledge acquisition techniques.

- Are the results incomplete or inaccurate?
- Is clarification or specific information needed?
- Does there seem to be an inadequate solution description?
- Does there seem to be an inadequate or inefficient domain conceptualization?
- Is the domain framework inappropriate?
- Is the background knowledge (e.g., concepts, terminology) incomplete?

For example, if the evaluation determines that the functional goals, and therefore the objectives, have been met, the system may be frozen and termed a baseline. The formal verification and validation process may begin in concert with system test efforts. If, however, evaluation uncovers any type of inadequacy or failure to meet preset goals, development efforts continue. The path that the developer takes at this point will depend on the type of inadequacy that has been observed. Development efforts may iterate to revisit the conceptual analysis stage to refine conceptual definitions or relationships. Knowledge engineers may then work with a domain expert, using a technique such as

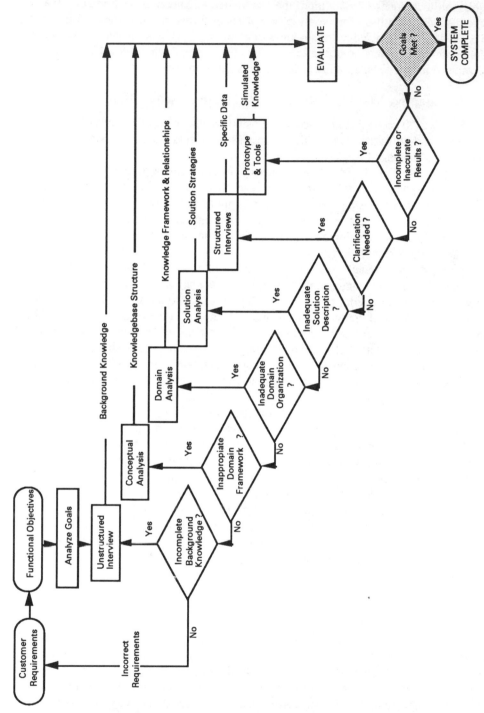

Figure 2-10. An Adaptive Waterfall Model for Knowledge Acquisition

concept sorting to refine critical conceptual relationships. On the other hand, the system may simply need more specific information, which can be isolated through the application of increasingly more focused knowledge acquisition techniques, such as the structured interview.

Knowledge Acquisition Techniques in the Systems-Based Approach

The initial task in knowledge acquisition is *identifying* the important domain knowledge, knowledge subsets, and vocabulary that both the knowledge engineer and the expert system will need. Techniques that are effective in this phase of knowledge acquisition include unstructured interviews or tutorials. These may consist of an open-ended "interview" with a domain expert or may be organized as more formal domain-related training seminars that are presented to knowledge engineers by a domain expert. While the unstructured interview is not effective nor recommended when the knowledge engineer needs to isolate *specific* data, its informal, open atmosphere can allow the knowledge engineer to become familiar with the domain and to identify important terminology and knowledge sources for later investigation.

Conceptual Analysis. Using conceptual analysis techniques, such as concept dictionaries or concept sorting, the knowledge engineer seeks to understand and graphically represent the way in which a domain expert has mentally organized the concepts within the domain. This development stage can yield a wealth of valuable information that is critical to the eventual functionality of the system. Information about domain concepts and their organization can be used in planning the overall architecture and in refining the overall system requirements for functionality. Using this information, knowledge engineers can also estimate knowledge acquisition needs, including forecasting the number and type of domain experts anticipated and the number of knowledge acquisition sessions that will be required for a given area. Conceptual analysis also can help the knowledge engineer identify other areas in which knowledge needs to be acquired and can provide tips on knowledge base design.

Domain Analysis. After the background knowledge has been identified, knowledge engineers use various types of analysis techniques to identify the framework of the domain and the basic relationships in the domain. These techniques allow the knowledge engineer to evoke and graphically depict important information that the domain expert may not be able to express verbally. For example, domain analysis techniques, (e.g., task analysis) provide the knowledge engineer with a foundation or structure that depicts the major tasks and subtasks, prerequisites, constraints, and actions an expert uses when attacking typical domain problems. Isolating these entities provides areas for questioning and other information that can be used to structure the domain and identify and plan future knowledge acquisition sessions.

Structured Interviews. The structured interview, unlike its unstructured counterpart, yields specific data (often declarative in nature) in response to focused questions. With this step, refinement of potential knowledge base content and actual design work begins. Structured interviews may be used to clarify or refine information originally elicited during domain, conceptual, or protocol analysis. While this process is portrayed sequentially in the model, knowledge engineers may use the structured interview technique in combination with other techniques at any other stage. Once accurate, refined information has been acquired, the knowledge engineer begins the translation of critical declarative and procedural knowledge into another representation. Suitable representations may include pseudocode, a selected knowledge representation language, or actual code itself.

Solution Analysis. After the knowledge engineer has identified a structure for the domain, major tasks or subsets within the domain, and the manner in which subsets, concepts, and attributes seem to be related, he or she analyzes the expert's solution strategies. At this point the knowledge engineer has some understanding of the domain and its organization. This knowledge enables him or her to select or generate problems for the domain expert to solve. The focus at this stage is on isolating clues to decision-making strategies. The primary goal of this stage is for the knowledge engineer to identify the priorities, heuristics, alternatives, attributes, and critical values that the domain expert uses. Thus, the techniques that are appropriate during this phase are not significantly different from those used in decision analysis (Matheson, 1977) and include process tracing and induction-oriented techniques. The knowledge that these techniques yield provides content for rules that specify how declarative knowledge is used to solve problems.

Knowledge Acquisition Tools and Prototypes. At this stage, the knowledge engineer may use a variety of knowledge acquisition tools to tackle the implementation task that is suitable for the given stage of development. Selected tools may vary along a continuum ranging from domain-related software simulations, intelligent editing programs, induction programs, and prototypes of the developing expert system itself. Reviewing the performance of early prototypes enables the knowledge engineer and domain expert to investigate the accuracy and completeness of the knowledge base and the inference procedures that were applied. Refinements that emerge from this type of knowledge acquisition session result in increased functionality and the identification of "holes" in the knowledge base. In addition, prototypes allow the evaluation of the efficacy of selected representations and knowledge-base design.

Putting it All Together

To summarize, the approach we propose is a systems-oriented methodology for knowledge acquisition. Selected techniques range from unstructured tools (e.g., unstructured interview) to those whose purpose and target knowledge is quite specific (e.g., structured interviews, prototype review). Their appropriateness for any given application depends on the development phase, the type or level of knowledge that has been targeted for elicitation, and overall knowledge acquisition plans. The systems orientation (emphasizing iterations of ever-more-specific analysis and design efforts) provides a manageable structure for the knowledge acquisition process.

Concurrently, this orientation emphasizes ongoing documentation throughout each cycle and technique applied. Program-wide documentation is suggested, both for the purpose of internal communication and for later verification and validation efforts. The documentation system we propose includes a central "knowledge acquisition database," which is updated to reflect knowledge acquisition plans, session notes, and domain expert participation. Specifically, templates within the database system include knowledge acquisition forms, which document plans for, and notes from, knowledge acquisition sessions, domain expert files, and rule content forms. (See Chapter 3 for suggested procedures in setting up and using these templates.)

As the development cycle iterates, its focus is on continual refinement (e.g., accuracy, completeness) and performance (e.g., interactions of established rules, time constraints, equivalence to human expert's reasoning). Because of the structure, standardization of approach, and the documentation of knowledge acquisition efforts across a program, the developing knowledge base reflects ongoing verification and validation efforts and enhances maintainability and modifiability.

The remaining chapters within this text address specific guidelines and procedures for putting the systems-oriented knowledge acquisition program in place and issues that relate to the different segments or techniques shown in Figure 2-10.

ENDNOTES

[1] In more recent ACM publications, Boehm has described the "spiral model."

[2] A comprehensive explanation of each of these components can be found in a number of software engineering texts.

[3] Information on these and other design notations and techniques is available in numerous software engineering texts, such as those appearing in the "Suggested Readings" section of this chapter.

[4] For further information, see Hayes-Roth and others (1983) and Frost, 1986.

[5] Chapter 1 provides a definition and description of knowledge engineering.

[6] If conventional problem-solving meets the same criteria, it too can be successful without good software engineering practices. The knowledge-intensive problems outside this category have the same difficulties as conventional problems.

[7] See Chapter 1 for more information on this model.

[8] These questions match the characteristics of AI problems that were discussed in the previous section. Notice that the questions are not as formal nor as specific as design notations and structured analysis methods available for conventional problem-solving analysis.

[9] Chapter 3 describes the suggested guidelines and procedures in detail.

SUGGESTED READINGS

Fairley, Richard E. Software Engineering Concepts. New York, N.Y.: McGraw-Hill, 1985.

Boehm, Barry W. Software Engineering Economics. Englewood Cliffs, N.J.: Prentice Hall, 1981.

Gane, C., and T. Sarson, Structured Systems Analysis: Tools and Techniques, Englewood Cliffs, NJ: Prentice Hall, 1979.

3

Organizing a Knowledge Acquisition Program

Getting Started

> **Domain Familiarization**
> **Knowledge Acquisition Facilities and Equipment**

Developing Knowledge Acquisition Procedures

> **Knowledge Acquisition Procedures**
> **Record-Keeping Procedures**
> **Review Procedures**

Orienting the Participants

> **Knowledge-Engineer Orientation and Training**
> **Domain-Expert Orientation and Training**

The Anatomy of a Session: A Case Study

> **Planning the Knowledge Acquisition Session**
> **Conducting the Session**
> **Reviewing the Session**
> **Session Follow-up**

INTRODUCTION

Large-scale expert system development projects complicate the process of acquiring knowledge because they typically have the following characteristics: (1) multiple knowledge engineers (both "acquirers" and "programmers"), (2) multiple domain experts, (3) customer requirements for knowledge-base traceability, and (4) domains that are complex in nature.

Knowledge engineers on large programs may function primarily as knowledge acquisition experts, programmers, or both. However, these areas of expertise typically require diverse types of skills. Thus, training in the use of knowledge acquisition techniques, methodology, and/or the implementation tool may be required prior to beginning knowledge acquisition. Second, the use of multiple domain experts is usually necessary, owing to demands on their time and the need for diverse subsets of knowledge. Yet these experts often do not understand expert system technology or the role they will play in knowledge acquisition. Third, knowledge traceability is important to both customers and developers of large-scale expert systems. Customers want to be able to review knowledge base content and be aware of knowledge sources. Developers require the ability to modify current knowledge base content, understanding the effect a change in one rule has on others. Finally, the complexity of the domains represented by most large expert systems requires that the knowledge engineers become familiar with domain concepts, vocabulary, and structure. Special organizational techniques and record-keeping procedures are required to enable developers to meet these demands.

This chapter presents guidelines that enable developers to approach knowledge acquisition in an organized manner. While this approach was designed for use on large programs that require more organization, it can be adapted for use on smaller programs. Initially, we suggest ways developers can organize the domain familiarization activities, including establishing a reference center, compiling a knowledge dictionary, and providing domain training. Next, we offer considerations for the selection of facilities and equipment for knowledge acquisition. We then present guidelines for setting up the knowledge acquisition program, including establishing knowledge acquisition procedures, selecting knowledge acquisition techniques, and developing record-keeping and review procedures. In the final section we offer guidelines for the development of orientation and training to increase the effectiveness of knowledge acquisition. We conclude the chapter with a case study that demonstrates the application of our knowledge acquisition guidelines.

Objectives

This chapter presents guidelines for the development of a structured knowledge acquisition program.[1] Specifically, it enables readers to accomplish the following:
- Define a domain familiarization program
- Suggest facilities and equipment needs for knowledge acquisition
- Identify a set of knowledge acquisition techniques that match program objectives and structure
- Develop management procedures for knowledge acquisition
- Construct appropriate forms to implement record keeping procedures

- Develop an orientation and training program for knowledge engineers and domain experts.

Key Terms

domain familiarization	simulation	knowledge dictionary
needs assessment	audit trail	
knowledge acquisition database	acquisition expert	implementation expert

GETTING STARTED

Prior to beginning an expert system development project, considerable attention should be given to its costs, benefits, and feasibility. In particular, this includes assessment and identification of a "do-able problem," an estimation of needs (costs, equipment, personnel) and schedule, and the formulation of high-level goals for system functionality. Previous authors (Mittal & Dym, 1985; Prerau, 1987) have outlined sets of guidelines for selecting a target system for development.

Once a project has been selected, the program enters what Buchanan (1983) has termed the identification phase of development. During this phase important components of the problem are identified or characterized. Specific tasks that should be completed during this phase include the following:
- Identify functional goals and expectations for the resulting expert system
- Identify subgoals or subtasks from the initial goals
- Define the type of problems the system will be required to solve
- Define expectations for solutions
- Outline known concepts that will be required to meet solutions
- Identify types of human expertise that are used to solve these types of problems
- Identify typical problems experts currently experienced in solving these types of problems.
- Estimate necessary time, equipment, money, internal personnel, and type/number of knowledge sources (e.g., texts, human experts).

The start-up phase of an expert system development program has enormous impact on later knowledge acquisition effectiveness. Knowledge engineers should work with program management during this phase to (1) plan domain familiarization efforts, (2) establish facilities, (3) develop knowledge acquisition program procedures, and (4) develop orientation plans for participants. Figure 3-1 illustrates these major tasks and related sub-tasks. Subsequent sections of this chapter provide detailed information to guide developers in attaining these goals.

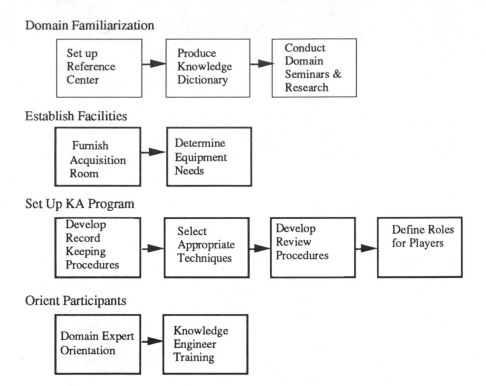

Domain Familiarization

| Set up Reference Center | → | Produce Knowledge Dictionary | → | Conduct Domain Seminars & Research |

Establish Facilities

| Furnish Acquisition Room | → | Determine Equipment Needs |

Set Up KA Program

| Develop Record Keeping Procedures | → | Select Appropriate Techniques | → | Develop Review Procedures | → | Define Roles for Players |

Orient Participants

| Domain Expert Orientation | → | Knowledge Engineer Training |

Figure 3-1. Major Start-up Tasks

Domain Familiarization

During the identification phase of knowledge acquisition, program management and knowledge engineers become familiar with aspects of the domain for which the expert system project will be developed. Initial familiarization efforts will produce only rudimentary knowledge, which must then be expanded to complete the tasks outlined above. There are two ways to approach **domain familiarization**. One approach is to attempt to hire a domain expert who is able to act also as knowledge engineer. The second approach is to (1) make use of seasoned knowledge engineers who can be trained to elicit domain expertise from a human expert or (2) train current system analysts to handle the task.

Developers should not assume that it will be less costly or problematic to hire one individual to serve in the dual roles of both domain expert and knowledge engineer. First, it is difficult or impossible for an individual to accurately tap his or her own knowledge. Second, requiring one person to act as both knowledge engineer and domain expert may contaminate the system by imposing a preconceived structure on the knowledge base. Third, few organizations can afford the overhead necessary to hire new experts for each system and then bring each of them "up the learning curve" with computer science, AI, cognitive science, and communications training. Therefore, we suggest that domain familiarization activities be established to meet the goals of expert system development during the identification phase of knowledge acquisition. The goal of these activities is *not* to turn knowledge engineers into experts, but to increase the effectiveness with which they communicate with experts and conceptualize the domain.

Since most projects have more on-staff knowledge engineers than experts, the importance of domain familiarization cannot be minimized. Most knowledge engineers will not be familiar with the domain with which the completed expert system must deal. As Prerau (1987) notes, "It is useful to invest some time up front discussing the domain in general without focusing on the task the expert system will perform" (p. 46). Through this extension of the identification phase knowledge engineers are trained to "speak the language" and understand basic concepts in the domain. Thus, they are better prepared to make the best use of the domain expert's valuable time. Domain experts appreciate a knowledge engineer's efforts to make communication more effective and sessions more constructive.

For small projects in well-defined or structured domains, knowledge engineers may be able to enroll in some of the training courses domain experts take. Refresher courses coupled with a review of existing training materials are particularly effective. In a large-scale project, however, developers will find it advantageous to organize domain familiarization. Tasks that enhance domain familiarization include

- Establishing and stocking a project reference center
- Developing a knowledge dictionary
- Planning seminars, lectures, or other training opportunities.

Establishing a Reference Center
Imagine a large expert system development project with multiple knowledge engineers, each assigned specific subtasks or subsystems. While many of them will need information that is unique to their assignment, all of them will need general, foundation-building information. As the project matures, personnel changes may necessitate that new personnel be assigned to replace original engineers or that responsibilities be altered to meet project needs. In this common scenario, knowledge engineers would almost certainly duplicate efforts in researching and ordering domain-related information. Establishing a project wide reference center can eliminate duplication, reduce costs, and encourage a "standardized" set of required readings. Printed material can provide valuable background information that knowledge engineers can use to build a foundation in the domain. Texts provide an extraction and organized presentation of an expert's (or a set of experts') knowledge (Prerau, 1987) and enable knowledge engineers to learn basic information prior to meeting with experts.

Establishing a reference center isn't difficult, but it does require a commitment by project management for time, space, and acquisition costs. The following steps summarize the major tasks involved.

1. Appoint someone to be the project "librarian." This individual is responsible for establishing a working relationship with corporate or university libraries, compiling requests for acquisitions, ordering materials, and keeping a current file on center contents.

2. Locate a central location for the reference center. A small room with a locking door and adequate area for files is most appropriate. Overestimate the area you will need for storage; acquisitions grow quickly!

3. Acquire a computer system and database software that will allow the project librarian to enter each acquisition according to important fields. Suggested fields include: title, author, publication, date, location in library, key words for searching, and a short abstract or description.

4. Meet with corporate librarians to determine available facilities, costs involved, and services provided. For example, a corporate librarian probably will have access to several external databases (e.g., Dialog). If so, he or she will be able to search them according to topics you specify and send you varying levels of information (title/author only, title/author/abstract) on "finds." Many corporate librarians are able to run the initial search and then update that search on a quarterly basis. In addition, many companies have arrangements with area libraries that will allow them to gain access to titles you request that may not be housed internally.

5. Establish procedures for project engineers to request searches or specific titles. For example, if you have electronic mail facilities, this information can be sent directly to the project librarian, who compiles and distributes search or title acquisition requests to all project personnel on a weekly basis. Each person reviews the titles and responds if he or she has already possesses them. This helps reduce duplication and costs.

6. Order selected materials for the reference center. Do not limit yourself to the articles requested from topic searches. Include books, videotaped training materials and copies of printed training materials (e.g., user's manual) used in the domain.

7. Determine the filing system to be used in the reference center. For example, files may be set up in alphabetical order by author's name, by content or functional area, or by a combination of approaches.

8. Use the computer system and database software to input key information for each acquisition as it arrives. Project engineers should be able to review alphabetical listings by author and title, as well as topic listings.

Producing the Knowledge Dictionary

Traditional systems engineering suggests the use of data dictionaries for software development projects. A requirement for a large-scale expert system program is a similar "domain knowledge" dictionary (Figure 3-2). Ask any student learning a second language and you will find that a translation dictionary is a must. Likewise, to accurately scope the expert system, define its functionality, and work effectively with domain experts, knowledge engineers must understand the domain's terminology and basic concepts. Since concepts are closely tied to the vocabulary we use to represent it, a **knowledge dictionary** is a useful tool to compile important information. Once compiled, it serves as a reference throughout the program, reflecting a common base of understanding for all team members.

Knowledge Dictionary
Desktop Publishing Advisor

em space
> A space that is the width of the type height

en space
> A space that is one-half of the type height

figure space
> A space that is the width of the numeric digits "0" through "9"

graphic elements
> Content-free visuals such as bars, bullets, boxes

hyphenation
> The process of connecting 2 words or dividing long words between 2 sides. Must first decide whether or not you want it to occur.

inside margin
> The margin nearest the binding; should never be closer than 1/2".

kerning
> The process of altering the natural spacing between letters.

leading
> The amount of space from the baseline of one line of type to the baseline of the line of type directly beneath it. Expressed in points.

Figure 3-2. Sample Page from a Knowledge Dictionary

The knowledge dictionary may be produced in printed format, with each new version assigned a different release number or date. However, it will be even more useful if it can be maintained electronically on a bulletin board system or a program wide account on a computer system. In the latter case, a single person coordinates getting the initial version on the system. Once established, individual knowledge engineers can update the system. In this accessible format the dictionary may be revised and printed as needed. The suggestions that follow may help compile the knowledge dictionary in either format.

1. Instruct knowledge engineers to keep a running list of all unknown words, key terms, and acronyms (plus the source in which they were presented) they encounter while researching the domain.

2. Add to the list any words or phrases that commonly occur in discussions of the domain, either in print (training material, etc.) or in meetings with domain experts or customers.

3. Compile the list for presentation to a domain expert or assign portions of the list to multiple domain experts. Ask the experts to offer a clear, concise definition for each entry and where feasible, to provide any interrelationships, constraints, etc. (If the expert prefers, this may be handled orally and videotaped for later transcription.)

4. Compile and alphabetize the list, including information received from the experts. Send the revised list to the experts for their review and edits.

5. Encourage knowledge engineers to make this a "living" list, adding new terms and definitions to the list as they are discovered.

Domain-Related Training

As the materials that will allow domain familiarization to occur arrive, project management should attend to the issue of knowledge engineer "training" in the domain. Training in the domain is one way that domain familiarization (Hayes-Roth, et al., 1983) can be approached. This type of training should occur in both individual and group settings. If the expert system project has been divided into tasks so that one or two engineers are assigned to develop a specific functional area, each team will need background in its specific area. In addition, there will be general needs that can be met by training presented to all project personnel.

Most individual or small team domain training goals can be attained using appropriate reference center materials. To extend their domain understanding, some customers may allow selected engineers to attend training courses. During this phase of development, knowledge engineers should also have access to a domain expert who can answer specific questions about the domain. Prerau (1987) suggests that an initial period should be devoted to tutorials on the domain and a review of domain terminology for all staff knowledge engineers.

The format for group-based training can vary from lecture-style seminars by domain experts on selected topics to group presentations of training videotapes. In some cases, knowledge engineers may benefit from actual domain experience. Regardless of its extensiveness, this experience can enable knowledge engineers to better plan the system and communicate with the experts. Project management may wish to organize opportunities for knowledge engineers to learn vicariously from close observation or personally from actual participation.

Knowledge Acquisition Facilities and Equipment

Small expert system development projects need few facilities and equipment. If the project has a single expert and that expert can keep interruptions to a minimum, knowledge acquisition sessions could take place at his or her office. For a project with one or two knowledge engineers, little additional equipment is required. One knowledge engineer may take notes as the other conducts the knowledge acquisition session. Although we encourage videotaping knowledge acquisition sessions, an audiotape may be sufficient for small projects. This tool serves to jog the knowledge engineer's memory and enhance his or her interviewing skills.

The Knowledge Acquisition Environment

Projects in which multiple knowledge engineers, each representing different parts of the system, work with multiple experts (either individually or in groups) place additional requirements on facilities and equipment--for several reasons:

- Large projects take longer to complete and thus experience higher turnover. Videotaping sessions with experts allow new project personnel to get important information without asking the expert(s) redundant questions.

- Large projects may have portions of the system divided between multiple knowledge engineers. While these engineers may be seeking dissimilar information from experts, there will be some areas of overlap. Scheduling knowledge acquisition sessions in rooms of reasonable size and videotaping them allows others engineers to participate in the session or view a recorded session. This also results in a reduction in redundant questioning.

- Large projects will experience more problems in tracking, tracing, or auditing knowledge. Eventually it will be important to know which piece of information came from which expert. Taping the sessions and following other procedures in this chapter can help meet this need.

Facilities should ideally include a closed-off, quiet area in which to conduct knowledge acquisition sessions. Figure 3-3 details some suggested requirements for knowledge acquisition environments.

Knowledge Acquisition Room Wish List

- Comfortably accommodate at least 3 people (seating, space)
- Contain a table or writing surface
- Be equipped with writing/communication aids
  (e.g., whiteboard, overhead projector, markers)
- Accommodate appropriate placement of videotaping equipment
  (e.g., camera, monitor, remote control)
- Be free from distractions (e.g., noise)
- Be equipped with "drop" microphones, if possible
- Be equipped with an observation window, if possible

Figure 3-3. Facilities for a Knowledge Acquisition Environments

Equipment for Knowledge Acquisition Sessions

A well-trained knowledge engineer, a communicative, well-versed domain expert, and a quiet setting can result in an effective knowledge acquisition session without any other "props." However, experience has shown that certain props make the job easier the first time and/or allow for later review of the knowledge acquisition session. Figure 3-4 specifies some useful support materials for knowledge acquisition sessions. The following sections provide rationale and considerations for the use of some of these items.

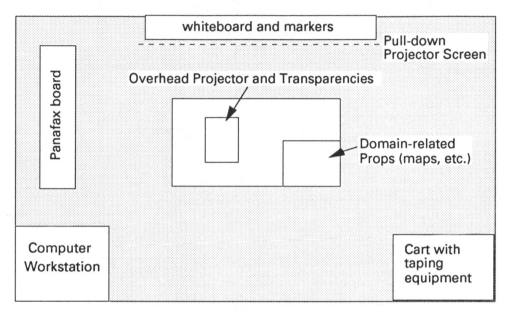

Figure 3-4. Knowledge Acquisition Environment

Videotape Equipment. If it is labeled to indicate knowledge acquisition session, topic, and date, a videotape of the session can be very useful in later review or clarification. It also frees the knowledge engineer to interact more directly with the expert instead of furiously copying down what is said. Additionally, videotaping enables the sharing of information among knowledge engineers on a program.

Videotaping does have disadvantages. First, it can be distracting to some experts (Hart, 1986), interfering with their ability to provide information. Second, it requires some orientation. Knowledge engineers must learn how to run it and experts must be briefed on why and how tapes will be used. Third, transcribing a session from a videotape is time-consuming. In fact, previous experience indicates that it will take from two to three times as long as the session itself to review it. For example, as Figure 3-5 illustrates, a 1-hour session may require 2 to 3 hours of an engineer's time for review and transcription.

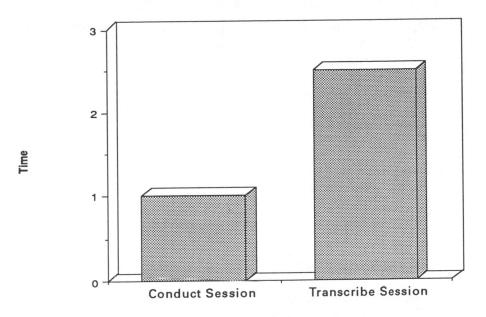

Figure 3-5. Time Requirements (in hours) for Sessions with Transcription

Audiotape Equipment. While video is superior to audiotape in its ability to capture nonverbal cues, interaction, and context, not every program will have videotaping equipment. Not only is it expensive, but it also is harder to transport and is more conspicuous than audiotape equipment. Some experts who are distracted by videotaping equipment may not find audiotaping equipment as intrusive. Although it cannot capture the nonverbal cues that are so important to specific types of knowledge acquisition sessions, audiotaping does free the engineer to focus on guiding the session. In addition, it can be carried to and from knowledge acquisition sites easily and takes up little storage space.

Writing boards and Transparencies. Whiteboards, blackboards, flip charts, or overhead transparencies all enable experts or engineers to draw diagrams or keep "community" notes during a session. Electronic boards, such as the Panaboard™, go a step further. They allow knowledge acquisition-session participants to write, draw, or post information on the board. The board is scanned electronically, producing a hard copy of board contents. This eliminates trying to copy from the board after the knowledge acquisition session and makes it possible to file related session information together.

Computer/Terminal. A computer with appropriate software (e.g., word processor, spreadsheet, graphics program, HyperCard™) and a printer can be a multipurpose knowledge acquisition tool. Knowledge engineers can use the word processing capability to take notes on the session in progress or take notes while reviewing a videotape and can use the graphic program to develop mental models or taxonomies based on domain expert input. Later, knowledge engineers can use spreadsheet and/or database programs to catalog session material and source. If given adequate training, experts can (and often will enjoy) also provide domain-related information in this manner. In fact, Chapter 9 recommends the use of more than one computer with a common projection mechanism to encourage communication and cooperation among knowledge acquisition session participants.

Models/Props and Simulations. Each domain has its own special models and props. Having these on hand before knowledge acquisition sessions saves the "last minute rush" to secure the desired equipment. For example, domain experts for route planning expert systems will need a map showing a variety of detail or from different altitudes or views. A **simulation** tool or a mock presentation of an actual domain event is also useful as it can stimulate the expression of cues (verbal, kinesthetic, etc.) to domain heuristics that might be difficult to obtain otherwise. If simulation tools already exist for the specific domain of interest, make early attempts to secure them and gain access to the tools and equipment on which they run.

DEVELOPING KNOWLEDGE ACQUISITION PROCEDURES

Concurrent with setting up domain familiarization activities and facilities, knowledge engineers and program management personnel should establish the session guidelines and the record-keeping and review procedures that will make knowledge acquisition manageable.

Chapter 2 suggests that large-scale development efforts require some organization of the rapid prototyping cycle. Even more so than in small projects, management and knowledge traceability issues are critical. In projects with one or two developers and a single expert, it is relatively easy to provide an **audit trail** (e.g., trace mechanism) from source to code. In addition, the use of knowledge acquisition procedures and techniques will be fairly standard because of the small number of knowledge engineers.

This section suggests knowledge acquisition session procedures, record-keeping procedures, and review procedures that enable organization of the knowledge acquisition process. To set up a successful, manageable knowledge acquisition program for a large expert system development project, the following tasks should be undertaken:
- Participant roles and knowledge acquisition techniques should be specified
- Knowledge acquisition forms and guidelines for use by numerous individuals must be developed
- Procedures for tracking knowledge from source to code must be developed.

Knowledge Acquisition Procedures

Developing knowledge acquisition procedures entails at least two major tasks: (1) identifying key players and their roles and (2) determining the specific knowledge acquisition techniques that the program will suggest knowledge engineers employ.

Determining Roles: Who Does What, When?
"Too many cooks spoil the broth." This truism is packed with wisdom for large-scale expert system development projects. Multiple knowledge engineers, programmers, and management staff can complicate implementation unless each knows what is expected. Major development roles and responsibilities are described in the following paragraphs.

The Knowledge Engineering Coordinator. Large-scale projects with multiple knowledge engineers can benefit from the services of a knowledge engineering coordinator. The coordinator's responsibilities vary, depending upon the current development cycle and the abilities of the rest of the staff. Initially, this individual is responsible for (1) ensuring that the domain-familiarization activities proceed as required and (2) selecting appropriate knowledge acquisition procedures and techniques. Concurrently, he or she is responsible for setting up and/or delivering training in the selected procedures and knowledge acquisition techniques. Later, this person may be responsible for the following activities:

- Reviewing knowledge acquisition plans developed by knowledge engineers
- Setting up knowledge acquisition session schedules upon knowledge engineer request
- Monitoring knowledge acquisition session completion and effectiveness
- Reviewing knowledge acquisition forms or transcriptions
- Checking the knowledge acquisition notebook or database to evaluate organization of material and to confirm later expert review of summaries of knowledge acquisition sessions
- Overseeing the translation of knowledge from source to initial code
- Compiling knowledge-base documentation.

Knowledge Acquisition and/or Implementation Expert. Expert system "teams" within a particular project may be made up of a single individual who is responsible for knowledge acquisition, design, and programming. An alternative is for multiple individuals to share these tasks and/or to pool their expertise. For example, an **"acquisition expert"** might be responsible for eliciting or acquiring target knowledge, while an **"implementation expert"** might be responsible for coding it. The division of responsibilities depends on (1) the size of the program (and thus, other tasks such as document preparations, review, and meetings) and (2) the skills of the individuals on each team.

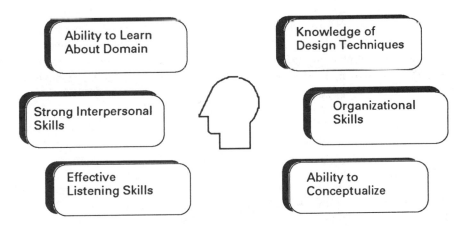

Figure 3-6. Desirable Knowledge Engineer Attributes

Tasks specifically associated with knowledge acquisition and design responsibilities require that the "ideal" knowledge engineer exhibit attributes such as those in Figure 3-6. Additional skills required for effective implementation of acquired knowledge include the ability to extract and abstract knowledge into a selected representation scheme, working knowledge of chosen expert system tool shell and/or programming language (e.g., LISP, Scheme), and ability to follow program coding guidelines and constraints (e.g., techniques to document code).

Domain Expert. Buchanan and others (1983) defined the role of the domain expert as that of an "informant" who tells knowledge engineers about personal knowledge or expertise. In this role, the domain expert does not necessarily present the information in an organized, carefully planned manner. On other occasions the domain expert may act as the "master" in the master-apprentice tradition. Regardless of the role desired, domain experts should be chosen carefully (assuming, of course, that the developer has a choice). Selection criteria include expertise, availability, and the ability to conceptualize and communicate effectively. Specific responsibilities include:

- Assisting as a mentor or guide in the domain familiarization phase (e.g., identifying key documents/materials, serving as the source for the development of the knowledge dictionary)
- Reviewing functional goals for various development cycles
- Reviewing knowledge acquisition plans to help meet functional goals
- Reviewing knowledge acquisition session forms prior to sessions
- Preparing for knowledge acquisition sessions
- Working with knowledge engineers to complete effective sessions
- Reviewing notes from knowledge acquisition sessions for clarification and verification
- Reviewing and evaluating prototype efforts.

Knowledge Acquisition Techniques

Establishing knowledge acquisition procedures also entails determining which knowledge acquisition techniques will be used and the degree of structure that will be applied to the process of knowledge acquisition. For example, unstructured knowledge acquisition would be exemplified by a session in which a knowledge engineer meets informally with an expert. In this type of session, questions are determined by conversation flow and resulting information may be transferred directly to code after the session. In comparison, a more structured knowledge acquisition approach might include

- Presession determination of technique, goal, and possible questions
- Expert preview of planned knowledge acquisition-session structure and questions
- Coordinator review of knowledge acquisition-session plans
- Suggested procedures to write up the knowledge acquisition session
- Suggested procedures to track the translation of acquired knowledge to code.

The field of all possible knowledge acquisition techniques is vast. It includes techniques borrowed from the field of communications (e.g., consensus decision making), psychology (e.g., construct analysis), instructional design, and education (e.g., lecture). Hoffman (1987), who analyzed knowledge extraction from the perspective of experimental psychology, suggests that knowledge extraction methods fall into a handful of categories. Other authors uniformly mention the interview as the standard technique. Still others list the analysis of expert solutions to sample problems and the use of automated knowledge acquisition techniques. Some of these techniques are more effective with single experts; others can be used with multiple experts in a single session. While some techniques require special training or communication skills on the part of the knowledge engineer, others require special hardware or software. Figure 3-7 summarizes a sampling of techniques that may be used in knowledge acquisition sessions. Each is briefly described in the next section. Later chapters describe specific techniques in greater detail.

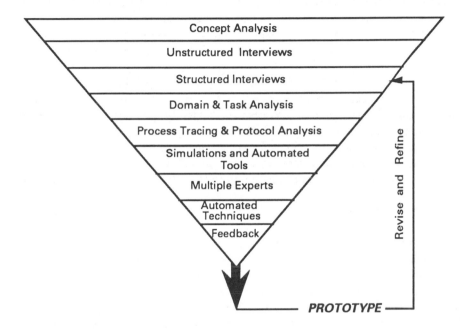

Figure 3-7. A Sampling of Knowledge Acquisition Techniques

Concept Analysis. Concept analysis techniques help knowledge engineers determine the classification and categorization techniques an expert is using. They may be used once the knowledge engineer is familiar enough with the domain to select sample problems. Knowledge engineers present the expert with a specific problem or situation. Problems using these techniques include required knowledge engineer training in the various techniques. Additionally, these techniques are very subjective. They often result in an understanding of a single expert's model of his or her "world" during a solution to a problem (Hart, 1986).

Unstructured Interview. Given the general knowledge acquisition session goal, the expert functions as a lecturer. The knowledge engineer asks questions to clarify understanding and takes notes in an outline format. This interview method is often used in initial knowledge acquisition efforts. Problems include lack of focus, dependence upon the domain expert's ability to "teach," and the possibility of not using the expert's time efficiently.

Structured Interview. The knowledge engineer outlines specific goals and questions for the knowledge acquisition session. The expert is provided with session goals and sample lines of questioning, but may or may not be provided with specific questions to be asked. This type of interview is a mainstay of knowledge acquisition. It is used in all phases of the process to clarify or extend information received via other techniques.

Domain and Task Analysis. Domain and task analysis can be used to structure the knowledge acquisition process (McGraw & Riner, 1987). Initially, the knowledge engineer identifies the type of knowledge the expert appears to be using and selects an appropriate analysis technique, such as mission decomposition or information flow analysis. The knowledge engineer works with the expert to refine the resulting analysis and the levels of information presented. Problems with this technique include a general lack of knowledge engineer training in analysis techniques and thus, an increase in required learning time. Additional problems depend on the knowledge engineer's ability to conceptualize and break down tasks into manageable chunks that may be represented in the analysis and later used in design.

Process Tracing and Protocol Analysis. Adapted from psychological techniques, protocol analysis and process tracing techniques involve asking experts to report on, or demonstrate, their decision-making process for a specific problem. The knowledge engineer then develops a structure or framework that can be used to represent the information, actions, alternatives, and decision rules the expert is using (Svenson, 1979; McGraw & Seale, 1987). These techniques are effective for knowledge acquisition sessions focusing on the elicitation of routine procedures, facts, or heuristics (Gammack & Young, 1985) for any phase of knowledge acquisition. Problems include the difficulty experts have reporting on their cognitive processes and required knowledge engineer training.

Simulations and Automated Tools. Especially effective in later phases of knowledge acquisition, these techniques allow an expert to interact directly with an automated tool to solve a problem. These tools can be used for knowledge acquisition, refinement, validation, or testing (McGraw & Seale, 1987). Tools may include software programs that are appropriate to the domain, "props" (such as models of various aircraft for tactical flight maneuver discussions), maps, or schematics for a system that the expert will "troubleshoot" to determine the probable cause of a malfunction. Problems include tool and equipment availability and training in their use. In addition, for simulations to be useful, they must be a close match to the problem at hand. And finally, the effective transfer of information received from these types of sessions to the knowledge base must be well-planned in advance.

Multiple Expert Techniques. Any of these aforementioned techniques may be adapted for use with multiple experts who will be consulted individually or in small groups. However, special techniques may be required when experts are consulted in a small group situation (McGraw & Seale, 1987b). These techniques include brainstorming, consensus decision making, and the nominal-group technique, all of which are described in Chapter 9. In addition to the selection of techniques, acquiring knowledge from multiple experts requires that knowledge engineers plan in advance for the resolution of conflict among the experts and techniques to represent the diverse knowledge that may be forthcoming.

Variables Influencing Technique Selection

Many variables will influence the selection of specific knowledge acquisition techniques and the degree of structure with which they are applied. For example, it may be advantageous to use a specific technique if it enables meeting established program goals, makes efficient use of both the knowledge engineer's and domain expert's time, and is less threatening to the domain expert. Techniques that can be tailored to extract information on selected subdomains of knowledge or on the expert's strategies (e.g., process tracing/protocol analysis) are desirable because they are efficient. That is, the knowledge engineer can learn one technique and vary or adapt it to meet many different needs. In many cases, knowledge engineers must weigh advantages and disadvantages when selecting a technique. For example, while interviews may yield a tremendous amount of data, they are often time consuming, require a knowledge engineer with interviewing skill, and may result in surface-level knowledge.

General determinants for the selection of knowledge acquisition techniques include the following:

- Program size and goals
- Knowledge acquisition phase
- Availability of experts
- Number and background of knowledge engineers.

Program Size and Goals. Large-scale programs are in more need of structure and predetermined techniques than smaller, more informal programs. Program goals and required expert system functionality impact the type of knowledge acquisition techniques that are selected. For example, if your customer requires that the resulting expert system function as a decision aid for an aircraft system maintenance troubleshooter, you may prefer to use techniques like structured interviews, process tracing, and problem simulation to extract knowledge.

Knowledge Acquisition Phase. For each development cycle, discernible knowledge acquisition phases exist. In most cases, these phases track with the level of specificity of information that is required. Figure 3-8 portrays one view of knowledge acquisition phases, major responsibilities for each phase, specific tasks to be conducted during each phase, and estimates for the percentage of total manpower required. These percentages represent the division of time required of each participant--knowledge engineer and domain expert--to complete the tasks. For example, Phase I knowledge acquisition efforts in a given development cycle are more general in nature and, when completed, provide a foundation for the knowledge that will be extracted. Important tasks to be completed during this phase include developing a knowledge dictionary of domain terms and concepts. In this phase, techniques like unstructured interviews and task analysis may be appropriate. Of the total manpower required for this phase, the knowledge engineer can be expected to expend the most effort. As the information sought becomes more specific and development enters Phase 2, techniques like process tracing, followed by structured interviewing are more appropriate. In Phase 3, knowledge acquisition tasks for the current development cycle may include requiring experts to work with a simulation or prototype to refine knowledge.

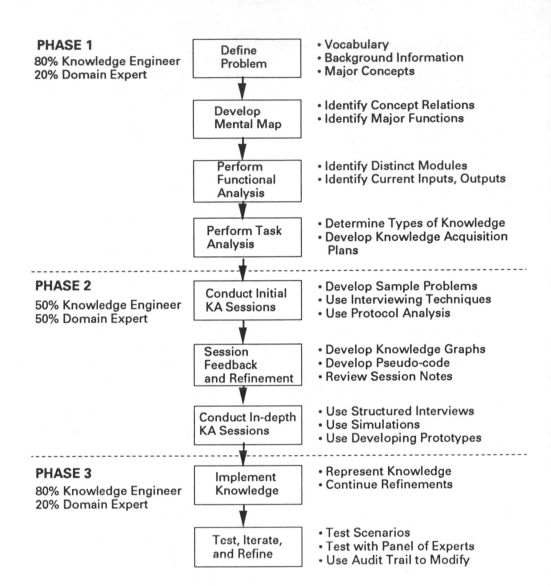

PHASE 1
80% Knowledge Engineer
20% Domain Expert

Define Problem
- Vocabulary
- Background Information
- Major Concepts

Develop Mental Map
- Identify Concept Relations
- Identify Major Functions

Perform Functional Analysis
- Identify Distinct Modules
- Identify Current Inputs, Outputs

Perform Task Analysis
- Determine Types of Knowledge
- Develop Knowledge Acquisition Plans

PHASE 2
50% Knowledge Engineer
50% Domain Expert

Conduct Initial KA Sessions
- Develop Sample Problems
- Use Interviewing Techniques
- Use Protocol Analysis

Session Feedback and Refinement
- Develop Knowledge Graphs
- Develop Pseudo-code
- Review Session Notes

Conduct In-depth KA Sessions
- Use Structured Interviews
- Use Simulations
- Use Developing Prototypes

PHASE 3
80% Knowledge Engineer
20% Domain Expert

Implement Knowledge
- Represent Knowledge
- Continue Refinements

Test, Iterate, and Refine
- Test Scenarios
- Test with Panel of Experts
- Use Audit Trail to Modify

Figure 3-8. Knowledge Acquisition Phases and Activities

Availability of Experts. The amount of time that a program "needs" an expert is a function of knowledge acquisition techniques and the degree of structure reflected in the knowledge acquisition program. For example, a small program that requires one two-hour meeting with an expert weekly for six weeks for information gathering and prototype review is less dependent on the expert. In comparison, a large program that requires experts to help plan knowledge acquisition cycles, review plans, prepare for knowledge acquisition sessions, interact in sessions, and review session notes is more dependent.

Number and Background of Knowledge Engineers. A function of program size, the number of knowledge engineers also impacts the organization of knowledge acquisition efforts. A further consideration is the degree of perceived match between the desired knowledge acquisition techniques and current knowledge engineer background or capabilities. For example, few novice knowledge engineers have been trained in structured interview techniques. However, if the knowledge engineer has good interpersonal skills, he or she may become adept at conducting structured interviews after brief training and practice sessions. Conversely, poor interpersonal skills or the selection of a more complicated technique (e.g., protocol analysis, construct analysis) will increase training time and, possibly, decrease the effectiveness of the knowledge acquisition session.

Hoffman (1987) proposes the following criteria for the comparison and selection of knowledge acquisition techniques: task and material simplicity, task brevity, task flexibility, task artificiality, data format, data validity, and method efficiency. Techniques may be rated on each of these criteria by applying questions such as those that follow.

Task Simplicity
1. How easy is the technique to use?
2. How much training does a knowledge engineer require prior to using the technique?

Material Simplicity
3. How easy is it to use the materials (e.g., props) that accompany the technique?
4. What are the ease and the cost of acquiring the materials that accompany the technique?

Task Brevity
5. How much time is required to complete a knowledge acquisition session with the technique?
6. How much follow-up time (e.g., transcription) does a technique require?

Task Flexibility
7. Is the technique adaptable?
8. Can the technique be modified?
9. Can the technique be used with a variety of materials?

Task Reality
10. How closely does the task required of the expert match the real world?

Translation Ease
11. How easy is it to translate information acquired using this technique?

Data Validity
12. How valid is the data acquired using this technique?

Technique Efficiency
13. How much useful data is acquired compared to time expended?

Record-Keeping Procedures

After program management has defined knowledge acquisition procedures, it should focus on the record-keeping procedures that the program plans to use. Record-keeping procedures enable knowledge engineers to accomplish the following:
- More effectively use experts' time
- Provide an audit trail for acquired knowledge
- Summarize acquired information for later use, either by the originating knowledge engineer or by engineers interested in related information
- Organize project-related work in a systematic fashion.

Most developers make use of some type of "knowledge document" or data dictionary like that suggested by Prerau (1987). This document is continually updated as the knowledge is acquired, is time-stamped, and reflects established program conventions for recording and coding expert knowledge (e.g., color coding, language use). Our experience has been that the use of a knowledge document is not in itself enough, especially on large-scale programs. Larger programs require that multiple engineers extract, annotate, and record essential information in a standard fashion. Additionally, the procedures used to instigate knowledge acquisition sessions, complete them, and later analyze them should (1) make efficient use of participants' time and (2) enable developers to audit or trace knowledge from source to code. The next section examines some of the management procedures and knowledge acquisition templates that we have found useful.

Knowledge Acquisition Database (or Notebook)

How will knowledge engineers keep track of session goals, areas of focus, and session results? Can knowledge engineers produce a list that details what each knowledge acquisition session in a cycle covered, when the knowledge acquisition session was completed, what materials were used, and who the knowledge source was? Additionally, can information in the knowledge base be traced to a particular knowledge acquisition session or source? Many projects will require that knowledge engineers keep track of knowledge acquisition-related information. The suggestions that follow are based on experience in both both large and small expert system development programs (McGraw & Seale, 1986) and may be adapted easily to meet additional, or lessened, requirements.

The concept of a **knowledge acquisition database** was derived from the engineering notebooks that most projects require engineers to keep during software development. Its purpose is to provide ongoing documentation on the state and results of knowledge acquisition. Although the concept may be expanded, a knowledge acquisition database should include the following sections:
- Knowledge dictionary for the specific system, detailing key terms, concepts, and/or examples
- Knowledge acquisition template and forms identified sequentially by date and functionally by subsystem
- Rule contents template and forms, detailing the derivation of rules from specific knowledge acquisition sessions

- Domain expert template and files, providing identifying information on domain experts (e.g., phone, address), their specialty, commitment to provide project assistance, and comments (e.g., sessions cancelled, late arrival, preparation, etc.).

Whether residing in an actual database or kept as hard copy in a notebook, an organized record can help knowledge engineers document knowledge acquisition sessions, verify session conclusions, and trace rule development to its source. Using a standard set of templates, knowledge engineers enter key information that helps identify the knowledge acquisition session, session date, domain expert or other knowledge source, session goals, session conclusions, and resulting rules. Templates or forms that are especially useful in providing a documentation trail from knowledge source to knowledge base content include the Knowledge Acquisition Form and the Rule Contents Form (examples are provided in subsequent sections of this chapter).[2]

The Knowledge Acquisition Form. The key template in the knowledge acquisition database is the form that documents plans for, and results of, knowledge acquisition sessions. This form initially may be used to plan the knowledge acquisition session and alert the domain expert to the topics that will be discussed. Later, it is expanded to document the major conclusions of the session, future plans, and/or an intermediate representation of possible rules for the knowledge base. After it has been completed, it becomes a permanent record in the knowledge acquisition database (or notebook).

Figure 3-9 provides a sample Knowledge Acquisition Form for an expert system development project. This particular form was created with the dBaseMac[TM] tool from Ashton-Tate. It is one of the templates in a knowledge acquisition project database that also includes a Domain Expert File and a Rule Contents Form. Important fields within the forms are linked or related to each other to enhance the amount of information that can be extracted from the database. The contents in the database are then used to print out reports of rules (e.g., a knowledge base document), knowledge acquisition sessions, and other information.

To increase the usefulness of the Knowledge Acquisition Form, it should be designed to include fields such as

- Knowledge acquisition session number
- Portion or function of the expert system that the information feeds
- Session date, time, and setting
- Knowledge engineer in charge of the session
- Session source(s) (e.g., materials and experts)
- Session documentation (e.g., audiotape, videotape, notes, other attachments)
- Knowledge acquisition technique used (e.g., structured interview, protocol analysis)
- Summary of main points and resulting action items
- Specific heuristics or rules specified by the expert
- Expert verification of session notes.

```
┌─────────────────────────────────────────────────────────────────┐
│                 Financial Planning Expert System                  │
│                  Knowledge Acquisition Form                       │
│                                                                   │
│  ──────────────────────────────────────────────────────────────  │
│  KA Session #:FP101                    KA Session Date: 5/5/88     │
│                                                                   │
│  Session Topic:CD Heuristics                                      │
│                                                                   │
│  Knowledge Engineer:Jan Schmidt        DE/Knowledge Source:Bill   │
│                                                       (1st Bank)   │
│                                                                   │
│  Session Location:1st Bank; 1:00-2:30  Elapsed Time:1 1/2 hrs.    │
│                                                                   │
│                                                                   │
│  Session Type                                                     │
│       ___interview   __X_process tracing    ___simulation         │
│       ___review     _____other             ___construct analysis  │
│  ──────────────────────────────────────────────────────────────  │
│  Major Session Goals:                                             │
│                                                                   │
│  Review terminology in "dictionary". Use protocol analysis to     │
│  observe/videotape Bill working                                   │
│  with client to determine if CDs are good.  Use retrospective     │
│  verbalization with tape as Bill                                  │
│  explains basis for the path his discussion tool.  Analyze:       │
│  • Why CDs were/were not recommended                              │
│  • Identify specific decision points                              │
│  • Isolate values that serve as cut-off points for decision points│
│  • Compare/contrast with other investments to determine attributes│
│    specific to CDs                                                │
│  ══════════════════════════════════════════════════════════════  │
│  Session Summary:                                                 │
│                                                                   │
│  See attached flow of decision paths and attributes.              │
│                                                                   │
│                                                                   │
│  ──────────────────────────────────────────────────────────────  │
│  Rules Derived from Session:                                      │
│                                                                   │
│                                                                   │
└─────────────────────────────────────────────────────────────────┘
```

Figure 3-9. Sample Knowledge Acquisition Form

Completing the Top of the Knowledge Acquisition Form. The following guidelines provide suggestions for the use of the Knowledge Acquisition Form. The purpose of its use is to increase the efficiency and organization of the knowledge acquisition process and to provide ongoing documentation of knowledge acquisition activities.

1. The knowledge engineer analyzes functional plans, previous research, and current development or design efforts to determine the information that will be required to meet development cycle goals.

2. The knowledge engineer fills in identifying information (e.g., session number, date, domain source). This information will later be used to provide knowledge acquisition history and enable auditing of the knowledge base.

3. Next, the knowledge engineer depicts the major goals or objectives of the session and selects the type of session that is planned. Session goals should be completed at a level commensurate with anticipated knowledge acquisition techniques. For example, goals for an unstructured interview would display less information at a higher level than for a structured interview, which would include specific questions to be asked.

4. When completed, the Knowledge Acquisition Form should be submitted (either electronically or as a hard copy) for review to the appropriate party (e.g., knowledge engineering coordinator, team leader). This individual returns the form with comments, if applicable, and provides the knowledge engineer with information needed to schedule rooms, equipment, and experts.

5. A copy of the Knowledge Acquisition Form is then sent to the selected domain expert for review prior to the knowledge acquisition session. The expert is encouraged to clarify or refocus session goals and prepare for the described session.

6. The knowledge engineer makes updates to the form based on domain expert input.

Completing the Bottom of the Knowledge Acquisition Form. In addition to helping plan a knowledge acquisition session, this form provides a record of session notes, conclusions, possible heuristics or rules for inclusion in the knowledge base, and tasks for later follow-up.

Knowledge engineers should follow these suggestions in compiling a review of the knowledge session (McGraw & Seale, 1986).

1. Keep informal notes during the knowledge acquisition session itself and use audiotape, videotape, or another knowledge engineer to capture more detailed information.

2. Review the knowledge acquisition notes or tapes as soon as possible (e.g., within 24 hours) following the session itself. Less information is lost or altered if this guideline is followed.

3. Begin the written review with a short summary statement. Use an outline format to record main points throughout the knowledge acquisition session.

4. Tie all specific information back to videotape or audiotape positions, if applicable. For example, the expert may provide detail on some information that is irrelevant to current development goals but may be useful at a later date. To avoid information loss or copious note taking, note the point on the tape at which this information is presented and jot a brief description of its content on the form.

5. If the knowledge engineer has questions about any information, annotate the session notes with a question or comment. Using *****, [ ], or other markers before and after such information helps differentiate it. For example, at some point the knowledge engineer might wish to ask the expert (who will review the notes) if specific information was interpreted correctly. To do so, the knowledge engineer could embed comments within markers: [Mr. Evans, please clarify and provide an example here].

6. Attach any Rule Content Forms that you create from the information derived from this knowledge acquisition session.

7. Conclude with a brief action item statement (who will do what, and by what date).

8. Send the form, plus supporting Rule Content Forms, to your domain expert for review. Attach a brief cover letter requesting the review and suggesting a return date.

9. Review the Knowledge Acquisition Form when the expert returns it. Make appropriate changes to the knowledge acquisition database. Derive rules from the acquired information.

Mechanisms to Translate Knowledge to Code

Since the focus of this book is on knowledge acquisition as opposed to representation, we will not dwell on specific forms of representations. However, there are intermediary techniques that the knowledge engineer might consider in the difficult task of translating knowledge to a formal representation mechanism. On a small program, the knowledge engineer may choose to work from the Knowledge Acquisition Form, directly translating recorded knowledge into rules. On a large program, in which the knowledge engineer who acquires the knowledge and the one who codes it may not be the same person, other techniques need to be considered. Knowledge engineers or program management personnel may choose from the following mechanisms to assist in this translation:

- An informal knowledge representation language
- English-style translations of heuristics
- Printed or computer-based Rule Content Forms
- Computer-based headers.

Guidelines based on our experiences and others (Prerau, 1987) include:

• Use English-style "pseudocode" IF-THEN rules to record domain expert knowledge during knowledge acquisition sessions whenever possible

• Agree upon conventions (e.g., indentation, capitalization, explanations, justifications) for recording rules from knowledge acquisition sessions

• Use terminology within rules that is consistent with that used in the knowledge dictionary

• Name rules rather than numbering them whenever possible for the increased specificity this allows and because of the number of changes the knowledge base will go through

• Include explanations for the rule, a summary of the rule, and a justification of the rule within its documentation

• Note any certainty factors or factors that impact the rule's validity

• Document the source and knowledge acquisition session from which the rule was acquired

• If possible, run through the prototype as soon as is feasible to determine other rules that a specific rule uses and rules that use it.

The selection of program wide techniques and standards to assist in the translation process depends on many factors. Some considerations include the target representation scheme, communication between knowledge engineers and programmers who will implement the code, personal preference, and the degree of desired documentation and formalism in the program. Each mechanism has positive and negative factors. For example, teams may choose to use an informal knowledge representation language (KRL). If so, they will need to define appropriate structures (e.g., IF-THEN-ELSE) into which knowledge from the knowledge acquisition form is to be mapped. In addition, a program data dictionary must already exist so that knowledge can be reported with accepted terminology. A KRL provides a common set of structures that can be used by all team members. However, it takes time to develop. More importantly, at the beginning of a project team members may not know all the structures they will need to define.

Requiring knowledge engineers to extract knowledge from the Knowledge Acquisition Form and translate that knowledge into English-style representations is usually easier to accomplish. The success of this arrangement, however, depends partially on the structure of the program, the communication abilities of individual team members, and working styles. For example, if the person acquiring the knowledge is not also responsible for coding it, the "acquiring" knowledge engineer must state the knowledge so that the programmer can code it (without translation problems). A typical problem with this arrangement is that the acquiring engineer may not understand the way the programmer has structured the code. Thus, the representation used may not fit the established pattern. Problems may also result from assumptions on the part of the programmer when translating expert knowledge into this representation. The success of this approach is also affected by adherence to the data or knowledge dictionary and frequent interaction between knowledge engineers.

Perhaps the biggest problem with the use of either of these approaches on a large-scale program is that neither includes any mechanism to audit the attained knowledge. Thus, while the acquiring engineer has that information on the Knowledge Acquisition Form, it may or may not find its way into the code itself. However, customers of large-scale expert system projects often require that the code show documentation that details source information to enhance modifiability. Two related techniques, Rule Content Forms and Rule Headers, can help meet this requirement.

A Rule Content Form is a mechanism to transfer origination and other historical information with the semantic content of the rule as it is translated into code. Figure 3-10 displays a sample Rule Content Form from the Knowledge Acquisition Database. Each form represents one rule. The domain expert may be asked to verify the rule and to provide information such as explanation, justifications, or special circumstances. This information then becomes a part of the Knowledge Acquisition Database and is coded into the developing expert system. Links within the database itself allow the knowledge engineers to review rules produced by specific sessions, review summaries from knowledge acquisition sessions in which rules were derived, etc. Printouts of existing rules in formats such as that in Figure 3-10 may be obtained on a scheduled basis and organized by module. Knowledge base documentation such as this enables both internal and external reviews.

DTP Rule Content Form	
Rule Identification:	Source:
Rule Type:	Context:
Rule Content:	
Associated Certainty:	Used By:
Exceptions / Special Cases:	
Comments:	
Approval:	Date:

Figure 3-10. Sample Rule Content Form

Computer-Based Rule Headers. This technique provides a standard format for comments that are appended directly to rules in the knowledge base. This format may include information that allows a knowledge engineer to trace a rule back to its knowledge source (e.g., knowledge acquisition session number). Other slots include explanations or justifications, certainty ratings, interdependency with other rules, etc. (Figure 3-11). Usually a macro is set up to allow easy access of these headers from the keyboard.

```
RULE NAME: SMOKE-DETECT          RULE TYPE:      PROCEDURAL
CODED BY:  CPH                   ACQUIRED BY:    RTG
DATE CODED:  12/9/87             DATE ACQUIRED:  10/7/87
KA FORMS(S):  OIL 203            SOURCE:         KKS
-------------------------------------------------------------
DESCRIPTION: This rule detects oil smoke. It checks for some type of smoke.
Then it checks for oil system pressure. If found, the rule concludes that the smoke
is oil. Diagnosis is recorded in database, which will trigger appropriate procedure.
RESTRICTIONS:            Multiple failures may impact follow-on procedure
RELATED UNCERTAINTIES:  none
COMMENTS/CONSTRAINTS: none
REVISION HISTORY: 9/27/87 (upgraded procedure for linking oil pressure with
smoke)
```

Figure 3-11. Sample Rule Header

Review Procedures

Established review procedures can help make verification and validation an ongoing process and can increase the viability of the developing knowledge base. Procedures should be established for both internal and external reviews.

Establish Internal Reviews

Internal reviews are those that are accomplished by expert system development personnel. Although each project must set up procedures that meet with its specific corporate requirements, we suggest the following techniques.

Peer Review. The completion of knowledge acquisition forms and other tasks related to design should be reviewed by other members of the expert system development team. This review can be informal or may require more formal approvals (e.g., signatures). The peer review works well if the originating knowledge engineer electronically transmits a completed plan for a knowledge acquisition session to other team members. Team members review the major goals and, if needed, respond concerning possible duplication of efforts or to suggest related questions that could be included in the knowledge acquisition session.

Management Review. In large programs, someone from program management may want to review the knowledge acquisition forms before transmittal to the domain expert. This review helps ensure that appropriate knowledge acquisition techniques are being used, that the requested domain expert is suitable, and that information is being sought at the desired level of detail for current design efforts. Management is also urged to schedule reviews of knowledge acquisition "notebooks" (e.g., printouts from the database) and code at least once during each prototyping cycle.

Other Reviews. As with the development of traditional code, practices that mirror good software engineering (e.g., code walkthroughs, design reviews) should be pursued in each prototyping cycle.

Establish External Reviews

As tedious as they can be, external reviews are a fact of life on customer-sponsored expert system development projects. Reviews will run the gamut from system design reviews to demonstrations of prototypes. In addition to these, the program may wish to establish other review mechanisms (e.g., domain expert review) that will may assist in later verification/validation efforts.

Domain expert review is the simplest type of external review. If the customer has "authorized" your domain expert, plan to include that expert in reviews of all resulting design and code efforts. If your customer has not authorized an expert, or if you need opinions from more than one person, you may convene an expert review panel. Select experts for this panel who can help you meet specific knowledge base needs. Establish the desired degree of formality and the meeting schedule well in advance. This panel can then be called on to review existing knowledge base documentation at regularly scheduled interviews. Panel input can be valuable in planning prototyping cycles, refining design, composing sample problem scenarios, verifying or clarifying knowledge base content, and later, in more formal validation procedures.

ORIENTING THE PARTICIPANTS

Procedures are now in place and session guidelines are established. What can possibly go wrong? Unless key team members all start from a common base of understanding, the answer is "quite a lot." An upfront orientation of both knowledge engineers and identified domain experts can make a difference in how well the procedures and guidelines work and thus, how smoothly knowledge acquisition progresses.

Knowledge-Engineer Orientation and Training

Even though some of the knowledge engineers on your team may be experienced in expert system development, they still will require orientation to the current program. Knowledge-engineer orientation should include the following content areas:

- Background on the current program (e.g., information from the proposal, statement of work, contract)

- Prerequisite domain background (e.g., domain training materials, videotapes, terminology)

- Introduction to knowledge acquisition procedures (e.g., sample forms, checklists for procedures)

- Training in specific knowledge acquisition techniques.

The first three content areas may be presented either through training sessions or through written documents that are distributed to all knowledge engineers on the project. A considerable amount of training can be presented in a series of short (approximately 45-minute) seminars that are based on the results of a **needs assessment**.

Developing a Needs Assessment

A training **needs assessment** can be as simple as a form that you compile to assess the areas in which knowledge engineers perceive they need training. Figure 3-12 is an example of such a form. Knowledge acquisition techniques that are expected to be used on the program are listed on the form. The knowledge engineer is asked to respond to indicate the level at which he or she feels training in the technique is needed.

Training Needs Assessment

Use the scale below to rate the degree to which you feel you could benefit from training in the following procedures and techniques. The selections that you make will influence the topics that are selected for the training seminars.

5 = Of great benefit   4 = Of moderate benefit   3 = Undecided
2 = Of little benefit   1 = No known benefit

___1. Knowledge acquisition procedures
___2. Knowledge acquisition techniques
___3. Interviewing domain experts
___4. Planning knowledge acquisition sessions
___5. Using analysis procedures in knowledge acquisition
___6. Conducting a prototcol analysis
___7. Using automated tools, simulations, and prototypes
___8. Ongoing verification and validation
___9. Transcribing knowledge acquisition sessions
__10. Refining knowledge base content
__11. Translating knowledge to pseudocode and for graphic feedback

---

Figure 3-12. Sample Training Needs Assessment

Training in Knowledge Acquisition Techniques

Once the completed needs assessment forms have been returned, training can be structured at the level that most frequently is requested. In many cases, a 45-minute training seminar on each knowledge acquisition technique, combined with a practice exercise and job aid (e.g., a checklist for the specific procedure) is sufficient.

Using Self-Appraisals. The effective use of knowledge acquisition techniques depends on both training and the application of the technique. To be an effective interviewer, for example, knowledge engineers must practice the technique. Likewise, without practice, few knowledge engineers will feel comfortable conducting a process training session. Project management may not have time to review each knowledge engineer's delivery of every knowledge acquisition technique. However, the engineers themselves can evaluate their performance prior to meeting with domain experts.

Self-appraisals offer an extension of training sessions. Provide checklists and exercises that help knowledge engineers practice each technique. For example, Figure 3-13 is a checklist that was used as a self appraisal tool for an interview. Requiring knowledge engineers to review and evaluate videotapes of selected techniques in use (by themselves or others) also can be very useful. Reviewing the videotaped delivery of selected knowledge acquisition techniques allows the engineer to refine his or her delivery and become more comfortable with the technique before working with an expert.

Interview Self-Check

During the interview, did you:
__Introduce the session
__Structure the interview by the use of questioning techniques
__Keep the expert on track
__Summarize the session at its end

View the tape and select a 10-minute segment to analyze. Mark each occurrence of open and closed questions. Figure the resulting ratio.
Open_____   Closed_____
Ratio __:__

Mark each occurrence of secondary questions.
Secondary Questions_____

How many times in the 10 minutes did you make an observable nonverbal response to an expert's comments. Did these behaviors seem to enhance or detract from the communication?
Nonverbal behaviors_____

What type of closing technique did you use?_____
Did you encourage the expert to clarify or revise during closing?____
Did you identify any tasks that would occur in the near future?_____

Figure 3-13. Self Appraisal Checklist

Domain-Expert Orientation and Training

An effective domain expert-knowledge engineer relationship depends on a common understanding of development goals. Chapter 4 presents information that will enhance the working relationship. One way to get it off to a positive start is through a program orientation. This orientation can help domain experts understand what the team is attempting to build, what their role in the program will be, and what they can expect from "knowledge acquisition." The following topics should be discussed in the domain expert orientation and training program and are described in Chapter 4:

- General introduction to expert systems
- Program background and goals
- The domain expert's role
- An overview of knowledge acquisition procedures and techniques.

Determining Expert Expertise

Either as the experts arrive or at the completion of the orientation, ask them to complete a Domain Expert Information Sheet. This form, explained in more detail in Chapter 4, allows each expert to detail past experience and training and to note phone numbers and addresses at which he or she can be contacted. This information can be entered in a database and can then be used to select the domain expert(s) most appropriate for a specific session.

Gaining Commitment

Before adjourning the orientation session, it is useful to gain some commitment from the domain experts. Knowledge engineers can gain commitment by having the expert respond verbally (in a small group) or by completing a form (in a large group). This psychological "sign-up" communicates to potential domain experts that the project is important and that they are critical to its success. It allows them to specify upfront how much time they can devote to the project, whether or not they can attend knowledge acquisition sessions at your site, how they should be compensated for their time, and if anyone else (e.g., supervisor) needs to approve the association.

THE ANATOMY OF A SESSION: A CASE STUDY

The brief scenario that follows is intended to help you integrate the information that has been presented in this chapter. It details the tasks and considerations that Jan, a knowledge engineer, confronts as she plans, undertakes, and follows up on a knowledge acquisition session. Jan is in charge of an expert system that will assist in financial planning. The total time Jan spends on this session is approximately 9 hours, broken down as shown in Figure 3-14.

Planning the Knowledge Acquisition Session

Initially, Jan refers to the contract she has to develop Planner, a financial planning expert system. According to the schedule, she will be fleshing out the knowledge base for CD and IRA investments during the first six weeks. Breaking the program plans down to determine knowledge acquisition plans, she identifies the CD module as her initial goal.

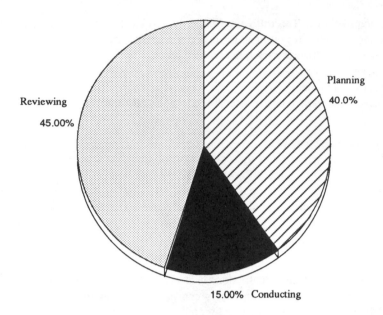

Figure 3-14. Breaking Down a Knowledge Acquisition Session

Contacting the Expert

Since she doesn't know a lot about CDs herself, she has consulted the Knowledge Source Database. It indicates that a financial planner named Bill attended the orientation session and currently specializes in CDs, IRA, and money market funds. His entry in the database lists his phone number and indicates that his time is provided by the customer.

Jan checks with program management before calling Bill to make sure no other knowledge engineers are currently working with him. She calls him to discuss his assistance as a domain expert for the next 4 to 6 weeks. Bill agrees to serve as the primary knowledge source and to send Jan some background reading material on CDs.

Session Background

Next, Jan begins the planning process. She studies the material on CDs that she received and sketches a cognitive model of the domain for her use. This model illustrates the important concepts and issues one must consider when contemplating CDs and how these seem to be related to one another. Because this is her first session on CDs, she decides to plan an overview knowledge acquisition session instead of focusing on a single element from the cognitive model.

Jan sets the major goals for her knowledge acquisition session. First, she wants Bill to review the mental model she has drawn, allowing him to help her clarify and extend it. Second, she wants to understand how Bill uses information about CDs and a person's finances to suggest that CDs are a viable investment.

Developing the Knowledge Acquisition Form

Jan enters the Knowledge Acquisition Database to complete a Knowledge Acquisition Form on the first session she is planning. Working from her session goals, Jan determines that the format will be unstructured interview (reviewing the mental model) followed by a brief process tracing exercise (to identify how Bill determines whether CDs are a good investment). Jan fills in the top portion of the Knowledge Acquisition Form, indicating the session number, system function (CDs), date/time, knowledge engineer and source, type of session, and techniques to be used. She briefly summarizes the major goals of the session and provides a tentative session agenda. The agenda refers to a list of specific questions that will help Bill refine her mental model and a request for Bill to plan a 10-minute scenario that will illustrate (1) features of CDs that make them good investments for a fictitious person and (2) how a financial planning session with this person might progress.

Reviewing the Knowledge Acquisition Form. Jan asks her program management to review the Knowledge Acquisition Form. The knowledge engineering coordinator signs off on the form after suggesting a minor change. She schedules a room and videotape equipment for the date and time Jan requested. Jan sends the form to Bill for review and preparation for the session. Later, Jan contacts Bill to confirm that he received the form and to solicit his suggestions, if any, for changes to the proposed format.

Conducting the Session

Bill arrives early for the session. Jan has already checked the videotape equipment and inserted a blank tape. She has used markers to write information on the whiteboard. Included is the identifying information (e.g., session number and date). This will appear in the first frame of the videotape to identify the knowledge acquisition session. The board also displays an agenda for the session. For Bill's comfort, she has adjusted the air conditioner and provided a glass of water. Jan has also secured writing materials for note taking and illustrating.

Jan welcomes Bill, thanking him for his promptness. She helps him get his material set up and reviews the agenda, topic area to be pursued, how the information will be used, and the special techniques (unstructured interview and process tracing) that will be used. Jan initiates the session by turning on the videotape, introducing the session, and reiterating session goals. The session proceeds according to the agenda and is finished within an hour.

At the close of the session, Jan summarizes their accomplishments and the main points. During the debriefing, she elicits clarification on any issues discussed. She tells Bill that she will work from the tape to write up notes on the session. She requests that he review her notes when they are complete. Action items for both Jan and Bill are written on the whiteboard and assigned an estimated completion date.

Jan thanks Bill and escorts him out of the area. Upon her return to the knowledge acquisition room, she runs the tape back to the beginning and labels the tape with identifying information (e.g., session name, date, source, function). She straightens the room and takes the tape and notes back to her area.

Reviewing the Session

On the following day Jan uses the computer and videotape equipment in the knowledge acquisition room to review the videotape and annotate the Knowledge Acquisition Form. Since the session was one hour, she has set aside two and one-half hours to review and write up the session. Initially, she writes a brief summary of the session's main points as she concurrently reviews it. Next, she takes notes in a general, outline format. When information is given that represents the expert's actual heuristics, she writes out an English version of the rule he seems to be using. When Bill offers advice that will be useful much later in development, Jan notes the numbers on the tape counters and writes these down beside her comment that he mentioned this topic at this point. At some point she realizes that she needs clarification on a specific issue and makes a special note to Bill to provide more information on the issue. She saves and prints out her session notes in a format that lists session name, function, date of the session and review, knowledge source, and knowledge engineer.

Upon completing her writeup of the session, Jan submits the Knowledge Acquisition Form (1) for internal review to the knowledge engineering coordinator and (2) for external review via the domain expert. After sending the form to Bill, she calls him to confirm that he received it and to get a commitment for an estimated return date. During this phone call, she reiterates the importance of his review and urges him to call her if he has questions.

Session Follow-up

Bill returns the annotated Knowledge Acquisition Form to Jan by the promised date. Jan updates the Knowledge Acquisition Database She reviews the form itself to extract (1) rules that she can derive from the session and (2) to identify areas that require further knowledge acquisition sessions. She uses Rule Content Forms to specify an English-language version of rules; when satisfied with their contents, she enters them into the developing knowledge base.

ENDNOTES

[1] Many of the procedures and guidelines suggested in this chapter were adapted from previous work by Dr. Karen L. McGraw and Mary R. Seale, "Pilot's Associate Knowledge Acquisition Session Guidelines," Texas Instruments Defense Systems Artificial Intelligence Lab, 1986.

2 Cognitive Technologies has developed a HyperCard[TM]-based knowledge acquisition management tool for the Macintosh[TM]. For more information, contact P.O. Box 15598, Alexandria, VA 22309.

Panaboard is a trademark of Panafax.

HyperCard and Macintosh are trademarks of Apple Computer Corporation.

dBaseMac is a trademark of Ashton Tate.

SUGGESTED READINGS

Freiling, M., J. Alexander, S. Messick, S. Rehfuss, and S. Shulman. "Starting a knowledge engineering project: a step-by-step approach." AI Magazine 6:3 (1985), 150-163.

Hoffman, R. "The problem of extracting the knowledge of experts from the perspective op experimental psychology." AI Magazine 8:2 (1987), 53-67.

Prerau, D. "Knowledge acquisition in the development of a large expert system." AI Magazine. 8:2 (1987), 43-51.

4

Working Effectively with Domain Experts

Building the Domain-Expert Pool

> **Factors Affecting the Selection Process**
> **Selecting the Initial Pool of Experts**
> **Selecting Specific Experts for Sessions**

Developing and Maintaining Rapport

> **Managing the Environment**
> **Managing the Session**

Common Problems

> **Analyzing Problem Behaviors**
> **Types of Problems**

Techniques for Difficult Situations

> **Reflective Listening**
> **Documenting Problems**

INTRODUCTION

To select appropriate domain experts, developers must identify the experience, characteristics, and attributes that will allow them to meet knowledge base development goals. Identification of requirements for domain experts is only the first step. Few of the selected experts will be knowledgeable concerning expert system development in general and knowledge acquisition specifically. The importance of their role in knowledge base development requires that they become an integral part of the team. This necessitates that their interactions with development personnel be characterized by professionalism and good rapport.

Most knowledge engineer-domain expert interaction takes place in the knowledge acquisition session. As the focal point of the program, the session must be managed and controlled in a manner that enables knowledge transfer and enhances the expert's willingness to participate. These requirements necessitate that knowledge engineers be trained in various areas that can improve their ability to manage sessions, communicate with experts, and effectively handle minor problem situations. In this chapter we address the issue of effective knowledge engineer-domain expert relationships and present techniques for enhancing this working relationship throughout the life of the program. We begin by describing some factors that affect the selection of domain experts, including background, customer authorization, availability, and personal characteristics. Then we present considerations and techniques for selecting the domain-expert "pool," as well as an individual expert for a specific knowledge acquisition session. In the next major section we discuss the application of management and communication principles to develop and maintain rapport between knowledge engineers and domain experts. Next, we discuss some of the more common problems that knowledge engineers will face. We conclude the chapter with a description of techniques that knowledge engineers can use to defuse difficult situations.

Objectives

This chapter presents information that can assist in developing and maintaining effective knowledge engineer-domain expert working relationships. Specifically, it enables readers to accomplish the following:
- Apply techniques to build the domain expert pool and prepare experts for knowledge acquisition sessions
- Develop and use tools to select and monitor domain experts
- Establish conducive physical, spatial, and temporal climates for knowledge acquisition sessions
- Apply leadership and listening skills to function as effective knowledge acquisition session facilitators
- Identify common knowledge acquisition session problems and apply appropriate techniques to lessen their effect.

Key Terms

practicing experts   experienced experts   participant analysis
temporal control   spatial control   nonreflective skills
nonverbal communication   reflective listening   upward-ripple paranoia
attending skills   communicator style

BUILDING THE DOMAIN-EXPERT POOL

Effective working relationships between knowledge engineers and domain experts are characterized by: (1) openness, (2) respect, and (3) interdependence. Openness describes the degree of honesty or directness each party can use with the other and is important to the knowledge engineer's ability to secure valid information from the domain expert. Mutual respect refers to each participant's ability to feel valued by the other. While this does not imply that they must *like* each other, it does imply that each should recognize the other's professionalism and abilities. Interdependence is important in this working relationship as the knowledge engineer and domain expert must work together to meet session goals. Each must be an active participant.

The development of relationships that embody these and related characteristics requires work that begins with the initial selection of domain experts who will contribute to the knowledge base development efforts. Initially, this section discusses expert-related factors that developers must consider as they begin the selection process. Next, techniques for selecting and preparing the initial pool of experts are presented. The final entry in the section provides tips for selecting specific experts from the pool for individual sessions.

Factors Affecting the Selection Process

Mittal & Dym (1985) note that the identification of appropriate experts is one of the areas of expert systems activity that is least discussed in existing literature. Yet the importance of "team building" is recognized as a critical factor contributing to success in many domains. For example, the task of selecting domain experts for knowledge acquisition sessions is analogous to the task an athletic coach faces when selecting the starting roster. Numerous personal and professional (e.g., skill) attributes must be weighed during the decision making process. Merely choosing the most highly skilled players may not be effective if the selected individuals are unable to assume the required positions or cooperate to accomplish the goal. Attributes that should be considered when choosing domain experts include domain background, customer authorization, availability, personal characteristics and attitudes (e.g., willingness). The sections that follow address the impact of each of these variables and discusses selection techniques.

Domain Background
Domain background includes not only what experiences an individual has had, but how long ago they were compiled and in what capacity the person used this knowledge. Although an individual with 20 years of experience in a field could be considered an

expert, the length of time he/she had been out of "active" work in that field has an impact on the accessibility and possibly, the accuracy of the domain knowledge. This is the "experienced vs. practicing" issue in domain expert selection (McGraw & Seale, 1987c). **Experienced experts** are those with domain expertise who are not presently practicing in that domain. **Practicing experts** are those who are currently active in domain tasks. This "practice" includes formal education and training as well as practical experiences. The ease with which knowledge engineers can extract knowledge is affected by this distinction. For example, an expert who is currently operating a specific piece of machinery is more likely to be able to describe the heuristics and specific procedures used to accomplish a domain task using that equipment.

Yet another consideration is what type of experience the domain expert had. Was it confined to the completion of domain tasks, or was the expert ever called upon to teach the tasks and underlying concepts for a domain? Experts who have served in a dual mode of "doer" and "trainer" may be better equipped to translate domain knowledge during knowledge acquisition sessions than those who have never (consciously) considered the basic objectives and concepts that comprise a specific task. More specifically, experience in the role of "doer," followed by experience in the role of "trainer" may make it easier for the expert to express the deep structure of his or her knowledge (where "doing" skills and "training" skills are equally competent).

Knowledge verification and validation are also impacted by the issue of experienced versus practicing experts. Consider the case of the experienced expert who cannot recall all the details of a situation. Metaknowledge research (Gentner & Collins, 1981) indicates that an expert will tend to discount the importance of the unrecalled information, surmising that if something was important, it would have been remembered.

Customer Authorization

Authorization of experts refers to the issue of who proclaims an individual "expert". If individuals say they are experts we do not automatically ascribe them validity. If our customer identifies the experts, or if they are selected on the basis of some sample problem solving task or test, we ascribe more validity to what they tell us. Ideally, developers would select domain experts based on their background and experience, ability to communicate, availability, and willingness. In some cases, however, the contracting agency or a combination of the contracting agency, customer, and developer may be responsible for designating or authorizing an individual as an "expert" (McGraw & Seale, 1987b). If selected experts are customer "authorized" early in development efforts, the customer is more willing to accept the refined knowledge that becomes the heart of the expert system.

Availability

Limited access to domain experts is a common problem in knowledge acquisition. Hart (1986) notes that most acquisition-related problems are caused by time demands on an "already-busy" expert. Regardless of an individual's suitability (e.g., background, characteristics, willingness), he or she should not be selected as a key domain expert if problems with access are anticipated. The more renowned the experts are, the more difficult it will be to gain access to them for knowledge acquisition sessions.

For knowledge acquisition sessions to be effective, selected domain experts must be available on a regular, scheduled basis. To help alleviate problems caused by lack of access, some authors suggest the use of *experienced* experts for the acquisition of initial knowledge, followed by input from *practicing* experts for knowledge base refinement (McGraw & Seale, 1987c). This technique allows knowledge engineers to meet initially with the more desired experts to build the foundation for later knowledge acquisition efforts, then work with experienced, but less "valued" experts to flesh out the skeletal structure. Once knowledge engineers have a better understanding of the domain or problem, they meet with the practicing expert to review and refine previous work. In this way practicing experts are used efficiently, and access to them has not become a major inconvenience to the knowledge engineer.

As another guard against access or availability problems, Reiss (1986) advises gaining upfront management commitment to allocate the expert's time to the project and suggests blocking out 3 to 4 hours per week for regularly-scheduled knowledge acquisition sessions. Based on our experience, this figure is a low estimate during the knowledge acquisition phase of any development cycle. On large projects a domain expert may spend 3 hours in sessions per week, but at least 2 more hours in review of session material or preparing for upcoming sessions. As each project's needs will be different, this number will vary, as will the intervals with which the knowledge engineers and experts conduct sessions. The important idea here, however, is to anticipate availability problems and alleviate their impact by planning and carefully scheduling blocks of knowledge acquisition time. Then once the domain expert selection process is complete and access has been granted, knowledge engineers must make excellent use of the time allowed.

Personal Characteristics and Attitudes

While proficiency in the domain is an important attribute for a domain expert to possess, other characteristics may influence the efficiency with which important information is transferred to the knowledge engineer. Desirable personal attributes for domain experts are summarized in Figure 4-1.

Domain experience	Ability to communicate ideas and concepts
Sense of humor	Introspective of own knowledge
Good listener	Willingness to prepare for session
Sense of commitment	Honesty with self and others
Patience	Persistence

Figure 4-1. Desirable Attributes for Domain Experts

Of equal importance with domain knowledge itself is the expert's ability to communicate concepts and ideas effectively to the knowledge engineer. In reality, this is a very difficult task. Notice the line of questioning and responses in the brief scenario described below. This knowledge acquisition session could be more efficient (e.g., better information obtained in less time) if the domain expert responded in a more appropriate way.

KE: Given the symptoms in the sample problem, what would you first suspect as the cause of the problem?

DE: Probably a clogged fuel injector.

KE: You said "probably." What are some other possible causes?

DE: Maybe needs some timing work. Or could need valve work.

KE: It would be helpful if you could rank order these possible causes in order of likelihood or frequency of occurrence.

DE: Sure. It would probably look something like this.

KE: What in the sample problem led you to believe that the problem was due to a fuel injector rather than the second most likely prospect?

DE: Just because that is most common.

KE: What were the main indicators that pointed you to the clogged fuel injector?

DE: Well, it would be the hesitation, combined with what I know about how often this happens.

KE: Could you estimate a percentage that would describe how often these symptoms might indicate that this was the problem?

DE: Yes, I guess it is *most* often the case.

KE: Would you be 75% sure, 85% sure, or so forth?

DE: I would be 80% sure, but this might be right or wrong, depending on the make of the car.

KE: So "make of car" is an important variable. Let's attempt to construct a graph to indicate frequency of this problem across makes of cars.

In the scenario, the knowledge engineer had to keep prompting the expert to communicate at the appropriate level. Although not overly communicative, the domain expert is patient and cooperates with the knowledge engineer to achieve the session goals. Finding a domain expert who is patient, cooperative, and able to provide the required information at the right depth, or within the appropriate context can be tedious. However, time spent selecting such experts is offset by the increased effectiveness of knowledge acquisition sessions.

Selecting the Initial Pool of Experts

Expert system development teams must select domain experts who will enable them to meet functional goals. Large-scale expert systems may require functionality across numerous subsystems, necessitating expertise in more than one area. It is rare that one individual embodies the total knowledge required for a large system.[1]

The selection of domain experts can be viewed at both a macro and a micro level. At a macro level, selection refers to the initial identification, authorization, and orientation of the pool of suitable domain experts. At a micro level, selection refers to the ongoing selection of specific domain experts for particular knowledge acquisition sessions. The following section describes techniques to help manage each of these selection processes to increase the effectiveness of the knowledge engineer-domain expert relationship.

The requirements analysis phase of an expert system development project provides a suitable environment in which developers can request customer input on domain expert selection. Once the required functionality for each part of the system has been identified, enablers to assist in attaining the functionality can be specified. Since the success of the completed expert system itself will depend on the quality of the knowledge that it represents, the identification of appropriate domain expertise is a critical component. Developers can also specify the level of support they desire for the domain expert selection. For example, on one program it may be politically advantageous for the developer to request only that the customer or contracting agency identify characteristics or types of experts whose knowledge and experiences would be considered acceptable. As an example, the customer for an expert system that diagnoses engine failures would be well advised to specify the type of engine (e.g., diesel or gasoline), makes of cars, etc., with which domain experts should have had experience.

Customer Identification

Developers may wish to request that the customer actually identify key individuals whose input would be considered "expert." For example, when Campbell Soup decided to investigate the development of an expert system to diagnose cooker failures, they had a specific expert in mind (Artificial Intelligence Letter, 1985). Mr. Aldo Cimino, a Campbell engineer with decades of experience designing hydrostatic sterilizers (i.e., "cookers"), was handling cooker troubleshooting for corporate headquarters. Troubleshooting required that Mr. Cimino consult by phone with site personnel or take a trip to the troubled cooker, which kept him in great demand. To complicate matters, Mr. Cimono was nearing retirement age. When the company contracted with Texas Instruments to build a prototype Cooker Maintenance Advisor, they specified Mr. Cimino as the expert who was to be emulated and made him available to the knowledge engineer.

Internal Selection

Although requesting customer input into the domain selection process is advantageous, it may not always be feasible. Customers may be hesitant to identify or authorize an expert. It is often the case that in the requirements phase, developers may not have the necessary domain background to work effectively with customer-specified experts. However, domain expertise is necessary during this phase and in some cases may be secured from within the developing organization. For example, for a recent expert system in the avionics domain developers needed expertise but were not ready to meet with customer-selected experts (to whom they had limited access). Company personnel with avionics expertise were contacted by "word of mouth" and an intercompany bulletin board. They received summary information about the expert system to be developed, examples of target functionality, and a rationale for the need for expertise from people who were experienced in the target areas. Individuals who perceived that they had appropriate experiences and training in any of the target areas and were interested in finding out more about being a domain expert were urged to complete and return an attached "information sheet" (McGraw & Seale, 1987b). When completed, it provided information on type, recency, and extent of experience, areas of related interest, and data on how to contact the individual. Developers then sorted the sheets, selected individuals who seemed appropriate, and invited these internal experts to an orientation seminar (explained later in this chapter) that refined the selection process.

Test and Select

Another selection technique is to interview possible candidates to determine domain expertise, communication abilities, and willingness to help. Mittal & Dym (1985) suggest that it is possible to gain an understanding of the different kinds of expertise prevalent in the domain by talking to a variety of experts early on in the project. They developed a selection approach based on interviewing a diverse group of experts. To prepare for these interviews, (1) resident experts collected typical design problems they had encountered and (2) other experts (aside from those who collected the design problems) from diverse background were identified. (Chosen problems were applicable to the domain, but were not familiar to the other experts.)

Once the sample problems and participating experts were selected, systematic interviews were completed. In these interviews, the resident experts presented the design problem to each potential domain expert, who was asked to complete the sample problem in as much detail as possible within the two-hour time limit. Not only did this approach provide important information for the design of the resulting expert system, but also it allowed developers to observe experts as they completed a domain problem. While Mittal & Dym originally used this technique to help identify the requirements of the expert system and select the design problem, it is adaptable to the selection of suitable domain experts.

Domain Expert Orientation

Once candidate domain experts have been identified, developers must prepare to cultivate effective working relationships that should extend throughout the life of the expert system project. A factor we have found to be pivotal concerns the expectations the domain experts hold for the expert system and their role in its development. Domain-expert orientation can help refine the list of possible domain experts and prepare experts for project development efforts. Once they learn what will be expected of them, they may decide *not* to participate. Those who do decide to participate are more aware of expert system technology, specific goals for functionality, and the amount of work they will be asked to do.

An orientation program has at least two major purposes. First, it allows developers to meet and talk to a group of potential domain experts in a group setting. Introductory information on AI and expert systems in general, and specific functional information on the expert system to be developed can be presented once. Additionally, developers may use this opportunity to make sure that each attendee has completed an information or data sheet that may be used at a later time to select and contact an appropriate expert for a session. Second, an orientation program affords developers a forum in which they can communicate the importance of domain expertise and the subsequent level of commitment (e.g., time, preparation) they desire from a domain expert.

In many cases the candidate experts may have appropriate domain backgrounds but may lack even a general understanding of artificial intelligence, expert systems, and knowledge acquisition. They may be flattered that they have been considered an expert. Or they may be concerned that their jobs will be replaced by a machine. In either case, they need specific training if they are to enter the program with realistic expectations. Many domain experts experience similar concerns upon being notified that they have been selected to serve as a knowledge source. To alleviate these concerns and refine the expectations that domain experts have, development teams should plan and present a domain expert orientation program prior to the first knowledge acquisition session. Figure 4-2 offers a general outline for an orientation session.

ORIENTATION TOPICS

1. Introduction to Artificial Intelligence and Expert Systems

2. Introduction to the Functional Goals of the System

3. Importance of Domain Knowledge to System Functionality

4. Knowledge Acquisition Techniques--What to Expect

5. Preparedness of Domain Experts

    a. Time, Role, and Responsibilities

    B. Videotape or Slides of Sample Sessions

Figure 4-2. General Topics for Domain Expert Orientation

Orientation
The orientation should be designed to answer questions similar to those that follow:
- What will the resulting expert system be required to do?
- At what level will the system be required to operate (e.g., job aid or decision-making tool)?
- Who will use the system (e.g., novices, experts in the domain)?
- What does an expert system development cycle "look" like?
- What kinds of expertise will be needed?
- How does knowledge acquisition fit in the development process?
- What types of techniques will knowledge engineers use in knowledge acquisition sessions (e.g., interviews, simulations, prototype review)?
- What happens in a knowledge acquisition session?
- How much time can a knowledge acquisition session be expected to take, from reviewing the planned agenda through reviewing notes from the actual session?

At the completion of the orientation, domain experts should have the opportunity to see knowledge acquisition facilities and to meet informally with knowledge engineers with whom they will be working.

Selecting Specific Experts for Sessions

We have previously discussed the selection of a domain-expert pool. Members of this group will represent diverse types of experience and will vary in (1) the recency of their experience, (2) their communication abilities, and (3) their ability to commit time to the program. A core group of domain experts will emerge from the orientation program to meet most development needs. This section discusses a technique to help manage the selection of a single domain expert from this group for the purpose of providing information for a *specific* knowledge acquisition session. While this level of selection may be handled informally, in large-scale programs with multiple potential domain experts (often representing different subsets of knowledge) it is useful to use a selection aid such as the Domain-Expert Information Sheet (Figure 4-3).

DOMAIN EXPERT INFORMATION SHEET

Name_____   Title or Position_____

Phone_____   Mail_____

Years in Current Assignment_____ Current Rating_____

Experience and Training
Please rate your expertise with the following product lines. Place one of the marks below in the blank beside the product to indicate your level of experience with that product. "Experience" is defined as a combination of: period of time handling the product, complexity of claims handled for that product, and quantity sold and handled.

3=Very experienced   2 = moderately experienced   1 = little experience

Personal Lines ____   Term Life ____   Whole Life _____
Commercial Lines ____   Annuities ____   Automobile _____
                                         Homeowner's___   Special Riders ____
                                                                      (computers, jewelry)

Comments:
Please provide any additional information that you think would be helpful. Thank you for your time.

Figure 4-3. Sample Domain-Expert Information Sheet

Using the Domain-Expert Information Sheet

The Domain-Expert Information Sheet (Figure 4-3) has a dual purpose. It presents (1) information on how to access a domain expert (e.g., telephone number, mailing address) and (2) information on areas of expertise, experience, and domain interest. Experts may be asked to complete and return an information sheet prior to a program orientation or immediately after it. In either case, they should be guided to provide as specific information as possible. The Domain-Expert Information Sheet should be designed to capture as much specific information pertaining to experience and expertise as possible so that knowledge engineers can review the sheet to determine the suitability of an expert for a particular session. The actual content of an information sheet will be determined by the expert system program it supports.

Domain-Expert Files in the Knowledge Acquisition Database

If each domain expert who has agreed to serve as a knowledge source completes a Domain-Expert Information Sheet (as described in the previous section), developers can include this information in the knowledge acquisition database. This portion of the database can be used in numerous ways. Primarily, it is an aid in the selection of an individual expert for a knowledge acquisition session. This use can be expanded to incorporate knowledge sources other than human experts.[2] It also can be used to document ongoing work with the experts, keep track of knowledge acquisition sessions attended or missed, and note any problems or concerns.

To develop domain expert files in the knowledge acquisition database, first design a form that contains the information from the Domain Expert Information Sheets that meets your program's needs. Figure 4-4 displays a design for a sample domain expert database form.

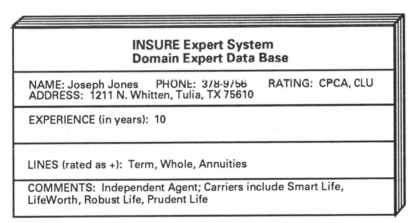

INSURE Expert System
Domain Expert Data Base

NAME: Joseph Jones   PHONE: 378-9756   RATING: CPCA, CLU
ADDRESS: 1211 N. Whitten, Tulia, TX 75610

EXPERIENCE (in years): 10

LINES (rated as +): Term, Whole, Annuities

COMMENTS: Independent Agent; Carriers include Smart Life, LifeWorth, Robust Life, Prudent Life

Figure 4-4. Sample Domain Expert File

Finally, type in the information from the sheet into the knowledge acquisition database. In doing so, make sure you retain the ability to search easily through experience and interests fields. Once in place, knowledge engineers planning a knowledge acquisition session may search through the files to find a listing of experts who seem to have appropriate experience, interests, and training. The list can then be culled based on availability and past session history (some experts may be more frequent "no-shows" or may cancel sessions more often than others). Thus, the use of such a tool helps increase the effectiveness of domain expert selection. Domain experts' time is used more efficiently and knowledge acquisition sessions yield more useful information at what tends to be more appropriate levels. The result can be not only better information for the knowledge base, but better domain expert attitudes toward participation in sessions.

DEVELOPING AND MAINTAINING RAPPORT

Once the domain experts have been selected and appropriately oriented to the program, development personnel should apply the guidelines and procedures described in Chapter 3. Concurrently, project personnel should begin building effective working relationships with the domain experts who will be so critical to eventual program success. The following sections address developing and maintaining rapport between knowledge engineers and domain experts. We first present suggestions for establishing and controlling the knowledge acquisition session environment. Next, we explore objectives which when met, can help knowledge engineers effectively manage a knowledge acquisition session. Later, we attend to common problems knowledge engineers will face and techniques that can be used to maintain effective working relationships even in difficult situations.

Managing the Environment

At least one author states that the most important objective of project control is to "retain the willing involvement of the expert" (Hart, 1986, p. 46). Yet there is little in the literature to guide knowledge engineers, the focal point of most projects, in "managing" knowledge acquisition sessions. A knowledge engineer's inability in this area can manifest itself in disgruntled domain experts, frustrated knowledge engineers, and surface-level knowledge. Knowledge acquisition session management techniques can be extrapolated from previous experience and relevant work in the fields of business, psychology, and communication. The session management issue can be examined from two major perspectives: (1) initially establishing the session environment and (2) controlling the session once it has begun.

Establishing the Environment
Prior to a knowledge acquisition session, the knowledge engineer should attend to a set of presession tasks. One of the first of these, **participant analysis** (Auger, 1972), refers to the selection of a domain expert who is well-suited to the topic and will arrive prepared for the session. Other equally important presession tasks include the following:
  • Confirming the knowledge acquisition session with the expert
  • Preparing to use the selected knowledge acquisition technique
  • Reserving a room for the knowledge acquisition session

- Arranging for appropriate taping equipment
- Securing necessary materials and/or "props"
- Posting the agenda in the room.

Auger (1972) notes that a blueprint for a successful meeting of any kind includes "make-ready" tasks such as these, as well as courtesy reminders to help maintain good relationships and increase the probability of success. We have adapted his suggestions for the knowledge acquisition session to include (1) making sure the expert is well-informed as to the purpose of the session, (2) avoiding surprise sessions, (3) telling experts how long the session will last, and (4) making sure each expert knows what role he or she is to play.

Controlling the Environment

At least fifteen minutes prior to the scheduled start time, the knowledge engineer should ensure that the environment is conducive to meeting session goals and should test any equipment that is critical to the session (e.g., videotape). Environmental factors can influence the length of a knowledge acquisition session, the domain expert's attitude toward the session (and the program), and the depth or quality of acquired knowledge. Some of these factors include
- Room size
- Room arrangement
- Room cleanliness
- Room temperature
- Proximity to restrooms and drinking fountains
- Planned length of the knowledge acquisition session
- Seating arrangements.

Physical and Spatial Climate. Figure 4-5 portrays guidelines for controlling the physical and spatial climate. If possible, the knowledge engineer should be allowed to suggest initial room design, including such niceties as observation windows, individual thermostats, and drop mikes. Room size, arrangement, and temperature contribute to the comfort factor. The room should appear neither too large (too impersonal and hard to videotape) nor too cozy (too threatening, lack of flexibility in using multiple experts). Room arrangement should include issues such as the number, size, and shape of working

- The room should comfortably accommodate 3-4 people.

- The room should be able to accommodate taping eqiupment and props.

- The room temperature should be between 72 and 76 degrees.

- The room should have easy access to break rooms and restrooms.

- The room should have a working surface and comfortable chairs.

- The room should have a white board, electronic scanning board, or other "community" writing surface.

Figure 4-5. Guidelines for Controlling the Physical/Spatial Climate

areas or tables, proximity to writing boards and/or projection tools, and placement of taping equipment. Temperature should be moderate and should allow the expert to remain in the room for the duration of the session (approximately one hour, in most cases). Proximity to restrooms and drinking fountains (and offers to break for their use) further extends the comfort factor.[3]

Temporal Control. While it is important to establish the physical and spatial environment, it is also imperative that the knowledge engineer attend to temporal elements. **Temporal control** refers to controlling the duration of the knowledge acquisition session. A partial framework for control is established when the knowledge engineer completes a knowledge acquisition session form. A reasonable guideline would be that no knowledge acquisition session last more than one hour, with a 90 minute session being the longest allowed. Even with an hour session, participants will experience attention span problems and important data may be lost. Thus, no session should be scheduled for over an hour (unless extenuating circumstances such as limited domain expert access are involved) and even hour-long sessions should be broken up into shorter segments of activity and brief "breaks" when possible.

Figure 4-6. Preferred Cooperative Seating Arrangement

Spatial Control. Finally, knowledge engineers should attend to **spatial control**, which is determined in large part by seating arrangements made prior to the domain expert's arrival. Seating arrangements are influenced by factors including leadership or dominance and the task at hand. If the knowledge acquisition session includes multiple experts and/or knowledge engineers, seating arrangements help establish leadership and dominance (e.g., who is in control, who talks the most). This phenomenon is discussed at length in Chapter 9. If the session participants include a single knowledge engineer and a single domain expert, seating arrangements are less affected by dominance but are more affected by the task at hand. For example, research in spatial ecology compared preferred seating arrangements for the following types of tasks: conversation, cooperation, co-action, and competition. Knowledge acquisition sessions most closely fit the "cooperation" task, in which both parties sit and work together to meet a common goal. Sommer (1969) concluded that when parties indicated a preferred seating for cooperative tasks, one of the arrangements in Figure 4-6 was most often chosen.

Managing the Session

Both to maintain effective knowledge engineer-domain expert relationships and to elicit quality information from a knowledge acquisition session, knowledge engineers must manage the session. Management includes techniques to control the knowledge acquisition session and requires the knowledge engineer to function as both an effective facilitator and listener.

Knowledge Engineer as Manager

The following objectives provide guidelines for the management of knowledge acquisition sessions to increase the effectiveness of the session and enhance the domain expert-knowledge engineer relationship:

OBJECTIVE 1: Establish active leadership upon greeting the domain expert.

The knowledge engineer should establish control of the environment early in a knowledge acquisition session. This can be handled explicitly, implicitly, or by a combination of approaches. Explicit control includes welcoming the expert, introducing the session, presenting the agenda, and keeping the expert on track. Implicit control includes body language subtleties and seating behavior. For example, implied leadership/dominance can be communicated via seating behavior in the following ways:
- Seating the domain expert in a position that allows him or her to best meet session needs (e.g., near the board if he or she will need to sketch, in the seat that is most easily videotaped, etc.)
- Positioning yourself near the door, lights, videotape equipment, or other elements of control.

OBJECTIVE 2: Control the introduction of the knowledge acquisition session and establish its purpose.

The knowledge engineer's inability to appear "in control" during a knowledge acquisition session compromises the domain expert-knowledge engineer relationship and the usefulness of the knowledge that may be acquired. We have observed cases in which the domain expert arrives for the session, notes the identifying information on the board, waits for the videotape to roll, and takes charge, introducing the session and stating its purpose. At this point, the expert is in control of the session and the knowledge engineer must work harder to regain its focus. It is much more effective if the knowledge engineer greets the expert, indicates where to sit, manages the taping equipment, and introduces the session. In this situation, the knowledge engineer is in control, having set the tone, outlined the agenda, and stated the session purpose. The psychological climate becomes more professional and task-oriented.

OBJECTIVE 3: Guide the expert through the knowledge acquisition session, following the agenda as closely as possible.

As explained in Chapter 3, the Knowledge Acquisition Form is useful in detailing session objectives, structure, and sample questions. If the recommended methodology is followed, the domain expert should arrive prepared for the session. Posting the agenda on the board in the room, or providing a hard copy for both parties to follow helps establish the fact that the session has a definite purpose and goals. Following the agenda communicates to domain experts that the session has been well-thought-out and organized to make the best use of their time.

Do not preclude the introduction of information that, while outside the scope of the session, is still important. Creating a special file (electronic or printed) of items to investigate or related ideas communicates that the material is important and will be explored in more depth at a later time (Martin, 1986).

OBJECTIVE 4: Focus the expert on the appropriate levels and points.

Know what type of information should emerge from the knowledge acquisition session. For example, as a knowledge engineer are you currently focusing on indepth information on a specific type of diagnosis (depth-first), or are you most interested in gaining a general view (breadth-first) of the problem and its related concepts? Requiring an expert to come prepared to answer questions on both of these levels is not usually effective; the session most likely ends without a clear feeling of accomplishment on either level.

Once you have identified the type of information you require, pursue it. If a question is not answered at the desired level, do not be afraid to follow up. Setting goals for levels or types of knowledge and actively pursuing them increases the professionalism with which the knowledge engineer is credited.

OBJECTIVE 5: Actively summarize the knowledge acquisition session and debrief the expert at the close of the session.

Does the session just taper off and end because there is no more to say, are you just out of time, or have you covered the major points in the plan well enough to understand current information and anticipate future needs? Domain experts' reactions to the situations just posed will vary; they will leave with different attitudes about the session, its effectiveness, your ability to manage sessions, and their attitudes toward participating in future sessions. Debriefing offers an opportunity for the knowledge engineer to summarize major points in the session, focus on the accomplishments, point out new areas to explore, and lets domain experts know what to expect as a follow-up.

Initial goals for a debrief include summarizing and correctly recording the major problems, solutions, and ideas discussed during the session (Figure 4-7). During this summation, the domain expert should be encouraged to request or suggest clarification on issues raised. Additionally, debriefing provides an opportunity to identify follow-up or action items that the session triggered, parties responsible for completion, and suggested completion dates. Finally, debriefing allows the session participants to outline near-future knowledge acquisition session plans and to leave with a positive attitude about their contributions.

MESSAGE PURPOSE	KNOWLEDGE ENGINEER'S COMMENTS
Initiates close	Let me summarize what we have accomplished today. As I do so, please feel free to revise any conclusions or assumptions I might make.
Sequential description	First, our session focused on the decomposition of software for a single mission area -- Armament. Our purpose in decomposing the systems for armament is to identify the main categories of software each system represents. This information will later be used to determine applicable software quality factors.

Based on the conceptual analysis we did, Armament seems to break down functionally into 3 main systems: threat systems, missile systems, scoring systems. |
| **Notes a chance for expert to refine** | Next, we refined our decomposition to determine the functions performed within each system. (Hands the list to the expert). I will be attaching this list to the completed knowledge acquisition form. I'd like for you to review these when you receive the form and let me know if any categories or entries should be changed. |
| **Future plans**

Action items | I'll try to get the form to you by next Tuesday. Meanwhile, can you send me the testbook you mentioned? I look forward to discussing this further at our next meeting. Can you meet Friday for about an hour to continue our decomposition? |
| **Gratitude** | Thank you for coming today. I appreciate your assistance. |

Figure 4-7. Sample Debriefing Transcript

Knowledge Engineer as Facilitator

As the knowledge engineer manages the progress of a knowledge acquisition session, he or she acts as a facilitator. The knowledge engineer uses nonverbal and verbal behaviors to act in ways that enable session goals to be attained. Auger (1972) recommends the following tips that a facilitator could use to coax a knowledge acquisition session along:

- Stimulate discussion
- Balance the discussion if there is more than one expert so that more than one

view is addressed
- Keep discussions on track
- Break up "hot" controversies
- Watch your timetable and stop on time
- Make sure there is some conclusion and positive actions.

Leadership Skills. To function as an effective facilitator, the knowledge engineer must be able to employ various leadership skills and communication techniques. Although these skills may be discussed or grouped in numerous ways, the leadership skills we have found to be most important to knowledge engineers include those in Figure 4-8.

GOAL ACHIEVEMENT	Contributing and evaluating ideas Isolating issues Gaining consensus Synthesizing ideas of others
INTERPERSONAL	Controlling emotions and resolving conflicts Setting the communications climate Regulating contributions Promoting interaction

Figure 4-8. Knowledge Engineer Leadership Skills
Raymond S. Ross. Speech Communication: Fundamentals & Practice, 6/e © 1983, pp. 350. Adapted by permission of Prentice-Hall, Inc. Englewood Cliffs, New Jersey.

Each knowledge engineer will use these skills differently, depending upon personal style and the environment of the knowledge acquisition session. Leadership styles range from behaviors that evidence no control to those that evidence extreme control, as illustrated in Figure 4-9.

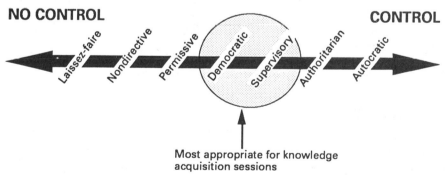

Figure 4-9. Leadership Styles

Laissez-faire style represents no control, a situation in which "anything goes" and would be ineffective for knowledge acquisition sessions. Both the *nondirective* and *permissive* styles would represent the use of additional control mechanisms, but neither could be considered to be as directive as most knowledge acquisition sessions require. *Democratic* and *supervisory* styles represent those most often evidenced by knowledge engineers conducting knowledge acquisition sessions. Strict *authoritarian* and *autocratic* control of a knowledge acquisition session are inappropriate for good interpersonal relationships and for the production of high-quality, creative exchanges of information. While most individuals are most comfortable using a single leadership style, knowledge engineers need to be able to select the style that is most appropriate for the situation. For example, while the knowledge engineer may most often use a democratic style, he or she may need to resort to a supervisory style to re-direct or re-task an expert who is "off track."

Communication Style and Facilitation. Many variables affect one's ability to function as a facilitator, but perhaps no variable is as pervasive in its influence as is interaction style of the communicator (in this case, the knowledge engineer). **Communicator style** includes the signals that are provided to help process, interpret, filter, or understand literal meaning. In the knowledge acquisition session, much of the knowledge engineer's message could be described as feedback. In a communication episode, both the sender and receiver can demonstrate feedback that is explicit or implicit and direct or indirect (Norton, 1983). Figure 4-10 depicts a matrix representation of the major types of feedback. The elements depicted in the figure may be intrinsic to the receiver or they may be inferences drawn from the environment, context, situation, or time. For example, attentive style is exemplified by feedback that is direct, as opposed to feedback that is indirect and implicit.

	EXPLICIT	**IMPLICIT**
DIRECT	Indicates immediate understanding; to the point.	Nonverbal/paralanguage signals of understanding; passive but responsive
INDIRECT	Immediate, responsive; some ambiguity present	Inferential; ambiguous information

Figure 4-10. Feedback Matrix
Adapted from Robert Norton, <u>Communicator Style</u>, p. 179. Copyright © 1983 by Robert Norton. Reprinted by permission of Sage Publications, Inc.

Direct, explicit feedback communicates immediately that the receiver has understood the message or that the receiver requires more information to clarify his/her understanding. *Direct, implicit* feedback is nonverbal or paraverbal messages that are apparently responsive to the communications currently taking place, but the success of the communication is only implied. *Indirect, explicit* feedback is responsive and immediate, but may have an ambiguous nature; the original sender may need to decode it. In other words, the sender may not be able to understand the feedback or may fail to recognize that feedback has occurred. Finally, *indirect, implicit* feedback represents feedback that should not be used by knowledge engineers. Not only does it not allow the sender (expert) to conclude whether or not the engineer is paying attention, but it also does not signal whether understanding has occurred.

Knowledge Engineer as Listener

Effective listening can play a major role in enhancing both the interpersonal relationships between knowledge engineer and domain expert and the quality of information garnered for the knowledge base. Listening encompasses a wide range of skills, which are depicted in Figure 4-11. Complete body listening requires that we minimize distractions, pay attention, establish and maintain eye contact, and use positive body language (Atwater, 1981).

SKILL SET	ATTRIBUTE
ATTENDING	Minimize distractions Exhibit attentiveness Establish eye contact Display positive body language
NONREFLECTIVE	Use attentive silence Use conversation starters Use minimal responses
REFLECTIVE	Clarifying Paraphrasing Reflecting feelings Summarizing
NONVERBAL COMMUNICATION	Interpret facial expressions Interpret gaze and eye contact Interpret posture and gestures Interpret personal space messages
MEMORY	Concentration Short term memory Long term memory

Figure 4-11. Listening Skills
Adapted from R. Bolton, People Skills, copyright © 1979, Prentice-Hall, Englewood Cliffs, New Jersey.

Attending and Memory Skills. Knowledge engineers who are good listeners pay attention to domain experts during knowledge acquisition sessions. As obvious as it seems, this task is most difficult because of our tendency to shift our attention. Attending to verbal messages, like those comprising most knowledge acquisition sessions, is even more taxing. Yet, if mastered, **attending skills** heighten listening skills, producing expectations for what will be heard next. One of the first enablers for attending is concentration, a memory skill. Concentration helps listeners block out distractions, which are major roadblocks to attending. Establishing eye contact and using a forward-thrust, open body language also helps encourage and exhibit attentiveness.

Nonreflective Skills. **Nonreflective skills** refer to those behaviors that are meant to initiate or guide communication. Key among these is the use of conversation starters, the high-level statements that serve to initiate, guide, or transition communication. If the conversation has begun and is progressing appropriately, knowledge engineers should practice "attentive silence," using only minimal responses when possible. Silence can be conducive to reflective thought, during which time the domain expert may think of other, extended, relevant information. In addition, not responding evaluatively to each comment the domain expert makes encourages the expert to work more at providing information and less at gaining the knowledge engineer's acceptance.

Nonverbal Communication. Listening involves more than attending to and interpreting verbal messages. **Nonverbal communication** can act strengthen, lessen, or in some cases, offset messages that may be simultaneously sent through verbal channels. In fact, when the nonverbal messages does not reinforce the articulated message, the nonverbal message will be accepted by the listener in over 90% of the cases. Thus, knowledge engineers should be attuned to the messages that are being conveyed facially, vocally, and kinesthetically.

COMMON PROBLEMS

Regardless of a knowledge engineer's abilities, the interpersonal nature of the knowledge acquisition session, coupled with the difficulty of the task ensures that problems will arise. The following expected difficulties will be most likely to evidence themselves:
- Negativism and apathy
- Lack of commitment
- Verbal and nonverbal communication blocks
- Hostility and defensive reactions
- Clashes between expectations and realities.

Analyzing Problem Behaviors

When problems occur, the knowledge engineer should analyze them in an effort to understand the behaviors that are being manifested. Negative behavior on the part of a domain expert often results from one of three major reasons: attention, inadequacy, and power.

Attention-getting behavior may signal that the domain expert wants to feel important and appreciated. If *inadequacy* is the motive, experts may be attempting to divert attention from the task at hand because they fear that they might be found inadequate. If *power* is the motive, experts may be "saying" that they feel most comfortable when they can control the knowledge acquisition session.

Knowledge engineers should take a methodological, impersonal approach in attempting to understand the domain expert's problematic behavior. Although few of us are psychologists, most of us, with the aid of taping equipment or careful attention, can use the procedure outlined in Figure 4-12. If applied systematically, it can help identify the problem and serve as the first step to alleviating its cause.

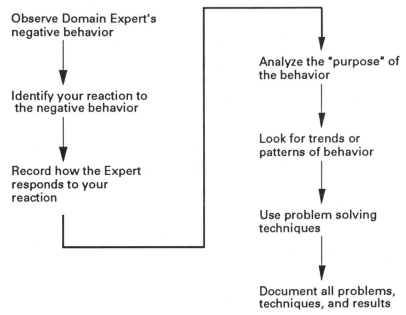

Figure 4-12. Controlling Negative Behavior

Types of Problems

Infrequently, domain expert-related problems will be manifested by what could be termed problem participants. Sometimes problems arise because of an expert's cancellation of a knowledge acquisition session or his or her failure to answer questions or supply information. Most problems are born of fear or from complexities involved in tapping "knowledge." For example, a review of actual domain expert comments following knowledge acquisition session includes the following:

- I was afraid at first that they were trying to build a computer to take over my job. It was only after I understood that this expert system would help people do their jobs better that I felt comfortable.

- At first I felt kind of important being a domain expert. But then I found out how tedious it is. Sometimes I couldn't understand why he was asking me such picky questions. It seemed like the more questions I answered, the more I got asked.

- My knowledge engineer was really nice and a very fast learner. He flat out admitted that he didn't know anything about the system and that I would need to teach him what was important for the system to know. The only problem was that we didn't have much time to start from scratch like that.

- My supervisor chose me to be a domain expert for this project. Neither of us knew how much time would be involved. He could not understand when I went in and asked for help prioritizing my activities so I could do the job I needed to as a domain expert. I felt really pressured to do my regular job plus serve as the domain expert until I convinced him I needed help.

- I would like to have known before hand just what being a domain expert meant. I mean, my boss came in and told me I would be a domain expert on this system and that I'd be talking to some people about what I do the next day. I didn't know what AI was, what an expert system was, or what they would be expecting of me. I was really nervous at first.

- They asked me if I'd review the notes from our knowledge acquisition session and initial that they were accurate. I didn't mind doing the review, but I was a little afraid to initial that everything was correct. What if the system didn't work right and my boss blamed me? Or what if someone else told them that it was incorrect. How embarrassing!

The following sections briefly discuss some of the more common types of problems that knowledge engineers may encounter.

Problem Participants

In each pool of experts there will be problem participants with whom the knowledge engineer must work to meet the goals of the session. Although problem behavior (e.g., "show boating", negativism) may manifest itself in numerous ways, roots of most problem behaviors are similar. Problem behavior can often be linked to either fear and/or the inability to tap knowledge.

Problems Based in Fear

There will be occasions when even an enthusiastic expert is not able to attend knowledge acquisition sessions and complete postsession tasks. These instances should be handled in a professional manner. However, if absences or other problems stem from an expert's fear, hostility, or inadequacy, the knowledge engineer should identify the cause and correct the situation before invalid information is transferred to the knowledge base.

Fear-based problems manifest themselves in a number of diverse ways. After observing over fifty hours of taped knowledge acquisition sessions, we can categorize indications of fear-based problems as follows:
- Lack of commitment prior to the knowledge acquisition session; expert may act noncommittal toward session topic or specific questions

- Curt, general responses during knowledge acquisition sessions; expert seems unwilling to commit himself or herself to an answer; communication seems superficial

- Overconsciouness of taping equipment, including comments and questions about what the tape will be used for, attempts to move outside of camera view, reluctance to make eye contact with the knowledge engineer and/or to look at the camera

- Approval-seeking behavior, including glancing at fellow experts during an answer, and intonation patterns that indicate the expert is seeking confirmation.

Many of these fear-based problems can be traced to a phenomenon McGraw and Seale (1987b) have called **upward-ripple paranoia**. It can be described as a discomfort that is rooted in a fear of negative repercussions from supervisors, peers, or significant others. In most organizations domain experts have regular jobs; they report to their own supervisory personnel. In fact, in military organizations they may be out-ranked by individuals who may either be present in knowledge acquisition sessions or may be asked to review and verify extracted information. Thus, participating domain experts may be concerned that their responses could endanger their regular jobs, or another person's perceptions of their expertise.

The atmosphere in the knowledge acquisition session (and, in fact, the entire project) must be such that domain experts feel comfortable contributing and evaluating ideas without fearing negative repercussions from superiors and/or peers. Knowledge engineers can lessen the impact of this phenomenon by attending to the following:

- Explaining the reasons for taping knowledge acquisition sessions
- Minimizing interference from taping equipment (e.g., not drawing undue attention to it)
- Preserving the "sanctity" of the knowledge acquisition session by monitoring who reviews session tapes and why
- Handling knowledge acquisition sessions with multiple experts with care (see Chapter 9)
- Reinforcing appropriate domain expert behavior
- Using reflective listening to approach possible problem situations.

Problems due to Inability to Tap Knowledge

Another common cause of problems is the difficulty humans have in tapping, expressing, and evaluating their own knowledge. We humans are not particularly astute in our ability to "know" what we know and how we use what we know. Much human activity is not accessible to awareness (Dixon, 1981). Some researchers (Bainbridge, 1986) even contend that there is little correlation between verbal reports and mental behavior. Although people seem to be able to estimate what they need to do to commit something to memory, they are systematically overconfident about the accuracy of their general knowledge (Fischoff, Slovic, & Lichtenstein, 1977). Results of one study indicated that the more expert an individual, the more strong the tendency to assume that if something was important he or she would be able to remember it (Gentner & Collins, 1981). This suggests that metajudgments based on the importance of the material and the subjective expertise of the expert affect the way in which inferences are made and combined in reasoning.

Anticipating these problems can encourage the knowledge engineer to set up some "check points" to minimize the negative effects. For example, domain experts need to be told that while their expertise is valued, they are not expected to be able to recall everything about a topic or to know all the answers. They must be encouraged to be honest about a failure to remember or a lack of knowledge. Questions must be framed to lessen negative effects on experts' egos. Domain experts should be encouraged to take time to research an area, consult with others, and report back at a later time. And finally, knowledge engineers must have a methodology to deal with uncertainties, probabilities, and vagueness.

TECHNIQUES FOR DIFFICULT SITUATIONS

The inevitable problems will occur, some more often than others. The knowledge engineer in charge should be prepared to defuse the problem and facilitate successful completion of session goals. In this section we discuss techniques that have proven effective in resolving problematic sessions or relationships. These techniques include using reflective listening and documenting problems.

Reflective Listening

The difficulties inherent in the communication process necessitate the use of reflective listening skills. **Reflective listening** skills are most valuable when the knowledge acquisition session is off-track or when there are potential problems between the knowledge engineer and domain expert. Atwater (1981) proposes three reasons for the use of reflective listening.

First, words have multiple meanings. Consequently, it may be hard to determine what someone means by a word unless you know its particular connotation to the speaker. As Atwater notes, words are "imprecise vehicles for conveying the personal meaning of speakers." Domain experts may find it hard to select the word they need to say what they want to say because the meaning is implicit (i.e., not embodied in the actual word itself). Thus, knowledge engineers should use reflective listening skills to clarify or check the meaning of the words the domain expert uses.

Second, the message in a communication has been coded from the intended meaning in the speaker's mind, requiring the knowledge engineer to "decode" the message to determine the intended meaning. Speakers may fail to communicate the message so that the listener understands. Therefore, the knowledge engineer playing the role of listener/facilitator must give feedback (e.g., "I don't understand.") to the speaker to decode the coded message.

Third, personal characteristics and background such as attitudes, training, experience, and emotions may contaminate a domain expert's communication. We tend to be biased toward things that we know and are familiar to us. Domain experts, for example, will tend to support certain procedures, behaviors, or heuristics and condemn others that may be perfectly acceptable but not in their background. In a like manner, knowledge engineers may listen to the expert's message but filter out certain components. Reflective listening can help ensure that the message being communicated (and perceived) is not based solely on personal factors. Atwater (1981) notes the following four basic types of reflective listening responses, each of which we have adapted for use in knowledge acquisition sessions: (1) paraphrasing, (2) clarifying, (3) summarizing, and (4) reflecting feelings.

Paraphrasing
When a knowledge engineer uses paraphrasing responses, he or she restates the perceived meaning of the speaker's message using his or her own words.[4] The goal is to check the accuracy with which the speaker's message was conveyed and understood. It should be used when the knowledge engineer is fairly confident that the paraphrase expresses the domain expert's original meaning. To paraphrase a domain expert's message, try to convey the main idea(s) and content (as opposed to feelings) of the message the domain expert has conveyed. Examples of clarifying responses include:
"What I believe you said was. . ."
"If I am wrong, correct me, but. . ."
"In other words, . . ."
"As I think I understand it. . ."

Clarifying
Requests that knowledge engineers may use to let domain experts know that their message was not immediately understandable are called clarifying responses. These responses encourage experts to elaborate or clarify the original message so that the knowledge engineer gets a better idea of the intended message. Guidelines for the use of clarifying responses include (1) focusing on the message as opposed to the expert's ability to communicate and (2) encouraging experts to elaborate or explain the original message by using open questions when possible. Examples of clarifying responses include
"I don't understand. . ."
"Could you please explain. . .?"
"Please repeat that for me. . ."
"Could you give me an example. . .?"

Summarizing
Summarizing responses can help the knowledge engineer compile discrete pieces of information from a knowledge acquisition session into a meaningful whole. They sum up the main ideas and feelings the domain expert has expressed. Also they let knowledge engineers confirm that they have heard the expert's message and conversely, let domain experts know that they have communicated appropriately. Summary statements should be expressed in the knowledge engineer's own words. They typically begin with phrases such as these examples:

"To sum up what you have been saying ..."
"What I have heard you say so far. . ."
"I believe that we have agreed to. . ."

Reflecting Feelings

This response mirrors back to the speaker or domain expert the feelings that seem to have been communicated. The main focus is on the expert's feelings, attitudes, or emotional reactions, not on the content of the message. The purpose is to clear the air of some emotional reaction or problem that is negatively impacting the message the expert is trying to communicate. Knowledge engineers will at first feel that their "reflected feeling" messages are artificial. However, they can be extremely useful in addressing problem situations. Sample reflected feeling messages include:

"You seem frustrated about. . ."
"You seem to feel you have been put on the spot. . ."
"I sense that you are uncomfortable with. . ."

Documenting Problems

Regardless of attempts to plan for effective working relationships with domain experts, difficulties will occur. Developing a plan to document problems allows project personnel to review problems looking for trends and to effect positive change. We have used a combination of the following techniques to document problems:

- "Comments" in a domain expert's file in the Knowledge Acquisition Database. This section can be used to document problems or concerns about a particular expert (e.g., noting chronic tardiness, uncooperativeness, ineffectiveness in group situations)

- Randomly requesting that domain experts complete a Knowledge Acquisition Session Evaluation Form (See Chapter 11) to get feedback on their perceptions of knowledge acquisition session effectiveness

- Keeping active communication going in the form of an electronic bulletin board on which experts and engineers can record problems and/or frustrations.

Domain Expert Files

As described earlier in this chapter, each domain expert should have a file in the Knowledge Acquisition Database. We suggest that one of the fields on each file be reserved for comments. We have used this field to record problems, including an expert cancellation of a session, an expert's complaints about a session, and an expert's effectiveness in a small group session. The Knowledge Engineering Coordinator periodically reviews the files for trends in an effort to identify and defuse problems before they erupt.

Knowledge Acquisition Session Evaluation Form

Session effectiveness is discussed at length in Chapter 11. An instrument proposed for evaluating effectiveness is a Likert-style attitudinal survey form that domain experts, knowledge engineers, and program management personnel periodically use to review and rate sessions. The form allows respondents to rate the overall effectiveness of a session and to respond to specific items that seem to correlate with perceived effectiveness. Tracking responses to this form can help head off problems between knowledge engineers and domain experts and to provide feedback to customers.

Electronic Problem File

Not all problems will be easily solved; not all can be. However, having a mechanism to express them can help. A domain expert can get a problem "off his or her chest" or a knowledge engineer can express a concern in a general way, as opposed to direct confrontation. One useful technique is to set up an electronic "bulletin board," which can be used for project-wide review of documents, schedules, and various files. One useful file is a problem file (Martin, 1986). As a problem is uncovered or confronted, it is expressed and posted to the problem file on the project bulletin board. Knowledge engineers, domain experts, and management personnel should all have access to the file and be encouraged to contribute both problems and solutions. Not only does the use of this file result in an on-going record of difficulties, but also in an awareness that others are experiencing similar problems and that shared solutions are valuable.

ENDNOTES

[1] Chapter 10 provides more information on the need for management of multiple experts.

[2] See "Reference Center" in Chapter 3.

[3] It has been our experience, however, that the knowledge engineer must take the lead in suggesting a break.

[4] Note that paraphrasing is not synonymous with parroting or repetition, which in fact, constrict communication.

SUGGESTED READINGS

Conrad, C. Strategic Organizational Communication: Cultures, Situations, and Adaptation. New York, NY: Holt, Rinehart, and Winston, 1985.

Knapp, M. Nonverbal Communication in Human Interaction. New York: Holt, Rinehart, & Winston, 1978.

Wolvin, A. and C. Coakley. Listening. Dubuque, IO: Wm C. Brown, Publishers, 1982.

APPLICATION

1. Review the major goals for negative behavior described within this chapter (attention, inadequacy, power). Read the scenarios that follow and attempt to identify which goal seems to be driving the behavior. Be ready to defend your identifications and describe how you might handle such a situation.

    a. During an initial interview with a potential domain expert who has excellent professional credentials, she tells you that she is very busy and probably will not be able to be a domain expert for your system. Further questioning reveals that she has never been a domain expert.
Behavior Goal_____
Response_____

    b. Your 'star' domain expert is less than serious during interview sessions you videotape with him. He responds to the camera instead of to you, sidesteps important issues that he seems unable to answer, and cracks jokes.
Behavior Goal_____
Response_____

2. The following scenarios depict typical problems that have occurred during knowledge acquisition sessions. Review the scenario and suggest a technique (e.g., reflective listening) that might be effective to solve each problem.

    a. The Knowledge Engineering Coordinator calls you into her office to inform you that the domain expert complained about the quality and effectiveness of your sessions. You explore his comments and discover that his main complaint is that the sessions with you are tedious and boring.

    b. The expert arrives on time for the acquisition session but once it has been introduced and the tape started, she pulls out packaged cookies to eat. Her responses to your questions are hard to understand and she seems less than interested in your agenda.

    c. During a protocol analysis session the expert becomes frustrated and angrily responds that this is a waste of his time.

5

Conceptualizing the Domain

The Role of Domain Conceptualization

> **Initial Understanding**
> **Estimating Knowledge Acquisition Needs**
> **Knowledge Base Design**
> **The Challenge of Domain Conceptualization**

Techniques for Evoking Domain Conceptualization

> **Evoking Concept Identification**

Techniques for Organizing and Analyzing Domain Conceptualizations

> **Defining Concepts**
> **Using Maps and Models**
> **Identifying Relationships**
> **Moving On**

INTRODUCTION

The success of knowledge acquisition efforts depends in part on being able to conceptualize the domain. The process of conceptualization involves evoking and abstracting concepts and heuristics that are represented in a given domain. Inaccurate or incomplete conceptualization negatively impacts subsequent knowledge acquisition activities and, of course, the resulting expert system. Although conceptualization is often identified as an important stage in the knowledge acquisition process, knowledge engineers may not be familiar with techniques that they can use to work through this stage.

The process of conceptualization is tied closely to a variety of related fields, including communication, psychology, and fields in which classification is a critical task. Techniques that have been used in other fields can be adapted to enable knowledge engineers to analyze and abstract concepts. For example, content analysis is a discipline that provides mechanisms to analyze the content of communication. Similarly, cluster analysis and construct sorting frequently are used to depict similarities, distances, and relationships of concepts, attributes, or other elements.

Conceptual-analysis techniques can be used in the early stages of knowledge acquisition, in order to (1) identify the important attributes possessed by examples of a concept and (2) determine the interrelationships of relevant concepts and attributes in the domain. Knowledge engineers may apply these techniques informally (e.g., requests for domain experts to graphically depict the major groupings of elements in their domain) or formally, (e.g., using algorithms and computers to measure similarities and distances between elements).

In this chapter we introduce the use of concept analysis in knowledge acquisition. Initially, we discuss the importance and difficulty of domain conceptualization. Next, we present techniques (e.g., concept dictionaries, conceptual frameworks, maps, models, and concept sorting) that knowledge engineers can use to evoke, document, and organize domain conceptualizations. The presentation of each of these techniques includes guidelines for its use. Finally, we discuss the use of manual and computer-based techniques to identify the interrelationships of domain concepts and their attributes.[1]

Objectives

This chapter presents techniques to assist knowledge engineers in conceptualizing the domain for which an expert system is being developed. Specifically, it enables readers to accomplish the following:
- Recognize the usefulness of conceptualizing the domain under consideration
- Identify major approaches to classifying domain knowledge
- Apply a variety of manual procedures to evoke knowledge of the expert's conceptualization of a domain
- Use a variety of manual tools to conceptualize, structure, and graphically represent domain knowledge
- Identify opportunities to use computer-based tools in the conceptualization process.

Key Terms

cluster analysis

density search

concept dictionaries

repertory grid

taxonomies

clumping techniques

discrimination tree

construct

concept clustering

concept sorting

conceptual framework

cognitive maps

THE ROLE OF DOMAIN CONCEPTUALIZATION

One of the most important and difficult knowledge acquisition tasks is to abstract the target domain to discover its primary concepts, attributes, and values. The section that follows describes some of the benefits that adequate conceptualization of a domain can afford developers, including
* Enhanced understanding of the domain
* A means to estimate knowledge acquisition needs and plans
* Preliminary ideas for knowledge-base designs.

The section concludes with a brief examination of some of the challenges involved in the conceptualization process.

Initial Understanding

When a knowledge engineer begins domain familiarization he or she is often confronted by a seemingly unrelated mass of unfamiliar terms, objects, and applications. One of the primary tasks in this phase of development is to work with a domain expert to identify categories in the domain and discriminate among them using a given feature set. Completion of the domain conceptualization phase results in an initial "mental map" of the domain, which can enhance the efficiency of subsequent knowledge acquisition tasks.

During this phase, the knowledge engineer should have the domain expert create an initial framework within which concepts can be identified and fleshed out. Once they have been identified, the knowledge engineer determines how these concepts are differentiated. This task requires that the knowledge engineer study domain materials and/or consult with a domain expert. After the primary concepts have been identified and differentiated, the knowledge engineer can develop a personal representation of the concepts and related terminology. Later, the knowledge engineer can enhance the initial, skeletal framework by deepening the knowledge represented within it.

Estimating Knowledge Acquisition Needs

As the knowledge engineer decomposes the domain, primary domain subsets and interrelationships become evident. Working with a domain expert, the knowledge engineer can depict graphically, the areas that will require major knowledge acquisition efforts. Each individual area within the domain can then be dissected to identify potential knowledge acquisition session needs, first at a general, and later at a deeper level. This information is invaluable in scoping knowledge acquisition needs and providing answers to the questions posed in Figure 5-1.

• Approximately how many domain experts will be required?

• What types of skills and expertise should the selected experts have?

• Approximately how many knowledge acquisition sessions might this topic trigger?

• How much time might be required (e.g., knowledge acquisition planning, delivery, and review time) of knowledge engineers and domain experts?

• What type of (and how many) knowledge acquisition sessions will be required on a weekly, monthly, or quarterly basis?

Figure 5-1. Using Domain Conceptualization to Identify Knowledge Acquisition Session Needs

Knowledge Base Design

Developing a conceptualization of the domain can also provide a preliminary framework for the design of the knowledge base. Because they can reveal an organization of domain knowledge that facilitates human access and retrieval, techniques to evoke and document domain conceptualization also may provide clues to system architecture, knowledge base design, or representation. While it is not necessary to emulate the mental structure a human expert brings to a problem, recognizing the major concepts within the domain (and their interrelationship) can provide a rough estimate of the knowledge base structure.

The Challenge of Domain Conceptualization

Eliciting, analyzing, and graphically depicting concepts is not simple. Problems related to the inability of humans to express knowledge make it difficult to isolate the "appropriate set of basic concepts that characterize the task domain" (Buchanan, et al., 1983, p. 143). To achieve this task, many hours of interaction between a domain expert and a knowledge engineer may be required. To compound this problem, there is a tendency for the knowledge engineer to make one of two classical mistakes during the conceptualization stage of knowledge acquisition. First, because the conceptualization of a domain can be a highly iterative process, the knowledge engineer may engage in "wheel-spinning." Knowing how to depict the information that is retrieved and how to provide feedback on that information to encourage refinement is critical. Knowing when *enough* knowledge has been conceptualized to map the concepts into "formal" representation schemes that allow the organization to be tested is equally critical.

The second common error is for knowledge engineers to attempt to analyze the problem correctly and completely before implementing some type of a trial system (Buchanan, et al., 1983). It is imperative that the knowledge engineer work through conceptualization activities, develop a mechanism for depicting developing organization schemes (either on-line, through a prototype, or using a printed copy), and share this with domain experts for use in mini-problem solving scenarios. This allows knowledge engineers to sample the efficacy of the conceptual organization prior to major knowledge acquisition and representation efforts.

Major difficulties that knowledge engineers have during conceptualization are due to basic unfamiliarity with
- Techniques for the elicitation of conceptual knowledge
- Methods for analyzing and depicting conceptual knowledge for refinement and later representation.

The next sections of this chapter provide background in these areas and present the knowledge engineer with a stable of methods and techniques that can be used in working through this vital stage of knowledge acquisition.

TECHNIQUES FOR EVOKING DOMAIN CONCEPTUALIZATION

A knowledge engineer faces at least two primary tasks when attempting to form a domain conceptualization. First, the primary concepts and attributes that differentiate concepts within a domain must be identified or defined. Second, the relationships between these concepts and attributes must be discerned. The following sections discuss techniques that can be used to accomplish the first task.

Evoking Concept Identification

Knowledge engineers can extract major concepts or subsets of knowledge within a domain from texts and training materials, domain experts, or both. Texts and training materials are a good place to start because they represent the author's attempt to present critical domain information in a logical manner. In most cases, this presentation will parallel a breakdown of the domain into its functional subsets and/or concepts. As the knowledge engineer struggles to abstract and understand the domain knowledge that is represented in source materials, he or she will find it desirable to work with a human expert.

Planning a knowledge acquisition session whose purpose is to identify or validate domain concepts and organization proceeds in much the same manner as was reported in Chapter 3. In particular, knowledge engineers should be attune to the fact that while all domain experts will have an internal organization for key concepts, tapping that knowledge so that it can be related verbally will be tedious. Several iterations may be required before conceptual organization can be abstracted graphically, refined, and accepted or verified by the domain expert.

The domain, program needs, and domain expert will impact the selection of techniques that the knowledge engineer will use to evoke conceptual information. Consequently, the techniques presented in the following section differ in their degree of formality, the type/level of information they will elicit, and the role played by the domain expert. Figure 5-2 summarizes a comparison of techniques that knowledge engineers can use to identify domain concepts.

TECHNIQUE	STRENGTH	REQUIREMENT
Generate Concept Definitions	• Informal • Few requirements on KE	• Requires DE who can conceptualize & communicate • Requires that KE have interview skills
Compare & Contrast Tasks	• Good for isolating salient features of concepts	• Requires selection of appropriate concepts prior to the session • Effectiveness may depend on KE's questioning techniques
Using Generalizations	• Demonstrates use of primary concepts & heuristics • Uses actual domain data	• KE must be able to use domain terminology • Requires inference of reasons • Requires selection of appropriate tasks prior to session
Using Predictions	• Uses actual domain data	• DE must be confident & willing to predict • Requires selection of appropriate task prior to session

Figure 5-2. Techniques to Evoke Concept Identification

Generating Concept Definitions

Requesting that a domain expert generate a concept definition is one of the least formal methods of concept identification. Because this technique requires only that the knowledge engineer have command of the critical terminology within the domain, it is useful during initial meetings with a domain expert. Using this technique, knowledge engineers prod the expert to provide an initial categorization and classification of elements within the domain. Thus, concept definition helps the knowledge engineer abstract and conceptualize the domain and identify the primary interrelationships among its major elements.

Because it is an informal technique, few specific guidelines exist for using concept definition. General suggestions include the following:

1. First, the knowledge engineer identifies key domain terminology.

2. Before meeting with the domain expert, the knowledge engineer graphically depicts the "top level" concepts in the domain in preparation for the knowledge acquisition session.

3. The knowledge engineer sends this preliminary information, along with the Knowledge Acquisition Form, to the domain expert prior to the session itself.

4. As the knowledge acquisition session begins, the knowledge engineer describes the purpose and use of concept definitions.

5. During the session itself, the knowledge engineer works with the domain expert to elicit the expert's reaction to the information compiled by the knowledge engineer or to elicit the expert's own grouping or abstraction of these important concepts.

6. Upon completion of the session, the knowledge engineer summarizes what has been accomplished and presents any supporting graphics to the expert for clarification and refinement.

Tasks During the Session. During the knowledge acquisition session itself, the knowledge engineer will find it helpful to use a structured-interview format. This format (described in detail in Chapter 7) helps to focus the session, avoiding long-winded discussions of the domain that may not be pertinent at this stage. In the course of the session, the knowledge engineer may use questioning techniques to guide the expert in depicting or explaining the elements and their association. Sample questions that the knowledge engineer might use to prod a domain expert to generate concept definitions include

"List the elements that help define _____."

"Now that you have listed the major types of ____, please circle those that somehow go together."

"You have listed these items in a group. Please identify the common thread that runs among them."

"Please provide a label for each of the groups you have formed."

The domain expert's actions in response to the use of this technique include the following:

- Grouping items
- Labeling items
- Labeling a new group
- Offering an alternative for a grouping
- Identifying a common factor among items
- Identifying complexities in the groupings.

Knowledge engineers may vary this technique to prompt the domain expert to categorize and classify specific elements within the domain. In this case, questions that can be posed involve labeling groups of concepts. Typical questions that knowledge engineers might ask include those that follow:

"Why did you group the elements in this manner?"

"Which additional elements or ideas might be added to the initial grouping?"

"Which elements do not seem to be appropriate for either the label or the group?"

Comparing and Contrasting

Once the domain expert and/or knowledge engineer has identified the basic elements within a domain, the expert can be asked to *compare and contrast* specific entities. This technique represents an adaptation of a type of questioning technique and can be effective when the knowledge engineer needs to isolate the salient features of primary concepts. Salient features, those attributes that discriminate between concepts, may not always be obvious. Isolating them is an important step in forming precise descriptions for elements or items.

To use this technique the knowledge engineer works through the following steps:

1. First, the knowledge engineer selects concepts, functions, or other items that previously have been identified as being important in the domain. (The knowledge engineer may wish to work with an internal domain expert to accomplish this task prior to conducting the knowledge acquisition session with another expert.)

2. The knowledge engineer summarizes the information to depict it in either text or graphic form and attaches the summary to the Knowledge Acquisition Form that will be sent to the expert.

3. The knowledge engineer sends the form to the expert and explains that the purpose of the session is to identify and discuss key attributes that distinguish elements or groups of elements from one another.

4. Once the session begins, the domain expert is asked to provide a top-level description of the items under discussion. This description should include primary attributes, uses, and distinguishing features and will be the basis for later comparison and contrast activities.

5. Now the expert is asked to compare or contrast the major, essential elements. During this activity he or she focuses on differentiating the components that have been listed previously for each item.

6. The knowledge engineer uses questioning techniques to keep the expert on track and refine differentiations among elements. Discussions should be accompanied by lists, diagrams, etc.

7. At the end of the session, the knowledge engineer summarizes the main points, presents diagrams or lists that depict the comparison completed during the session, and requests clarification or refinement.

Using Compare and Contrast. Suppose, for example, that a knowledge engineer had completed the presession activities, requesting that the domain expert bring to the session a grouping of the essential components of each element, idea, or event in the target domain. The components that the expert identified are posted on a whiteboard or on notes that both the domain expert and knowledge engineer can view easily. Next, the knowledge engineer requests that the domain expert compare or contrast the major, essential elements that have been abstracted from the domain. The domain expert should be encouraged to state explicit reasons for the similarities and or differences that are specified. The knowledge engineer might use questions such as:

How is ITEMA different from ITEMB?

In what way(s) are ITEMA, ITEMB, and ITEMC alike?

Is there any relation between the way ITEMA and ITEMB are used?

Describe possible areas of overlap between ITEMA and ITEMB.

When would the concepts in GROUP1 be most important? When would the concepts in GROUP2 be most important?

If more information is desired, the knowledge engineer asks the domain expert to repeat the process, offering comparisons and contrasts according to minor elements or less salient features.

Generalizations

As children form concepts to help categorize their world, they display a tendency to generalize. This tendency is so strong that children attempt to generalize the attributes and definitions of one concept to others that *appear* in some way similar (which results in a phenomenon known as over generalization). As the knowledge engineer identifies and structures the concepts that make up a specific domain, he or she can make use of the human tendency to generalize. Generalizations may be evoked in either a structured or unstructured knowledge acquisition interview sessions. The primary requirement for the use of generalization as a method to evoke domain concepts is that the knowledge engineer have a working knowledge of the domain's terminology.

The guidelines that follow suggest one way to use this technique:

1. Prior to the knowledge acquisition session, the domain expert receives a Knowledge Acquisition Form summarizing session goals and may be asked to select a typical event or set of data that will help the knowledge engineer generalize critical concepts.

2. The domain expert should be told that during the session he or she will be asked to form or share generalizations.

3. As the session begins, the knowledge engineer describes the purpose and goals of the session.

4. During the knowledge acquisition session itself, the domain expert describes the pre-identified event or set of data.

5. The domain expert is then asked to infer reasons for the events, which are noted by the knowledge engineer.[2]

6. Next, the knowledge engineer requests that the domain expert use analogies to describe a *similar* event.

7. Comparing the events and the concepts delineated in each set of data, the knowledge engineer prompts the domain expert to develop and state a generalization that connects separate points from this discussion into one statement or heuristic.

At the end of the session, the knowledge engineer summarizes the completed tasks and presents resulting statements or heuristics for clarification and refinement.

Using Prediction

Recent research (Klein, 1986; Hoffman, 1980; Lakoff & Johnson, 1980) suggests that people often use analogies and metaphors to solve problems. Klein (1987) suggests that this is so because analogies and metaphors can be used to derive inferences and make predictions. Knowledge engineers can request that domain expertsuse prediction to isolate the concepts, facts, attributes, and parameters that are used to solve a problem in the domain. This technique is a corollary to the previous exercise in developing generalizations. Information used in making generalizations will also be used in making predictions. Guidelines for using this technique include the following:

1. Before using the prediction technique, the knowledge engineer develops a situation or scenario that contains information that will act as a trigger for the target knowledge. The scenario should be short, easy to explain, and should require the use of the concepts or element groupings under examination.

2. The knowledge engineer completes a Knowledge Acquisition Form describing the technique that will be used and presents the general scenario that will be worked with during the knowledge acquisition session.

3. As the session begins, the knowledge engineer explains its purpose and goals. The domain expert is told that whether or not his or her predictions are correct is *not* the most important part of the process. The emphasis will be on the information that the expert uses to form the prediction.

4. During the session the knowledge engineer presents the pre-identified situation to the domain expert and asks him or her to predict the probable consequences (to the desired level) of the situation.

5. Next, the knowledge engineer prompts the domain expert for facts or generalizations that support his or her prediction.

6. The knowledge engineer then asks the domain expert to provide an alternative situation, complete with predicted outcome and suspected consequences of that prediction. This information is posted for discussion.

7. The knowledge engineer uses questioning techniques to lead a discussion on similarities and differences between the predicted outcomes or consequences. The goal of the discussion is to isolate pivotal occurrences, distinguishing features, or important factors that are used to discriminate concepts or determine consequences.

8. At the close of the session, the knowledge engineer summarizes conclusions and presents those to the expert for clarification and refinement.

Variations to setting up this procedure include
• The knowledge engineer and domain expert work together to depict a scenario or situation prior to the knowledge acquisition session
• The knowledge engineer requests that an 'internal' (e.g., "in-house") domain expert compile the situation for the knowledge engineer to present.

TECHNIQUES FOR ORGANIZING AND ANALYZING DOMAIN CONCEPTUALIZATIONS

Typically, an evaluation of the organization of domain concepts occurs at the end of a prototype stage, as domain experts and program personnel demonstrate system performance. Problems identified at this stage require that the prototype be debugged, at best and completed restructured, at worst. DeGreef and Breuker (1985) have already established that changing conceptual structures requires less effort than debugging a prototype, is less time consuming, and is equally effective as prototype evaluation.
The next section presents techniques that knowledge engineers and domain experts may use to analyze and evaluate the conceptual structure of information The focus here is on key information and relationships, rather than on the performance of the system.

Defining Concepts

Concepts are abstract representations that define objects, elements, or events according to attributes and values. They are exceedingly difficult to speak about, much less to represent in a knowledge base. Few of us are aware of the techniques we have used to organize information about which *we* are experts. Yet if asked to train another individual in our field of expertise, we tap into that knowledge.

Similarly, if the domain expert is asked to verbalize knowledge about his or her field of expertise, he or she must convey the concepts (with their attributes and values) and the interrelationships among them. Much of this information will be conveyed verbally and is subject to typical problems inherent in communication (e.g., differing meanings of the same words, differences in backgrounds of sender and receiver, etc.). Therefore, the knowledge engineer needs a mechanism through which to "capture," abstract, and represent domain concepts. Such a mechanism enables interaction with the domain expert for feedback and refinement prior to translation into rules. Figure 5-3 provides a comparison of some of the techniques that a knowledge engineer might use to analyze or define concepts.

TECHNIQUE	STRENGTH	REQUIREMENT
Concept Dictionaries	• Displays interrelatedness of key domain terms or concepts • First step toward classification of primary concepts	• KE must have working knowledge of domain • Appropriate terms must be selected prior to session
Conceptual Frameworks	• Standard format for the analysis of domain material	• Appropriate structure must be selected and distributed to team

Figure 5-3. A Comparison of Concept Definition Techniques

Concept Dictionaries

The vocabulary used in a domain represents major concepts within the domain. Chapter 3 suggests that project development personnel establish a knowledge dictionary during the domain familiarization phase of knowledge acquisition. The development of the knowledge dictionary stimulates the definition of the primary terms and acronyms that the knowledge engineer will be required to use and understand.

The fields of communication and content analysis use a tool called the **conceptual dictionary** (Carney, 1972) that can be adapted for use in the conceptualization stage of knowledge acquisition. It provides a mechanism to visualize an abstraction of the primary concepts in a domain and the terminology used to label them. Such a "dictionary" is based on the notion that words may be grouped by common elements of reference into recognizable concepts. Some concepts are very closely aligned with one another, while others will be more unrelated. Once they have been exposed, conceptual associations or groups may be classified together under a broader umbrella that reflects all of the concepts that should be depicted. Figure 5-4 presents a partial concept dictionary.

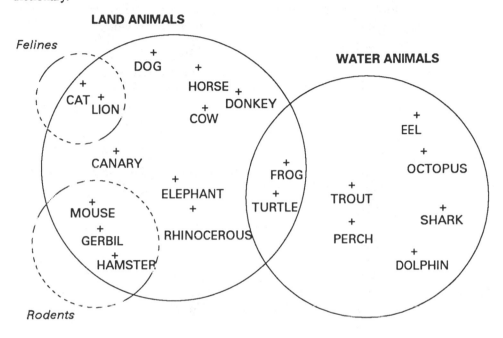

Figure 5-4. Conceptual Dictionary Structure

Developing a Concept Dictionary. To develop a concept dictionary, a knowledge engineer could follow these basic guidelines. Notice that this technique may be applied either manually (hand-drawing), or using a computer-based graphic or design tool. The computer more easily accommodates the changes that occur during the course of this task.

1. The knowledge engineer completes the Knowledge Acquisition Form that describes the planned knowledge acquisition session, including introductory information on the goals and purpose of this technique.

2. Before the session begins, the domain expert provides or is presented with a set of terms within the selected domain.

3. During the session the domain expert is asked to list these words together in the manner that is most appropriate, compiling groups or "families" of words when possible.

4. The knowledge engineer reviews the resulting conceptual groups.and uses questioning techniques to stimulate the domain expert to explain reasons for grouping, overlapping, or isolating groups.

5. As these discussions occur, the knowledge engineer and domain expert formulate and refine a graphic depiction of group relationships.

6. At the close of the session, the knowledge engineer presents the resulting graphic, summarizing the major considerations and reasons for the current structure.

A variation of this technique is to use conceptual dictionaries to compare the organization of concepts among multiple domain experts. For example, a knowledge engineer might be interested in comparing the groupings of a domain practitioner who is a novice with those of a domain expert. Similarly, the abstractions of two domain experts may be compared. The purpose of this exercise is to pinpoint those words and groupings that are common to both representations, as well as those that are different. Differences that are noted are used as springboards to discussion that can clarify and extend the knowledge engineer's conceptualization of the domain.

Conceptual Frameworks

The notion of using **conceptual frameworks** to depict the elements an individual monitors when drawing conclusions is adapted from the technique of standardized frameworks for the content analysis of communication (Carney, 1972). Standardized frameworks provide a specific structure for depicting categories of critical information that are later analyzed to determine how an individual drew conclusions. Originally, Carney defined the categories for the framework as follows:
- Subject matter categories
- Frequency of mention
- Length of mention
- Intensity of the discussion.

Knowledge engineers can adapt the technique to use as a tool when analyzing either written (e.g., domain texts or training manuals) or oral communication (e.g., knowledge acquisition interviews). The conceptual framework allows the knowledge engineer to abstract key information from the communication to determine the concepts, attributes, and values that are important in the subset of the domain under scrutiny. Because they offer a means to structure the analysis process, they may be useful on a large program with multiple knowledge engineers, or on a program that is required to consult multiple domain sources. Used in these situations, conceptual frameworks provide a synthesized view of the domain across sources.

Figure 5-5 represents a sample structure for using conceptual frameworks in the knowledge acquisition session. The heading labels are program-driven. That is, while a program may prefer to use Carney's original labeling scheme, the scheme may be adapted to meet the needs of each specific program. Whatever structure is selected, it should be standardized for use throughout the expert system development effort or teams so that information attained may be depicted in a systematic manner and shared easily.

OBJECT/ELEMENT	FREQUENCY	ATTRIBUTE VALUES	IMPORTANCE
Age of Investor	7 in 5 min Above 30	Below 30	9 (Scale 1-10)
Amt. to Invest	5 in 5 min	Below 5K	7 (Scale 1-10)

Figure 5-5. Sample Structure for Conceptual Frameworks

Using Maps and Models

Extracting a representation of a domain expert's "mental model" provides for a common frame of reference for later interviews or analysis and can also provide clues for knowledge-base design. Many of the methods discussed in later sections of this chapter, including the use of scaling technique and conceptual clustering, can provide graphs or "networks" of key concepts. Other, less formal techniques that can be used to provide conceptual feedback to domain experts include cognitive maps and models.

Cognitive Maps

Cognitive maps are tools that represent a domain expert's ideas concerning primary concepts and interrelationships in a domain. These maps may be constructed manually, by sorting cards on a table or wallboard, or drawn on a computer using a drawing program. The benefits of using cognitive maps are that they allow the knowledge engineer to
   • Become familiar with major concepts and relationships
   • Reduce the amount of time he or she spends pouring over domain documents.

The primary drawback is that they are based on the domain expert's perception and thus, are subject to inaccuracies (caused either by the initial perception or its translation to a graphic representation).

Cognitive maps provide a tool that can be used as a foundation or framework for knowledge acquisition sessions. They can be constructed during or after initial interviews with a domain expert. To develop a cognitive map, the knowledge engineer may use the following guidelines:

1. The knowledge engineer completes the Knowledge Acquisition Form, specifying the purpose and goal of the knowledge acquisition session and describing the cognitive mapping process.

2. During the knowledge acquisition session the knowledge engineer presents the expert with a list of objects or concepts and ask that they be organized to reflect the domain. Alternately, the knowledge engineer may request that the domain expert come to the session with a first draft of the map completed.[3]

3. As the knowledge engineer and domain expert review the cognitive map, they should refine the level of detail of the "map." The knowledge engineer should be able to use the map to identify critical objects and concepts in terms of their relationships.

4. The knowledge engineer uses questioning techniques to stimulate the domain expert into revealing some of the reasoning behind the structure provided.

5. As the session concludes, the knowledge engineer presents the finalized mapping and summarizes the critical objects, concepts, and relationships. The domain expert refines and clarifies the resulting map.

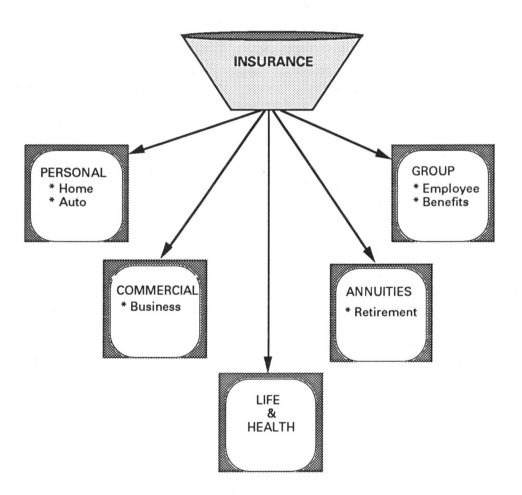

Figure 5-6. Sample Cognitive "Map" for the Insurance Domain

Conceptualizing the Domain   **Chap. 5**

Figure 5-6 represents a top-level cognitive map for the insurance domain that was developed during an introductory knowledge acquisition session.[4] To create the graph, the domain expert was asked to help us depict graphically the organization of the major areas within the insurance domain. Because it was created using a graphics program on a computer, our "map" could be changed easily to enable refinement. The resulting graph became a springboard for subsequent knowledge acquisition sessions. For example, in follow-on sessions, we used the graph as a discussion tool and worked with the expert to

- Refine each node within the graph
- Schedule the most important components for early knowledge acquisition sessions
- Begin identifying documents and experts that can serve as knowledge sources for each major area
- Plan knowledge acquisition time
- Begin initial design efforts for the knowledge base.

Models

Many problems are solved by abstracting data, heuristically mapping higher level problem descriptions onto solution models, and refining these models until specific solutions are found (Clancey, 1986). A number of theories or models exist that can provide a mechanism to help organize domain knowledge to convey it to expert system designers. Expert system designers can benefit from a syntactic/semantic model of user knowledge. Such a model relates to the idea that domain experts have both syntactic and semantic knowledge about the way tasks are currently performed. Syntactic, surface-level knowledge is described as requiring rote memorization and being fairly device- or context-dependent. Semantic knowledge (e.g., "deep" knowledge) is more device- and context-independent, is stored in long term memory, and is stable. The syntactic/semantic model has been used to describe user behavior in many fields, including programming (Schneiderman & Mayer, 1979; Schneiderman, 1980).

Mental models can be structured and graphed according to any scheme that meets the requirements of the domain.. An alternative to the syntactic/semantic model discussed earlier, for example, is the use of a knowledge acquisition tool to develop a process model (Reeker, Blaxton, & Geesey, 1987), and transition diagrams (Kieras & Polson, 1985). Other researchers (Card, Moran, & Newell, 1983) suggest the GOMS (goals, operators, methods, and selection rule) model.

Identifying Interrelationships

The ability to classify objects such as events, states, or observations as members of object families or concepts is the basis of all inferential capacity (Fisher and Langley, 1985) In addition to identifying major domain concepts, knowledge engineers must be able to relate and abstract them for later representation in the knowledge base. The following techniques provide vehicles for depicting the interrelationships of concepts and their attributes:

- Taxonomies

- Concept sorting
- Scaling techniques
- Conceptual clustering
- Repertory grids.

Because each of these techniques can be a field of study in itself, the descriptions here are not meant to be all-inclusive. The focus of this presentation is on methods that a knowledge engineer can use to detect interrelationships or groupings of concepts. Throughout the discussion, pointers are provided to other sources that provide in-depth coverage of each technique.

Taxonomies

Taxonomies are basic classification systems that enable designers or knowledge engineers to describe conceptual identifications and dependencies. For example, a knowledge engineer assigned the task of acquiring knowledge for an expert system that will to assist in selecting an appropriate mix of landscaping plants for optimum color and survivability might first develop a taxonomy that represents the different types and characteristics of landscape plants (Figure 5-7). The resulting taxonomy would initially depict major distinctions or types of landscaping (i.e., flowers, shrub, trees). Beneath these nodes would appear more specific types or subgroups of each category (i.e., perennials, ground cover, evergreen). Nodes beneath these nodes would "inherit" attributes (i.e., "loses leaves" would be an attribute of DECIDUOUS) from the parent node and become increasingly more specific until instances of various types or landscaping (i.e., "Red Oak" as a child of DECIDUOUS) are depicted in the graph.

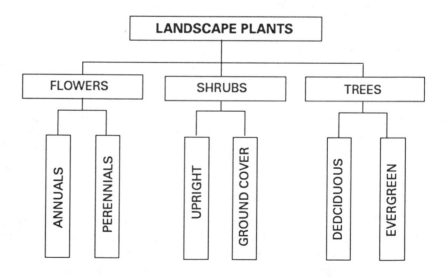

Figure 5-7. Partial Taxonomy for Landscape Plants

Regardless of whether or not a knowledge engineer selects them as the major analysis technique, taxonomies are important conceptual tools. Taxonomies are most useful in the organization of declarative knowledge, such as that embodied by knowledge-based diagnostic systems. Shannon (1980a, 1980b) believes that the validity of any analysis (and thus, the system that is based on that analysis) seems to depend on the use of a valid taxonomic model.

The construction of a taxonomy involves identifying, defining, comparing, and grouping elements. During taxonomy construction, the knowledge engineer is advised to work with a domain expert to make decisions concerning elements, attributes and salient features, and values. To construct a taxonomy, knowledge engineers may follow these guidelines

1. First, the domain expert and knowledge engineer create a classification process or heuristic that allows each element within the domain to be defined by its attributes.

2. Each of the elements that has been identified as important to the domain is further defined. This definition process includes associating a value with the set of attributes that define each element (Galloway, 1987).

3. Next, the knowledge engineer subdivides existing elements into classes of elements that have equal values for each of a select set of attributes.

4. The knowledge engineer works with the domain expert to clarify his or her understanding of the domain.

The resulting taxonomy can be used to depict the knowledge engineer's understanding of the domain, aid in training new knowledge engineers, planning knowledge base structure, and planning knowledge acquisition sessions.

Concept Sorting

Concept sorting is a psychological technique that is useful in tapping organizational knowledge (Chi, Feltovich, and Glaser, 1981). The elicitation of the concepts and constructs can be handled manually, or at least partially automated. Gammack and Young (1985) describe a manual application of concept sorting that is easy to use and requires no statistical procedures or other tasks requiring a computer. Using this technique in the domain of central heating systems, they and their domain expert were able to construct a "tree" of related concepts. Concepts within the tree included a primitive set of 75 basic components of the domain, structured into five levels of abstraction. This hierarchical organization allowed them to comprehend the expert's personal domain organization and abstract it into subsystems that represented the flow of gas, water, electricity, and heat (Gammack & Young, 1985, p. 110).

To apply this technique manually, the knowledge engineer follows these basic steps.

1. First, the knowledge engineer consults a textbook, training manual, or in-house domain expert to identify the major top-level concepts represented in the domain.

2. The knowledge engineer completes a Knowledge Acquisition Form, stating the goal and purpose of the knowledge acquisition session and attaches the list of top-level concepts that will be sorted.

3. When the expert arrives, the knowledge engineer works with him or her to place each of these concepts on a note card (if working with paper) or on a magnet-backed strip (if working with a magnetic board). Because of the difficulty in shuffling large numbers of note cards (and keeping them in place), we recommend the use of a large magnetic board or wall that allows objects to be stuck in place.

4. Next, the knowledge engineer asks the domain expert to begin sorting the cards, placing them in groups according to those that "belong" together.

5. As the domain expert sorts the cards, the knowledge engineer uses questioning techniques to determine *why* they are placed together. (Note that this step may be combined with techniques previously mentioned in this chapter, such as concept labeling and definition.)

6. The knowledge engineer periodically summarizes how items have been grouped, stimulating discussion and refinement activities.

Rarely will the domain expert be satisfied with the first structure or hierarchy that results from this process. More commonly, the expert will iteratively shuffle and combine "concepts." Once in place, however, the resulting structure can provide the knowledge engineer with a tool to stimulate further discussion of concept interrelatedness, individual attributes and values, and other analyses.

Automating the Process. The concept sorting procedure just outlined entails several tasks that may be more easily handled, processed, and stored using a computer program. For example, when implementing concept sorting, a computer graphics program, design program, or knowledge acquisition tool could be used to depict the labeled objects that may then be linked graphically. As the knowledge engineer works with the expert to refine the structure, the "objects" may be moved around into different groups, linked together as groups and labeled. When the knowledge acquisition session is over, a dated printout may be obtained and sent back with the expert for further refinement. The resulting work is stored for later use.

Scaling Techniques
A number of researchers (Cooke & McDonald, 1986; Butler & Carter, 1986) have suggested the use of psychological scaling techniques. Cooke and McDonald (1987) contend that these techniques are more objective than manual knowledge elicitation methods. While we do not support their use as the sole elicitation method, scaling

techniques can be valuable tools for use in both the conceptualization and refinement phases of knowledge acquisition.[5]

Scaling techniques may be useful in providing a method of feedback with which domain experts can work during initial knowledge acquisition sessions. Abstracting and representing domain concepts and conceptual relationships can spur the expert to refine, extend, and clarify the knowledge engineer's initial understanding of the domain. Cooke and McDonald (1987) suggest that scaling techniques could also provide information that can serve as a basis for knowledge representation. Finally, scaling mechanisms can provide one way to compare and analyze knowledge derived from multiple sources.

There are a variety of scaling techniques, including the following:

- **Multidimensional scaling** (Kruskal, 1977; Kruskal & Wish, 1978). Based on the least-squares fitting technique, these programs are fairly complex. They require that the knowledge engineer both input a symmetrical distance matrix and detail the number of dimensions into which the data must fit. This technique's usefulness as a knowledge acquisition and conceptualization tool is limited primarily by the fact that dimensions must be known prior to the analysis.

- **Hierarchical cluster analysis** (Johnson, 1967). Less complex than multidimensional scaling, hierarchical cluster analysis is the most common application of scaling techniques to knowledge acquisition. It requires that (1) each of the two closest objects in a matrix be combined into one "cluster" and (2) distances to the cluster be computed (i.e., either as the minimum, maximum, or average of the distance from each of the objects). The result of this process is a tree with links between clusters and items.

- **Network scaling** (Schvaneveldt & Durso, 1981; Schvaneveldt, Durso & Dearholt, 1985). Network scaling requires that the knowledge engineer or domain expert identify concepts that are then expressed as nodes. Working from these nodes, links are then formed between select pairs of nodes to represent their relationship. Next, the knowledge engineer must present some estimate of "relatedness" or distance between pairs of concepts. Using an algorithm (e.g., *Pathfinder*, Schvaneveldt & Durso, 1981; Schvaneveldt, Durso & Dearholt, 1985), the knowledge engineer can determine whether or not a link will be present between concepts in pairs. If present, links are assigned weights that represent the strength of their relationship. If the minimum distance between the concepts is greater than the distance estimate for the pair, a link is constructed.

Conceptual Clustering

Conceptual clustering, a methodology for organizing and summarizing domain data, is the process of grouping "exemplars" in logical ways, such as in a hierarchy of categories or a tree structure (Stepp, 1987). It enables an expert system developer to produce an abstraction of the domain under investigation. Defined for use in knowledge acquisition by Michalski (1980), conceptual clustering is based on the analysis of clusters. **Cluster analysis** is a generic term for a "set of techniques which can produce classifications from data that is initially unclassified" (Everitt, 1980). Ball (1971) reports that cluster analysis techniques are commonly used for a number of purposes, from model fitting and prediction based on groups to data exploration and hypothesis generation and testing. The fields in which cluster analysis is used range from psychology and biology to artificial intelligence.

Regardless of the specific purpose for which it is used or the field in which the technique is applied, cluster analysis focuses on this task:

Given a certain number of concepts, devise a classification scheme to group the objects into a number of classes (with the following constraints).

(a) Each of the concepts is described by a set of numerical measures (and if inductive tools are used, qualitative values, as well).

(b) Objects within classes or groups must be similar in some respect.

(c) Objects within classes or groups must be unlike those from other classes.

Because cluster analysis is used in a variety of fields, it has been applied using numerous techniques. Cormack (1971) has analyzed and categorized the most prevalent of these techniques. The categorizations that seem most appropriate for use in analyzing domain knowledge include those that follow:

Hierarchical Techniques. The classes themselves are subdivided and classified into groups. This process iterates until an inverted tree is formed. The resulting "tree" structure depicts the fusions or partitioning that has occurred at each step of the analysis. It is important to note that, unlike a taxonomy, which may simply illustrate similar ideas, the dendogram (Figure 5-8) is based on a mathematical procedure in which the similarity or distance matrix between elements is computed. Specific techniques that are used to produce these hierarchical representations include

- Nearest neighbor method (Johnson, 1967)
- Group average method (Sokal & Michener, 1958; Lance & Williams, 1966; Everitt, 1977)
- Median cluster analysis (Gower, 1967)
- Centroid cluster (King, 1966)
- Association analysis (McNaughton-Smith, 1965).

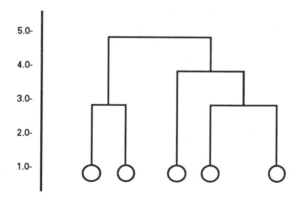

Figure 5-8. Dendogram Structure

Density Search Techniques. Imagine that elements, such as concepts, are represented as specific points in a domain expert's "world." It stands to reason that some of these concepts would be clustered or grouped together (high density), while other portions of this "world" would be sparse, illustrating a low density of related concepts. Carmichael and others (1968) and Gengerelli (1963) have applied this **density search** technique to discover "natural" clusters or subgroups. The taxometric map technique (Carmichael & Sneath, 1969), is an attempt to emulate the procedure that a human observer uses to detect clusters in more than one dimension. In this situation, humans seem to compare the relative distance between a pair of points and to search for densely-populated areas that are surrounded by sparcely-populated areas. Other techniques include mode analysis (Wishart, 1969) and unimodal fuzzy set detection (Gitman & Levine, 1970).

Clumping Techniques. While some concept-analysis techniques yield an inverted tree-like structure, others may allow a less disjointed or distinct grouping of clusters. As Everitt (1980) noted, fields such as language study must allow class overlap because words frequently have more than one meaning depending on how they are used and the speaker's background. **Clumping techniques** commonly are initiated by producing a matrix that depicts similarity to provide an estimate of similarity between pairs of elements on the basis of some property. Then one of several methods may be applied to identify partitions between groups (Needham, 1967; Jones & Jackson, 1967; Bonner, 1964; Jardine & Sibson, 1968).

Because conceptual clustering is algorithmically-intensive, the computer can enhance the precision of clustering methodologies and the speed with which they can be applied. To date, a number of systems have been developed to aid in the task of clustering domain concepts. Conceptual clustering systems typically take input (e.g., events, observations, facts) and generate a classification scheme that incorporates the data that was provided. Fisher and Langley (1985) report on two views of the conceptual clustering task: (1) applications described by Michalski and Steep (1983) as an extension of numerical taxonomy and (2) conceptual clustering as an example of concept formation (i.e., learning by observation). Each of these views has spawned a number of conceptual clustering algorithms and the construction of entire conceptual clustering systems. A description of each of these systems would be beyond the scope of this text. Instead, the reader is encouraged to investigate literature related to conceptual clustering in the field of machine learning (Michalski, 1980; Michalski, 1983; Michie, 1982). However, to provide readers with an overview of the types of systems that have been developed for this purpose and the use of computer programs in conceptual analysis in general, we will describe two examples. COBWEB (Fisher, 1987) and TAXI (Galloway, 1987).

COBWEB. COBWEB is a system for conceptual clustering that is based on the assumptions that critical properties are dependent on the regularities that exist in the environment and that these may be extracted and organized (Pearl, 1985; Cheng & Fu, 1985; Dietterich, 1981). COBWEB uses a evaluation function to guide class and concept formation. Termed "category utility," this function attempts to guide the formation of object classes and concepts by selecting classes that maximize the amount of information that can be inferred from knowing an object's class membership (Gluck & Corter, 1985).

Using category utility, objects are described and classified in terms of attribute-value pairs (Fisher, 1987), as illustrated in Figure 5-9.

```
NUMBER = seven
COLOR = blue
```

Figure 5-9. Attribute-Value Pairs

For each attribute-value pair and class, the similarity within classes is measured in terms of a conditional probability. Partition quality is then estimated, based on the predictability and predictiveness of the attribute value. COBWEB uses this utility to incrementally include objects in a classification hierarchy.

Within this hierarchy, nodes represent a probabilistic concept for a specific object class. Each element or object is included by classifying it during a descent of the tree. Elements may be partitioned by placing a new element in an existing class, creating a new class, or merging and splitting nodes.

An example is portrayed in Figure 5-10.

```
FISH = BodyCover = scales (probability of 1.0)
TRANSPORT = Swim (probability of 1.0)
```

Figure 5-10. Denoting Probabilistic Concepts

COBWEB has been used in the domains of soybean disease diagnosis (Fisher, 1987a) and thyroid disease diagnosis (Fisher, 1987b). Its designer claims that after being presented with five randomly-selected instances of soybean disease, COBWEB was able to use a classification it had developed to diagnose correctly 42 cases of soybean disease 88% of the time. After being presented with ten instances of soybean disease, COBWEB was able to achieve 100% diagnosis accuracy. Thus, within a limited domain, COBWEB does seem to suggest that computer-based classification systems can capture, summarize, and organize critical relations among concepts and their attributes.

TAXI. Swartout (1981) expressed doubt that it was possible to automate the construction of taxonomies because they require the processing of large amounts of domain knowledge prior to construction. For example, to develop manually a valid taxonomy in a given domain, humans must be able to accomplish quickly, tasks that involve complex reasoning, such as
- Identifying the primitive elements in a domain and their attributes and values
- Pinpointing generalities among them
- Tracking dependencies among the elements or objects
- Continually refining the developing taxonomy.

TAXI, the Taxonomic Assistant (Galloway, 1987) represents a first-generation knowledge-manipulation system for taxonomic representation. It was developed to aid in organizing domain knowledge. Its primary purpose is *not* to replace human analysis of concepts, but to enhance a developer's understanding of the domain and the relationships of knowledge it represents. TAXI was developed to assist in this detailed process by providing tools to alter the structure of a developing taxonomy, track the dependencies among the elements, and detect generalities in domain knowledge that is represented (Galloway, 1987).

TAXI uses a **discrimination tree** to represent the organization of domain knowledge because it is simple to comprehend, compute, and represent graphically. In such a tree, each node can have only one "parent." Sets of elements are divided into subsets based on discriminating evidence provided by attributes and their values. TAXI allows developers to create and edit each component (e.g., object, attribute, type, class, discriminator, taxonomy) and to manipulate the structure and interrelationships depicted by the taxonomy. The system presents knowledge engineers with control over the "construction, editing, exploration, and experimental processes for discrimination tree taxonomies" (Galloway, 1987, p. 418). While it was developed as a research tool as opposed to an operational system, the scheme upon which it is based is one worth further exploration. If fully developed, an automated assistant that handles "bookkeeping," graphical representation of taxonomies, and prompts for the definition and discrimination of objects, elements, attributes, and classes could be a valuable tool for the knowledge engineer.

Repertory Grids

Repertory grid analysis is a technique for eliciting and analyzing a model of the domain expert's world. Its origin can be traced to a psychologist named George Kelly (1955) who developed the *personal construct theory.* Although explained in more depth in Kelly's original writings, the theory states that each person functions as a "scientist" who classifies and organizes his or her world. Based on these classifications, the individual is able to construct theories of how the particular domain functions. Thus, he or she is able to predict and act in the domain based on these personal theories. Once the classifications have been identified and constructs isolated, a repertory grid can be developed to represent the expert's comprehension of a specific entity (e.g., problem, concept).[6]

Repertory grids have been used in a number of settings prior to their application to the development of expert systems. For example, Stewart and Stewart (1981) note that business applications using repertory grids have included the following:
- Counseling
- Training assessment
- Evaluation
- Job-related motivation
- Questionnaire design
- Market research.

The repertory grid technique can also be used to represent an expert's organization of basic concepts in a specific domain. To develop a grid, the knowledge engineer must first elicit a set of **constructs** (e.g., a bipolar characteristic, such as stable-unstable).

Next, the knowledge engineer must stimulate the domain expert to provide a set of examples, called elements, each of which can be rated according to the constructs that have been provided previously (e.g., various chemicals would be examples of elements that could be classified according to the construct *stable-unstable*). Once constructs and elements have been identified, the knowledge engineer requests that the domain expert rate (i.e., rank) each element according to the constructs that have been provided. This rating is often achieved by developing a linear representation similar to those used in Thurstone attitude scales, such as the one that appears in Figure 5-11.

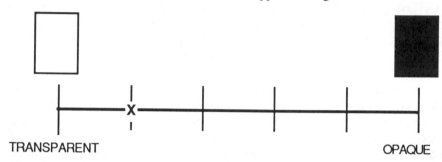

TRANSPARENT   OPAQUE

Figure 5-11. Rating Degree of Transparency Along a Bipolar Scale

After each element has been rated according to each construct, the results may be analyzed using a variety of techniques, including factor analysis and cluster analysis (Shaw, 1981a; Hart, 1986). Whatever technique is used, the purpose of the analysis is to measure similarities and distances among objects and to represent these graphically as a "grid." One set of researchers (Ford, Chang, Petry, Adams-Webber, 1988) describes repertory grid elicitation using a spreadsheet paradigm to obtain knowledge about the radiology domain. In this application, the elements of the domain are used to define the scope of the problem domain for the grid and the constructs are used to help the expert make useful distinctions among the elements.

The completed grid becomes a cross-referencing system between critical constructs and domain elements and can be used to find patterns or relations during initial knowledge acquisition efforts (Hart, 1986). Once developed, the knowledge engineer can use the grid to better understand the domain. For example, Ford and others (1987) loaded the initial set of rules produced from repertory grid data into an automated mechanism for machine learning which continually adjusted the degree of confirmation associated with a hypothesis regarding a diagnosis in the radiology domain.

Moving On

After a conceptual-analysis technique has been used, the results should be presented to the domain expert for review and refinement. During this process the domain expert may be able to offer information not previously tapped and can clarify any misconceptions. Not only can the refinement process enhance the ability of the knowledge engineer to plan knowledge acquisition sessions and begin preliminary knowledge-base organization, but it can also provide information that is essential to ongoing validation and verification. It offers the knowledge engineer an early opportunity to establish that

- The expert system is being designed to meet the appropriate functional goals
- Knowledge base design will reflect an expert's perception of the domain
- The target knowledge for the system has been identified and verified by an expert prior to formal knowledge acquisition sessions.

In some respects, domain conceptualization continues throughout the life of the expert system development project. Defining domain concepts and their interrelationships provides a set of data with which the domain experts interact to refine and clarify the portrayal of key entities. As knowledge acquisition and design plans are made based on this data, interaction continues with the domain experts and the initial conceptualization is expanded and deepened. Concepts originally thought to be unimportant become important in specific contexts. Relationships defined for one application or context differ when investigated under different constraints. Conceptualizations outlined by one domain expert may differ from those portrayed by another of a different level of expertise.

Although they typically undergo metamorphosis, conceptualizations of a domain serve as guideposts to the knowledge engineer who structures and organizes knowledge acquisition efforts for expert system development. Their use can make the difference in an expert system that fulfills a fragment of its goals and one that review panels (see Chapter 11) will find acceptable in its coverage and depth.

ENDNOTES

[1] For more information on concepts and attributes, refer to Chapter 1.

[2] Research in cognitive psychology suggests that inferring reasons is extremely difficult. Responses to this request should be used as a springboard to the next step, but should not be viewed as infallible.

[3] Note that the context in which a cognitive map is elicited influences the structure of a graph that reflects cognitive organization.

[4] Special thanks to Mr. S. T. Kennedy of Lubbock, TX for acting as our domain expert for this activity.

[5] An excellent methodology for applying scaling techniques to the knowledge-elicitation tasks is provided in N. Cooke and J. McDonald, "The application of psychological scaling techniques to knowledge elicitation for knowledge-based systems," International Journal of Man-Machine Studies, 26 (1987), 81-92.

[6] See Think Again (M.E. Shaw, 1981) for a set of examples and Chapter 9 of Knowledge Acquisition for Expert Systems (Hart, 1986) for a complete description of the use of repertory grids in knowledge acquisition.

SUGGESTED READINGS

Everitt, Brian. Cluster Analysis. Halsted Press, a Division of John Wiley & Sons, New York, 1980.

Smith, E.E., and D. L. Medin. Categories and Concepts. Cambridge: Harvard University Press, 1981.

Shaw, M. E., ed. Recent Advances in Personal Construct Technology, New York: Academic Press, 1981.

Shaw, M. E. and C. McKnight. Think Again. Englewood Cliffs, NJ: Prentice-Hall, 1981.

Kowalik, J. Knowledge-Based Problem-Solving, Englewood Cliffs, NJ: Prentice-Hall, 1986.

Bannister, D., ed. Perspectives in Personal Construct Theory, London: Academic Press, 1970.

APPLICATION

The ideas and techniques presented in this chapter provide the knowledge engineer with tools to evoke, structure, and analyze the organization of a domain. Before working with domain experts or other knowledge sources, we advise knowledge engineers to practice some of the techniques. The following activity suggests one possible application of conceptualization techniques that can be completed in small groups.

A. Identifying Concepts

Work in pairs with another individual to practice using at least one of the techniques described to evoke concept identification: concept definitions, comparing and contrasting, using generalizations, or using prediction. Each member of the pair takes turns role playing domain expert and knowledge engineer. When acting as domain expert, the individual selects a fairly restricted domain in which he or she knows a great deal (e.g., hobbies, recreational activities, previous jobs). The knowledge engineer uses one of the aforementioned techniques to elicit the identification of primary concepts in the domain.

B. Organizing Conceptualizations

Once the domain and its primary concepts have been isolated, the domain expert and knowledge engineer should select a technique for defining the concepts and their interrelationship. Techniques may include concept dictionaries, conceptual frameworks, models and graphs, and concept sorting, in addition to taxonomies (Note: scaling techniques, conceptual clustering, and repertory grids, although useful techniques, may be unavailable due to limited time and resources).

Using the selected techniques, the knowledge engineer works with the domain expert to depict and refine an appropriate representation of the domain's major concepts. Recall that tools used during this process may include whiteboards, overhead transparencies, and software programs (e.g., drawing programs).

6

Structuring the Knowledge Acquisition Process

Extending Systems Analysis to Expert System Development

>   **Knowledge Engineer as Systems Analyst**

The Role of Analysis in the Knowledge Acquisition Process

>   **Anaylysis Procedures for Knowledge Base Development**

Using Analysis Tools and Techniques for Knowledge Acquisition

>   **Using Templates**
>   **Using Diagrams**
>   **Laying the Groundwork**
>   **Structuring the Domain**

Completing the Analysis

>   **Refining the Initial Task Analysis**
>   **Planning Knowledge Acquisition Sessions**

INTRODUCTION

Just as outlining is an important precursor to the writing process, structural analysis is a precursor to the knowledge acquisition process. In conventional system development, software engineers use analysis to help define the problem that is to be solved, identify the set of solution variables for the problem, and delineate any existing restrictions on the solution (Jensen & Tonies, 1979). In expert system development, the problem may be more difficult to define and the solution set not as readily identifiable. These increased difficulties underscore the importance of the analysis phase of software development. The less is known about the problem and/or the domain, the more difficult the knowledge engineer's task as he or she begins the knowledge acquisition process.

As one of the initial elements in a systems-oriented knowledge acquisition methodology, analysis serves at least three major purposes: (1) setting boundaries on the domain being examined, (2) actively introducing the knowledge engineer to the domain, including its major concepts and vocabulary, and (3) imposing an initial structure on the knowledge base, (McGraw & Riner, 1987).

This chapter presents two types of analysis techniques that knowledge engineers can use in the initial phases of knowledge acquisition for a large-scale development effort.[1] To begin, we compare the task of traditional systems analysis with related procedures and needs in expert systems development as we discuss similar goals, requirements, and personnel. In doing so, we liken the role of the knowledge engineer to that of the systems analyst, present background on the use of analysis in a number of different fields, and summarize some of the information on "expertise" that affects the analysis task. Next, we outline a set of considerations and procedures that knowledge engineers can use during the analysis process. These include reviewing background domain information, decomposing the domain, identifying knowledge types within the domain, and selecting an appropriate analysis technique. We then present two types of techniques a knowledge engineer might use to accomplish an analysis. We conclude with information intended to help the knowledge engineer refine an initial analysis and use the analysis to plan knowledge acquisition sessions.

Objectives

This chapter presents information on the use of analysis techniques in the knowledge acquisition process. Specifically, it enables readers to accomplish the following:
- Compare and contrast the roles of systems analyst and knowledge engineer
- Distinguish between analysis techniques based on purpose and knowledge acquisition phase
- Select an appropriate analysis technique based on knowledge type, task nature, and knowledge acquisition needs
- Outline procedures to complete an analysis prior to knowledge acquisition
- Work with a domain expert to produce one of several types of analyses
- Use a completed analysis to plan follow-up knowledge acquisition sessions.

Key Terms

task nature	task analysis	timeline analysis
functional analysis	job analysis	interaction analysis
information flow analysis	mission decomposition	
decision/action analysis	operational sequence analysis	

EXTENDING SYSTEMS ANALYSIS TO EXPERT SYSTEM DEVELOPMENT

Knowledge acquisition is intertwined with and dependent upon the knowledge represented in the domain. Structuring knowledge in a way that allows the knowledge engineer to identify targets for knowledge acquisition can help increase the efficiency of the knowledge acquisition process. Once targets have been identified, the knowledge engineer can build a structure or framework that can help drive the knowledge acquisition plans and activities that follow.

To analyze knowledge is to analyze the way "experts categorize a chunk" of their domain (Tiemann & Markle, 1984). Analysis of knowledge implies that the job, task, or episode under investigation can be partitioned into parts or aspects. Analysis concerns the cognitive and evaluative processes that designers use to uncover primary factors from a set of factors and enable the knowledge engineer to build a foundation for understanding the relationships among them. Thus, a valid analysis can aid in the decision making process concerning expert system organization and functional requirements (McGraw, 1987).

Analysis for knowledge base design and knowledge acquisition planning has its roots in systems theory. General systems theory emphasizes the need to examine all parts of a system and enables communications among specialists in diverse fields. As defined by Lucas (1981), a system of any kind is an "organized, interacting, interdependent, integrated set of components or variables" (p. 5). To further complicate development, a system is comprised of many components (e.g., jobs, goals, system parts) that interact to meet the system's objectives (some of which may be hard to observe). Numerous theorists have contributed to lists of components for general systems theory (Schroderbek, 1971). Those components that seem most applicable to *expert* systems are paraphrased below:

1. System components are interrelated and interdependent. Pre-design goals include determining the relationships among components.

2. Systems should be designed within an overall framework. Thus, we may break it down into subsystems for development, but we should not ignore the overall picture.

3. Systems are goal seeking, interacting to reach a final state or goal. Systems often have different ways to reach goals.

4. Systems have inputs, outputs, and processing.

5. Systems generally consists of smaller subsystems.

Knowledge Engineer as Systems Analyst

The goal of traditional systems analysis is to understand a complex system well enough to extend or enhance its functionality to improve efficiency. In the case of expert systems, the goal is to understand the functions, inputs, outputs, and processing of the *current* way of completing a task to design a knowledge-base system that can serve as a job aid, management, or training tool. Systems analysis consist of a series of steps, including the following (adapted from Lucas, 1979):

1. Defining the problem.

2. Understanding the system, its definition (e.g., system components, interrelationships, system boundaries), and its functional requirements.

3. Identifying alternatives to system modification or implementation and selecting design objectives.

4. Implementing the selected alternative.

5. Evaluating the results of the implementation against the problem definition and requirements.

The individuals responsible for implementing these tasks in order to develop a *traditional* information system are referred to as systems analysts. Systems analysts are responsible for working with users to
- Identify goals, requirements, and structure of a new system
- Create plans or blueprints for system design, and later
- Examine decisions and information flow to flesh out system structure and enable system goals to be met.

The systems analyst constructs and iteratively refines a model of existing processing and decision making procedures.

The knowledge engineer in an expert system development project shares many responsibilities and traits with the systems analyst of conventional computer-based information systems (Figure 6-1). For example, to design an expert system that will be able to act as a decision-aiding tool that assists novices in the completion of a task, the knowledge engineer must work through a set of steps that parallel those of the systems analyst. Initially, the problem must be defined. That is, the task(s) the system will need to accomplish (e.g., the system's objectives) must be stipulated. Next, existing constraints or requirements on the system must be identified. In addition, a framework for the system must be derived so that the basic requirements, components, and interdependencies can be dealt with in an appropriate manner. Based on the system framework, an initial structure for the system can be designed. During this process, the designer makes initial decisions concerning modularity, representation, and language needs. Next, the knowledge engineer works with domain experts and end users to refine the system structure and framework and to develop a "first cut" of part of the knowledge base. Finally, the knowledge engineer implements initial system decisions, evaluates the results, and iteratively refines the developing system until it meets established requirements and objectives. To accomplish these tasks, the knowledge engineer works with the domain expert and end users.

KNOWLEDGE ENGINEER	SYSTEMS ANALYST
• Determine customer requirements	• Formulation of customer/system requirements
• Identify functional objectives for definition of the system	• Analysis of problem and criteria, specs, objectives
• Determine requirements for system functionality	
• Analyze goals to determine knowledge acquisition needs	
• Compile background knowledge of the domain	• Search for best system solution
• Determine appropriate domain framework	
• Determine knowledge base structure	• Decision on system design
• Determine expert's solution	• Specification of system
• Isolate specific data	
• Implement prototype	• Implement design and test for accuracy
• Evaluate accuracy of results	
• Determine if goals have been met	

Figure 6-1. Knowledge Engineer as Systems Analyst

The part of this process that is most like systems analysis entails problem definition, requirements analysis, and the development of system framework and structure. Effective completion of these tasks contributes to more organized expert system development and lays the groundwork for user acceptance of the resulting system. The premise of this chapter is that the metaphor of "knowledge engineer as systems analyst" (Hart, 1986) can enable structured, organized expert system development. When applied to knowledge acquisition, we contend that this organization can increase the efficiency of the process. The following sections provide a brief historical background on analysis techniques that are appropriate for use in knowledge acquisition and information on the relevance of expertise in analyzing tasks.

Historical Perspectives on Analysis

The idea of analyzing a system, procedure, or job by breaking it into its primitive components is not new. Educators/trainers (Mager, 1962), psychologists (Gagne', 1975), ethnoscientific researchers (Dougherty, 1982), and human factors engineers (Woodson, 1981) have all developed procedures that use some form of analysis. Consequently, these analysis techniques have experienced a wide range of application, from setting hiring and promotion standards to developing appropriate training materials and advanced systems.

Only recently has the idea of systems analysis been applied within the context of expert system development. In their early stages, expert systems tended to be small, "proof-of-concept" systems that were not necessarily intended to be "operational." It was not uncommon for the development team to be comprised of a single domain expert and a knowledge engineer. Little formal analysis or design was required prior to programming, as rapid prototyping allowed the programmer to determine system goals, design, and knowledge needs and to quickly test out his or her initial ideas. If they were not acceptable, the existing code was rejected and new structures or information entered. The emphasis was on implementation techniques (e.g., representation) as opposed to full functionality.

Current trends toward developing expert systems that are in fact operational, as opposed to simply "proof-of-concept" have re-focused developers on the task of structuring the development process to reduce the amount of rejected code and thus, development costs. In doing so, they have begun to apply more management techniques to the rapid prototyping task (Figure 6-2). While it still remains the primary expert system development philosophy, rapid prototyping can be adapted to benefit from some traditional software development methodologies, including analysis techniques. (See Chapter 2.) The application of analysis procedures to expert system development stems at least partially from the need to increase the validity of the deployed system, eliminate the subjectiveness of the knowledge base, and increase the maintainability of the knowledge base.

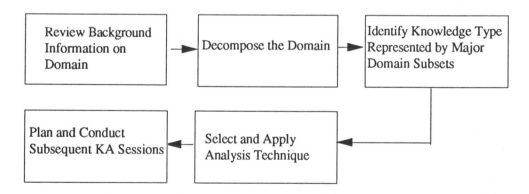

Figure 6-2. Using Analysis to Manage Development

Experts and Their Tasks

One of the knowledge engineer's primary responsibilities is to analyze and decompose the "expertise" of a domain expert. Consider, for example, the knowledge engineer who has been tasked with developing an expert system in the avionics domain. Before the knowledge base can be constructed, he or she must first study various flight tasks in terms of cognitive, behavioral, mission, and tactical requirements. Using analysis techniques, the knowledge engineer in our example can establish a framework to identify areas for initial expert focus, determine a preliminary structure for a knowledge base, and decompose tasks for analysis and subsequent discussion with the avionics expert.

Before exploring guidelines for using various analysis techniques with domain experts, we encourage readers to review some of the related issues from Chapter 1 and the Appendix. Issues such as memory and organization are important because the manner in which experts store and access task-critical knowledge affects the possible strategies an expert uses to solve a problem or complete a task. As we learn a task and practice or apply it in various situations, we may begin to recognize certain associated stimuli or patterns and begin to store these together as "chunks" (Newell & Simon, 1972). Experts commonly chunk or group information into episodes or "schemas" for both efficient storage and access. For example, a pilot may have a conceptual schema for a mechanical breakage that includes slots for indicators, possible causes, plans for reactions, possible results for each plan, and previous episodes that appear to apply.

Task nature (e.g., discrete, sequential) is another important feature that knowledge engineers should explore as they investigate the components that comprise an expert's repertoire of knowledge. Task nature is a salient feature in that it may determine the possible strategies that the expert uses to complete or solve a task (Hogarth, 1974). As Figure 6-3 illustrates, the response pattern for discrete tasks (tasks in which one step does not invariably lead to other specific steps in a sequence) can be observed or recalled with less difficulty than sequential tasks (tasks in which one step is but a single point in a sequence of many steps). The knowledge engineer's analysis of knowledge type, response type (e.g., cognitive, motor, or perceptual), and related attributes and constraints will be less complex for discrete than sequential tasks.

Discrete Tasks

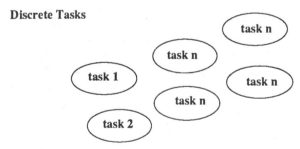

Sequential Tasks

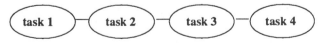

Figure 6-3. Discrete and Sequential Task Characteristics

Similarly, human experts tend to complete problem-solving tasks in a selective, serial manner. This means that as a domain expert solves a problem, his or her current state of cognitive processing partially determines the future state of cognitive processing. Analyzing the various processing states and considerations an expert applies as he or she performs a task or makes a decision is key to developing an initial understanding of the domain.

THE ROLE OF ANALYSIS IN THE KNOWLEDGE ACQUISITION PROCESS

A number of existing analysis techniques can be adapted for use in the identification and conceptualization stages of knowledge acquisition. Analysis techniques (e.g., task analysis) can be used effectively prior to more formal knowledge acquisition sessions (e.g., protocol analysis, structured interviews) (McGraw & Seale, 1987a). While some authors contend that analysis techniques are most effective with the type of knowledge represented by routine procedures (Gammack & Young, 1985), we believe that methods such as decision/action analysis are appropriate for the initial investigation of more complex processing tasks, such as decision making.

Information seems to be organized for everyday activity on the basis of goal-oriented tasks and strategies (Miller, Galanter, Pribram, 1960; Schank and Abelson, 1977). As human experts work, they create and revise organizations of many aspects of their knowledge that are appropriate or relevant to the specific task at hand (Dougherty & Keller, 1982; Barsalou, 1983). Thus, recognizing major domain expert tasks, responsibilities, knowledge types, and task nature are important foundations for developing the knowledge base and for enhancing the effectiveness of knowledge acquisition sessions. Analysis of this and other related information can help the knowledge engineer plan and focus knowledge acquisition efforts.

Analysis for expert system development requires painstaking attention to detail and a knowledge engineer who can ask questions to clarify what may seem to be a relatively simplistic procedure. For example, decisions an expert makes must be scrutinized to identify
- The cues that trigger an expert's attention or action
- The information that he or she required to make a decision
- The attributes and values of the variables that may affect the final decision.

For this reason, some authors (Tiemann & Markle, 1984) advise investing a large percentage of time in the process of analysis prior to software development. In some development programs, human factors engineers may be responsible for providing a detailed analysis, down to task element timing estimates (e.g., start and end times for tasks). Knowledge engineers can then use this analysis to identify knowledge needs and organize knowledge acquisition sessions. Where human factors engineers are not available, knowledge engineers should be responsible for preparing task analyses at the level of detail that meets their program's needs.

Analysis Procedures for Knowledge-Base Development

Successful end use of analyses developed by knowledge engineers for a specific domain depends upon the procedures used in the development process. There are two diverse types of analysis procedures

(1) Those whose purpose is to define functional requirements, thus laying the groundwork for knowledge base development

(2) Those whose purpose is to structure the knowledge acquisition process by investigating major components, tasks, and knowledge within the domain.

The following two sets of procedures are suggested for the use of both of these types of analysis techniques in the development of large-scale expert systems. Later sections discuss each of these steps in more detail. Figure 6-4 illustrates the use of analysis in knowledge acquisition, which is described in more detail throughout this chapter.

A. Lay the groundwork for knowledge acquisition by identifying the major functions your expert system will be required to perform.

1. Review background information on the domain or domain subset prior to beginning the analysis procedure. Use sources such as vocabulary lists and acronyms, articles, training manuals, training videotapes, books, and user documentation.

2. Decide upon a logical decomposition of your domain to allow you to focus on individual parts; conduct requirements analyses as needed.

B. Structure the domain to derive knowledge acquisition goals and plans.

1. Identify the different type(s) of knowledge (e.g, procedural, declarative, semantic episodic) that seem to be represented in the area for which you wish to elicit information.

2. Identify the analysis technique that seems most appropriate for the knowledge you wish to acquire.

3. Using the technique(s) you have selected, develop a framework for the information needed for the analysis session and complete a rough draft of the analysis for use with a domain expert.

4. Work with the domain expert to refine, adapt, or embellish the analysis. Target your next session and your knowledge acquisition plan to the information you anticipate needing.

Figure 6-4. Using Analysis in Knowledge Acquisition

Review Background Information on the Domain or Knowledge Subset

Before analyzing a domain or outlining functional requirements to meet customer specifications, knowledge engineers should complete the following tasks:

- De-scope the current problem
- Identify specific uses for the resulting analysis
- Set end goals related to the specific uses, and
- Outline a plan for meeting those goals.

For example, the level of detail in two task analyses may vary greatly, depending on the projected end-use of the individual analysis. An analysis whose purpose is to help a knowledge engineer structure and relate the various components of a domain probably will be less detailed than one that is intended to serve as a model for the development of a subsystem to automate pre-flight sequential procedures.

The knowledge engineer uses conceptual analysis (Chapter 5) to help delimit the domain and identify discrete components of the domain and surface-level relationships between them. To accomplish this task, the knowledge engineer must study the domain or selected subset using a variety of source material. Becoming acquainted with common vocabulary and acronyms associated with the domain during the domain familiarization period can help the knowledge engineer to identify major concepts more effectively. Reviewing both the structure and content of training manuals can be very helpful prior to task analysis, in that resource material (e.g., the table of contents) is an excellent cue to delineations within the domain. While learning the content within the manual is not usually possible, learning the terms and major areas of focus aids not only in the process of task analysis, but also in the later stages of analyzing concepts and interviewing a domain expert. Additional sources that we have found to be useful include training videotapes, videotapes of a domain expert working through tasks for which your expert system will be responsible, and initial conversations with a domain expert concerning the major roles and responsibilities of his or her tasks.

Design a Logical Decomposition of the Domain

Decomposing the domain involves both defining customer requirements and conceptualizing the domain to identify knowledge that must be acquired. Using the information gathered in the preceding phase of development (i.e., Conceptualization), the knowledge engineer should sketch out, either in graphic or outline form, a breakdown of the domain or subset under consideration. Committing the information that has been gathered to a rough graphic form aids in refining the initial understanding of the domain in terms of major subsets and relationships. Once developed, the knowledge engineer should review the graphic with a domain expert primarily to clarify or extend the domain structure. When completed, this tool allows the knowledge engineer to focus on specific areas or subsets within the domain, review information relating to them, and plan future knowledge acquisition sessions.

Identify Knowledge Types Represented by Major Domain Subsets

A preliminary goal of analyzing the tasks involved in an expert's solution process or job is to identify the type(s) of knowledge that the expert seems to be using to accomplish major objectives. Four types of knowledge that should be considered include procedural, declarative, semantic, and episodic (Refer to Chapter 1 for descriptions.).

Identifying the type of knowledge that is most prevalent in a given task or domain subset is important in that it can help determine the analysis technique that will be most appropriate. For example, tasks that are sequential in nature and represent knowledge that is primarily procedural or episodic may be analyzed using techniques such as timeline analysis. The resulting knowledge acquisition structure takes into account the temporal, sequential constraints that place additional requirements on the task. To ignore this aspect of the task may cause later knowledge base inequities and may result in expert system performance that does not meet the standard of "making decisions like an expert." In the same manner, tasks that represent deep semantic knowledge that is correlated with situational variables may be best analyzed using decision/action diagrams or task/subtask analysis. Figure 6-5 provides a suggested pairing of knowledge type to analysis technique. However, the reader is advised to use this figure only as a guideline; individual aspects of specific situations will require adaptations.

KNOWLEDGE TYPE	POSSIBLE ANALYSIS TECHNIQUE
Procedural knowledge	Timeline analysis Operational sequence analysis
Declarative knowledge	Functional analysis Information flow analysis
Semantic knowledge	Taxonomies Goal/sub-goal analysis
Episodic knowledge	Goal/subgoal analysis Task/subtask analysis Mission decompositions

Figure 6-5. Knowledge Type and Analysis Techniques

Choose an Analysis Technique

Once knowledge type has been considered, the knowledge engineer selects the analysis technique(s) that most closely meet the system requirements and knowledge acquisition phase. Two primary categories of techniques are for (Figure 6-6)
- Building design foundations
- Structuring a domain.

```
┌─────────────────────────────────────────────────────────┐
│                                                         │
│       Techniques to Build a Design Foundation           │
│                                                         │
│           • Functional Analysis                         │
│           • Information Flow Analysis                    │
│           • Interaction Analysis                        │
│           • Operational Sequence Analysis               │
│                                                         │
│                                                         │
│       Techniques to Structure the Domain                │
│                                                         │
│           • Task Analysis                               │
│           • Job Analysis                                │
│           • Timeline Analysis                           │
│           • Extended Decision/Action Diagrams           │
│                                                         │
└─────────────────────────────────────────────────────────┘
```

Figure 6-6. Sets of Analysis Techniques

USING ANALYSIS TOOLS AND TECHNIQUES FOR KNOWLEDGE ACQUISITION

Building a knowledge base is analogous to building a house. The initial stages of knowledge acquisition, including conceptualization and analysis, parallel the architectural-design and foundation construction phases of house building. Without appropriate conceptualization and design work, architectural specs may not approximate the desires of the owner/builder. Without an adequate foundation, the house will not stand. Similarly, without being built on an adequate understanding of the domain and a reliable structure, the knowledge base will not support the desired functionality of the expert system.

There are two types of analysis that can help a knowledge engineer structure the development process. They differ mainly in the purpose that they serve. The first we call *foundational* or *functional analysis techniques*. They help "lay the groundwork" or the foundation for the expert system's eventual functionality. The second are those that are more specifically targeted at the expert's domain and current responsibilities. They help the knowledge engineer "structure the domain" by capturing the major tasks, responsibilities, decision considerations and factors.

Regardless of the type of analysis that a knowledge engineer selects, preliminary work should determine a standard mechanism for representing major entities or components in the resulting diagram. For example, a knowledge engineer who is responsible for developing a functional diagram for one expert system subsystem should be able to view and understand a similar diagram for a related subsystem. To enable this sharing of information, developers should standardize not only what type of information each diagram should attempt to represent, but also the symbols that are used across each diagram.

Using Templates

We advise each expert system development team to define templates for the various analysis techniques that they intend to use during development. A template can be a simple electronic file that provides sample fields to flag the type of information that a particular type of analysis should yield and suggestions for structure or format for the analysis. Templates such as these can then be accessed by all project personnel and can be maintained on a project-wide bulletin board or mail system. For example, using the information presented in the section on functional analysis, a template might look like Figure 6-7.

TEMPLATE FOR FUNCTIONAL ANALYSIS

1.0 Describe or depict overall system and major subsystems
    1.1 Detail major system functionality
2.0 Define each major subsystem within the overall system
    2.1 Detail the functionality for each major subsystem within the system
    2.2 Detail or depict expected inputs to each major subsystem
    2.3 Detail or depict expected/required outputs for each major subsystem
    2.4 Specify processing requirements based on domain expert input.

Figure 6-7. Sample Template for Functional Analysis

Using Diagrams

It is also useful for each project to standardize the way in which components of analysis diagrams will be represented. For example, regardless of the type of analysis that is being done, the resulting diagram should be readable by all members of a project. This means that the symbol selected to indicate a decision point should be the same across diagrams. Each organization may have its own standards for flowcharting symbols (e.g., diamond for decision point, etc.). If internal standardization guidelines are not available, the American National Standards Institute (ANSI) publishes standards that may be used as guidelines.

In addition to the standardization of symbols, the following suggestions can facilitate diagram construction and usefulness (Chapin, 1976):

- To enhance readability across a project or within an organization, define or use existing standards for construction

- Keep the diagrams as simple as possible, while attempting to convey intended functionality

- Investigate the possibility of hierarchies of diagrams in order to keep each diagram from becoming too cluttered

- Develop the diagram according to the needs and abilities of the reader (e.g., knowledge engineer, domain expert).

Laying The Groundwork

The first step in the system design process for the development of conventional or knowledge-base information systems is to generate an initial structure of the system. The purpose of this structure is to reflect the primary functionality the user desires from the system (Enos & Tilburg, 1979). The results of this process define the necessary operations that must be performed to accomplish the goals of the system or the worker. A number of analysis techniques exist that the knowledge engineer can use to structure system requirements and outline functionality. The end product of this type of analysis is an agreed-upon framework for the expert system that is being developed, which serves to define system functionality and manage user expectations. Analysis techniques that we will consider in this category include
- Functional analysis
- Information flow analysis
- Interaction analysis
- Operational sequence analysis.

Functional Analysis

If the expert system being developed is required to perform tasks related to specific system functions (e.g., diagnosis or maintenance), we advise that knowledge engineers develop a **functional analysis** of the system tasks prior to knowledge acquisition sessions with domain experts. Functional analysis yields functional flow diagrams similar to those that systems designers have used with conventional software systems. Typically, a functional flow diagram is a structure of the primary functions of a system. According to Enos and Tilburg (1979), these diagrams consist of standard flowcharting symbols that show the flow of data from inputs to the function being performed and the resulting outputs from the functions. The emphases at this stage is on (1) translating customer requirements into an initial functional diagram and (2) depicting the basic relationships among the functions.

Using functional flow diagrams, the knowledge engineer can depict major systems, subsystems, system requirements, interactions between components, important parameters for functional acceptability, and common faults (Waldron, 1985). In fact, functional analyses may be required in program contracts and their results used in development documents such as the System Requirements Analysis and Software Requirements Specification. The information that results from either a formal or informal functional analysis provides important foundations for development efforts, but is not intended to provide detailed design information. Specific information that developers commonly describe in this type of analysis include:
- Major system decompositions (e.g., hydraulic, electrical, fuel)
- System responsibilities or functions
- Subfunctions that contribute to system functionality
- Major or required inputs to each system
- Major or required outputs from each system
- Domain expert or user interaction with each system.

In addition to these typical inputs, knowledge engineers should also consider factors that impact functionality, such as domain expert (end user) interaction with each system or subsystem, purpose of the system (e.g., used for advice to a human or as input to another system, and processing requirements that may impact functionality (e.g., the need for "real-time" processing).

Information Flow Analysis

The **information flow analysis** technique can be used if the knowledge engineer needs to diagram the operations and binary decisions that may be required to complete major system functions. It is a type of dataflow diagram and is very similar to flowcharting techniques that programmers commonly use. The level of detail that the diagram depicts can vary, depending on the purpose of the analysis and the knowledge engineer's needs. Woodson (1981) contends that the flowchart need not reflect a uniform level of specificity. One decision point may be stated in general terms based on engineer needs, while another point that is important in later knowledge acquisition and design efforts is broken down into a series of specific decisions.

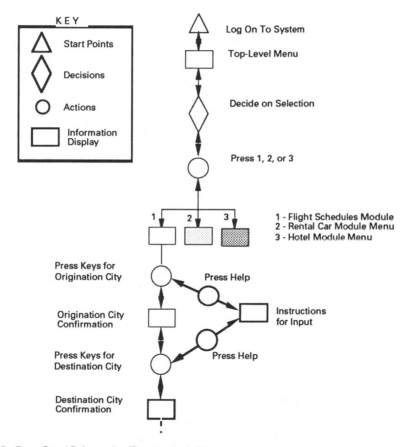

Figure 6-8. Gross Level Information Flow Analysis Diagram

Figure 6-8 illustrates one method that may be used to diagram the analysis of information flow within a system. As this information-flow diagram depicts, symbols have been selected to represent major actions (circles), start points (triangles), and decisions (diamonds). The chart itself appears on one side of the page so that a textual description can support and extend the meaning of the graphic symbols. While an information flow-analysis can result in a much more detailed chart, illustrating more specific information, the gross level shown here generally suffices for use in the identification and conceptualization stages of knowledge acquisition.

Interaction Analysis

An extension of the information flow analysis technique, **interaction analysis** enables knowledge engineers to specify crucial interactions required for a specific system or job. The interactions that this type of analysis may reflect include the following:

- Functions that relate to or constrain an action or decision point
- System or subsystem goals that relate to or constrain an action or decision point, or
- Knowledge that is needed before a decision can be made or an action taken.

Operational Sequence Analysis

Operational sequence analysis traditionally is used to investigate and represent a more specific level of system functionality than the techniques that have been described previously. Used in conjuction with a sample scenario, these diagrams allow the knowledge engineer to analyze in detail the interrelationships in an information system between actions and processing tasks (Enos & Tilburg, 1979). The scenario that is used can be as simple as a narration of a typical chain of events that is likely to occur as an end user interacts with the expert system in its operational environment.

A variation of this technique, **decision/action analysis**, can be particularly effective in the analysis of knowledge acquisition needs. The decision/action diagram depicted in Figure 6-9 portrays major tasks, cues, alternatives, and decisions within the selected scenario at a gross level.

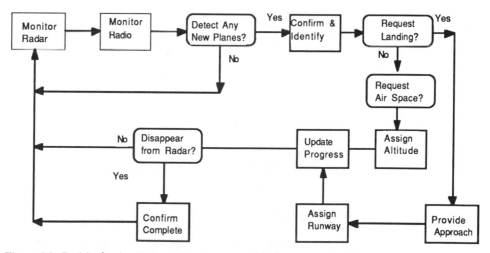

Figure 6-9. Decision/Action Diagram Based on Operational Sequence Analysis

Structuring the Domain

Once the initial analysis has been completed, the knowledge engineer structures the domain to determine knowledge acquisition needs. Analysis techniques for this phase include the following:

- Task analysis
- Job analysis
- Timeline analysis (and a variation, mission decomposition)
- Extended decision/action analysis.

The knowledge engineer is not expected to use all, or even the majority of these techniques for any one development effort. The presentation of numerous techniques is intended to provide the knowledge engineer with a set of tools and techniques that can be selected based on situation and need.

Task Analysis

Task analysis can help the knowledge engineer decompose an expert's major tasks in a given area. According to Shannon (1980b), task analysis is a methodological tool that can be used to (1) describe the functions a human expert performs and (2) determine the relation of each task on a certain dimension to the overall job. Originally, task analysis was considered to be a form of systems analysis. Among human factors engineers, it has been used to investigate what a design requires of an operator or product user and whether or not the intended design is optimum from a user's standpoint. Additionally, system-level task analyses have been used to establish requirements for training and user documentation because they usually provide task descriptions, necessary responses, considerations and constraints. Their ability to help provide structure makes them effective tools for knowledge engineers to use during the initial phases of knowledge acquisition.

Woodson (1981) states that there are no established rules for the completion of a task analysis and implies that function should determine form. Miller (1971) is more specific, suggesting that although there are no set rules that reduce the technique to a routine endeavor, there are guidelines. However, most users of task analysis techniques would agree that form follows function. For example, if the knowledge engineer needs general information on specific tasks and task descriptions for an emergency procedures expert system, a task analysis like the one pictured in Figure 6-10 would suffice.

Task 3.1.2   Respond to Temperature Alert
Identified Constraints: Time limit = 7 seconds from alert buzzer

Task Description: Alert buzzer and visual cue indicate emergency temperature situation. Operator must recognize signal, identify cause, observe gauge settings, and respond. Response involves moving flap over PAUSE key to up position and pressing the key.

Follow on Tasks: Deciding whether or not to shut the system down or to continue with higher than normal temperature, making minor changes (See Tasks 3.1.3).

Figure 6-10. Initial Analysis of a Task

Task/Subtask Analysis.   Using task/subtask analysis, the knowledge engineer defines major tasks involved in an operator's current activity to determine what the expert system will be required to handle and what types of information it will need. Figure 6-11 represents an example of this type of analysis for an emergency procedures expert system. This analysis provides knowledge engineers and system designers with additional, more useful information than the analysis depicted in Figure 6-10.

FUNCTIONAL COMPONENT	TASK	SUBTASK
Activate temperature emergency response	1. Identify situation.	a. Recognize buzzer. b. Check gauge for 202+
	2. Make PAUSE input	a. Lift key flap. b. Press PAUSE.
Activate test procedures	3. Initiate Analysis	a. Set TEMP to GRN. b. Clear READ-OUT display. c. Press SELF TEST.
	4. Monitor Read outs.	a. Check READ-OUT display for malfunction code. b. Compare code with codes. in SYSTEM CODES table.

Make corrective inputs, including GO/NO-GO decision, suggestion for part replacement, etc.

Figure 6-11. Task/subtask analysis

What Should it Look Like?   Primary determinants of the final form a task analysis takes includes variables such as those that follow:
- The purpose of the task analysis
- The desired detail within the task analysis
- Existing information of a similar nature.

The following scenarios illustrate the interaction of these determinants. In scenario A, the purpose of the task analysis is to help the knowledge engineer structure or identify major human expert tasks and response modes. The analysis will be used to conceptualize the domain. The major source of the analysis is relevant information that will be derived from training manual objectives. To meet the needs expressed by this scenario, the task analysis need not reflect great detail. Now consider scenario B, in which the purpose of the task analysis is to provide a guide or design for overall system response. In this instance, no relevant printed material exists. To meet the needs of this scenario, a more detailed analysis, indicating timing estimates, critical factors, decision point attributes, and constraints is needed.

In considering the required amount of detail, the knowledge engineer should recognize that expanded task analyses can be very time consuming, may require extensive observation of the human expert, and may require assistance from a human factors engineer. Typical information that may be desired in an expanded task analysis is presented in Figure 6-12. Selection of any of these will, of course, depend on the purpose the resulting analysis is to serve.

Task Title	Short, descriptive, title describing a function
Task Number	Indexing number for easy reference
Task Description	Information including displays, gauges, controls, and equipment that is used; actions, aids, and feedback
Task Type	Classification of task, including motor, interpretation, etc.
Knowledge Required	Types/levels of knowledge required to complete task
Performance Time	Typical completion time; critical, permissible response time
Related Tasks	Other tasks related to, depending on, or interacting with current task performance

Figure 6-12. Basic Task Analysis Information

Task Analysis Terminology. One way to approach task analysis is to classify tasks according to types of human behavior. This allows the knowledge engineer to study the major functions currently performed by human experts and identify those that can be emulated by the expert system. Additionally, this structure allows knowledge engineers to identify important information that the human operator or expert uses in making decisions. The resulting analysis depicts behaviors of human operators on the basis of major tasks.

One problem with behavioral or task analysis relates to the lack of guidelines previously mentioned. Unless system developers devise a structure or task vocabulary to be used across the program, the usefulness of resulting task analyses may be threatened. Devising a program-wide set of acceptable behavioral classifications and task verbs enables knowledge engineers other than those who originated the analysis to study and use the information within the analysis diagram. In addition, such documents may then become a portion of the overall system documentation and later can even be used to support system test plan development. Previous authors (Berlinger, 1964; Woodson, 1981) have suggested process classifications (e.g., perception, mediation, communication, motor) and corresponding activities or behaviors (e.g., perception = detect, inspect, observe, etc.). Typical words that are used to describe tasks of various classifications are presented in Figure 6-13.

PERCEPTION	MEDIATION	COMMUNICATION	MOTOR
Detect	Categorize	Advise	Activate
Inspect	Calculate	Answer	Close
Observe	Encode	Communicate	Connect
Read	Compute	Direct	Disconnect
Receive	Interpolate	Indicate	Join
Scan	List	Inform	Move
Survey	Tabulate	Instruct	Press
Discriminate	Translate	Request/Ask	Set
Identify	Analyze	Transmit/Send	Raise/Lift
Locate	Select		Regulate
	Compare		Hold
	Estimate		Lower
	Predict		Adjust
			Track
			Align
			Synchronize

Figure 6-13. Suggested Task Verbs and Classifications
(Adapted from Woodson, W.E., "Behaviors, Measures, and Instruments for Performance Evaluation in Simulated Environments, Human Factors Handbook, p. 93, © copyright McGraw-Hill, 1981. Used with permission.)

Job Analysis

Job analysis is a technique that is used to specify the major responsibilities of a job or, on a gross level, the tasks that a given job entails. Such analyses are often used to determine job descriptions or performance evaluation tools. Job analyses may be useful to knowledge engineers who are developing an expert system to assist a human operator in completing a portion of his or her job. In many cases, such analyses will already exist and can be requested for use in the initial stages of knowledge acquisition. If, however, a job analysis does not exist, is not specific enough, or no longer reflects major tasks or responsibilities, the knowledge engineer may devise one.

To arrive at a job description, the knowledge engineer should first detail the complete set of task statements that describe what an individual performing the specific job should be able to do. Securing job description documents and using onsite interviews and observation methods may help knowledge engineers conduct a job analysis. Specialized survey-style questionnaires, including the Likert scale (Likert,

1932a, 1932b) can help knowledge engineers gather and compare information from diverse individuals. Riner (1982) reported success with the use of both questionnaire survey forms (open and closed questions) and group discussion techniques (e.g., Delphi) for the purpose of determining job descriptions. Turoff (1972) has successfully used a modified Delphi technique for computer-based group discussions that may be effective in initially defining job or task descriptions.

Creating the Job Analysis. The success of the job analysis depends on the quality of the basic unit, the task statement. Each task statement must consist of three parts: the behavior, conditions for the behavior, and standards against which the behavior is evaluated (Mager, 1962). Critical to the behavior section of the statement is adherence to the following guidelines:

- The use of an action verb
- The existence of only one behavior per task statement, and
- The ability to observe or measure the behavior that is described.

The conditions portion of the statement must describe the performance environment and the resources an individual uses to complete the task. Task performance standards should include minimum acceptable performance levels, time limits, and any applicable quality and quantity levels. The following guidelines were established for constructing task statements (Riner, 1982; McGraw & Riner, 1987)

1. Each task has a definite beginning and end. It is performed in a relatively short period of time.

2. A task statement describes a finite, independent part of the job.

3. Each task is mutually exclusive and is completed for its own sake.

4. Each task statement should be clearly understood by anyone doing the job. Its description should use terminology that is consistent with current usage by the target group.

5. Each task should be rateable in terms of time spent doing it.

6. A task statement should elicit differences among respondents; there should be those who do it and those who do not.

7. A task is begun by an observable cue.

8. A task statement is brief.

9. A task statement avoids qualifiers. Only when there is more than one way to perform a task is a qualifier allowed.

10. A task statement uses one verb, except when several actions are invariably performed together.

11. A task must be measurable. The end result or product can be estimated or measured as having been done correctly/successfully.

Shannon (1980a) suggests some slightly different mechanics for the development of task descriptions. These guidelines include:

1. Develop a statement of purpose to provide structure.

2. Attain a detailed knowledge of the job, environment, and, if applicable, the system. To do so, use expert opinions, on-site observations, existing literature, open-ended questions, existing task descriptions, and procedural systems handbooks.

3. Develop a task inventory that outlines increasingly detailed information (e.g., from general to specific). For example, define a job by its role, a role by its duties, a duty by its tasks, a task by its elements.

4. Develop a task statement that contains action verbs with a definite objective, required personnel, required equipment, and other requirements (e.g., processing, environmental).

While the use of either of these methods will result in a job analysis that paves the way for knowledge acquisition, standardization of methods and vocabulary increases the usefulness of the technique.

Timeline Analysis

Timeline analysis may be an effective way for a knowledge engineer to structure tasks that are highly sequential in nature. As the name implies, this analysis technique focuses on the relation or effect of *time* on the completion of a task. Originally, human factors engineers used timeline analyses to help derive human performance requirements by diagramming the functional and temporal relationships between tasks. This allowed them to isolate intervals during which a human operator might be overloaded. Although timeline analysis may be less effective for knowledge acquisition than some of the other analysis techniques, it can enable developers to get an initial picture of the sequential nature of required performance. In addition, developers can use timeline analysis to isolate temporal performance requirements of tasks that the expert system may need to emulate. Later, knowledge engineers may use this information to estimate temporal processing requirements.

Creating the Timeline Analysis. A timeline analysis may be continuous, from the start to the end of a series of tasks, or may be compiled from several individual analyses, each of which represents a discrete task or task segment (Woodson, 1981). To construct the timeline analysis diagram or chart, the knowledge engineer first solicits information on (1) accepted task sequence and (2) time for task completion. As depicted in Figure 6-14, the major function or task number should appear as a label for the chart, with subtasks and their associated numbers and time estimations or sequencing information comprising the body of the chart. While sequential information may be all that is needed in most knowledge acquisition cases, if the knowledge engineer chooses to represent time estimates, a standard interval (e.g., 5 minutes) should be selected for use throughout the chart.

Timeline Estimation	Task Name: React to Possible Targets											
Task #	Subtask Name	Seconds of Time										
		5	10	15	20	25	30	35	40	45	50	55
1.1	Scan for Targets											
1.2	Detect Target											
1.3	Identify Friend/Foe											
1.4	Monitor/Track Target											
1.5	Determine Stores											
1.6	Select Weapon											
1.7	Calculate Trajectory											

Figure 6-14. Sample Modified Timeline Analysis

Mission decompositions are a special type of timeline analysis that may be useful in depicting major phases, actions and decision points for a military mission or related activity. Like timeline analyses, mission decompositions are valuable tools for graphically depicting sequentially-bound information or knowledge that may be episodic in nature. In this type of analysis, the particular stage of a mission or tasks influences future goals and therefore determines the tasks that subsequently must be completed. Once the stage or task has been identified, the knowledge engineer may establish acquisition session goals to "fill in" information associated with each stage or sequential task.

Extended Decision/Action Diagrams
Decision/action diagrams that initially were created during the first phase of analysis may be extended to derive additional domain and knowledge base structure. One purpose of extending these diagrams is to enable knowledge engineers to conceptualize the expert's domain based on information, decisions, and resulting actions for specific tasks or subtasks. This type of analysis can help the knowledge engineer identify the major tasks and decisions required of the human expert.

Extending the Diagram. The knowledge engineer begins with any existing decision/action diagram. Next, he or she reviews background domain material (e.g., training documents, training tapes, etc.) and meets with appropriate domain experts to clarify or revise initial conceptualizations of major decision points, cues, and resulting actions. With the help of the domain expert, the knowledge engineer then attempts to extend the initial graph or diagram by noting the isolated actions, alternatives, decision points, and key factors or constraints that contribute to each decision.

COMPLETING THE ANALYSIS

The result of each type of analysis technique will be a tool that can assist in the design of the overall expert system and in the identification of knowledge base needs. However, the process of analysis and design is iterative, especially in expert systems development. Thus, the initial result should be considered preliminary in nature. Once the ideas derived from analysis are represented in a graphic form, the process of refinement begins.

Refining the Initial Task Analysis

After the knowledge engineer has selected an analysis technique and completed an initial framework for the domain, he or she should request that a practicing domain expert review the material. This review allows the expert to ask questions that may detect false assumptions, offer clarification to areas of possible confusion, or extend the information represented to a more specific level of focus. This procedure allows the expert to reflect on the information that the analysis depicts. In some cases the diagrams and graphs we have compiled based on analysis have made the process seem more "real" to the expert. Typical responses from domain experts include:
"Oh, so that's what you wanted. . ."
"No, I guess now that I see it I think it is really more like this. . ."
"Actually, we should include the following as considerations at this point. . ."

Once the goal has been clarified, useful information usually is forthcoming. In fact, the knowledge engineer may need to set specific limits as to the type and extent of the desired review. Otherwise, the domain expert may provide information at a level of detail that may not yet be appropriate.

Videotaping the domain expert's review of the resulting graphic analysis can provide valuable information.[2] Important organizational and design issues may be brought to the surface during an analysis review session. As the domain expert walks through the diagram or other analysis end product, he or she asks questions and offers suggestions for revision. Taping the session frees the knowledge engineer to interact with the expert, answering his or her questions and responding to other communication (e.g., nonverbal) signals. Other aids that have proven valuable during an analysis review include whiteboard or a Panaboard™ electronic board, which enables the digitization and printing of drawings that have been created or placed on its surface.

Once the review has been completed and appropriate revisions compiled, we suggest that the knowledge engineer meet with other personnel on the development team for a systems-level review. Systems review helps to ensure that system development plans, customer requirements, and knowledge acquisition plans are consistent. For example, in early development efforts for a system to advise students on curriculum based on their needs and goals and course objectives, it was discovered that the current registration system was a bottleneck. This discovery did not directly impact development, since the contract did not include an analysis of the course registration system. However, it was identified to the customer and added to an enhancements "wish list" for follow-on work.

Planning Knowledge Acquisition Sessions

The refined analysis now can be used as a structuring mechanism. The analysis process has served to identify and delimit major sections of the domain, thus providing developmental focus. At this point, knowledge engineers can identify whether or not they want development to proceed in a breadth-first or depth-first manner. Once decided, they can use the resulting analysis as a planning tool in several ways. First, the analysis has yielded an identification of the major functions or tasks for which the expert system will be responsible. Similarly, it has helped the knowledge engineer define the major sections of the domain. Using this information, knowledge engineers can extend domain familiarization efforts, specifically focusing on the elements that the analysis identified.

Second, the analysis has helped the knowledge engineer identify specific areas for knowledge acquisition sessions. Knowledge engineers can use this information to estimate the required knowledge acquisition time and to plan or schedule knowledge acquisition for the upcoming prototyping cycle. While these are estimations, they do provide benchmarks or goals that can then be reported to management or customers.

Third, the existence of the analysis and a knowledge acquisition plan can help knowledge engineers elicit the help of the domain experts who are most appropriate for upcoming sessions. For example, within a given domain, it is not uncommon for available experts to specialize in particular areas or subfunctions. If the analysis outlines specific functionality and tasks, the knowledge engineer may seek the services of individual experts who specialize in these areas. Additionally, accessing a true "expert's" time for knowledge acquisition purposes is quite difficult. Even in-house experts (and their management) will want to know an estimate of the number of hours they will be needed each week, and the period of time (e.g., January, first quarter) during which sessions will occur. This is even more true in instances where the domain expert is external to the knowledge engineer's company, especially if he or she is employed by the customer.

Finally, knowledge acquisition sessions can be managed more effectively. With plans outlined, knowledge acquisition session goals can be specified in a more organized fashion. Management can monitor knowledge acquisition progress by comparing "sessions held" to "sessions planned." Setting specific plans helps identify gaps, needs, and future plans.[3]

ENDNOTES

[1] Some of the content of this chapter was adapted from K. McGraw and A. Riner, "Task analysis: Structuring the knowledge acquisition process," Texas Instruments Engineering Journal, 4:6 (October 1987), pp. 16-21.

[2] See issues relating to videotaping in Chapters 3 and 7.

[3] Management personnel should be cautioned not to force adherence to the "plan" or schedule at all cost. It has been our experience that knowledge engineers will always find that knowledge acquisition sessions breed more sessions. In addition, once a session with a well-prepared expert has begun, developers will find that there is always more information than expected. Thus, it is not unusual for the knowledge acquisition process to require a greater number of sessions than previously anticipated.

Panaboard is a trademark of Panafax.

SUGGESTED READINGS

Hart, A. Knowledge Acquisition for Expert Systems. McGraw-Hill: New York, 1986.

Lucas, H. The Analysis, Design, and Implementation of Information Systems. McGraw-Hill: New York, 1981.

Shachter, R.D. and D.E. Heckerman, Thinking backward for knowledge acquisition, AI MAGAZINE, 8,3, (Fall), 1987, pp. 55-61.

APPLICATION

1. Assume that you are the knowledge engineer in charge of developing most of the knowledge base for an expert system that will be required to assist in determining and ranking risks for people who request health insurance. The job of reviewing applications for those who wish to sign up for the company's insurance is currently done by a team of humans who have subdivided the various tasks. Persons are ranked according to risk based on a number of pre-identified characteristics, including sex, age, amount of insurance requested, smoking history, health history, and familial health history.

You have been asked to analyze the current process to determine (1) system requirements and (2) an initial structure for the domain. Sketch out a plan for accomplishing these goals.

    A. Identify which analysis technique(s) you would use for each of the two types of analysis that has been requested.

    B. Defend your choice of technique based on knowledge type, knowledge acquisition phase, etc.

C. Determine what scenarios or process you might use to accomplish each of these analyses.

D. Summarize how you would use the resulting analyses to begin planning the necessary knowledge acquisition sessions.

2. Compare and contrast the role of systems analyst with that of knowledge engineer. Consider training, responsibilities, tools of the trade, interaction with users, etc.

3. Specify analysis techniques that you think would be appropriate for structuring the domain for the following types of expert systems:

A. Emergency procedures (in-flight emergencies) for commercial jet liners

B. Diagnosis of types of skin diseases

C. Route planning for a mail delivery corporation

D. Monitoring gauges at nuclear plants.

7

Interviewing for Content and Clarification

The Interviewing Process

> **A Model for Knowledge Acquisition Interviews**
> **Interviewing for Knowledge Acquisition**
> **Planning the Interview**
> **Beginning the Interview**
> **The Body of the Interview**
> **Closing the Interview**

Special Interview Skills and Techniques

> **Using Questions Effectively**
> **Levels of Questions**
> **Sequencing Questions**
> **Important Questioning issues**

After the Interview is Over

> **Transcribing Session Information**
> **Deciding What is "Important"**
> **Moving Towards Representation**

INTRODUCTION

If polled to determine the most common technique for the elicitation of domain knowledge from an expert, expert system developers probably would reply, "the interview." Some would even confide that they interviewed an expert for a few hours a week and went "straight to code" with the acquired information. Perhaps this methodology was effective if the expert system being developed was small, research-oriented, and required knowledge from a single domain expert. In this case there was less need to contend with issues such as making efficient use of an expert's time, tracking knowledge from source to code, or the application of a systems approach to knowledge acquisition. Code was through-away, and rapid prototyping was the accepted methodology.

As expert system development has moved from pure research projects into the research and development world, it has became important to work with experts in a timely fashion. The increased emphasis on knowledge validation and verification has made it important to be able to trace information in the knowledge base back to specific knowledge acquisition sessions. In addition, the application of the approach to the knowledge acquisition process that this text suggests necessitates that rapid prototyping efforts be managed. These issues affect the manner in which knowledge engineers select and apply various knowledge acquisition techniques. Interviewing, for example, needs to be reexamined as a technique for the elicitation of knowledge.

In this chapter we initially describe a model for knowledge acquisition interviews, investigate the anatomy of an interview session, and discuss the use of both unstructured and structured interviews.[1] In doing so, we address the related issues of nonverbal and verbal communication, feedback, and appropriate record-keeping procedures. Next, we attend to special interviewing skills and techniques that influence the effectiveness of the interview and the usefulness of information elicited from the interview. Specific discussions include types of questions, question phrasing determinants, levels of questions, and question sequence. Subsequently, we present information on the use of five interviewing techniques that can contribute to a knowledge engineer's repertoire and increase interviewing ability. In closing, we discuss other important questioning issues, such as wait time and strategies for handling common interview problems.[1]

Objectives

This chapter presents information that will enable knowledge engineers to use interviewing as an effective knowledge acquisition technique. Specifically, it enables readers to accomplish the following:

- Select and conduct the appropriate type of interview, according to knowledge acquisition session goals
- Identify specific phases of a knowledge acquisition interview and the tasks associated with each
- Determine the appropriate record-keeping technique for a knowledge acquisition interview
- Recognize and produce specific types (open/closed) and levels (primary and secondary) of questions

- Select the most appropriate question phrasing, based on terminology, level, and complexity
- Design a knowledge acquisition session agenda based on the funnel and inverted-funnel sequence
- Demonstrate various interviewing techniques.

Key Terms

structured interview	unstructured interview	closed questions
phrasing	open questions	inverted funnel
funnel	directional control	primary questions
secondary questions	wait time	

THE INTERVIEWING PROCESS

Gammack and Young (1985) report that the interview is the most common technique used by knowledge engineers to elicit domain knowledge from an expert. This knowledge acquisition technique allows the knowledge engineer to quickly grasp important domain concepts and vocabulary. Interviews with domain experts are often used in the early stages of knowledge acquisition for expert systems development. However, we believe that interviewing may not always be the correct choice of technique and that it is often incorrectly applied. Unskilled knowledge engineers may envision the interview as the sole elicitation technique and may have an inaccurate perception of its purpose and structure. For example, when asked to describe interviewing, many knowledge engineers responded that it involved meeting and "talking" to the domain expert. Such an informal, unstructured approach is often ineffective and may result in poor quality of information. The sections that follow present a model for knowledge acquisition interviews, discuss the major components of interviewing, and contrast the types of interviews for knowledge acquisition.

A Model for Knowledge Acquisition Interviews

Figure 7-1 illustrates a model of interviewing within the field of knowledge acquisition. This procedural model is linear in nature and reflects an open oral communication system that describes the knowledge acquisition interview. This type of interview is a dyadic (e.g., two-person) interpersonal communication activity. The purpose is of the interview that is represented by this model is to allow the knowledge engineer to obtain deep-seated rule structure about the domain expert's performance on tasks.

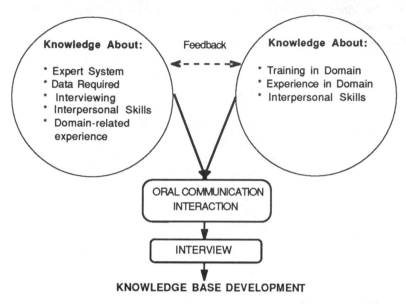

KNOWLEDGE ENGINEER'S
BACKGROUND OF EXPERIENCE

DOMAIN EXPERT'S
BACKGROUND OF EXPERIENCE

Knowledge About:

* Expert System
* Data Required
* Interviewing
* Interpersonal Skills
* Domain-related experience

Feedback

Knowledge About:

* Training in Domain
* Experience in Domain
* Interpersonal Skills

ORAL COMMUNICATION INTERACTION

INTERVIEW

KNOWLEDGE BASE DEVELOPMENT

Figure 7-1. A Model for the Knowledge Acquisition Interview Process
(Adapted with permission from Wm. Derr, 1986)

A brief description of the model itself provides a foundation for later sections in this chapter. Prior to the knowledge acquisition-session interview, the domain expert may have spent years gaining knowledge about a particular domain through continuing professional education and exposure to problem solving in the domain itself. This extensive "background of experience" and knowledge is brought to the knowledge acquisition session. Likewise, the knowledge engineer previously has acquired knowledge of (1) artificial intelligence and expert systems and (2) the data the knowledge base will require. Additionally, the knowledge engineer's background of experience should include the effective use of knowledge acquisition techniques, including interviewing for knowledge base content.

When the two session participants meet, the knowledge engineer conducts in-depth interviews of the domain expert, using effective listening, communication, and interviewing techniques. Primary interview goals expressed by this model are to obtain enough information about task performance to increase foundational knowledge and/or to structure and refine already-acquired information. For this model to be effective, knowledge engineers must complete specific tasks prior to the interview itself. They must determine the data or knowledge that will be required, based on the goals of the current prototyping cycle. In addition, they must conclude that the interview is the most effective knowledge acquisition technique to enable the retrieval of the desired knowledge. Considerations for this decision include (1) the type of knowledge needed (Gammack & Young, 1985) and (2) the time required for preparation, interviewing, and reviewing the knowledge that is transferred during the session.

Interviewing for Knowledge Acquisition

The interview remains a primary knowledge acquisition technique (Hart, 1986; Waldron, 1986) in spite of attacks on it as inefficient. Cooke (1986) has deemed it a less than optimal knowledge acquisition technique. Other authors (Gammack & Young, 1985) complain that informal interviews may not be the appropriate approach for the acquisition of domain knowledge. In its defense, Waldron (1985) contends that if the knowledge engineer implements a sound, structured strategy, the knowledge acquisition interview can be an efficient tool. In fact, the knowledge engineer's ability to interview effectively is a significant factor in determining the success of the interview and the usefulness of the acquired knowledge.

From a knowledge acquisition perspective there are two types of interviews: unstructured and structured. Each can be appropriate, given the goals of a session. An unstructured interview may be appropriate when the knowledge engineer wants to explore an issue (i.e., during the initial stages of a topic's consideration). A structured interview is appropriate when the knowledge engineer desires specific information (i.e., content or issue clarification) and results in more useful knowledge-base content.

The Unstructured Interview

Hoffman (1987) surmises that many expert system developers have relied on the **unstructured interview** as the central knowledge acquisition method. As already illustrated, it is tempting for developers to think of knowledge acquisition as a knowledge engineer talking to appropriate domain experts about their tasks. The knowledge engineer's role in this type of "interview" would be to ask spontaneous questions.

Unstructured interviews are seldom this simple, however, and may present the knowledge engineer with some very problematic after effects. Unstructured interviewing seldom provides complete or well-organized descriptions of cognitive processes (Waldron, 1985). One problem is that expert system domains are generally large and complex; thus, the knowledge engineer *and* the domain expert must actively prepare for interview situations. Unstructured interviews generally lack the organization and structure that would allow this preparation to transfer effectively to the interview itself. Second, domain experts usually find it very difficult to express some of the more important elements of their knowledge. Third, domain experts may interpret the lack of structure in this type of interview as requiring little preparation on their part prior to the interview. Fourth, data acquired from an unstructured interview is often unrelated, exists at varying levels of complexity, and is difficult for the knowledge engineer to review, interpret, and integrate. A fifth problem concerns training. Because of a lack of training and experience, few knowledge engineers can conduct an efficient unstructured interview. Thus, they appear unorganized and may unwittingly allow the expert to pursue tangents and diverge from desired session goals. This informality does little to build a domain expert's confidence in the knowledge engineer's, nor does it enhance the rapport that is needed to work together on a large-scale development effort. Most importantly, unstructured situations generally do not facilitate the acquisition of *specific* information for expert system knowledge bases.

The Structured Interview

Structured interviewing forces an organization of the communications between a knowledge engineer and domain expert. As opposed to the informal, wandering nature of the unstructured interview, the **structured interview** is goal-oriented. Waldron (1985) believes that the structure provided by goals reduces the interpretation problems inherent in unstructured interviews and allows the knowledge engineer to prevent the distortion caused by domain expert subjectivity. One reason that structured interviewing is more effective is suggested by Hoffman (1987): it "forces the domain expert to be systematic" in attending to interview tasks.

Structuring an interview for manual delivery requires attention to a number of procedural issues:

1. The knowledge engineer studies available source material on the domain to identify major demarcations of domain expert knowledge.

2. The knowledge engineer reviews planned expert system functionality and schedules. He or she identifies gaps in the knowledge base that become the basis for the questions designed for the knowledge acquisition session.

3. The knowledge engineer works with team members to schedule and plan the structured interview. Planning includes attending to physical arrangements, defining knowledge acquisition session goals and agendas, and identifying or refining major areas of questioning.

4. The knowledge engineer completes a planning form, such as the knowledge acquisition form as described in Chapter 3. This tool, or one like it, provides an excellent method for structuring and organizing the interview.

5. The knowledge engineer may extend this preparation by writing out sample questions, focusing on question type, level, and questioning techniques.

6. The knowledge engineer ensures that the domain expert understands the purpose and goals of the knowledge acquisition session and is encouraged to prepare prior to the interview (Question areas and/or sample questions may be given to the expert to as a preparation aid).

7. Upon the domain expert's arrival and the start of the interview, the knowledge engineer follows guidelines (Chapter 3 and 4) for conducting knowledge acquisition sessions.

8. During the interview the knowledge engineer uses **directional control** (Nott, 1984) to retain the interview's structure.

Planning the Interview

When planning an interview, knowledge engineers are advised to adhere to a systems approach, whereby functional goals for the current prototype cycle yield areas of questioning for subsequent structured interviews. Once topics have been selected, the knowledge engineer develops an agenda and sample questions for use during the interview. The knowledge engineer also must plan to have any necessary tools (e.g., paper, whiteboard, taping equipment) in place prior to the interview. Tools may also include those that the domain expert will use as props, such as models or actual pieces of equipment, maps, documents, and even computer simulations.

During the planning stage, knowledge engineers should also consider how much information can be covered during the session (approximately one-hour length) and how that information is to be recorded. It is imperative that the knowledge engineer (1) decide before the interview what note taking process will be used, (2) ready the appropriate equipment before the session plan is put in place, and (3) announce the notetaking methodology to the domain expert before the knowledge acquisition session.

Preserving session information can be accomplished in one of three ways: manual note taking, audiotape, and videotape. Whether a knowledge engineer should rely on manual notes, uses an audiotape or videotape recorder, or combines these approaches depends on the individual. Some knowledge engineers feel that they should take few notes during the actual interview; others warn that taking selective notes is worse than none at all. Some contend that the audiotape is sufficient to capture information and relieve note taking responsibility; others feel that the videotape is far superior. Still others advise against using taping equipment owing to its intrusive nature.

Each method has its pros, cons, and considerations. The method and style of data recording must meet the needs of the knowledge engineer and the purpose and structure of the knowledge acquisition session. For example, during a high level research session in which the knowledge engineer hopes to obtain initial domain information, it may not be necessary either to take extensive notes or to use taping equipment. Simple, outline format notes are sufficient in most cases. If, on the other hand, the session's purpose is to determine the decision-making procedures an expert uses in completing a simulated activity, the knowledge engineer may need to videotape the session for later review with the expert. The sections that follow will investigate the various types of note taking and the considerations for using each.

Handwritten Notes

Handwritten notes enable knowledge engineers to be self-sufficient during the interview; they do not have to prepare tape labels, test taping equipment prior to the session, or monitor whether or not taping is successful during the session. However, few knowledge engineers have been trained to take *efficient* notes (i.e., knowing what to write down and when to do so). In addition, note taking during an interview may pose several communications-oriented problems that can interfere not only with the flow of information but with the expert's train of thought.

Pros. Handwritten notes offer control. Whether taken by the knowledge engineer conducting the interview or a second knowledge engineer in a supporting role, they allow specific information to be saved. This reduces costs in both equipment and time.

Manual note taking also reduces the need for later transcription time and effort. The knowledge engineer need not wade through an hour of tape to extract and transcribe the information that is genuinely critical for current knowledge base development needs. Finally, handwritten notes provide flexibility of location. This method may be used regardless of where the knowledge acquisition session is conducted.

Cons. Knowledge engineers must be responsible for both the note taking and the management of the interview. Increased focus on note taking decreases the effectiveness with which a knowledge engineer focuses the expert, guides the questioning, and ensures that the interview progresses according to the agenda. Notetaking can interfere with communication. The knowledge engineer who is concentrating on manually recording the expert's verbal responses may miss cues for follow-up communication. The use and quality of secondary, probing questions may suffer from the knowledge engineer's preoccupation with note taking. Additionally, knowledge engineers who rely solely on manual notes may respond by trying to write down everything that the domain expert says and does in response to a question. Or they may find it difficult to anticipate what will be important in what is said. To compensate, they scribble notes to record *each* idea that is offered. Finally, knowledge engineers must be concerned about the effect of manual note taking on the domain expert. Certain experts may become so preoccupied with what the knowledge engineer records that they may begin interrupting, identifying which information is important (and should be written down) and which is not.

Guidelines for Manual Note Taking. Figure 7-2 lists basic guidelines that will increase the effectiveness of manual note taking in the knowledge acquisition session.

---

1. Prior to the interview, tell the domain expert that you will be taking notes and how you expect to use them. This provides an opportunity to diffuse an expert's hesitation to having his or her ideas recorded.

2. Have on hand a plentiful supply of pens, sharpened pencils, paper, and a hard writing surface.

3. Maintain eye contact as much as possible during the notetaking intervals.

4. Do not cue the domain expert as to what is or is not important by furiously scribbling in response to an answer. Maintain as steady a level of notetaking activity throughout the interview as is possible.

5. To make the expert feel more at ease, allow him or her to view the notes instead of trying to hide them.

6. Code the notes to phases or sections of the interview to help you restructure the interview as you are refining your notes.

7. Review the notes soon (within 24-48 hours) after the interview to aid in recall.

Figure 7-2. Guidelines for Manual Note Taking

Tape-Recorded Notes

We have used both audio and videotaping in knowledge acquisition sessions. Combined with selective manual note taking, they can be highly effective methods to record information. In addition, if catalogued and stored for later access, they provide a desirable archive of knowledge base development efforts. They should not be used indiscriminately; tape recordings should be reserved for lengthy or complex knowledge acquisition sessions or for sessions that other knowledge engineers or staff personnel will need to view. Considerations for their use must include techniques to later mark, store, catalog, review, transcribe, and check out the resulting tapes.

Pros. Taping the knowledge acquisition session frees the knowledge engineer to focus on making brief, structural-level notes, responding effectively to the domain expert, and managing the interviewing process. After the knowledge acquisition session is over, the knowledge engineer can review the tape and extract what is important from what is not without having the pressure of doing so during an actual interview. Another reason we have used taping is that it allows us to share information among knowledge engineers. This virtually eliminates the need to bother the domain expert with duplicate or related questions from more than one knowledge engineer. By the same token, we are able to compare the responses of multiple experts to a similar issue or simulation. Finally, the tape plays an important role in archiving knowledge acquisition sessions and may be of use in later verification and validation efforts.

Videotaping a knowledge acquisition session offers additional benefits over audiotaping. Audiotaping may be effective with a single knowledge engineer and domain expert, but is much less effective when multiple experts are involved, owing to the problem of identifying speakers during a review of the tape. Also, with audiotaping one is not able to pick up on nonverbal cues. Such cues are very important when multiple experts are responding to the knowledge engineer or to each other, when the knowledge engineer is using protocol analysis techniques (see Chapter 8), or when the knowledge engineer attempts to discern an expert's degree of certainty concerning a particular statement or response.[2]

Cons. Both audiotaping and videotaping have disadvantages that must be dealt with prior to their use in an expert system development project. To defend the costs (e.g., time, money, equipment) involved, developers initially should identify the purpose for taping the sessions . Before taping makes sense, the program must be large enough, the information complex enough, and the sessions numerous enough; also, there must be adequate tape storage space. Once the decision to tape is made, developers must secure the necessary equipment, make arrangements to initiate specific taping, transcription, and storage procedures, and provide knowledge engineer training in the use (including troubleshooting) of the equipment and resulting procedures.

Another disadvantage in the taping of knowledge acquisition sessions is the effect on the domain expert(s) who will be taped. We have seen two undesirable effects. On one hand, domain experts may be overly concerned that what they say might be attributed directly to them in a situation that could cause embarrassment or harm. Behaviors triggered by this concern include
- Reluctance to commit to an answer
- Excessive hemming and hawing

- The use qualifiers that invalidate the answer given
- Rurtive glances at the taping equipment during the interview
- Requests that the equipment be turned off
- Refusal to participate.

On the other hand, we have observed domain experts who "take center stage" in response to being taped. They talk *at* the taping equipment instead of the knowledge engineer, seem to "showboat," and appear reluctant to reply "I don't know" in response to any question. The knowledge engineer may have trouble guiding these types of interviews and as a result, may lose valuable information. During subsequent reviews of tapes in which the expert "showboated," we found that the knowledge conveyed was surface-level. Obviously, these problems impact the validity of the acquired information and must be controlled.

Taping may encourage knowledge engineers to become too dependent on automated record keeping. As they manage the interview, they refrain from making any notes at all, marginal or otherwise. Yielding to this temptation makes them very vulnerable. Not only are they totally reliant on equipment that may or may not function properly, but they are also restricting their access to the interview material until after it has been transcribed. Although we recommend that transcription be done promptly following an interview, this may not always be practical. The time lag that total dependence on taped sessions creates can result in a loss of some data that the knowledge engineer may infer, but not record. Thus, we strongly suggest that the knowledge engineer use some form of manual notation, even with taped interviews. Simple notes that outline the knowledge acquisition session and allow the knowledge engineer to add comments (1) serve as mental organizers and later, as memory jogs and (2) allow for immediate review by both knowledge engineer and domain expert.

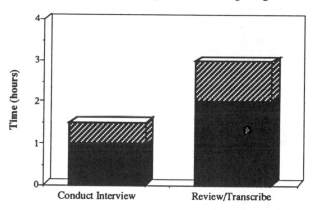

Figure 7-3. Estimation of Time Required to Record and Review Interviews

Finally, a major disadvantage in the exclusive use of taping is the time it consumes. Reviewing (and transcribing) tapes can require twice as long as the actual session itself, an estimate that does not include training and set-up time. This is especially true of videotapes, which may provide nonverbal cues that are recorded with the verbally delivered information. As Figure 7-3 illustrates, if a knowledge engineer videotapes a one-hour knowledge acquisition session and makes marginal, outline-format notes, he or she can expect to spend at least two hours reviewing the tape after the interview. This review includes making more complete notes, coding the notes to the counter on the tape, rewinding to catch a phrase or fast forwarding past irrelevant information, and labeling the tape for storage.

Guidelines for Taping Knowledge Acquisition Interviews. Figure 7-4 lists guidelines that will increase the effectiveness of automated (audio or videotaping) note taking in the knowledge acquisition session.

---

1. Make sure that you have been thoroughly trained in the use of audio and videotaping equipment prior to setting up the knowledge acquisition session.

2. When you send the Knowledge Acquisition Plan to the domain expert for review, notify him or her that the session will be taped.

3. Explain to the domain expert why you would like to tape the session and how you plan to use the tape.

4. Check your taping equipment well before the interview. Have extra tapes on hand.

5. Check your viewing and/or sound sensitivity range; arrange the placement of microphones and cameras prior to the knowledge acquisition interview.

6. To reduce distraction, put microphones, cameras, and monitors in as inconspicuous a place as is possible. If you are videotaping, put the monitor where you can see the visual but the domain expert does not have to look at himself or herself.

7. If the domain expert is reluctant to answer a question because of the tape, offer to turn it off.

8. Support taped information with some manual notes. Use an outline format and summary statements if possible. Code notes to the counter on the tape machine for ease in finding key information at a later date.

9. Rewind tapes and return equipment to readiness states after their use.

Figure 7-4. Guidelines for Taping Knowledge Acquisition Interviews

Beginning the Interview

A critical phase of any interview is the introduction or opening. According to Zunin (1972), the major function of this phase is to motivate the participants to communicate actively. What an interviewer says and does during this time sets the tone for all that follows. The tone conveyed should be perceived as professional, nonthreatening, and relaxed. To convey otherwise could discourage the attending domain expert from participating freely and honestly or from taking part in subsequent interviews.

Knowledge Acquisition: Principles and Guidelines 193

Stewart and Cash (1984) suggest a two-step interview initiation process that is also appropriate for knowledge acquisition sessions. The order in which these steps are completed may vary, depending on personal preference, the relationship between the interview participants, and the specific situation. The first of these involves establishing rapport, or trust, between the knowledge engineer and domain expert. Establishing rapport can include the following verbal messages, accompanied by appropriate nonverbal messages (e.g., eye contact, handshake):

- Introduction, using names as opposed to titles
- Attempts to deal with any initial anxiety on the part of the expert
- Personal inquiries or "small talk."

The second step is the interview orientation. This involves providing the expert with the purpose of the knowledge acquisition session and an overview of the session goals and agenda. As discussed in Chapter 4, the knowledge engineer should take charge of the knowledge acquisition session by actively introducing the session and setting the tone. It is helpful if the knowledge engineer can refer to a posted or printed agenda during the orientation phase. Other techniques include providing a verbal summary of the problem at hand or the purpose of the session, mentioning the anticipated amount of time the session will require, and asking a "starter" question that is related to the overall session topic.

The Body of the Interview

The knowledge acquisition form suggested in Chapter 3 can serve as a guide for the body, or main section of a knowledge acquisition interview session. Appropriately constructed, this form can be used to accomplish the following:

- Provide the expert with a presession overview of topics to be discussed
- Help the knowledge engineer recall important areas and/or questions
- Serve as a re-focusing tool if the interview gets "off-track"
- Serve as a tool against which the knowledge engineer can gauge interview progress.

Most importantly, the form provides planned areas of coverage as opposed to random questions that may not provide adequate inquiries in a topic or area.

Verbal Communication in the Interview

Figure 7-5 illustrates the communicative process, in which both verbal and nonverbal play a role. The next two sections briefly discuss these components and their importance in the knowledge acquisition interview. Verbal communication is the more overt form by which meaning is conveyed during the interview. Both the domain expert and the knowledge engineer express internal meanings through their choice of words. Thus, verbal communication is imperfect because the meaning *one* person ascribes to the words used may not be the meaning that is extracted by the *other* party. Verbal ambiguity is a factor that each knowledge engineer must consider, as it can have far-reaching negative effects. Consider the way most of us verbally quantify information, using words such as the following: most, much, a majority, little, average, none. Each person has his or her own meanings for these words, but few of us agree on percentages that would correlate with these words. Thus, if the expert with whom we are working uses the term "average" to describe a speed or the chance of something occurring, he or she has introduced verbal ambiguity into the conversation. Unless the knowledge engineer actively seeks to reduce this ambiguity by responding with focusing questions, the value of the information is questionable.

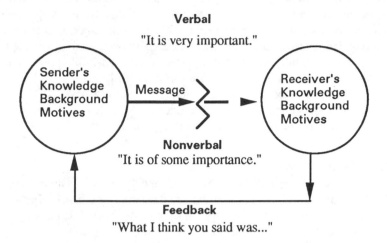

Figure 7-5. Verbal and Nonverbal Communication

The manner in which a verbal message is 'understood' depends in part on the similarities of the backgrounds, vocabularies, and experiences of the communicators. Disparity in these communication foundations results in interference. Concurrently, other signals (e.g., intonation, voice, pitch) accompany and may distort or clarify the verbal message. For example, varying the level of stress placed on different words in the following sentence changes the meaning it conveys:

The *training* manual does not say to do that.
The training *manual* does not say to do that.
The training manual does not say to do *that*.

Verbal communication also is affected by the disparity in the meanings of the words the interview participants use. During a knowledge acquisition interview, each party may use similar words differently. To decrease the impact of this disparity a knowledge engineer can

- Study the domain vocabulary, acronyms, and concepts prior to conducting the interview.

- If the expert uses a word differently than expected, watch for other cues before interrupting him or her. If used judiciously, active listening techniques can help in refining and clarifying intended meanings.

- Guide the expert if necessary, but allow him or her to do most of the talking.

Nonverbal Communication in the Interview

The domain expert watches the knowledge engineer for communicators such as head nods, pauses, inflections, body movements, and facial expressions. Nonverbal communication conveys meanings that may enhance, substitute, or contradict the accompanying verbal communication.

Knowledge engineers should be cognizant of the nonverbal communication that they use and should attempt to send consistent verbal and nonverbal messages to domain experts. Additionally, they should learn to read nonverbal communication from domain experts to detect frustration, lack of interest, motivation, and other messages. Communication texts generally agree that an interviewer transmits certain nonverbal messages during an interview. For example (Stewart & Cash, 1984):

- Fast-paced, clipped speech may indicate importance or urgency
- A breathy voice may communicate nervousness;
- Halting speech may communicate a general level of uncertainty

Feedback During the Interview

Feedback is the "give and take" by which the knowledge engineer receives, understands, and communicates that understanding has occurred. Feedback is continuous and immediate. Its generally takes one of three forms, verification, disagreement, and revision. Generalized examples of feedback include

- Feedback that verifies --"Yes, that is what I said."
- Feedback that states disagreement --"No, that is not what I said"
- Feedback that revises --"Actually, what I mean is. . ."

Guidelines to the effective use of feedback in the knowledge acquisition session are:

1. Provide the domain expert with appropriate feedback to illustrate your degree of understanding. Use both nonverbal and verbal prompts for clarification when it is needed. Don't hesitate to use supportive and appreciative "noises."

2. Do not attempt to provide feedback for every comment the expert makes; ask probing questions or make clarifying statements when appropriate.

3. Review a videotape of your interview behavior. Analyze the purpose of your feedback to the domain expert. Feedback should be used for the sake of enhancing communication (e.g., making the expert feel positive about himself and the value of his contributions), not for showing how much you know, defending your ideas, or arguing ideas.

Closing the Interview

Interview closings resemble the concluding and debriefing activities suggested for any knowledge acquisition session. After an hour-long session of intense concentration and active listening, a knowledge engineer may be tempted to cut the closing activities. In fact, observation of knowledge acquisition-session videotapes indicates that this is a common tendency. Activities involved in session closing and debriefing tend to receive low marks when rated by knowledge engineers and domain experts. The problem is not that these activities are handled poorly but is that they frequently are ignored.

Closings can be an important part of the interview. Psychological research reveals that people tend to remember based on a primacy-recency scheme. They tend to remember what happens first in an interaction (e.g., "first impressions"); they also have a tendency to remember or judge an interaction based on what happened last. If the knowledge engineer does a good job summarizing the major points and purpose of a knowledge acquisition session, provides an opportunity for the domain expert to clarify or revise these points, and tells him or her what to expect next, the domain expert is likely to leave feeling that the time was well spent. This enhances rapport, the expert's propensity to take part in later sessions, and the expert's inclination to speak well of your program to others.

Communications researchers (Knapp, Hart, Friedrich, & Shulman, 1964) contend that a number of verbal and nonverbal techniques can be used to close an interview. Most interviewers combine verbal and nonverbal signals. Figure 7-6 adapts and summarizes some common verbal closing techniques for a knowledge acquisition session.

TECHNIQUE	EXAMPLE
Time's Up	"It's now 4:00 and our scheduled stop time."
Appreciation	"I feel good about what we have discussed today and I appreciate your obvious preparation."
Declaration	"I think we have covered everything we had scheduled."
Prompt	"Do you have any questions?"
Checkpoint	"That seems to cover the agenda. Did we miss anything?"
Personal Concern	"Be sure to call me if you have any concerns with the session notes I'll be sending you next week."
Future Plans	"Let's meet the week of the 10th to talk more about the basic planning constraints."
Summary with Tasks	"We've agreed on these points. . . . You will provide me with the Training Manual by the 21st. I'll send you the notes before next Wednesday."

Figure 7-6. A Sampling of Verbal Closing Techniques

Nonverbal closing techniques are commonly combined with verbal closing techniques, either purposefully or unintentionally. Knowledge engineers should analyze their own closing techniques to ensure that nonverbal signals are not being used unintentionally, conveying unwanted messages to the domain expert. Many physical actions serve as signals that the interview is at its psychological end. Some of the more commonly used nonverbal closing signals include the following:

- Continually looking at one's watch
- Closing, arranging, or otherwise moving one's materials
- Shutting off and rewinding taping equipment
- Straightening in one's chair; pushing the chair back to stand
- Standing up; prompting the domain expert to shake hands.

Figure 7-7 summarizes guidelines for knowledge acquisition interview closings.

---

1. Even if you have run overtime, do not cut short the closing.

2. Verbally state that the interview has come to a close, using a technique with which you feel comfortable.

3. Briefly summarize the knowledge acquisition session's major points or areas of discussion.

4. Briefly mention any major area of misunderstanding or disagreement between participants and its resolution.

5. Use questions that offer the expert an opportunity to respond to a point, clarify an issue, or revise a conclusion.

6. Summarize any action items or tasks that either of you is to complete prior to a specific date; plan briefly for the next session.

7. Let the expert know what to expect next.

Figure 7-7. Guidelines for the Closing of Interview Sessions

SPECIAL INTERVIEW SKILLS AND TECHNIQUES

Many variables will determine the success of the structured knowledge acquisition session interview. Skills that impact success include being able to present various types of questions and sequence the selected questions in a manner that enhances the specificity of the elicited information. Being able to manipulate multiple types of questioning techniques can help knowledge engineers select those that are best suited to the elicitation of information for a particular knowledge acquisition session.

Using Questions Effectively

The sections that follow explores the types, levels, and sequencing of questions in more detail and present suggestions for improved phrasing of interview questions.

Types of Questions

Questions can be categorized or classified in numerous ways. One of the most common ways to categorize interview questions is as open and closed. The following discussion reflects the difference in the amount of structure that each question type conveys and the advantages and disadvantages of each. Figure 7-8 provides examples of each type of question.

QUESTION TYPE	EXAMPLES
Open	"How does that system work?" "What do you need to know before you can decide?" "Why did you choose this one rather than that one?" "What do you know about the fuel system?" "How could your training have been improved?" "What is your general reaction to this statement?"
Closed	"Which of these planes have you maintained?" "How many hours in the cockpit have you had?" "Which of these types of investments do you consider strongest?" "Will this cause the oil pressure to be higher or lower?" "What is the target speed or window for this maneuver?" "Is 225 degrees the upper limit?"

Figure 7-8. Examples of Open and Closed Questions

Open Questions. **Open questions** tend to be broad and place few constraints on the responding domain expert. Open questions are not followed by choices; they encourage free response (Oppenheim, 1966). Open questions are appropriate when the knowledge engineer wishes to observe high level responses to discern the domain expert's scope of understanding, response certainty, and what he/she thinks is important about the topic. They also enable the domain expert to offer information that the knowledge engineer did not know to ask for, a probable situation in knowledge acquisition sessions. Answers to open questions enable knowledge engineers to observe the expert's use of key vocabulary, concepts, and frames of reference.

Open questions also have disadvantages. Key among these is that, while answers to open questions are time-consuming, they may reveal little information *at the level required* for knowledge-base development. The knowledge engineer will be required to work harder to control the interview, including focusing and redirecting the expert, using probing or follow-up questions to garner specific information, and determining whether or not the domain expert has omitted information that he or she thinks would be irrelevant. Open questions also may cause difficulties in note taking and/or coding of the information that may be embedded in a response. For example, if the respondent rambles on in a highly unorganized fashion, the knowledge engineer will have trouble not only recording the information, but also in coding and organizing it.

Closed Questions. Closed questions set limits on the type, level, and amount of information a domain expert provides. They provide a choice of alternatives or level of reply (Oppenheim, 1966). They may vary in the degree to which they are closed. A moderately closed question allows the domain expert to respond with a specific piece of information but does not limit the set from which he or she responds. For example, a question like the following specifies particular information but does not limit the expert to select a bipolar response (e.g., yes/no) or multiple-choice option:

"Which symptom led you to believe the problem was in the fuel system?"

In most cases, knowledge engineers who need to use closed questions as follow-up probes or clarifiers are advised to construct moderately closed questions. Bipolar questions, which limit the respondent to one of two choices, can be used as a feedback mechanism to establish accuracy. Because they are often misused, their use should be limited.

Closed questions are most effective when the knowledge engineer needs a specific piece of information. Closed questions (1) enable the knowledge engineer to control the progress of a knowledge acquisition session more effectively, (2) make note taking and answer coding easier, and (3) are less time consuming to use than open questions.

Closed questions also have disadvantages. First, there is the knowledge engineer's tendency to overuse this easier type of questioning, receiving too little information and necessitating more follow-up questions or knowledge acquisition sessions. Second, closed questions may preclude the domain expert from volunteering important information that has not been directly specified in the question. Third, a knowledge acquisition session in which more closed questions are used (in comparison to open questions) results in the knowledge engineer's doing most of the talking and thus, dominating the session. Finally, closed questions require that the knowledge engineer have an excellent command of the domain's vocabulary and concepts, as well as an awareness of the domain expert's abilities and frames of reference. Because knowledge engineers typically are not experts in a domain themselves, this requirement is difficult to fulfill.

Using Open and Closed Questions. Determinants to selecting a question type include

- Level of knowledge required
- Purpose of the knowledge acquisition session
- Knowledge engineer's background and abilities.

Because each type of question has advantages, knowledge engineers must be able to use both. Most sessions will require the use of a variety of both open and closed questions with varying degrees of restrictions. As he or she constructs a knowledge acquisition session plan, the knowledge engineer should consider the following points concerning the mix of open and closed questions.

1. The amount of information offered by a domain expert in response to a question decreases with increased question restrictiveness.

2. The knowledge engineer's degree of control over the knowledge acquisition session increases as the amount of information offered by the domain expert decreases.

3. The amount of information offered by the domain expert increases as the knowledge engineer decreases the amount of control by asking less restrictive questions.

4. Domain experts are more likely to offer valuable, but unasked information, in sessions that are less restrictive and in which the knowledge engineer uses less overt control.

Knowledge engineers should practice using both types of questions in a mock session atmosphere and, if possible, review a videotape of their questioning behavior. This will allow them to observe their ability to transition smoothly between open and closed questions. As they do so, they should watch for what Lazarus (1975) terms one of the most common conversation obstacles, the double question (e.g., combined open and closed question), which makes the respondent's job difficult and the answer uncodable. In analyzing the questions asked during a session, a knowledge engineer can look for signals in the questions themselves and in the levels of response to the question. Figure 7-9 depicts trigger words that act as signals for open and closed questions.

```
OPEN
discuss...      interpret...    explain...      evaluate...     compare...
if...           what if...

CLOSED
who...          what...         when...         where...        name...
```

Figure 7-9. Trigger Words for Question Types

Phrasing Tips

Some authors contend that after selecting the appropriate type of question, **phrasing** the question is the second and most important step. Knowledge engineers should consider at least three factors as they determine question phrasing: terminology, level, and complexity.

Terminology. Most importantly, knowledge engineers must be able to use key domain terminology in phrasing questions. Using the language of the domain enables the domain expert to expend less time translating questions and more time providing answers for them. The knowledge engineer's mastery of critical domain vocabulary enhances rapport and maximizes the time allotted for knowledge acquisition sessions. In addition to the terminology selected, knowledge engineers should consider the guidelines in Figure 7-10 when phrasing questions that will be posed to domain experts.

---

1. Avoid words that may have multiple meanings.

2. Avoid using vague words (e.g., most, much, average).

3. Control the use of words that may express unintended synonymity (e.g., could, should).

4. Offer contexts to guard against misunderstandings caused by words that may sound similar but have very different meanings.

5. Eliminate bias in question phrasing.

Figure 7-10. Tips for Phrasing Questions

Level. What is the background of the domain expert? What types of knowledge is he or she likely to possess? What type or level of knowledge will the particular knowledge acquisition session require and elicit? The way knowledge engineers answer these questions affects the phrasing of session questions. Questions that require responses above an expert's level of ability, outside of his or her area of expertise, or at a level that he or she finds difficult to access may cause embarrassment, reluctance to participate, or lack of honesty. Questions that are phrased in too elementary a manner or require levels of knowledge that appear "beneath" the expert may result in a feeling that time has been wasted and lead the expert to respond in a less-than-adequate manner.

Complexity. A major phrasing fault is question complexity. Knowledge engineers, in attempts to provide question contexts, often construct very complex questions that are difficult or impossible to answer. The following example illustrates this tendency:

> I need your opinion on the parts of this display that you find most useful. Take a few minutes to look at the display and envision yourself in the situation we talked about earlier. You need to rate each lettered part of the display to indicate usefulness. This is so I can analyze information flow and later color selection. Rate the portions using the scale attached, where the number 1 indicates most important or critical and the number 5 indicates least important or of little value.

Common phrasing errors include providing too much explanation or context, embedding one question in another so that the expert does not know how to respond, and using the question to "soapbox" or put forth a belief the knowledge engineer holds. A related phrasing error occurs when the knowledge engineer attempts to "out-story" the storyteller (Derr, 1986), using the knowledge acquisition session to explain or describe an idea or to practice one-upmanship in response to the expert's description of experiences.

Levels of Questions

There are two levels of questions, primary and secondary (Kahn & Cannell, 1964). **Primary questions** are those that an interviewer uses to introduce topic areas or transition to other areas. A reviewer could analyze a transcription of a knowledge acquisition session and understand primary questions out of the normal interview context. The question,"Given the symptoms, what cause would you *first* be inclined to suggest?" is a primary question. It can be taken out of context and be understood. It introduces the question set that follows.

Secondary questions are often termed probing questions. Their purpose is to find out more about information offered in response to a primary or a preceding secondary question. They allow the knowledge engineer to follow up on a topic area, requesting more specific information. Situations in which the use of secondary questions is suggested include domain expert responses which seem to be vague, uncertain, superficial, or irrelevant. The following are some types of probing questions:

Silence Probe. If the expert does not seem to have completed a response, use active listening techniques (e.g., eye contact, body language) and remain quiet to encourage further response.

Prompting Probe. If a nonverbal probe does not stimulate further response, use verbal techniques such as "Please continue...", "Yes?" (Stewart & Cash, 1984).

Last-Chance Probe. To make sure all relevant information has been elicited on a topic area, use a probe such as: "Is there anything more we should know about this fuel system malfunction?"

Depth Probe. If the domain expert has provided surface-level information, follow up with probes such as: "Explain further why you diagnosed it in that manner", "Tell me more about..."

Specifying Probe. If the domain expert has provided information that is not specific enough or not at the appropriate level, direct or focus later efforts with probes such as: "What does 'BVR' mean?" "What value would you set for 'fast enough'?"

Reflective Probe. If you suspect that the domain expert has provided inaccurate information, restate the answer that was provided, emphasizing the part of the probe that contains the information to be checked for accuracy: "Do you mean *MPH* or *KPH?*", "Did you mean may *not*?"

The effective use of secondary questions is a trait of an effective knowledge engineer. A skilled knowledge engineer listens to responses to primary (and later, secondary) questions, compares answers against expectations, analyzes meanings that have been communicated, determines if the answer is satisfactory (as measured by session goals and requirements of the current development cycle), and generates probing questions for follow-up.

Sequencing Questions

Various communications specialists describe techniques that interviewers use to connect questions that comprise an interview session. Any one of these connective techniques may describe a whole knowledge acquisition interview or may be used within specific subsets of a knowledge acquisition interview. Sequencing techniques that are most appropriate for knowledge acquisition sessions include the funnel and inverted-funnel technique.

Funnel Sequence
Figure 7-11 depicts the **funnel** sequencing technique, in which the knowledge acquisition session begins with broad, open questions, continues with probing or focusing questions, and concludes with more restrictive, closed questions. The funnel sequence can be very effective--for several reasons. First, because it begins with open questions, rapport is more easily established and the session begins on a less-threatening note. Second, beginning with open questions allows the knowledge engineer to evaluate responses and refine secondary follow-up questions. This maneuver allows the discarding of intended questions that are no longer necessary owing to the expert's volunteering of information in response to an open question.

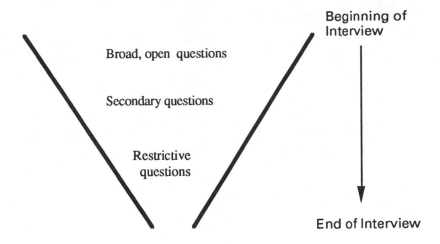

Figure 7-11. The Funnel Questioning Sequence.

Inverted Funnel

As one would expect, the **inverted-funnel** approach is opposite to that of the sequence described above (Figure 7-12). When using the inverted funnel, the knowledge engineer begins with restrictive, closed questions and offers progressively less restrictive ones as the interview concludes. While the funnel sequence is most commonly used in knowledge acquisition sessions, there are times when the knowledge engineer might wish to use the inverted funnel sequence. For example, this sequence allows the knowledge engineer to begin with a specific, well-focused question, beginning the interview on a very business-like note. Such a question may enable the domain expert to refresh his or her memory, setting the stage for the topics to be discussed. Finally, as noted by Stewart and Cash (1985), the inverted funnel allows the interviewer to use closed questions to draw out an interviewee and end with a generalization or summary statement.

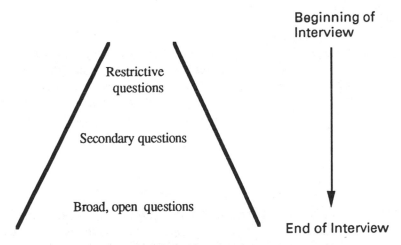

Figure 7-12. The Inverted Funnel Questioning Sequence

Knowledge Acquisition: Principles and Guidelines

Important Questioning Issues

Knowledge engineers will discover quickly that even armed with proper questioning know-how, they still may feel uncomfortable and ill-at-ease with the interview. As noted by Derr & Brown (1987), practice is an enabler in conducting efficient, structured interviews. Breaking up into small groups, in which each knowledge engineer takes turns acting the role of knowledge engineer, domain expert, and recorder, is an effective means of practice. If possible, knowledge engineers should videotape themselves conducting a mock knowledge acquisition interview session and immediately review their behavior prior to their first meeting with a domain expert.

During these practice sessions, knowledge engineers should look for opportunities to practice using techniques to stimulate appropriate responses from the domain expert. The section that follows addresses the issue of "wait time" in questioning and suggests techniques to handle common interview problems.

The Concept of Wait Time

"If the knowledge engineer talks, the domain expert cannot." This simple statement summarizes the idea of **wait time,** a normal convention of two-party conversations. As its name implies, wait time refers to that period of time after the knowledge engineer has asked a question. In some ways, it can be thought of as the expert's "think time." Research in other fields indicates that wait time increases of as little as 3 to 5 seconds increased the length of responses and decreased the failure of an individual to respond (Rowe, 1974). Knowledge engineers are advised to remain quiet after posing a question and to guard against using nonverbal cues that might communicate impatience. Allowing the domain expert to retrieve the required information will result in a better quality answer. If, after a number of seconds, the domain expert still has not answered or indicated that he or she is searching, the knowledge engineer may use the restatement technique. This takes some immediate pressure off the domain expert while still indicating that the information is desired. During this additional time, the domain expert continues to "retrieve" requested information and formulate a response.

Handling Common Problems

During knowledge acquisition interviews, situations will arise that will interfere with meeting session goals. Many of these problems (e.g., refocusing the expert, the occasionally difficult expert) are common to any knowledge acquisition session and are discussed in the latter sections of Chapter 4. Additional problems that can negatively impact the usefulness of material acquired from the knowledge acquisition session include:
- "Yes, but. . ."
- Irrelevant remarks
- Global answers.

"Yes, but. . ." This is a simple technique that an expert may use to dodge a difficult question. It sends two diametrically opposed messages. "Yes" indicates that the expert agrees or responds affirmatively. However, the addition of "but," followed by some line of reasoning or exception, negates the initial response. The resulting expression is deceptive and hard to code. Since most respondents who use this technique may not even realize the problem, the knowledge engineer may subtly rephrase the initial question to trigger a response. If this does not elicit a more appropriate response, the knowledge engineer may consider telling the expert the problem of coding such an answer or may ask the expert to review portions of the videotape in which the technique was used. During this review, the knowledge engineer is advised to focus on an incident and ask,"Exactly what did you mean in that situation?"

Irrelevant Remarks. These remarks have no bearing on the question at hand and may even result in a defocusing or in a diversion from the planned agenda or structure. Most knowledge engineers find it very difficult to deal with irrelevant remarks because they think it requires that they be assertive or aggressive. An alternate response is to use a more subtle approach. For example, in response to an irrelevant remark, the knowledge engineer can ask the expert,

"Please tell me how that is related to _____?"

"I'm not sure I understand how that is connected to ____. Could you explain?"

Typically, the domain expert will respond that it isn't related and allow the session to resume. In some situations, it actually may *be* related, and the domain expert can pursue a more complete explanation.

Global Answers. Global answers are those that are so general that they are difficult to translate into a knowledge base. In some cases, these answers do provide useful information for the knowledge engineer to use in structuring his or her understanding of a domain and the relatedness of concepts. In most, however, they are inadequate. Knowledge engineers should respond to a global, surface-level answer by using secondary questioning techniques discussed earlier in this chapter. The use of different kinds of probing techniques enables the knowledge engineer to focus the expert on the type and level of information that is needed without embarrassing the expert. For example, the clarifying probe lets the knowledge engineer pursue greater depth of information in a minimally-threatening manner, such as

"Say more about..."

"What steps would you use to do ___?"

"How did you arrive at that?"

AFTER THE INTERVIEW IS OVER

When the interview ends, the knowledge engineer's work is only partially complete. After the expert has been debriefed, important information summarized, and future tasks or expectations outlined, the knowledge engineer enters the follow-up phase. The follow-up phase for a knowledge acquisition session in which the technique was a structured interview is not very different from a session that was characterized by the use of protocol analysis or simulated activities. After the use of any of these techniques the knowledge engineer still must deal with translating session data into a usable format.

Transcribing Session Information

Program management must first decide whether to transcribe session tapes (weighing costs and benefits). *If* transcription is required, the format of the knowledge acquisition session transcript must be specified. Some projects may require that a transcription clerk type out *everything* that was said, attributing the statement to the appropriate party, as Figure 7-13 depicts.

Knowledge Acquisition Form
KA Session: Product Development #204   7/18/87
Knowledge Engineer: KLM   Domain Expert:BAM
Session Type: Interview

LINE TRANSCRIPTION
001   KLM: This is knowledge acquisition session 204, in which we will be
002   discussing the major factors that are used to decide whether or not to bring a
003   new ideaor product to market.

004   BAM: First we would study each to determine if they are right for our
005   company's image. Will we be able to market this idea within the "family"
006   of products that we already have or are planning?

007   KML: BAM, to help us identify the factors you use in selecting a product for
008   development, I have mocked up two different ideas that your company is
009   currently considering.

Figure 7-13. Line-By-Line Transcription

One can easily observe that this format and detail will require extensive time and will result in a mass of unprocessed material. It is not a cost effective task--taping the interview for posterity and review is a more reasonable approach.

Other projects may decide to tape the session and transcribe only the most important portions. The tape is kept for archive purposes, but notes are filed to summarize and index the information for easy access. For example, Figure 7-14 presents a transcription (in reality, a summary) in which each major section represents important data. Note that the information is tied to the identifying characteristics (e.g., date, session number) and to the appropriate reading on the tape counter. Indexing terms have been assigned to areas which knowledge engineers may need to review at a later point. These key index terms are agreed upon on a program-wide basis. They are later compiled in a database that allows knowledge engineers to review the sessions and transcription line numbers that reference any key word. This technique helps manage, and enhance the accessibility of, data compiled from knowledge acquisition sessions into transcripts.

KA Session: Product Development #204   7/18/87
Knowledge Engineer: KLM   Domain Expert:BAM

Tape Counter 104: Introduction to major issues in product development. Basic considerations. Notes the following factors: market niche, identifiability of target market, technological considerations, usability, current competition, expected competition, innovation. Index: *TAM, Brand Identification, Competition.*

Tape Counter 145. Discussion of the weightings of the considerations discussed in deciding whether or not to strongly consider an idea for product development. Discussed time factor involved in bringing a technologically-advanced product to market. Discussed "readiness" of the target market for the product. Index: *Development Time, Market Readiness*

Figure 7-14. A Sample Top-Level, Indexed Transcription Methodology

Developers must also resolve who will be responsible for the transcription of knowledge acquisition tapes. The knowledge engineer in charge of the session usually handles this; however, the resulting transcription mirrors only one person's interpretation of what in the session is important. Some authors (Hoffman, 1987) suggest the use of two knowledge engineers in transcribing the data from a knowledge acquisition session. The logistics of this set up will vary according to the program and time and computer constraints. For example, two knowledge engineers may both view the session tape and discuss what to transcribe while one handles data input to the recording form. While the use of two "judges" or knowledge engineers can help increase the validity of what is interpreted and transcribed, this method is extremely person-intensive and may not be suitable for many programs.

Deciding What Is "Important"

Deciding what is truly noteworthy, especially in the initial phases of knowledge acquisition, is not a trivial task. Here are a few guidelines to separate the wheat from the chaff:

• Follow the earlier guidelines concerning the knowledge acquisition plan. Insisting that the expert review the plan prior to the session increases the likelihood that he or she will come prepared to discuss the information that is most relevant to the current topic.

• Make frequent use of probing, secondary questions, as discussed in the "Problems" section of this chapter. These techniques help keep the domain expert on track and reduce the amount of information that is "out of bounds."

- During the session, take notes in an outline format and. place a star or check mark beside the topic areas that appear to be most relevant to your needs. Likewise, annotate those topic areas that do not seem to be as useful at this point in the development cycle. This will save time later, during a review of the tape for transcription purposes.

- Ask another knowledge engineer for assistance in selecting critical information during the transcription or summary process.

- During the transcription process, review all material using tools that will help determine data usefulness. Such tools include initial diagrams from task or functional analyses, functional descriptions of the current prototyping cycle, or of current knowledge acquisition plans.

- In particularly troublesome cases, call an in-house domain expert to assist in the review and transcription process; be prepared to handle some of the problems that might arise when consulting multiple experts.

- Tape the knowledge acquisition session. This will allow retrieval of what may initially seem to be superfluous data when, and if, it becomes important at a later date.

Moving Toward Representation

Once the transcription methodology and format have been established, knowledge engineers become responsible for making "sense" of the data that was retrieved so that they can work it into an appropriate format for use in the knowledge base. Some tasks involved in this phase include the following:
- Send knowledge acquisition forms to a domain expert for review and response.
- Follow up with the domain expert to make sure the material is reviewed and returned.
- Determine the important material for the current prototyping cycle.
- Translate the data into an agreed-upon knowledge representation language for coding.
- Complete appropriate rule design forms or other mechanisms to trace rules from the acquisition session into knowledge-base rules.

ENDNOTES

[1] The authors wish to acknowledge the helpful contributions of William Derr, Ph.D., and Barbara Brown to the content of·this chapter.

[2] McNeill and Levy (1982) found that an expert's nonverbal cues (e.g., facial expressions and gestures) may be used as cues to inference-making processes.

SUGGESTED READINGS

Stewart, C & W. Cash. Interviewing: Principles and Practices (4th ed.). Dubuque, IO: Wm Brown Publishers, 1985.

APPLICATION

1. Select an area about which you know a great deal. Use this domain to plan for a knowledge acquisition session that will use the structured interview as the elicitation technique.

   a. Develop a knowledge acquisition plan, complete with agenda and main topics.

   b. Using the funnel sequence technique, draft sample questions (open and closed) for the session.

   c. Select one area or sample question and break it down into a primary question, followed by possible secondary questions.

2. Based on the type and level of knowledge required, select one of the five interviewing techniques for use in this session. Defend your choice of technique.

8

Tracing the Decision Making Process to Acquire Knowledge

The Role of Decision Making in Knowledge Acquisition

> **Tracing the Decision Process**
> **The Usefulness of Verbal Reports**
> **Techniques to Compile Verbal Reports**

Managing Process Tracing in Knowledge Acquisition Sessions

> **Establishing a Methodology**
> **Sampling the Methods**

Extracting Knowledge from Process Tracing Sessions

> **Translating Sessions to Protocols**
> **Selecting the Analysis Framework**
> **Determining Decision Rules**
> **Refining the Analysis**

INTRODUCTION

Rolandi (1986) argues that the real job of a knowledge engineer is to determine what domain experts do as they make decisions. He contends that in knowledge engineering the knowledge engineer analyzes the flow of information that occurs during the expert's decision making behavior.

The task of analyzing decision making behavior is difficult, yet central to an expert system development project. To investigate an expert's decision-making behavior, the knowledge engineer may use both manual techniques and induction-oriented knowledge acquisition techniques. This chapter presents process tracing and protocol analysis, paired techniques that enable the knowledge engineer to trace or study a domain expert's decision making processes. These techniques can be effective knowledge acquisition tools because they provide a methodology that enables a knowledge engineer to focus on the important decision making elements of a task. After studying the expert's responses to the task and later, to questions about his or her performance, the knowledge engineer can compile decision heuristics, alternatives, attributes, and attractiveness values for the target task.

Although some authors (Waldron, 1985b) contend that process tracing may be the primary method for obtaining information about an expert's tasks, its effectiveness depends on a number of factors. First, knowledge engineers must be trained in its use. Second, knowledge engineers should complete the domain familiarization and conceptualization stages prior to using process tracing and protocol analysis. Finally, process tracing sessions require follow-up interviews to refine and clarify the analysis of the decision making information. Although time-consuming, these sessions can yield valuable information that is appropriate for knowledge-base development efforts.

In this chapter we present both background and applications-oriented information on techniques to trace and analyze an expert's decision making processes. Initially, we consider the task of tapping problem-solving expertise. Within this context we discuss the usefulness of verbal reports and present guidelines for establishing a process-tracing methodology. Next, we present verbalization techniques (e.g. concurrent, retrospective) and methods (e.g., constrained solutions) to stimulate the production of verbal reports. Subsequently, we propose guidelines for translating process tracing information into protocols and present information on selecting an analysis framework for determining decision rules.[1]

Objectives

This chapter suggests the use of process tracing and protocol analysis as techniques for acquiring decision-making or problem-solving knowledge. Specifically, it enables readers to accomplish the following:

- Recognize the usefulness of verbal reports for knowledge acquisition
- Define an overall process tracing methodology that helps control for some of the problems associated with verbal reporting
- Select appropriate process tracing methodologies and techniques according to knowledge acquisition goals
- Identify scenarios or problems that reflect a specific process tracing method (e.g., constrained information)

- Determine an appropriate analysis framework (e.g., alternatives, attributes, aspects, attractiveness) and decision rules for specific situations.

Key Terms

process tracing	protocols	protocol analysis
concurrent verbalization	memory aid	alternatives
decision rules	aspects	attributes
attractiveness	retrospective verbalization	

THE ROLE OF DECISION MAKING IN KNOWLEDGE ACQUISITION

The acquisition and representation of isolated domain facts does not produce an expert system that is considered to be very smart. Like the "idiot savants" of old, such a system would be able to regurgitate, but not apply, facts to solve problems. If the ability to apply knowledge to solve problems is an indication of intelligence, expert system knowledge bases must reflect decision making and problem-solving knowledge. Expertise in a given domain is related not merely to *what* is known, but also to how that information is *stored*, how it is *retrieved*, and how previous problem solving knowledge is *applied* to solve new problems.

The initial stages of knowledge acquisition often require only that the knowledge engineer identify domain subsets, concepts, vocabulary, and facts. As expert system development progresses, prototypes will be required to function more and more expertly. This degree of functionality requires that the expert system exhibit the ability to solve problems and make decisions--abilities that involve the interaction and application of numerous facts, constraints, and situational information. The following sections describe several techniques that can help a knowledge engineer tap problem solving and decision-making information.

Tracing the Decision Process

Process tracing is any of a set of techniques that allows knowledge engineers to determine a domain expert's "train of thought" while he or she completes a task or reaches a conclusion. Knowledge engineers who desire to investigate (1) information that an expert uses for decision making and (2) how the expert processes that information, may opt to use process tracing. **Protocol analysis** requires that the knowledge engineer use one of several techniques to analyze the **protocols,** verbal reports that have been generated by a domain expert, that result from a session. For example, in one type of process tracing session the domain expert may be asked not only to solve a problem, but also to "think aloud" while doing so. The resulting verbal report provides a transcript of the problem solving session. The knowledge engineer examines this protocol to identify decision-making sequences and alternatives.

Protocol analysis and process tracing techniques have been used by researchers in numerous fields (e.g., psychiatry, anthropology) to generate and study data that is reported verbally. Research in decision making and problem solving has applied similar techniques to study problem solving states, decision points, and considerations. For example, Newell and Simon (1972) used protocol analysis extensively to study how people solve cryptoarithmetic problems. Initially they used the technique to discern the subject's general problem solving approach. Once identified, they used protocol analysis to identify specific operations the subject was using to move from one knowledge state to another.

Process tracing sessions require some type of personal interaction between a knowledge engineer and a domain expert. However, unlike the interview technique, process tracing sessions typically are not interactive (Waldron, 1985b). Figure 8-1 illustrates this important difference.

Flow of Communication in the Interview

Flow of Communication in Process Tracing Session

Figure 8-1. Comparison of Communication Flow in Interview and Process Tracing Sessions

Prior to the session, the knowledge engineer does a considerable amount of work (e.g., selecting a suitable scenario or problem set based on task and concept analysis). During the session itself the expert does the talking as he or she interacts with data to solve a problem. Concurrently, the knowledge engineer records the process for later review, analysis, and follow-up interviews.

The session itself can be based on one of two basic techniques--concurrent or retrospective verbalization--and may reflect the use of any of a number of methods to present problem scenarios. For example, in a **concurrent verbalization** session, the expert "thinks out loud" as he or she solves a problem. In a **retrospective verbalization** session, the knowledge engineer records (with taping equipment or manually) the expert's procedure in the course of solving the problem. Later, the expert and knowledge engineer review the session to produce the protocol.

Process tracing and protocol analysis can provide useful insight into the knowledge and data states a domain expert works through in solving a typical domain problem. Knowledge acquisition sessions based on this technique require that the knowledge engineer preselect a sample scenario, problem, or other situation that will tap appropriate domain knowledge. In turn, this necessitates that the knowledge engineer demonstrate a solid grasp of the concepts, vocabulary, and tasks involved in the domain. Following the session itself, the knowledge engineer must be able to analyze, interpret, and structure the protocol into heuristics that can be reviewed by the domain expert. Figure 8-2 summarizes some of the pros and cons of verbal reporting measures.[2]

PROS	CONS
Expert consciously considers decision making heuristics	Requires that expert be aware of why he or she makes a decision
Expert consciously considers decision alternatives, attributes, values	Requires that expert be able to categorize major decision alternatives
Knowledge engineer can observe and analyze decision making behavior	Requires that expert be able to verbalize the attributes and values of a decision alternative
Knowledge engineer can record and later analyze with the expert, key decision points	Requires that expert be able to reason about the selection of a given alternative
	Subjective view of decision making
	Explanations may not track with reasoning

Figure 8-2. Pros and Cons of Verbal Reporting on Decision Making Behavior

Process tracing involves the analysis of verbal and observational data. It provides the knowledge engineer with a tool to extract problem solving and decision making knowledge that otherwise can be difficult to ascertain. Many expert systems are designed to serve as job or decision aids for use by personnel with novice- or intermediate-level abilities. To be useful to their target audiences, these expert systems require both basic declarative facts and decision making heuristics used by experts in the domain. These heuristics are critical to the acceptance of the resulting system's functionality, yet they are difficult to tap using techniques such as the interview. Process tracing provides a strategy that a knowledge engineer can use to investigate, analyze, and translate these heuristics.

The Usefulness of Verbal Reports

Researchers in psychology, psychiatry, and interpersonal communication have relied on data that is highly dynamic because the source was a human. Typical techniques that have been used to gather data in these fields include the analysis of eye movements and nonverbal behavior. While these techniques are effective, the data proved to be both very expensive to gather and difficult to analyze. As knowledge engineers work with domain experts to extract heuristics, we confront similar problems. For example, placing an expert fighter pilot in an aircraft simulator to gather precise data on body movements in response to changing displays is prohibitively expensive. As in the aforementioned fields, knowledge engineers find it necessary to rely, at least to some extent, on verbal reports as data.

Requesting that a domain expert answer a specific question or describe considerations as a task is completed may seem logical in our quest for problem solving knowledge. However, the use of verbal data (either alone or in combination with other data) presents special problems. In the case of knowledge acquisition, these problems include (1) structuring the setting to enhance the validity of the knowledge and (2) analyzing the resulting information for translation and inclusion in the knowledge base. If gathered and analyzed in an efficient manner, knowledge gained from process tracing can enable knowledge engineers to isolate decision making heuristics. Process tracing can help a knowledge engineer minimize interactions with the expert, streamline the knowledge acquisition process, and enhance accuracy.

Minimizing Interactions

Process tracing can also minimize unnecessary interactions between a knowledge engineer and a domain expert (Waldron, 1985a). Recall that whereas interviewing requires two-way communication, process tracing requires only that decision making information "flow" from the domain expert. The information produced in the session is recorded for later review and analysis. The heuristics presented or portrayed by the domain expert during the session can then be examined by multiple knowledge engineers without requiring each of them to contact the expert directly or to request redundant information. Finally, the use of process tracing as a precursor to structured interviews enhances the knowledge engineer's ability to compile decision making information efficiently.

Streamlining Knowledge Acquisition

Second, taped recordings enable the knowledge engineer to streamline knowledge acquisition efforts. Analyzing the taped process tracing session allows the knowledge engineer to identify future knowledge needs and plan follow-on sessions. Follow-on sessions are likely to be comprised of a series of structured interviews that focus on specific aspects of the information produced during the process tracing session. This "surgical" interviewing can help the knowledge engineer (1) refine the information provided during the process tracing session and/or (2) clarify any questionable areas that remain from the process tracing session. Thus, structured interviews are used only the knowledge engineer understands the domain, at least one set of its problems, and typical problem solving processes. Process tracing sessions and the information they provide facilitate more expedient selection of knowledge acquisition techniques for follow-on sessions.

Enhancing Accuracy

Finally, process tracing can enhance the accuracy of the developing knowledge base if the selected problem or scenario is realistic. Knowledge acquisition techniques, such as the interview and task analysis, yield valuable declarative knowledge and are useful in structuring the domain. However, they do not produce applications-oriented, problem solving heuristics. Process tracing and protocol analysis can be used to work from domain facts to develop problems and scenarios that require the use of domain facts.

Techniques to Compile Verbal Reports

There are two different frameworks upon which a knowledge engineer can develop process tracing sessions: concurrent and retrospective verbalization. The first requires that the domain expert provide an on-going commentary as he or she completes a selected task or simulation. Conversely, retrospective verbalization requires that the domain expert complete the task at hand without providing a concurrent verbal report. After completing the task, the domain expert views a **memory aid** (e.g., the session notes or tape) and reports on the behavior or considerations that occurred as the task was completed. Figure 8-3 portrays qualities of each verbalization framework. The following sections describe the major protocol elicitation techniques that can be used within each framework.

CONCURRENT VERBALIZATION
- Domain expert reports on his/her activity as the task or problem is completed
- Requires little equipment
- Requires selection of task or problem that may be completed in time allotted to the session
- Reporting may interfere with task completion

RETROSPECTIVE VERBALIZATION
- Domain expert completes a task prior to discussion of his/her activity
- Used when reporting is anticipated to interfere with task completion
- Requires that domain expert remember what he/she was thinking
- Recording equipment may be used to stimulate recall
- Requires selection of task or problem that may be completed in time allotted to the session

Figure 8-3. Comparing Protocol Elicitation Techniques

Concurrent Verbalization (Think-Aloud)

In the most widely used protocol elicitation technique, the domain expert provides a running verbal report of actions, considerations, decision points, and strategy while completing the sample task or the simulated problem. However, the act of reporting on these issues while the problem is being solved requires the use of cognitive resources. Thus, it is not uncommon for concurrent verbalization to interfere with the task that the expert is attempting to complete. To understand the problem that concurrent verbalization may cause, imagine that you were teaching someone as simple a task a tying a shoe. To do so, you want to concurrently "show and tell" them how to tie the laces. While you complete each step in the task, you describe it. In doing so, you may experience the sense of losing "where you are" in the sequence of steps, which may necessitate starting over or retracing a previous step to provide a mental trigger for the step that follows. Negative results may include incomplete or inaccurate information due to any of the following:

- Omission of steps in the problem solving task
- Lack of recognition of a step or consideration
- Interruption to the flow of information (i.e., "losing one's place").

These negative effects are more predominant with tasks that do not allow for interruptions, while they are less potent with tasks that can incorporate "breaks in action." An example provided by Waldron (1985a) is that more difficulty would result from requiring concurrent verbalization from a pilot (who may be required to respond quickly to changing conditions) than from a mathematics professor (who may pause to consider the next step in the solution to a difficult problem).

Discussions

An alternative to the concurrent verbalization technique is the discussion format. In the most common discussion-oriented technique, two or more experts work together to solve a problem. Their actions and communications are recorded for later review and analysis. In a variation of this technique, one expert communicates with another expert using networked computers to solve the problem. Another variation, termed "user dialogs" (Wielinga & Breuker, 1985), requires that a domain expert act as the expert system and a person with novice or intermediate skills act as the user. The "user" asks questions of the "expert system" to solve the problem.[3]

A primary benefit of the discussion is that problem solving information is provided in a less awkward fashion than with the think-aloud technique. A side benefit is that the knowledge engineer might later be able to retrieve important information to refine system functional and interface requirements. The discussion technique is not without problems, however. While two people may be more apt to communicate problem solving knowledge during a dialog than when working in isolation, they may not agree on the priorities, alternatives, important attributes, or strategy for solving the problem. This difficulty can be managed by analyzing the protocols each member generates and resolving disagreements by asking another authority to review and select the more appropriate decision rules.[4]

Retrospective Verbalization

Retrospective verbalization allows a domain expert to complete the task *before* discussing alternatives, considerations, and decisions. This technique can be useful when the knowledge engineer anticipates that the act of verbalizing might interfere with the cognitive processing that the domain expert will require in working through the sample problem, task, or scenario.

While eliminating the difficulties that may be evident with concurrent verbalization, retrospective verbalization presents both the domain expert and the knowledge engineer with other problems. Domain experts may find it difficult to remember what they were thinking when major decision points were considered and important problems solved. Knowledge engineers must attend to and somehow record information from the session that may provide cues to domain expert behavior. As important as the cues themselves is knowledge of the *context* in which they occurred.

After the session, the domain expert reports on actions, considerations, and justifications. If the report strays from information that seems important, the knowledge engineer should present the target behavioral cues and their contexts to guide the expert's verbal reporting behavior.

Cued Recall

A variation on retrospective verbalization, cued recall incorporates the use of a memory aid (e.g., videotape). Cued recall extends the usefulness of retrospective verbalization by lessening the problems associated with failed memory and manual note taking. Using this technique, a domain expert completes a task without providing verbal reports. The knowledge engineer audiotapes or videotapes the session and makes marginal manual notes of behavior to be explored during the subsequent discussion. Immediately after the task has been completed, the knowledge engineer plays the tape back for review. During this review the knowledge engineer can ask questions that probe for knowledge states, decision points, considerations, and data used for solutions. Obviously, a memory aid helps domain experts recall the information that was used to make target decisions.

MANAGING PROCESS TRACING IN KNOWLEDGE ACQUISITION SESSIONS

The sections that follow suggest techniques for structuring and managing process tracing sessions.

Establishing A Methodology

There are numerous ways that knowledge engineers can examine decision making procedures or problem solving priorities and strategies. Both Patton (1985) and Hoffman (1987) described techniques, including some that are similar to those discussed in the following section.

Few guidelines exist for the use of process tracing and protocol analysis in knowledge acquisition. To date, their use in expert system development projects has been haphazard. To complicate matters, each individual method can be presented with varying levels of structure and knowledge engineer involvement. The same method may be presented to the expert in such a way that it requires either concurrent verbalization or retrospective verbalization. Some general suggestions for a process tracing/protocol analysis methodology have been derived from experience on a variety of projects:

1. Select a "standard" set of methods from those described in the following section. Methods include observation, constrained information and solutions, simulated scenarios, episodic analogies, and difficult case analysis.

   (a) Select a method based on specific program needs, type of knowledge to be tapped, and knowledge acquisition session goals (e.g., data generation, data refinement).

   (b) Select methods that are flexible, allowing knowledge engineers to adapt them to scenarios or problems that may vary across domain subsets.

2. Develop a checklist for the use of each method. Encourage knowledge engineers to use the checklist as a job aid in planning and executing the knowledge acquisition session.

3. Provide knowledge engineers with training in each method and technique. Training should include not only background information and general guidelines but also practice in using selected methods. Pairing knowledge engineers for practice sessions (which may or may not be videotaped) increases their confidence and lessens their anxieties about using the technique with a domain expert.

4. Provide knowledge engineers with a suggested format that describes the presentation of these methods to a domain expert and steps for debriefing an expert.

5. Devise a set of guidelines for how the protocol is to be formatted. For example, will each line be numbered? How should engineers record verbalizations such as "uhmm...."? Will the knowledge engineer be expected to record notes or heuristics that derive from the protocol on the form? If so, the format should include a margin for the placement of this information.

6. Train knowledge engineers to derive protocols using the guidelines and formats established earlier. Provide information on how long transcription may take, how to record nonverbal information (e.g., body language), etc.

7. Establish suggestions for reviewing process tracing tapes, protocols, or conclusions with the domain expert.

Involving the Expert

Regardless of the process tracing method or protocol generation technique that is selected, it is crucial to involve the experts prior to the use of the technique. Few experts will have had experience with any of these techniques.

Initial Introduction. Knowledge engineers should submit the knowledge acquisition form to the expert before the knowledge acquisition session. The form should state that the method is process tracing and that the goal is to investigate the decision making or problem solving process related to a specific scenario. The form also should identify the area of consideration and as much description of the scenario as is possible. This information allows the expert to prepare beforehand and to feel less threatened by the task when the session actually takes place.

This Is Not a Test. Although the expert will have reviewed the knowledge acquisition form prior to arriving for the session, he or she may still feel some trepidation. Domain experts may be threatened by these techniques because they may fear "exposure" or that their ideas will be dissected for evaluation during the session. For example, methods that constrain the amount of information presented to the expert require the expert to "solve" the problem with less data than might normally be the case. While these methods help to identify heuristics and prioritization strategies in problem solving, they may make the domain expert feel very uncomfortable. Thus, when the expert arrives for the session the knowledge engineer should explain the goal of the technique in more detail. The knowledge engineer should introduce the scenario or problem and explain that some variable (e.g., information or time) may be restricted to help meet session goals. Upon the conclusion of the session, the knowledge engineer should debrief the expert. Debriefing tasks include summarizing the session for the expert, allowing him or her to express frustration with established limits, explaining what happens next, and thanking the expert.

Follow Up. After the scenario is completed or the problem solved, the bulk of the knowledge engineer's work begins. Tapes must be reviewed to produce protocols, which are analyzed to discern decision rules, alternatives, and major considerations. Follow up may include a variety of procedures, such as those that follow:

- The knowledge engineer and domain expert work together in a structured interview format to review the process tracing tape and derive decision making heuristics.

- The knowledge engineer reviews the process tracing tape and generates protocols before meeting with the domain expert to derive decision making heuristics from the protocols.

- The knowledge engineer reviews the process tracing tape, generates protocols and decision making heuristics, and meets with the domain expert to review the protocols in a structured interview format.

Recording the Experience

Regardless of the method that is selected to stimulate the production of a verbal report, the knowledge engineer will be required to make decisions concerning how that report will be recorded. Recording makes it possible for the knowledge engineer to produce a protocol that can be analyzed to determine decision rules the expert used to solve the problem. As the domain expert reports on decision making considerations, the knowledge engineer records the information by hand or by automatic means (e.g., audiotape and videotape). Producing handwritten records of the report can be tedious. The knowledge engineer will find it difficult to know what to record and may not be able to take notes fast enough to refrain from interrupting the expert's train of thought.

Additionally, note taking may interfere with a knowledge engineer's ability to observe the domain expert's behavioral or nonverbal cues.

Automated recording mechanisms free the knowledge engineer to concentrate on the expert's solution process. In most cases we suggest the use of videotape for process tracing because many cues to the decision process are not verbal. Eye movements and fixations, "fillers" (e.g., "uhmm," "let's see. . ."), and body movements (e.g., head scratching, doodling, pointing) are cues that the domain expert may be considering an issue or may be perplexed. Their occurrence can be noted by a reference to the tape counter reading at the time they occurred. Upon later tape review with the expert, the knowledge engineer can probe for issues under consideration that may have triggered the body movements.

As in the previous example, the knowledge engineer may wish to use a combination of recording methods. He or she may use handwritten notes to record questions that can be explored after the problem has been solved or the time limit is up. In addition, the knowledge engineer may increase the efficiency of tape reviews and transcription by noting decision points in terms of where on the tape they occur.[5]

Sampling the Methods

While each program may devise its own standard set of methods to tap problem solving or decision making knowledge, a number of methods already exist.[6] Most of these differ primarily in the amount of structure that the knowledge engineer imposes on the implementation of the selected technique. In the sections that follow we present a sampling of methods that can be used to observe and isolate a domain expert's problem solving heuristics.

Environmental Observation

Short term environmental observation submerges the knowledge engineer in the domain expert's world and can be a useful method for initial endeavors in the analysis and structuring of a domain (Figure 8-4). Similar techniques have been used in systems analysis prior to the development of a conventional software system. The primary advantage of this method is the increased domain familiarity and understanding afforded the knowledge engineer. Using this technique, the knowledge engineer observes the expert in the course of a "normal" working day, noting major tasks, interactions with other personnel, primary decision constraints, and required "processing" time. While this method may be useful during domain familiarization, it is less so if the knowledge engineer's primary interest is in decision making. Observation alone will not reveal appropriate information about decision alternatives, processes, and attributes. Thus, this method is recommended only in combination with one or more of those that follow.

> For a dam-diagnosis expert system project, knowledge engineers were having difficulty delineating major domain concepts and attributes and determining how they were related. It was then that they suggested a visit to the dam itself. During this trip the expert identified major components, provided labels, and noted associated gauges, and specified normal and abnormal readings. Additionally, the knowledge engineers were able to observe the expert in his day-to-day solution of typical problems and his interaction with peers as they did the same.

Figure 8-4. Environmental Observation Task

Constrained Information

Constrained scenarios or tests are those in which either the (1) problem to be solved or (2) amount of information available to the domain expert is limited. Unlike task analysis procedures, which investigate the expert's completion of a typical task, constrained scenarios require that the expert work with a limited set of information (i.e., some important information may be missing), under a strict time limit, or with a restricted scenario.

The method of constraining the information that is used to solve a problem can be effective in revealing a problem's most salient features and the strategies the expert uses to seek a solution. The knowledge engineer uses this method to isolate specific priorities and identify primary **alternatives** that are considered and their attributes. This analysis helps "fill in gaps" in the knowledge base. The goal is to allow the knowledge engineer to focus on the strategies an expert uses, as opposed to mere factual information, and to identify what the expert considers to be the data that is most critical to the solution. Solving a problem without all of the pertinent data stimulates the expert to think strategically and to select the heuristics and information that are most critical to the solution.

To use this method, the knowledge engineer works with a domain expert to fashion a problem scenario or task that can be solved within the session's time limit. Next, pivotal information is removed from the problem. For example, if the domain expert will be required to diagnose a skin disease, the problem may be constrained by purposefully *not* providing critical diagnostic information (i.e., photos of the rash, specific biopsy reports, etc.). When the task is presented to the expert, the knowledge engineer explains the purpose of the session and that some information intentionally has been removed.

As noted by Hoffman (1987), experts typically are uncomfortable with constrained or restricted situations. They may perceive these types of tasks as "challenges to their ego . . . or expertise" (p. 56). Thus, their first response may be to declare that there is no solution to the problem, given the restrictions that have been presented. Knowledge engineers may need to prompt the expert by reiterating that the process and the priorities and strategies that are revealed are as important as reaching a definitive solution. As the domain expert "solves" the problem, he or she should be encouraged to talk about the solution process unless verbalization will interfere with the decision making process (Figure 8-5).

The knowledge engineer and internal domain expert worked together to select a problem in the domain of dermatology in the development of an expert system to aid in the diagnosis of skin diseases. They chose a set of archive data detailing the diagnosis of dermatitis herpetiformis. Upon presenting the problem to the expert, they included photos of the rash, patient description of the symptoms, and information as to onset and prior treatment, but excluded biopsy reports.

The expert was asked to estimate a diagnosis with the information provided. The knowledge engineer was able to isolate what was most important in the diagnosis and to observe the expert as he related data. When the expert requested a biopsy, he specified what he suspected and what he would need to receive to verify his hypothesis.

Figure 8-5. Constrained Information Task

Constrained Solutions

Constrained solution sessions, a variation on constrained information problems, require that the knowledge engineer remove or manipulate a pivotal variable (e.g., time factor) from an otherwise familiar problem (Hoffman, 1987). For example, in the skin disease example discussed in the previous section, the domain expert was constrained by a lack of critical information. A constrained solution task for the skin disease domain might be structured such that the domain expert is provided with all of the necessary data, but is asked to reach a preliminary diagnosis within a compressed time frame (e.g., 5 minutes).

To conduct a session, the knowledge engineer explains the session's goals to the domain expert. The expert is told that the time factor has been compressed for the purpose of isolating the factors that seem most important (i.e., are considered first) in a diagnosis. The knowledge engineer specifies the arbitrary time window, allowing, for example, 2 minutes for the expert to review the diagnostic information and 3 minutes to formulate and describe the anticipated plan and the reasoning behind its selection (Figure 8-6). In follow-up interviews, the knowledge engineer can clarify the most critical decision factors and explore the effect of imposed constraints on the decision.

> The knowledge engineer and internal domain expert worked together to select a problem in the domain of dermatology in the development of an expert system to aid in the diagnosis of skin diseases. They chose a set of archive data detailing the diagnosis of dermatitis herpetiformis. Upon presenting the problem to the expert, they included photos of the rash, patient description of the symptoms, information as to onset, prior treatment, and biopsy reports.
>
> The knowledge engineer requested that the expert take three minutes to examine the information provided. After that period of time, the materials were put away. The expert they was given three minutes to forumlate hypotheses and supporting information for discussion.

Figure 8-6. Constrained Solution Task

Simulated Scenarios

Scenarios or problems can be simulated by using actual data from a task or problem that has already been solved. Hoffman (1987, p. 57) describes a method called "simulated familiar tasks," in which a common task is performed using archival data. This problem represents a modification of the concurrent verbalization technique discussed previously. Simulated scenarios have been used in knowledge acquisition sessions with physicians in developing an expert system for the diagnosis of a particular class of illness. Given an "illness" or a set of symptoms, physicians were asked to use archival data to estimate a diagnosis. Because the task was now simulated (i.e., not occurring in "real time"), the knowledge engineers were able to "stop the clock" during the session and probe the physician's reasoning strategies or information priorities.

To use this method, the knowledge engineer selects a familiar task (similar to one which may have been used for a task analysis). Next, the knowledge engineer extracts the actual data that comprised the problem and presents that data to the domain expert. (Experts should be told that the data is archival.) As with the other methods, the domain expert should be told the purpose of the session and the fact that his or her reasoning may be interrupted by probes from the knowledge engineer. Once the knowledge engineer presents the data and the scenario, the expert works through the data toward a solution and may or may not be asked to verbalize.[7] At any point in the reasoning process, the knowledge engineer may probe the expert about a specific point, strategy, data being used, or current priorities. Upon completion of the task, the knowledge engineer may wish to compare the original solution to that obtained by the domain expert, or to investigate solution differences with the domain expert or a supporting panel of experts (Figure 8-7). While neither solution will be all "right" or all "wrong," a comparison of features, parameters, and decision points between the decisions may enable the knowledge engineer to view the problem from different angles and develop the system based on this additional expertise.

> During the development of a route planning expert system, knowledge engineers gathered a pilot, navigator, and intelligence specialist together. These experts were presented with archival data including terrain and weather information, mission goals and requirements, known enemy activity in the area, and the original mission plan. They were then given updated information and asked to re-plan a route through the specified territory.
>
> As they worked together to solve the problem, the knowledge engineer noted interactions, questions asked, and information that seemed to be pivotal.

Figure 8-7. Simulated Scenarios Task

Episodic Analogies

This method draws upon experts' tendencies to use analogies to other problems or situations when confronted with a new problem. Researchers (Eberts, 1984; Hoffman, 1987; Klein, 1987) contend that when called upon to solve a problem, experts draw analogies to cases or situations with which they are familiar. Episodic memory of a specific situation's salient features (e.g., cues or indicators, alternative responses, selection criteria, selected alternative, results) can be used as a "benchmark" for comparisons to the new situation. For example, a human factors engineer who is asked to produce a user interface for a new computer system will compare this system to previous ones for which he or she has designed interfaces. Previously used interfaces will be "studied" mentally to extract features (e.g., font size, amount of white space, menus vs. command language) that can be extrapolated to the new interface. The knowledge acquisition sessions in which the physicians used archival data revealed a tendency to predict or estimate a diagnosis based on analogies to cases they had encountered previously.

When using this method, the knowledge engineer should familiarize the domain expert with the session's purpose. Specifically, the knowledge engineer should request that the domain expert note his or her use of analogies to previous problems (Figure 8-8). Items of particular interest include a comparison of similarities/differences to the current scenario, the types of previous scenarios that are triggered or recalled by the task at hand, the identification of the problem's salient features based on experience with other problems, and alternative selection criteria that may be stimulated by previous scenarios.

The knowledge engineer works with an internal expert to select a problem in the aircraft emergency procedures domain. They selected a problem involving the co-occurrence of two emergencies because procedural manuals often spell out actions in response to only one emergency at a time.

The domain expert is given the "emergency" and relevant supporting information and is asked to suggest solutions. In particular, he is encouraged to note analogies between this problem and similar problems he has solved. During the ensuing discussion, the expert's past experiences help to reveal salient features of the current problem. He then identifies alternative solutions and suggests anticipated consequences. As he works, criteria for selecting among the alternatives are posted on the board.

Figure 8-8. Episodic Analogies Tasks

Analysis of Difficult Cases

What really separates the behavior of an expert from that of an individual with intermediate skills? Both may be able to solve common problems and deal with tasks that are commonplace within the domain. Both may be equally able to provide domain facts and basic heuristics. When confronted with a particularly difficult problem or case, the individual with intermediate skills generally defers to the advice of an expert.[8]

If knowledge acquisition sessions are confined to discussions of the ordinary, the expert system can be expected to function only as an advisor with intermediate-level skills. Such systems may even be unable to reach effective solutions to mundane cases. If the kind of knowledge an expert uses when solving the really hard problems can be tapped, the expert system can function at a much higher ability level, which will enhance its acceptance in the user community.

The analysis of difficult cases is appropriate when the knowledge engineer realizes that the developing knowledge base lacks subtle aspects of expert reasoning. Knowledge engineers can structure a session to explore difficult cases in several ways. First, they may work with an expert (prior to the session with another domain expert) to compile archival data and a scenario from an actual case that could be termed "difficult." In the session itself, the knowledge engineer presents a brief description of a problem to the domain expert, using data from an actual case that has been solved. The domain expert uses the data to work toward a conclusion or a suggested approach to a solution. If more that one solution path is mentioned, the knowledge engineer should determine the **attributes** (i.e., characteristics) and values for each alternative solution. Once a solution has been selected, the knowledge engineer may present further data to investigate its effect on the suggested solution. In some cases it may be useful to present the actual case and its solution to the expert once a conclusion has been reached. If differences in solutions exist, they can be explored to identify the reasons behind diverse solution paths; however, many domain experts may be threatened by this type of exercise (Figure 8-9).

During development on an expert system to aid in decision making in the auto maintenance domain, the domain expert was asked to bring in archival data and a problem description for a difficult case. He provides a brief description of the case, detailing what made it "difficult" and what the primary solution paths were. The knowledge engineer prompts him to verbalize the attributes and values for the solutions. Following this discussion the expert explains why he chose the solution he did and what the result was.

If the knowledge engineer wanted more information, she could follow-up by presenting the same problem to another domain expert and comparing solutions.

Figure 8-9. Analysis of Difficult Cases Task

Hoffman (1987) suggests another approach to difficult case analysis, in which the knowledge engineer asks selected experts to record (e.g., audiotape or annotate) difficult cases as they experience them. These notations may include case description, alternative solutions, reasoning for solution selection, and results. In yet another variation, the knowledge engineer may ask key domain experts to describe tough problems they have solved, differentiating them from easy problems. Finally, domain experts may be asked to "criticize" or evaluate a solution that has been obtained from a novice or person of moderate expertise.

Combining Methods

Knowledge engineers may wish to combine elements of the aforementioned methods. For example, the knowledge engineer may devise a problem that gives only limited information and allows the domain expert only 5 minutes to suggest a solution. When using this method it is important that the knowledge engineer encourage the domain expert to verbalize about possible alternatives *and* the missing information that might have helped confirm or reject each alternative. While domain experts rarely like this type of problem, it can help the knowledge engineer isolate highly ranked solution hypotheses, key information to test each hypothesis, and general strategies for solving problems with uncertain or missing information.

Matching Method to Goal

Selecting a method for stimulating verbal reports depends on many variables, including the task to be explored, the session's goal, and the project guidelines. Each of these techniques produces specific types of information. Figure 8-10 presents a comparison of the different methods and portrays some of the strengths and weaknesses of each.

METHOD	STRENGTH	WEAKNESS
Observation	• Overall view of expert's tasks • Facilitates domain facilitation • KE views decision making	• Time-consuming • Inefficient for expert
Constrained Information/ Constrained Solution	• Reveals salient features of a problem • Reveals strategies	• Expert discomfort • Depends on task selection • Depends on variable restriction
Simulated Scenarios	• Use of archived data • Not "real-time" • Can interrupt solution process	• Requires access to archival data • Requires expert assistance in formulating scenario
Episodic Analogies	• Stimulates use of past experiences • Insight into salient features of a problem	• Requires expert to discuss past problem solving • May interfere with other strategies
Difficult Cases	• Access to data that is infrequently used • Access to methods of combining and prioritizing data	• Difficult to plan for • Relies on expert to record

Figure 8-10. Comparison of Methods
(Adapted from R. Hoffman, "The problem of extracting the knowledge of experts from the perspective of experimental psychology," AI Magazine, 8:2 (1987), pp. 53-76. Used with permission from AI Magazine and Dr. Robert Hoffman.)

EXTRACTING KNOWLEDGE FROM PROCESS TRACING SESSIONS

The goal of process tracing is to determine the decision making processes used in the completion of a task or the solution of a problem. Typically, process tracing requires that knowledge engineers translate verbal reports or other cues into protocols or notes that they can analyze. Using the notes, the knowledge engineer can trace the domain expert's decision making process from problem presentation to problem solution. The next section presents issues in translating sessions, discusses transcription techniques, and describes a framework for protocol analysis.

Translating Sessions to Protocols

Once the knowledge acquisition session has been conducted, resulting in a recorded or annotated "history" of the session, the knowledge engineer translates session information into protocols for later analysis. Session information that provides cues to the expert's decision making process may be both verbal and nonverbal in nature.

Using Verbal Cues

Verbal cues consist of both the actual words a communicator uses and the paralinguistic cues (e.g., "uhmm," tone of voice) that accompany a communication. Both types of verbal communication can be used to develop protocols from a process tracing knowledge acquisition session. For example, verbatim information can be represented in regular text, while paralinguistic cues that might indicate cognitive processing, confusion, or deeper thought may be represented parenthetically.

Analyzing Nonverbal Cues

A substantial amount of interpersonal communication is nonverbal in nature. While this type of behavior may be laden with information (i.e., eye movement analysis), it is difficult to monitor and interpret and may require the use of expensive equipment. Thus, the choice of whether to note their occurrence within protocols must be made by each individual project. Listed below are some nonverbal behaviors that (1) can be cues to cognitive processing or (2) may be used to stimulate discussion of the considerations that coincided with various cues:

- Pushing away from materials
- Moving options side-by-side
- Sighing, grunting
- Scratching/touching head, brow
- Chewing pencil, lip
- Squinting
- Doodling
- Crossing arms, legs
- Walking away.

Transcription Techniques

Because transcription is time-intensive and tedious, its value to the program must be weighed carefully. In our work and conversations with others who are transcribing knowledge acquisition sessions we have found that the transcription task takes *two to three times longer than the knowledge acquisition session itself.* This is because the knowledge engineer must

- Extract what the domain expert is saying
- Monitor to whom each comment should be attributed
- Indicate pauses and nonverbal cues, as well as conversation-based information.

Because transcription is so time-consuming, a decision must be made whether to follow strict transcription procedures to create formal protocols (i.e., transcribe every word) or to take informal notes from the session videotape (i.e., summarize major points). If transcription is required, the format used should enable easy access, indexing, and notation or coding. Figure 8-11 portrays one format for protocol development. The line numbers on the left-hand side of the page enable the knowledge engineer to access where a specific piece of information was encountered. This format can be useful in later reviews of session data with the domain expert and enables the knowledge engineer to document domain information from its elicitation.

LINE	TRANSCRIPTION	RULES/COMMENTS

KA Session #_____   Date_____ Time_____
KE_____   Expert_____

LINE	TRANSCRIPTION	RULES/COMMENTS
001	TAPE 000: Well (pause) if I was planning a	
002	trip from Dallas to Brownwood...(traces a	
003	route with finger) I (uhmm) would first consider	
004	what my priority was. I mean,...well...is it	
005	more important that I get there fast or...Give	
006	me a minute to check on some mileage.	
007		
008	TAPE 010:	
009	OK, well, I have added up mileage on the two	
010	routes that look to be the most direct. Now	
011	you see that this one (points) is actually a	
012	little shorter in distance. But you see that	
013	it goes right through Dallas and Fort Worth.	
014	Hmmm. Wouldn't want to do that during	
015	rush hour. (laughs)	
016		
017	TAPE 015:	
020	OK. Now, well, I think I am ready to list a	
021	couple of alternatives, like you asked (goes	
022	to board). Road A, there, and here are	
023	the reasons it is a good one (writes). Now	
024	road B, well, it may not look so good, but	
025	it doesn't go through major roads...well, I'm	
026	getting ahead of myself. Let's see. I'll...	
027	uhmm...I'll just jot down reasons it is good.	
028	There's two lists. OK. I'll prioritize the	
029	things under each road choice (writes).	

Figure 8-11. Sample Protocol Transcription Form

The text in the center of the form represents *either* the actual transcription of the session (formal procedures) *or* an interpretation of its primary content (informal procedure). On the far right-hand side of the page is an area that can be used for coding or making notes of specific session data.

After the protocol has been worked into the desired format, the knowledge engineer can analyze the propositional and decision-oriented knowledge it evidences. Hoffman (1987) reports that the time required to code the transcript for propositional content may take from one to five minutes per transcript page and initially requires at least two independent judges (until evidence shows that the frequency of their agreement is high).

While the inter-rater reliability can enhance knowledge verification and validation efforts, it is too expensive for many programs to implement. If sparing two knowledge engineers to 'code' or translate transcriptions into analysis frameworks and decision rules is prohibitive, programs should investigate the following options. First, on-staff knowledge engineers could all be trained to use a standard set of analysis frameworks and to analyze content based on an identified set of decision rules. Second, automated tools could be used to increase the efficiency of this task and to apply standards across a program. The sections that follow provide information on different types of analysis frameworks and decision rules that could be used to analyze protocols.

Selecting the Analysis Framework

After protocols have been generated, they can be analyzed to identify (1) the basic alternatives that the expert seemed to consider at specific decision points and (2) resulting actions on the part of the expert. Defining a framework that can be used to trace the decision making process is essential to the usefulness of process tracing and protocol analysis. Knowledge engineers should establish analysis frameworks (either automated programs or manual guidelines) that meet the following characteristics:

- Enable the identification of critical vocabulary or terminology for actions, dimensions of attributes, attribute values, and/or attractiveness weightings

- Enable the knowledge engineer to apply a preliminary structure to the data extracted from the protocols

- Provide a bridge between data evident in the protocols and the representation scheme into which the data will be required to fit.

Svenson (1979) presented a series of frameworks that knowledge engineers can adapt for use in depicting a domain expert's decisions. Knowledge engineers can classify an expert's decisions according to alternatives, attributes, aspects, and attractiveness (Waldron, 1985). Each of these elements is described in the following paragraphs.

Alternatives

At the simplest level of analysis, an expert's decision making can be classified according to the major alternatives that the expert identifies. **Alternatives** represent possible actions on the expert's part and probable outcomes as a consequence of the selection of an alternative. If an expert is monitoring gauge readings to troubleshoot a faulty system function, he or she will have several alternatives for a situation in which one of the readings approaches an "out-of-upper-range" reading. One alternative may be to consult readings of other gauges prior to taking action; another may be to respond by physically switching off a system or by manually decreasing some important input to the subsystem. Each alternative may have different outcomes, which the knowledge engineer should explore in terms of costs and benefits.

Attributes

Similar to the manner in which concepts can be defined by attributes, alternatives also can be defined by attributes. **Attributes** are the separate components or dimensions that define an alternative. For example, in buying a car, most of us analyze the problem by devising alternatives that are defined or expressed by attributes such as those that appear in Figure 8-12.

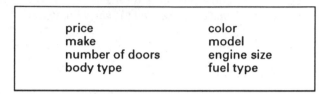

price   color
make   model
number of doors engine size
body type   fuel type

Figure 8-12. Attributes for Car Selection Alternatives

Aspects

Just as each alternative can be expressed more specifically by its attributes, so do **aspects** further define attributes. Aspects are the values that can be assigned to a specific attribute. In Figure 8-12, for example, eight car selection attributes are listed. Each can have a number of aspects that might be considered in our decision. *Model* , for example, might have aspects of *Tercel*, *Camaro*, or *Firebird*, among others. Other aspects for attributes are depicted in Figure 8-13.

ATTRIBUTE	ASPECTS
Car Color	Silver
	Candy Apple Red
	Sky Blue
	Dark Navy
	White
	Crimson
Fuel Type	Unleaded
	Regular
	Diesel
Make	Ford
	Chevrolet
	Toyota
	Pontiac

Figure 8-13. Aspects for Selected Car Attributes

Attractiveness

The analysis of an alternative's overall attractiveness provides another dimension that the knowledge engineer can explore by reviewing the protocols and probing the selection of alternatives with the domain expert. **Attractiveness** is the psychological value, weight, or strength of an aspect. Attractiveness should reflect the domain expert's analysis of an alternative's costs versus benefits. It usually is possible to represent attractiveness with a single value (Waldron, 1985), which can then be used to compare alternatives on a single aspect. Once the alternatives and their aspects have been compared, they may be rank ordered based on their overall attractiveness.

Using the car example, we can suppose that an analysis of a domain expert's protocol indicated an inclination toward two alternatives. Each alternative would represent the lease or purchase of a different type of car. Each type could be represented by numerous aspects, such as color, price, and fuel. More specifically, each aspect may be "rated" according to its attractiveness. Thus, if unleaded was the desired type of fuel, it might be rated a "2," while diesel might be rated a less desirable "1." When the aspects of an alternative have all been rated according to attractiveness, they may be rank ordered to assist in the selection process.

Determining Decision Rules

Protocols can also be examined by analyzing the **decision rules** (or overall approach) that a domain expert seems to be using throughout the decision making process. Research in the area of human decision making has identified typical, naturally recurring decision rules. Knowledge engineers can employ either process tracing or induction tools to extract the decision rules that an expert is using. Some of the basic "rules" that a domain expert may use in making decisions or solving problems appear in Figure 8-14. Brief directions for recognizing or using each rule are presented in the paragraphs that follow.

Dominance rule	Conjunctive decision rule
Disjunctive decision rule	Lexicographic decision rule
Elimination by aspects rule	Maximum attribute-attractiveness rule

Figure 8-14. Categories of Major Decision Rules

Dominance Rule

The dominance rule entails a comparison of the attributes for alternatives in search of the superior alternative (Lee, 1971).

1. The expert compares alternative A with alternative B by examining the attributes of each.
2. If alternative A is better than alternative B on at least one attribute (i.e., higher attractiveness values), and not worse than alternative B on all other attributes, the expert selects alternative A.

Conjunctive Decision Rule

The application of this rule depends on selecting criterion values for each critical attribute and discarding any alternative that has even one attribute that does not meet the preset criterion value (Coombs, 1964; Dawes, 1964a; Svenson, 1979).

1. The expert specifies a set of criterion values for each attribute that is critical to an alternative.
2. The expert compares the values of the attributes for the chosen alternative with the set of criterion values. The value of the chosen alternative attributes should equal or exceed the criterion value the expert initially set.
3. If an alternative fails to meet the criterion on any attribute, it is removed from consideration.

Disjunctive Decision Rule

This rule also requires that a set of criterion values be specified, but focuses on the selection of an alternative in which at least one attribute exceeds the criterion while all others fall equal to or beneath the criterion value (Coombs, 1964; Dawes, 1964a; Svenson, 1979).

1. The expert specifies a set of criterion values for each attribute that is critical to an alternative.
2. At least one attribute associated with an alternative must exceed the criterion value for the alternative to be acceptable.
3. All other aspects of other alternatives can be equal to or fall below the criterion values.

Lexicographic Decision Rule

The lexicographic technique is a simple rank ordering of attributes of each alternative according to importance (Fishburn, 1974).

1. The expert rank orders attributes of each alternative, listing the most important attribute first.
2. The expert compares the most important (e.g., top-ranked) attribute of each alternative.
3. The expert selects the alternative that is most attractive on the most important attribute.
4. If two aspects of this attribute are equally attractive, the expert compares the two competing aspects of the next most important attribute.

Elimination by Aspects Rule

This rule combines aspects of the lexicographic and conjunctive rules (Twersky, 1972).

1. The expert specifies a set of criterion values for each attribute that is critical to an alternative.
2. The expert rank orders the attributes of each alternative, listing the most important attribute first.

3. The expert compares the values of the rank ordered attributes.
4. If the attributes for an alternative do not equal or exceed the conjunctive criteria for its attributes, the expert eliminates it from consideration.
5. The expert repeats the procedure with attributes that fall lower in the lexicographic order to eliminate alternatives whose aspect values do not equal or exceed the conjunctive criteria.

Maximum Attribute Attractiveness Rule

This rule enables the identification of the most attractive alternative based on the sum of all values for an alternative's attributes (Svenson, 1979).

1. The expert sets criterion values for attributes for each alternative.
2. The expert rank orders the values for each attribute against competing attribute values. Ranking can be as simple as "equal to, better than, worse than."
3. The expert identifies the alternative with the most positive values.

Refining the Analysis

Cognitive psychologists have wrestled with the issues of accuracy and representation of decision making behavior and the information it provides for decades. Limitations around which they worked are similar to those facing knowledge engineers who use process tracing and analyze the resulting protocols. Omissions of important decision making data are probable. Data eventually must be provided to correct these omissions. Inconsistencies between verbal and nonverbal behavior may be noted and will need to be investigated. Inaccuracies must be expected, isolated, and alleviated. Thus, once the initial analysis is complete, the knowledge engineer works with the domain expert to refine it. Refinement of decision making heuristics should include tasking the domain expert to review not only the facts that were used, but also the *interrelationships* of those facts and the procedures that were undertaken or considered. While a domain expert's initial review of information derived from a structured interview may consist of verifying English-version session notes, information derived from process tracing sessions will require more complex analysis.

Coded representations of the knowledge may not be a good tool for the domain expert to use in refinement because they can be too confusing. On the other hand, text descriptions of the knowledge or pseudocode may be too lengthy and complex. Thus, the knowledge engineer and domain expert may wish to use a combination of protocols, graph techniques (i.e., cognitive maps), computer-based drawing and software design tools, and prototype system evaluation during review and refinement. Once the knowledge engineer has refined the information, he or she can plan structured interview sessions to acquire specific information that the knowledge base will require to solve domain problems.

ENDNOTES

[1] The authors wish to acknowledge Vince Waldron, Kathy Waldron, and Robert Hoffman, Ph.D. whose ideas and reviews contributed to the content of this chapter.

[2] Background information on the disadvantages of verbal reporting is summarized in Appendix B.

[3] The additional benefit of this variation is that not only is problem-solving information verbalized, but system designers also can view how a "typical" user might approach a sample problem.

[4] In addition, disagreements can be resolved by using some of the techniques provided in Chapter 9, which investigates the use of multiple experts in more detail.

[5] For a discussion of the pros and cons of manual, audio, and video recording, refer to Chapter 7.

[6] Knowledge engineers may recognize that they have used many of the methods described in this section. We have simply labeled and described a process for applying them. In doing so, we acknowledge the work of Robert Hoffman, Ph.D., who has reported similar methods in his article, "The problem of extracting the knowledge of experts from the perspective of experimental psychology," AI Magazine 8:2 (Summer 1987), 53-76.

[7] Whether or not the expert should verbalize as the problem is being solved depends on the nature of the task and the type of knolwedge the problem's solution taps.

[8] Experts' skills are more highly polished, not only because they know more and have gathered more cases to use in analogical problem solving, but also because they know how to use what they know to solve a problem.

SUGGESTED READINGS

Hoffman, Robert. "The problem of extracting the knowledge of experts from the perspective of experimental psychology." AI Magazine, 8:2 (1987), 53-67.

Puff, C. R. Handbook of Research Methods in Human Memory and Cognition, (1982) New York: Academic Press.

APPLICATION

Route Planning Exercise

Materials Required: Road map of your state, taping equipment (if desired), paper, pencil.

Directions: Work in pairs or groups of threes to complete this exercise. If you work in threes, let one person be the knowledge engineer and allow for the use of two experts. Take turns by rotating the role of knowledge engineer.

1. Select a city on the map to serve as your destination point. The destination point should be accessible by many different types of roads. The departure point for your exercise is the city in which you live.

2. Assign the roles of knowledge engineer and expert.

3. Role play a process tracing knowledge acquisition session in which the expert is asked to plan a route from the departure point to the destination point. (Many routes are possible; the goal is to find out how the expert makes decisions to choose one route over another.)

4. To complete the exercise, refer to the descriptions of activities for each participant.

Knowledge Engineer: Select any protocol analysis framework that you think would be appropriate (e.g., "think-aloud," discussion, retrospective verbalization, retrospective verbalization with a memory aid). Select a process tracing method. You may present this as a simulated scenario, or you may wish to constrain some information or solution variable. Introduce the session and its purpose. As the expert works through the problem, record notes for later discussion. Look for evidence of the types of decision rules being used. When the process is complete, question the expert to discover what alternatives were considered. Explore the attributes, aspects, and attractiveness of various alternatives.

Domain Expert: As you consider the task, verbalize about each idea that comes to mind. Let the knowledge engineer know what types of alternatives are available, what the attributes (e.g., miles, time on trip, countryside, road type, starting time) of the alternatives are, which attributes are more important than others, etc.

9

Acquiring Knowledge from Multiple Experts

Characteristics of Problems That Require Multiple Experts

    Inconsistency Between Problem Domain and Available Expertise
    Subdivision of Knowledge Among Multiple Specialists
    Alternate Solution Sets

Using Multiple Experts

    Considerations for Using Multiple Experts
    Multiple Experts -- Pros and Cons

Approaches to the Use of Multiple Experts

    Individual Consultation
    Group Consultation

Techniques for Working with Multiple-Expert Teams

    Brainstorming
    Consensus Decision Making
    Nominal-Group Technique
    Computer-Facilitated Sessions

Managing and Accommodating Multiple Knowledge Sources
    Documentation
    Conflict Resolution

INTRODUCTION

Most of the literature related to expert system development alludes to the troublesome nature of knowledge acquisition, even when only a single domain expert has contributed to the knowledge base. The already difficult knowledge acquisition process becomes even more complicated when the expert system being developed requires that knowledge engineers interact with multiple experts, either as individuals or in a group. "[I]f knowledge acquisition for an expert system with a single expert can be described as a bottleneck, acquisition from multiple experts, especially in a group setting, has the potential to become a 'log jam.' " (McGraw & Seale, 1987, p. 166).

As complex as multiple-expert knowledge acquisition is, it can be argued that multiple viewpoints can enhance the functionality of an expert system. Expert systems that are developed based on a single, perhaps narrow line of reasoning do not emulate most real-life decision making. Real-life decision making in the courts, financial, or other institutions rarely reflects a single viewpoint. Reboh (1983) notes that it is not uncommon for groups in these institutions to support opposite sides of an issue, enlisting the services of respected experts who may suggest conflicting courses of action (p. 145). Even if a group of experts in a given domain arrive at a similar conclusion, it is difficult to ascertain whether they used the same reasoning processes to do so.

Expert systems based on inputs from multiple domain experts may reflect multiple lines of reasoning. These multiple viewpoints may enable the expert system to function as a better *collective* expert than any one of the individual domain experts who contributed to its reasoning (LeClair, 1985). The content within this chapter addresses key issues in using multiple experts for expert system development. Initially, we discuss considerations for using multiple domain experts in knowledge acquisition efforts. Next, we provide general information on using multiple experts, as separate individuals or in small group settings (i.e., multiple expert teams or panels). Then we provide empirical information on the selection and application of knowledge acquisition techniques that are appropriate with multiple domain experts. Finally, we address ways to document and incorporate multiple lines of reasoning and conflict resolution within the knowledge base.[1]

Objectives

This chapter presents information that will enhance the use of multiple domain experts in the knowledge acquisition for expert system development. Specifically, it enables readers to accomplish the following:
- Recognize problems that may require the use of multiple experts
- Recognize considerations in the decision to use multiple experts
- Identify primary approaches to the use of multiple experts
- Identify requirements for the use of multiple experts, both for small groups and individual expert knowledge acquisition sessions
- Specify and use techniques that are appropriate for specific phases and goals of multiple expert sessions
- Identify methods that may be used to track and accommodate contributions from multiple domain experts.

Key Terms

multiple-expert team	brainstorming	nominal-group technique
uncertainty	probability	upward-ripple paranoia
consensus decision making	computer-facilitated session	multiexpert systems
meta rule		

CHARACTERISTICS OF PROBLEMS THAT REQUIRE MULTIPLE EXPERTS

Complex, real-life problems are seldom so simple that they can be solved based on consultations with a single expert. More often than not, a complex problem requires access to different types of knowledge and thus, to more than one expert. In circumstances where a single expert does exist, it is usually difficult to meet with that individual owing to demands on his or her time. The following sections create a framework for understanding the need for multiple experts in the solution of complex problems.

Inconsistency Between Problem Domian and Available Expertise

Although many expert systems seem to be developed with what could be termed the "single-expert" approach, closer investigation reveals contributions from a number of individuals. According to LeClair (1985), these multiple "cooperating" expert systems are typical. Although the knowledge engineer may rely on a single, predominant expert during knowledge-base development, the expert system's functionality ultimately results in the "aggregation of expertise from many experts" (LeClair, 1985, p. 187) who contribute during knowledge-base review and refinement.

The use of a single expert in the development of an expert system may be easier logistically but is often not practical, owing to an inconsistency between the problem domain and available expertise. This inconsistency may result from a mismatch between the the expert's expertise and knowledge base requirements, or from an inability to tap *the* identified expert. Access to an individual who represents the pinnacle of expertise in a given domain is extraordinarily difficult; demands on such an expert constrict his or her availability for knowledge acquisition sessions. This often necessitates the use of additional experts or special approaches to using multiple experts. For example, developers may identify a single expert as the "final" authority, who verifies the validity of information acquired from other experts (McGraw & Seale, 1987).

Subdivision of Knowledge Among Mutliple Specialists

The use of a single individual as the domain expert may be efficient when (1) the system is required to problem solve in restricted domains or (2) a single, easily identified expert embodies most of the expertise the system is required to emulate. A common stimulus for the use of multiple experts is the development of an expert system that requires diverse subsets of knowledge. In this case, it is unlikely that a single individual could be termed an expert in each of these knowledge subsets. Instead, different experts, each of whom specializes in a particular subset of the domain, would be consulted.[2]

LeClair (1985) refers to the use of multiple experts because of domain segmentation as a multiple-expert knowledge system.

As depicted in Figure 9-1, developing an expert system to provide diagnostic information for a single, specific area may require the services of only one qualified expert. However, developing an expert system to provide diagnostic information for both the hydraulic *and* electrical systems of a piece of machinery requires the services of individuals who are qualified in their respective domains.

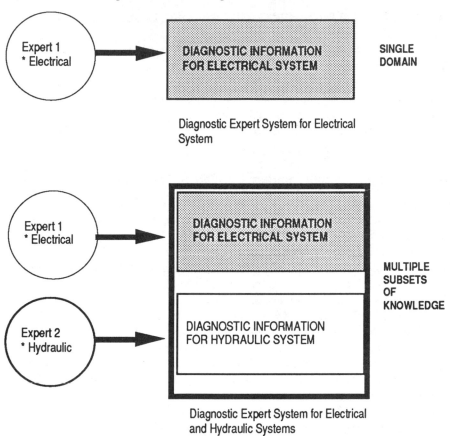

Figure 9-1. Multiple Experts and Subdivisions of Knowledge
Adapted from McGraw, K. and M. Seale, "Knowledge elicitation with multiple experts: Considerations and techniques," Artificial Intelligence Review 2:1 (1988), pp. 32. Used with permission.

For example, Hunter (TI Satellite Symposium, 1985) related the use of multiple experts in the development of diagnostic expert systems for an integrated circuit manufacturing facility. For one of these systems the experts consisted of a machine vendor engineer, an equipment engineer, a process engineer, and a senior equipment technician. Each represented a different specialty or area of expertise. As multiple experts, they provided the different subsets of knowledge that enabled a pervasive coverage of the diagnostic domain.

Grenander (1985) noted the need for multiple specialists or experts in the development of Devisor, a prototype deep-space mission planner developed by the Jet Propulsion Laboratory for unmanned spacecraft. Devisor integrates the information that was contributed from a total of seven technical and management specialists, including AI researchers, a spacecraft specialist, a sequencing expert, and three managers.

Another example of an expert system that required the use of multiple experts is FRESH, developed by Texas Instruments and BTG. This system required the acquisition of considerable naval knowledge, from the type and capabilities of various ships,[3] to operational expertise (McGraw & Seale, 1987b). Multiple experts were necessary because of the various subsets of problem-solving expertise that the knowledge base required.

Alternate Solution Sets

Previous authors (Mittal and Dym, 1985) have established that it is "simplistic" to assume that one expert's rules constitute expertise. Although some domain problems have restricted solution sets and thus, fewer alternatives to consider in the decision-making process, others may have numerous solutions and alternative paths toward those solutions. The use of a single domain expert for knowledge acquisition in complex, highly dynamic domains may not produce knowledge base content diverse enough to handle anticipated scenarios. Using more than one expert allows knowledge engineers to study different problem solving approaches, considerations, and applications of the same sets of knowledge.

For example, Ford Motor Company's robotic center in Dearborn, Michigan has developed an expert system for use in servicing and training their Asea robot system. According to the principal automation engineer in this facility, using more than one expert allows developers to consider more than one way of viewing the same problem. As he notes (TI Satellite Symposium, 1985), "A guy may be an expert, but that doesn't mean he is always right. He may be an expert, but that doesn't mean he can always *explain* what he means."

USING MULTIPLE EXPERTS

Many existing expert systems could be described as "single"-expert systems. That is, their knowledge bases primarily reflect input from a single expert, perhaps combined with other information from secondary knowledge sources (e.g., training manuals). Some circumstances preclude the exclusive use of a single domain expert, necessitating that the engineering team consider using multiple experts. Multiple experts may be used in any of several ways, including
- Individually
- As primary and secondary experts
- In small groups
- As a panel of experts.

To use multiple experts *individually* simply means that more than one expert is consulted on a regular basis during the development of the expert system, but these experts are not required to function as a group. Using multiple experts in this manner relieves the knowledge engineer from the stress associated with multiple expert teams (i.e., those who function as a small group). However, this approach requires that the knowledge engineer have an approach for resolving conflicts and handling multiple lines of reasoning. Owing to differences in background, training, communication abilities, and perception of the problem, each expert may have a different opinion and may disagree with information provided by another expert.

Primary and secondary experts refers to the use of a single domain expert as the primary expert, who is responsible for validating information retrieved from other domain experts. Knowledge engineers may consult the primary expert at the beginning of the program for guidance in domain familiarization, refinement of knowledge acquisition plans, and the identification of individuals who may be asked to serve as secondary experts. Content-oriented knowledge acquisition sessions take place with secondary experts, who are easier to access than the primary expert. The primary expert is consulted periodically to review the results of knowledge acquisition sessions (e.g., heuristics, resulting rules). This use of multiple experts has the same plusses and minuses as the use of multiple experts individually, except that the primary expert serves as the focal point for ongoing conflict resolution in the case of diverse responses from secondary experts.

Multiple experts who are consulted in a small-group setting provide the knowledge engineer with a "community of information." The knowledge engineer is able to provide information once, and then monitor responses from more than one domain expert. Working with small groups of experts allows the knowledge engineer to observe (1) alternate approaches to the solution of a problem and (2) the key points made in solution-oriented discussions among experts. However, working with multiple experts in a group situation requires special planning and skills on the part of the knowledge engineer.

To meet goals for verification and validation of on-going development efforts, some programs choose to establish a panel or council of experts. These individuals typically meet together at times scheduled by the developer for the purpose of reviewing knowledge base efforts, content, and plans. In many cases, the functionality of the expert system itself is tested against the expertise of such a panel. Key issues in the use of a panel that serves these purposes include member selection, scheduling constraints, and group type (e.g., distributed power, in which all members are equally powerful, or centralized power, in which a single leader is appointed or allowed to emerge). For purposes of the discussions that follow, knowledge engineers may consider expert panels to have the same benefits and problems as those associated with multiple experts in small- group situations.

Considerations such as available expertise, subdivision of the knowledge base, and customer requirements will impact the decision of how to use multiple experts. The following sections discuss (1) factors that should be considered in deciding how to use multiple experts and (2) some of the costs and benefits of using multiple experts.

Consideration for Using Multiple Experts

Three factors are important in the decision to use multiple experts individually, in small groups, or in a combination of settings. These include:
- The identification and separability of the knowledge subsets
- The issue of group versus individual judgement
- The knowledge engineer's abilities in knowledge acquisition techniques, group dynamics, and group leadership.

Identification and Separability of the Knowledge

Knowledge within a complex domain consists not only of basic definitions and concepts, but also of more intricate specificities and subsets of knowledge. The more complex the domain, the more numerous and detailed the subsets of knowledge. For example, some individuals may possess knowledge about submarines at a global or general level. Because submarines represent a complex domain, key individuals may possess a great deal of knowledge about a specific feature of the submarine, such as life-support systems. Others may know a lot about submarine tactics but nothing about life-support systems.

Knowledge engineering within a domain in which the knowledge subsets can be identified and, to some extent, separated exemplifies a situation in which multiple experts may be extremely useful. If subsets of knowledge, or subtasks within the domain can be isolated and identified, a domain expert with expertise in each of the identified areas may be consulted on an individual basis. If the subsets or subtasks seem inextricably interwoven, multiple experts still can be useful. However, since in this circumstance a decision concerning one subset may influence another subset or subtask, it may be more prudent to consult multiple experts in a small group setting. In this environment the knowledge engineer may observe the problem-solving techniques and "rules" used by each expert and the resulting interactions in the decision-making process.

Group versus Individual Judgement

The quality of the information that a knowledge engineer acquires from knowledge sources may be affected by the number of knowledge sources and by whether information was obtained from an individual or from a group. Some authors believe that on the average, small group judgment tends to be better than individual judgment (Eisenson et al., 1963). Others believe that group judgments are at least as good as the judgment of an average individual and may be superior. As Shaw (1932) discovered, the major advantage of using groups may be the group's ability to recognize and reject *incorrect* solutions and suggestions.

Whether or not group judgments are superior may depend on the type of task or problem that is being solved (Shaw, 1976). For example, a group of experts may be better able to solve a problem than an individual working alone when the task can be partially divided into related subtasks (i.e., "divide and conquer") and each individual member's skills matched with particular subtasks (Steiner, 1972). This approach allows the knowledge engineer to break the problem down into subproblems, which domain experts can then "solve" as they interact and share expertise. As the resulting solutions are integrated, dependencies among subareas and dissonant solutions may be discussed and resolved by the group.

The effectiveness of a group seems to be correlated with group size and type of task. For example, while Smith (TI Satellite Symposium, 1985) found that having a second expert helped clarify the communication between the expert(s) and knowledge engineer, having more than five experts would have been problematic. His intuition is supported by research indicating that groups of five or less are most effective for tasks in which members make decisions based on the evaluation of exchanged information (Slatter, 1958). In the Texas Instruments AI Lab, successful knowledge acquisition sessions with multiple experts have occurred with one knowledge engineer and up to three experts (McGraw & Seale, 1987).

Knowledge Engineer Capabilities

In addition to being able to use the knowledge acquisition techniques presented in this textbook, knowledge engineers should also be skilled in the areas portrayed in Figure 9-2 before working with multiple experts.

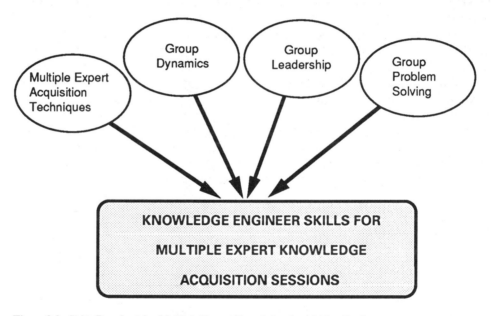

Figure 9-2. Skills Required for Multiple Expert Knowledge Acquisition Sessions

These skills are important, because as the number of members in a multiple-expert team increases, so do the subgroup relationships or interpersonal interactions (McGraw & Seale, 1987b, 1988). With a single expert, the only group-dynamics issue is the interaction between domain expert and knowledge engineer. As more experts are added, the knowledge engineer becomes concerned not only with the initial relationship (i.e., domain expert-knowledge engineer), but also with the relationship(s) (1) between each expert and the knowledge engineer and (2) among all of the domain experts in the group.

The type and quality of these intragroup relationships have a direct impact on the success of the knowledge acquisition session. In fact, they may even influence the expert's willingness to interact with the group or the knowledge engineer again.

Multiple Experts--Pros and Cons

The decision to use multiple experts is not trivial. It results in many subsequent considerations, such as how to handle the diverse opinions that may be forthcoming. Research that can help knowledge engineers weigh the benefits and costs of using multiple experts for knowledge acquisition is presented in the sections that follow.

Benefits of Multiple-Expert Participation

Who among us, if told that we have a fatal disease, would *not* seek a second opinion for either the diagnosis itself or the prescribed treatment? Likewise, presidents of large organizations typically confer with multiple experts (e.g., board of directors, senior management staff) during decision making. In real life, we rarely rely on the expertise of a single individual, because we know that experts differ in respect to training, background, specialties, and experience. Additionally, relying on a single expert may result in our being over-dependent on that expert; we are at the mercy of scheduling and access problems. The same arguments can be applied to knowledge acquisition for expert system development. If the purpose of the development process is to build a decision-aiding tool for use by experts and novices alike, extracting expertise from multiple domain experts can be beneficial. Primary benefits include increased ease of access and strengths associated with multiple lines of reasoning.

Increased ease of access. The use of a single individual as the domain expert in the design of an expert system is usually efficient when the system will be required to problem-solve in a restricted domain or when a single, easily identified expert embodies most of the expertise the system requires. However, access to a single person who is recognized as "the" expert in a particular domain can be very difficult; he or she is usually the person least likely to be able to spare the time required for knowledge acquisition. A single expert may have expertise in only a small subset of tasks in the domain. Multiple experts can alleviate these constraints. Using multiple experts enables the knowledge engineer to make the best use of each expert's time, while not completely usurping his or her working hours.

Weakness of single lines of reasoning. Expert system developers who consider only a single expert's heuristics and reasoning risk becoming "myopic." According to LeClair (1985), these developers force the decision maker who subsequently uses the expert system to view the problem and the solution from the perspective of a single expert. Being dependent on a solitary approach to problem solving can be inadequate in that it may make the decision maker prone to the same reasoning errors as the expert. Problem- solving expertise improves by being challenged and refined. A single expert may provide adequate, but not ingenious advice. Multiple experts provide the opportunity for the knowledge engineer to stimulate interaction that can be used to derive heuristics and reasoning reflecting a *synthesis* of expertise.

Member Equality. Factors affecting member equality include rank and status. During reviews of videotaped multiple-expert sessions, it is common to find a junior expert making a decisive statement and then looking over to the senior expert for nonverbal confirmation. A well-thought-out multiple expert knowledge acquisition methodology can help combat the potential negative effects of inequality due to rank and status. For example, cooperative group communication can be improved through training (Eisenson, Jon, et al., 1963).

Upward-ripple paranoia. "Upward ripple paranoia" (McGraw & Seale, 1987) is a term used to describe a domain expert's fear of repercussions from supervisors because of information contributed during knowledge acquisition sessions. This phenomenon can cause domain experts to be less than candid with the knowledge engineer or to be hesitant to verify that the notes on the knowledge acquisition form reflect the information he or she contributed during the session. Communication can help alleviate upwar-ripple paranoia. Prior to knowledge acquisition sessions with a domain expert, knowledge engineers should ensure that potential experts attend an orientation session that describes the goals and purpose of knowledge acquisition.[4] Supervisors of those who are selected as domain experts should be consulted concerning time and task requirements, responsibilities of domain experts, and the need for autonomy during knowledge acquisition sessions. Finally, the atmosphere within the multiple expert group must be such that each member of a multiple expert team feels comfortable contributing and evaluating ideas without negative repercussions from his or her superiors.

Confidentiality. The issue of confidentiality is not unlike concerns previously mentioned about upward-ripple paranoia. Domain experts may feel threatened by knowing that their contributions will be shared with and in some cases, evaluated or validated by other domain experts. A domain expert in a small-group setting should feel free to express his or her ideas without recrimination from the other group members. When working with multiple experts on an *individual* basis, knowledge engineers must ensure privacy and respect for each expert's contributions. All contributing experts should be confident that neither they nor their ideas will be ridiculed by other experts. Allowing key experts to review the expert system at various stages of development enables them to ensure that their knowledge was appropriately translated into code and that no external consideration or impact exists that was not anticipated.

Access. Obtaining access to a practicing expert is often a severe problem. When using multiple experts, either individually or in small groups, the problem of access is compounded by conflicting schedules. Once the scheduling problem is resolved and a meeting time set, however, multiple experts may be more likely to show up for the session that a single expert. Hunter (TI Satellite Symposium, 1985) noted that when she had a team of people scheduled to meet at a designated time, they came because they knew that other people had committed their time. If she was working with a single expert, the expert was more likely to request cancellation or rescheduling prior to the meeting itself.

Consensus versus diversity. Multiple experts will yield multiple opinions. Many of these opinions may be conflicting. Few knowledge engineers are uneasy about the prospect of managing a multiple expert group who agree on most issues and/or who reach consensus easily. On the other hand, most knowledge engineers would be at least somewhat apprehensive about being able to control knowledge acquisition sessions in which multiple opinions are expressed. The leadership style a knowledge engineer uses should be based on the type of knowledge acquisition session and the domain experts in attendance.[5] Democratic leadership style is effective in facilitating knowledge acquisition sessions in which only one expert is present or in which there is little controversy. Multiple-expert sessions may require the knowledge engineer to display a variety of leadership styles. During a discussion in which ideas are being generated and communications among members are positive and idea-inducing, knowledge engineers may be able to relax leadership efforts, displaying a more permissive style. As ideas are refined, issues clarified, and consensus gained, knowledge engineers may need to apply a more supervisory leadership style to keep the discussion on track, ensure that each member is able to express his or her ideas, and to control the progression of the session.

APPROACHES TO THE USE OF MULTIPLE EXPERTS

Whether domain experts are consulted as individuals, as primary/secondary experts, as a small group, or as a panel, there are basically two approaches to their use. The following sections outline issues related to the *individual* consultation of multiple experts and the *group* consultation of multiple experts.

Individual Consultation

Most knowledge acquisition programs will reflect this use of multiple experts, as it is fairly common for an expert system to be developed based on individual contributions from a number of people. In some cases, individual domain experts represent expertise in a variety of knowledge subsets. In others, they represent a primary expert who oversees efforts of a number of secondary experts. In either case, knowledge engineers can enhance the effectiveness of individual consultations with multiple experts by attending to the factors discussed in the next sections.

Selecting Multiple Experts for Individual Consultation

Techniques used in the selection of individual experts for a multiple-expert program include talking to the experts to determine domain expertise, communication abilities, and the willingness to work in a small group.[6] Feigenbaum (TI Satellite Symposium, 1985) believes that it is necessary to find people who are comfortable with a highly introspective, analytic approach to their discipline. As Feigenbaum noted, "You have to find people who are willing to meet the knowledge engineers halfway over the bridge between computer science and the target discipline. Some specialists are comfortable with that and some are not."

Ensuring Privacy and Individual Respect

A key to the effective use of multiple experts who are consulted on an individual basis is ensuring that the interaction remains private, if the expert desires, and that each individual's input is respected. Although videotapes may be made, the knowledge engineer should exercise caution in sharing videotaped sessions with other domain experts. When knowledge engineers anticipate the need to share videotapes with other experts, the original domain expert should be told in advance of the taping. If this need is evident only *after* the tape has been made, the domain expert should be contacted prior to its review by other individuals. In most of our experiences, the domain expert is not averse to other knowledge engineers or experts viewing his or her session tape as long as the needs, purpose, and goals of the review are made clear.

Debriefing Individually Consulted Multiple Experts

An important component of an effective knowledge acquisition session closing is the debriefing process.[7] Knowledge engineers are encouraged to hold individual debriefing sessions with each expert as soon as possible after the session has concluded. Meeting individually with an expert helps ensure that the expert is able to freely express agreement or disagreement with the knowledge acquired without fear of embarrassment or compromise. Confidentiality is ensured, valuable information may be acquired, and the expert's willingness to participate in future development efforts with multiple experts is enhanced.

After debriefing the expert(s), the knowledge engineer carefully summarizes or transcribes the information extracted from the session. This allows him or her to use this recorded information as a springboard to receiving feedback from the expert. Expert feedback is used to verify the information received, clarify major issues, and identify missing sets of knowledge. In addition to comparing and compiling agreed-upon knowledge for implementation, this information may be presented to other experts to begin the validation and verification process.

Group Consultation

The manner in which knowledge engineers manage multiple experts who are consulted in a group setting will vary according to development needs and philosophies. Some developers may feel that the goal of group sessions should be gaining consensus; others may feel that diversity breeds "better-than-average" ideas. For example, LeClair (1985) and Reboh (1983) support the pursuit of multiple lines of reasoning. Hunter (TI Satellite Symposium, 1985) feels that group settings focused on determining a single line of reasoning are productive because of the ensuing agreement on knowledge-base content. She does not believe that it is useful to meet with one expert and say, "Give me what you know," put that information in the system, and then direct another expert to "'Give me what you know but first look at what the first guy said and change anything you want." She concluded that it is best to consolidate the experts and "argue out" their differences before trying to embed the acquired knowledge into the system.

The selected system architecture also will affect the way that multiple experts are used. If the system is designed to handle multiple lines of reasoning, it is acceptable to acquire diverse information without demanding that experts reach a consensus. If the architecture is designed such that a combination or integration of expertise is required, knowledge acquisition sessions must be tailored toward reaching a consensus.

Selecting Multiple-Expert Team Participants

When qualified domain experts are asked to cooperate as part of a multiple-expert team, they should possess (or be willing to acquire) group interaction skills. (Figure 9-3) presents a set of characteristics of an "optimum" **multiple-expert team** participant.

Tactful	Enthusiastic
Exhibits a sense of humor	Cooperative
Friendly	Minimizes differences
Interacts	Identifies with group's goals
Works to help group	Considers rewards of membership

Figure 9-3. Characteristics of a Multiple-Expert Team Participant
William M. Sattler/N. Edd Miller, Discussion and Conference, © 1954/1968, pp. 221-223. Adapted with permission of Prentice-Hall, Inc. Englewood Cliffs, New Jersey.

Preparing the Multiple-Expert Team

The multiple-expert team consists of the knowledge engineers and domain experts who may be required to work together in the development of an expert system knowledge base. The effectiveness of knowledge acquisition with multiple experts depends on the preparedness of both the domain experts and the knowledge engineers. Issues that can increase the effectiveness of this team include orienting the experts who may be working individually or in small groups and training the knowledge engineer(s) in group leadership skills.

One approach to orientation for multiple experts who will be consulted on an individual basis includes ideas presented in Chapter 4. Suggestions for domain-expert orientation consist of an introduction to AI, videotapes of interviews in which domain experts discussed what knowledge acquisition was like, seminars on the goals, objectives, and structure of the expert system, and an overview of the domain expert's role in the expert system's development.

Multiple experts who will participate in group settings also should be briefed on group dynamics. For example, the knowledge engineer may distribute and discuss with experts some guidelines for small-group discussions. This may be accomplished in either a group seminar or one-on-one dialogue with the knowledge engineer.

For multiple-expert teams to succeed, the knowledge engineer must be able to function as an effective group leader. Major skills of leadership that are important to the knowledge engineer in a multiple expert knowledge acquisition session include being able to

- Keep the purpose or goals of the session in view
- Refocus domain experts as needed to work toward session goals
- Facilitate discussions among multiple domain experts
- Mediate negative or controversial discussions
- Develop and build a team environment.

Debriefing the Multiple-Expert Team

Debriefing a multiple expert team entails bringing closure to the knowledge acquisition session. Although debriefing should be a step in the knowledge acquisition process with an individual expert, it is especially important when sessions have involved small groups (Figure 9-4).

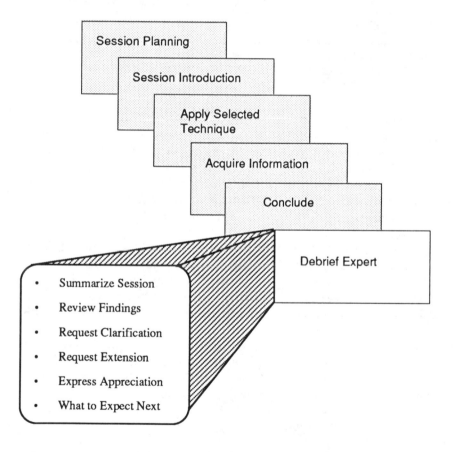

Figure 9-4. Debriefing as a Step in the Knowledge Acquisition Process

To encourage free expression of ideas from each participant, it may be necessary to debrief the group and later, to debrief each individual member of the group. Debriefings usually are structured to accomplish a series of separate objectives, including
- •Clarifying and refining knowledge
- • Defusing potential content or interpersonal problems
- • Partially verifying the acquired knowledge
- •Assigning agreed-upon certainties to acquired knowledge.

Initial goals for the debriefing address the tasks of summarizing and correctly recording the problems, solutions, and ideas discussed during the session. During this summation, experts should be encouraged to request or suggest clarification on the issues that were raised. The debriefing process offers knowledge engineers an opportunity not only to obtain consensus from experts (if desired), but also to elicit information concerning the experts' degree of certainty or a belief in the information obtained. While certainty or validity of rules for a knowledge base is always important, it is extremely so in situations where more than one expert may have contributed ideas or where ideas were consolidated based on discussion among experts (McGraw & Seale, 1987, 1988).

As the session concludes, the knowledge engineer should take the opportunity to identify action items, parties responsible for specific tasks, and target completion dates. For example, many of our sessions result in identifying a need for a specific manual, which our expert may be able to secure for us. By including "action items" in the closing or debriefing of the session, the expert is more likely to record the need and date for response.

Additional objectives for debriefing the multiple-expert team as a group include ensuring that the group members have a positive attitude about their contributions and participation and outlining future plans for the multiple-expert team.

TECHNIQUES FOR WORKING WITH MULTIPLE-EXPERT TEAMS

Knowledge engineers need not generate new techniques for working with multiple expert teams. First of all, many of the techniques described in earlier chapters can be adapted and used. For example, the process tracing methods may be altered such that two or more experts consult together to solve the problem scenario. This discussion scenario allows knowledge engineers to observe the consultation, key questions asked, alternatives presented and considered, and attributes and values that lead to the selection of a solution. Likewise, user dialogs (Wielinga & Breuker, 1985) are appropriate for multiple experts, in that at least two individuals are required to use this technique. As this technique is set up such that the participating experts represent different levels of expertise, it is easily adapted such that the experts represent different subsets of expertise.

In addition to the use of other knowledge acquisition techniques, numerous techniques used in the corporate world can be adapted for use with multiple expert knowledge acquisition teams. For example, the Delphi method (Linstone and Turoff, 1975) was designed for technological forecasting by a group who are geographically dispersed. The **nominal-group technique** provides a method for consensus-forming.

While some authors (Kraemer & King, 1983) have termed some group problem-solving techniques "rational but naive," we argue that the techniques described in this section provide a knowledge engineer with a set of workable tools. We cannot recommend the *exclusive* use of any of these techniques. Instead, we suggest that they be used for the knowledge acquisition phase and the intent for which they are best suited. For example, **brainstorming** is useful for initial multiple-expert team knowledge acquisition sessions, as its goal is to generate, but not evaluate, a set of solutions. Once the team has generated solutions, subsequent sessions can make use of the nominal-group technique and **consensus decision making** as the solutions are evaluated, ranked, and priorities for selection identified.

The sections that follow present guidelines for adapting brainstorming, consensus decision making, and the nominal-group technique for use in multiple-expert knowledge acquisition sessions. Any of these techniques can be implemented traditionally, or using a computer-based approach. Computer-facilitated approaches to collaboration among group members are presented in the final entry of this section.

Brainstorming

Brainstorming (Osborn, 1953) originated from concerns by top business executives that lower-level managers were too quick to parrot the conventional wisdom of their superiors. While this approach might have been politically safe, it was thought to preclude better decisions concerning company policies from getting a fair hearing. Brainstorming promotes the identification of a number of responses to an issue (Figure 9-5).

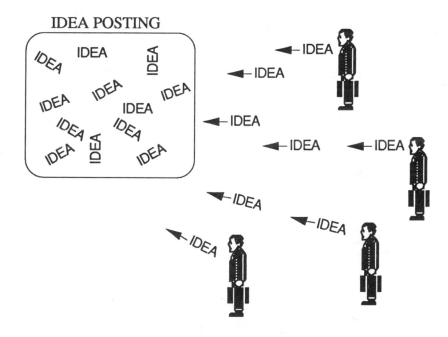

Figure 9-5. Brainstorming as a Knowledge Acquisition Technique

Brainstorming can also be used to help experts and knowledge engineers break loose from the obvious, or conventional, solutions to complex problems. Many experts get into an intellectual "rut" when they know one or two approaches to a problems. The knowledge of these approaches may make them reluctant to think that there might be other, more imaginative, and perhaps better, solutions. Brainstorming is designed to stimulate thinking and generate ideas in such a way that we do not get easily sidetracked to a quick acceptance of the ordinary and conventional. With multiple experts working as a team, brainstorming can help prohibit immediate criticism and reduce discussion-inhibiting comments.

Whether used in business or in a knowledge acquisition session with multiple experts, the guidelines for conducting brainstorming exercises are simple. Prior to the brainstorming-based knowledge acquisition session itself, select a problem to be brainstormed or the topic that the multiple-expert team will consider. Explain brainstorming rules to the members of the multiple expert team prior to, or at the beginning of, the knowledge acquisition session in which it is used. Conduct the brainstorming session using the following guidelines:

1. Introduce the brainstorming session with a brief discussion of the session's goals and major considerations.

2. Present the domain experts with a problem to consider or a topic to be brainstormed.

3. Prompt experts to generate ideas by one of two basic methods:
   (a) Invite experts to call out their ideas as rapidly as they can; allow experts to speak whenever there is an "opening."

   (b) Confine participation so that each expert is ensured a "turn." Each expert presents one idea; when an expert does not have a contribution, he or she may pass.

4. The recorder (i.e., the knowledge engineer or other designated individual) records all ideas on an overhead transparency, whiteboard, or chart pad. He or she will be required to work quickly to keep up with the experts if they are calling out solutions.

5. Continue brainstorming until all experts pass or until the knowledge engineer notices a reduction in the rate of idea presentation. (A high level of participation cannot be sustained for more than 10 or 15 minutes.)

6. The knowledge engineer and the multiple experts who participated in the session discuss and debrief the ideas that have been introduced. (The knowledge engineer may wish to use consensus decision making or the nominal- group technique at this time.)

Consensus Decision Making

Consensus decision making is a set of techniques that can be used by itself or as a follow up to brainstorming with a group of multiple experts. In contrast to brainstorming, in which the focus is on the *quantity* of the responses, consensus decision making focuses on finding the *best* solution to a problem. In brainstorming, an answer is not judged; all possible solutions are considered equally valuable. In consensus decision making, the advantages and disadvantages of each answer are weighed and measured by the multiple-expert team members. Even the fact that one "best" answer may not be agreed upon by the team can be significant for knowledge-base development efforts. Figure 9-6 illustrates the use of consensus decision making for knowledge acquisition.

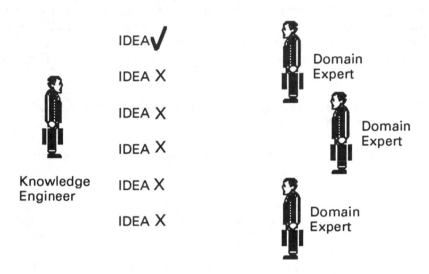

Figure 9-6. Consensus Decision Making as a Knowledge Acquisition Technique

Consensus decision making is effective only if each domain expert who participates in the team feels that his or her views and opinions have been heard. It is also vital that each expert has a commitment to the group decision even though he or she may have some reservations (Cragan et al., 1980). These considerations necessitate that the knowledge engineer take care introducing, explaining, and executing a knowledge acquisition session based on the use of consensus decision making.

Consensus decision making involves presenting a problem to the multiple-expert team and encouraging each member to vote on alternative solutions to the problem. Voting occurs in rounds, which provide a means of gaining commitment to the final solution. The number of rounds is determined by the number of alternatives or options that have been suggested. This unique method of voting ensures that each member of the multiple expert team has the opportunity to make his or her views and opinions known, regardless of rank or status. For the technique to be effective, the knowledge engineer must be aware of the possible effects of status, rank, or experience differences among the members of the multiple-expert team. Specific guidelines that can be followed to manage the consensus decision-making approach include the following:

1. The knowledge engineer describes the process of consensus decision making to the multiple-expert team and introduces the purpose of the technique in the context of the specific knowledge acquisition session.

2. The knowledge engineer outlines the problem and possible solutions (which may have been obtained prior to this exercise from other experts, or through brainstorming).

3. In ROUND 1, each expert has three votes and places no more than one vote beside any one option. After the voting is completed, the team decides to delete the options with less than some agreed-upon number of votes ("X")

4. ROUND 2 may begin if the list of options is still large. Otherwise, the knowledge engineer leads a discussion that is stimulated by questions such as "Does everyone understand each option? Is there any option that you cannot live with? Can any options be combined into one?"

5. During ROUND 2, each expert uses two votes, placing no more than one vote beside any one option. Options with less than a preselected number of votes ("Y") are deleted. and further discussion can occur as is necessary. [*Note:* The knowledge engineer sets the value of "Y" (e.g., 3, 5) with the cooperation of the experts.]

6. Rounds continue until only two options remain or unless one option emerges as a unanimous choice. During the last round, each expert votes for the final option.

7. The knowledge engineer follows up with questions such as "Does anyone feel that he or she cannot commit to this? Can everyone feel comfortable with this decision?" Those who wish to do so can examine further their choice by comparing it with the final option. This last look at alternatives may surface solutions to modify or address peculiar instances of the problem under consideration.

Nominal-Group Technique

The nominal-group technique (Huseman, 1973) is a problem-solving procedure that reduces negative effects (i.e., nonparticipation, conflicts) that may be triggered by face-to-face interaction among members of the multiple-expert team. This technique is useful if characteristics of the multiple expert team, such as status and rank, appear to threaten the effectiveness of the consensus decision-making approach. The nominal-group technique allows the multiple-expert team to become a "nominal" group. Thus, the group members are together but they are allowed to function independently and even anonymously, if desired (Figure 9-7).

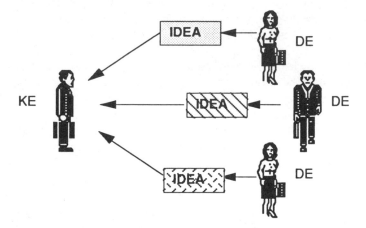

Figure 9-7. Nominal-Group Technique in Knowledge Acquisition

To conduct a knowledge acquisition session based on the nominal-group technique, knowledge engineers must first ensure that group members are familiar with the technique and the purpose of the session. Specific guidelines (adapted from Frank, 1982) for conducting the technique include the following:

1. Prior to the knowledge acquisition session in which it is used, the knowledge engineer introduces the nominal-group technique to the members of the multiple expert team and provides each member of the team with information on the problem or problem-solution alternative that will be discussed.

2. When the session convenes, the knowledge engineer asks each member of the multiple-expert team to list on paper (without any discussion) the advantages and disadvantages noted in the problem situation or problem-solution scenario that was presented prior to the session.

3. Without comment, the knowledge engineer compiles the advantages and disadvantages from all of the lists. The knowledge engineer may eliminate only those ideas that overlap and may reword only when it is necessary to clarify ideas.

4. Without prior discussion, group members anonymously rank-order advantages and disadvantages, revealing priorities that should be observed when searching for or considering solutions.

5. The knowledge engineer leads a discussion of the advantages and disadvantages and their respective ranks; discussion should focus on priorities that the members used to determine ranking.

6. Without prior discussion, the members of the multiple-expert team list possible solutions to the problem.

7. The knowledge engineer compiles a list of all solutions to the problem (as per Step 3 above).

8. The knowledge engineer leads a group discussion to examine the solutions to the problem. The primary goal of this discussion is to select the "best" solution.

The nominal-group technique can be used as a stand-alone technique, as an alternative to consensus decision making, or as an interface between brainstorming and consensus decision making. The technique can be varied to include more group interaction after group members have generated and ranked ideas. Increased interaction allows the knowledge engineer to draw upon the individual talents of the experts without the fear of counterproductive forms of communication. In addition, knowledge engineers (McGraw & Seale, 1987, 1988) have found that the combination of group interaction and the nominal-group technique enhances the creativity and quality of the resulting solution(s).

Computer-Facilitated Sessions

The techniques presented previously, as well as related techniques for idea generation and evaluation, may be adapted or aided by using computer technology. Researchers (Bush, 1945; Turoff, 1972) have devised numerous schemes to use technology to assist humans working interactively. It is a natural progression that computers be used as effective aids and focal points in meetings of a multiple expert knowledge acquisition team. Steflk and others (1987) note that use of media, such as overhead projectors, handouts, and whiteboards, can influence a meeting's progress and complexion because they interact with the participants' resources for communication and memory.

Static Communicative Devices
What we term "static" communicative devices include media that present a "frozen" view of group contributions, such as blackboards, overhead transparencies, and whiteboards. Although inputs may be erased and edited, they are not dynamic. Content that is displayed on the "board" represents the facilitator's interpretation or translation of an idea. The medium provides non-interactive communication, in that it displays "group" views, which are manipulated by the group facilitator. It generally does not stimulate input from individual members nor is the posted data usually edited or added to by members themselves. Additionally, storing or saving data that were contributed and transferred to static communicative devices is problematic. Other knowledge engineers may wish to use the knowledge acquisition room later in the day, which may necessitate

erasing posted information. Characteristics of static communicative devices that influence a knowledge acquisition session include the following:

- Entail facilitator's translation of participants' ideas as they are posted

- Allow posting of ideas to contribute to a community memory

- Help participants visualize and compare major issues

- Are affected by the recorder's interpretation and judgment

- Allow board-to-group interactive communication, but not member-to-member

- May or may not allow storage of posted ideas (i.e., members may take notes, or in using an electronic board the content may be scanned; otherwise, content is erased at the conclusion of the session).

- Modify content because of the need for space (i.e., new ideas may necessitate erasures) and the sharing of facilities (i.e., room used for other meetings)

Dynamic Communicative Devices

Dynamic communicative devices, such as networked computers with projection capability, provide individual members with the ability to view, expand, revise, or clarify content that has been posted. Views or data are posted by the members themselves; there is no need for the facilitator to act as an intermediary, who translates ideas to save display space. The ability to interact with each other may encourage less aggressive group members. Actually, using the computer to respond or post information is less threatening for some individuals than speaking to a group and risking the facilitator's rejection or translation of ideas. Finally, contributions may be saved or stored to disks, more than one version of a view may be saved, and stored views may be loaded for further discussion and revision at subsequent meetings. Characteristics of dynamic communicative devices are summarized below:

- Allow posting of ideas to a community memory

- Help participants visualize and compare major issues

- Allow "board"-to-group and member-to-member communication

- Are not affected by the group facilitator/recorder's interpretation and judgment

- Allow storage of numerous versions of the content

- Do not modify content because of the need for space and facilities sharing

Computer Conferencing and Collaboration

Computer conferencing and collaboration can provide a fertile environment for a multiple expert knowledge acquisition team. While the physical environment is basically a normal knowledge acquisition setting (e.g., room, table, chairs, presentation media), additional tools and specific arrangements of those tools differentiate this more collaborative setting. Figure 9-8 illustrates a room that is arranged for computer collaboration. In this setting, each member of the multiple-expert team is provided a workstation or computer terminal. The workstations are linked together over a local area network that can provide access to a distributed database. In this manner, group participants are provided with a multiuser interface. The seating arrangement encourages person-to-person communication, in addition to the machine-to-machine communication provided by networking. Additional equipment in the room includes projection equipment that can allow any member's screen or the facilitator's screen to be displayed.

Figure 9-8. Physical Environment for Computer-Facilitated Sessions

Nunamaker, Applegate, and Konsynski (1987) report success using computers in the decision-and-planning laboratory the University of Arizona. During interactive (i.e., all participants were in the same room) brainstorming sessions in the lab, they found that forceful personalities who tend to dominate traditional brainstorming sessions lose their "pulpits" when the discussions take place in an electronic medium. Specifically, the research team was interested in how integrated, computer-based systems could help groups solve problems. During their studies, they instructed participants in the lab to respond simultaneously on their keyboards to questions or issues. In addition to generating ideas, participants reviewed other participants' responses and appended their comments. Software was developed to consolidate the comments and organize them for display on a large screen. Sessions concluded with additional comments and analysis. Nunamaker (1987, pg. 5) describes the positive influence of computer-facilitation of brainstorming by stating that, "Computers force you to concentrate on the problem and allow you to express yourself. The system lets us focus on *ideas* rather than on the people who came up with them."

Another attempt to expand meeting effectiveness by the use of dynamic, interactive media is Xerox Parc's Colab. Colab is a computer lab whose purpose is to increase the effectiveness of meetings among computer scientists and to provide a research environment to investigate the effect of computer tools on meetings (Stefik et al., 1987). Within Colab, the available tools provide participants with a coordinated interface that the authors have described as WYSIWIS.[8] WYSIWIS allows members of the group to interact with shared and "tangible" objects.

The system Stefik and others (1987) describe provides both public, interactive windows (those that are accessible to other group members) and private windows (e.g., those with limited access). Furthermore, Colab tools support simultaneous action, allowing group members to work in parallel and to act on shared objects. Conflicts (i.e., more than one member attempting to act on the same image) are handled by noting a "busy" signal and by relying on social constraints. A variety of software tools, including Cognoter, Argnoter, and database paradigms extend the usefulness of Colab.[9]

If computer-facilitation techniques for multiple-expert teams can be thought of as existing on a continuum, the previous example indicates an extreme end. Unfortunately, very few knowledge acquisition facilities will be equipped with the tools that are the core of Colab. However, some of the important concepts embedded in Colab can be extracted and applied with variations to meet the needs (and equipment availability) of specific knowledge acquisition programs. Facilities may be able to provide terminals or personal computers with networking capability. This technology can enable group members (1) to communicate with each other or with the knowledge engineer using electronic mail, (2) to vote during the nominal-group technique, and (3) to generate brainstormed ideas for sharing with group members (thus reducing the knowledge engineer's need to serve as a group recorder). Other technologies, such as the Aquastar™ allow large-screen projection of computer screen content and would be useful in multiple-expert knowledge acquisition sessions.

MANAGING AND ACCOMMODATING MULTIPLE KNOWLEDGE SOURCES

Previous sections of this chapter have focused on approaches and techniques for *conducting* multiple-expert knowledge acquisition sessions. While the purpose of this text is to provide information on knowledge *acquisition* methodologies and techniques, we would be remiss in a discussion of using multiple experts if we did not briefly address some issues that could more appropriately be thought of as knowledge representation or system architecture. When translating information from multiple-expert knowledge acquisition sessions, knowledge engineers need to consider how they will represent and manage multiple expertise in the knowledge base. The following sections provide (1) tips for documenting the acquisition of information from multiple experts and (2) some pointers to some of the more prevalent techniques for accommodating or integrating multiple expertise.

Documentation

Knowledge engineers who consult multiple experts will not only be required to select and apply appropriate knowledge acquisition techniques but also will need to provide a means for documenting the acquired knowledge. Even more so than for an expert system that is designed from a single expert's input, **multiexpert systems** (LeClair, 1985) require that knowledge engineers document the source and circumstances of the information acquired during knowledge acquisition sessions. The increased importance of documentation is due to the following:

- Panels of experts may be required to assist in the verification and validation of rules in the knowledge base; knowing the source of information may contribute to this process.

- A domain expert's individual background affects the information he or she provides in response to a question or a problem; knowing the different sources for information helps provide a context for that information.

- Should a domain expert withdraw from the program, and information he or she provided is later questioned, documentation provides a means to identify the information provided by a specific expert.

- Documentation, such as standard templates for rule content and rule headers, may be designed to specify not only knowledge source, but also certainty or **probability** ratings that are important when multiple lines of reasoning are considered.

Chapter 3 provides detailed information on some suggested knowledge acquisition documentation, such as the knowledge acquisition form, rule content form, and knowledge acquisition database. Each of these enables knowledge engineers to incorporate the source of the knowledge and the context in which it was acquired. Tagging knowledge acquisition notes with source information is of obvious importance. Tagging knowledge acquisition notes with context information allows knowledge engineers to understand the conditions under which the information is applicable. This type of knowledge is useful when the expert system being designed will allow for multiple lines of reasoning or when expert system designers plan to associate certainty factors or probabilities with specific pieces of information.

Another form of documentation that can help knowledge engineers organize efforts to incorporate information from multiple knowledge sources is rule header documentation. This documentation provides a bridge between the information on the knowledge acquisition form and the information that becomes encoded into the knowledge base. Rule header documentation can be designed to meet the needs of a specific program, therefore there are few hard-and-fast rules governing its format. The slots that become most important when dealing with multiple experts include knowledge source and uncertainty slots. Rating certainties or probabilities based on a knowledge source, consensus of experts, and varying contexts enables knowledge engineers to make use of multiple lines of reasoning or alternate solution sets during the execution of the expert system.

Conflict Resolution

LeClair (1985, p. 145) notes that most of the approaches to dealing with multiple lines of reasoning tend to follow one of two paths. One is to integrate expertise from multiple experts *during* knowledge acquisition so that each rule action or consequence represents the consensus of a group of experts with an associated measure of certainty (Figure 9-9). Several techniques are available to accomplish this task. One technique is seeking group consensus for information that will be translated into a rule, so that all of the experts consulted agree on a rule that required their input.

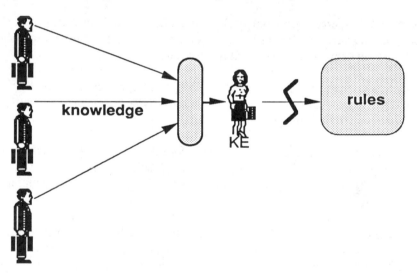

Figure 9-9. Integrating Expertise During Knowledge Acquisition

Other integration techniques used during knowledge acquisition include analyzing multiple-expert input, overlaying each input over the other, and investigating the areas of agreement and disagreement. Examples of these techniques include repertory-grid analysis and concept sorting (either manual or computer-based). For example, Boose (1985) describes the use of ETS, a repertory-grid based knowledge acquisition tool, to combine expertise from multiple experts. Several experts were allowed to build grids independently and then combine them into one consultation system. The grids provide both consensus and dissenting information. While in most cases users would want to receive consensus information, special cases and exceptions might necessitate that they review dissenting opinions. The end user could then select the expertise of any subset of experts during the consultation and receive both consensus and dissenting recommendations.

The other major approach is to segment the knowledge-base into subdomains and use a single, separate expert line of reasoning for each (Figure 9-10). The advantage of this technique is that each line of reasoning (i.e., problem-solving model) can contribute unique information that others can use in supporting the initial line of reasoning in deducing a solution. For example, experts in LeClair's (1985) research competed, offering overlapping, possibly redundant, but unique lines of reasoning. This technique allows developers to combine the strengths of different problem-solving models or alternate solution sets.

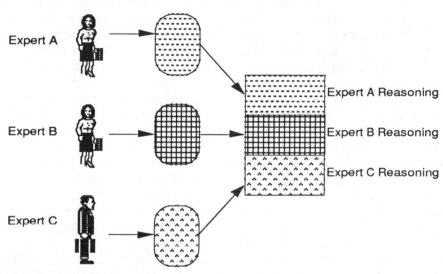

Figure 9-10. Segmenting the Knowledge Base

In addition to competing lines of reasoning, multiple expertise can be integrated cooperatively. Cooperative reasoning demands that the problem is one (1) where multiple models of the problem can be constructed and (2) the models are related such that they *collectively* contribute to solving the problem. Because they are all created from an initial line of reasoning, they must be consistent with that initial line of reasoning and with each other (Stefik, 1982).

Mayer (1987) describes a methodology in which the knowledge engineer is responsible for gathering, but not integrating the multiple expert input. His approach relies on distributed AI techniques to allow multiple sources or "agents" cooperatively to solve a single problem. Each "expert" within the system views current solutions to the problem. If it can provide input or wishes to modify the current solution, it notifies the system. In turn, the system shows the expert system user a list of experts available for "consultation." The user directs the course of subsequent reasoning by deciding "whose" advice to take at any given time.

The following sections introduce some of the techniques that developers use to alleviate or handle conflicts. A thorough coverage of any one of these techniques is beyond the scope of this book, however, sources for further information on each technique are provided.

Multiple Lines of Reasoning

Reboh (1983, p. 145) refers to the need to handle conflicting expert advice in an expert system:

> "An important issue encountered in the construction of expert problem-solving programs is how to deal with conflicting expert advice. This question arises even more tangibly in real-life decision making. Even when experts do arrive at the same conclusion, how do we know they reached it for the same reasons? The process by which the decision maker, who presumably is not an expert himself, finally decides whose advice to follow is at best highly subjective."

Hearsay-II, a speech understanding system, represents an early example of a system that uses multiple lines of reasoning (Barr & Feigenbaum, 1981). In this system the approach was to modularize the knowledge base into cooperating knowledge sources and to allow the knowledge modules to communicate using a blackboard. MYCIN and PROSPECTOR exemplify this approach, for in these systems if the experts differ or the reasoning is indefinite, certainty factors are used to quantify the likelihood of the result of a rule activation.

Research by LeClair (1985) determined that it is feasible to accommodate and resolve conflict among multiple viewpoints in a multiexpert expert system and that there are numerous techniques that designers can use to do so. His research focused on developing an architecture consisting of techniques to accommodate, recognize, and resolve conflict and to enable learning and knowledge-base maintenance. This capability is particularly useful in circumstances where there is no single expert and there are "tradeoffs" that must be considered by the decision maker among conflicting perspectives and/or goals (LeClair, 1985, p. 285). In regard to accommodating multiple lines of reasoning, his research conclusions included the following:

• Knowledge engineers should utilize 'kernel' knowledge bases to establish context for the problem domain of interest, thereby ensuring that each expert 'line of reasoning' will be addressing a commonly-understood problem domain.

• Conflict can be resolved by adding specific knowledge (i.e., knowledge about the particular problem being addressed), enabling the expert system to take advantage of all available knowledge regarding the problem of interest. This specific knowledge is used to identify that expert line of reasoning which is most appropriate, should conflict arise.

Meta Rules

A specific technique that is used to handle conflict resolution within a knowledge base is the **meta rule**. Resolving conflict with meta rules is useful in domains in which a higher-order policy maker dictates. Meta rules require that knowledge acquisition sessions produce information concerning the set of rules that should be followed to select the solution path from all those available. For conflicts to be resolved at all points in the system, the meta rules must (1) be sufficiently general to operate on all possible conflicts or (2) exist for all specific conflict points.

The difficulties in acquiring either of these types of meta rules are many. The expert must recognize that he or she *has* such a set of rules and be able to explicate them. Beyond this, the domain expert must have informed the knowledge engineer of the possibility of a conflict. A system designed with a set of meta rules must reflect the correct meta rules for each conflict situation and must be adequately tested to ensure that unanticipated conflicts do not occur.

When they are applied, meta rules are usually found in a hierarchical system. This enables the conflict-resolution rules to operate at a higher level than the domain rules. The simplest set of meta rules would be those that apply globally to any conflict. Unfortunately, global meta rules are often not appropriate. In more complex situations the meta rules can be separated into knowledge sources and applied according to the type of conflict or the context in which the conflict occurs.

Fuzzy Sets

The expert sometimes may experience difficulty assigning numbers representing the degree to which he or she "believes" the knowledge. For some problems the degree of belief may be represented more effectively by categories (rather than ranges). In either case, developers may use a mechanism that allows the expert to categorize (e.g., good, very good, greater than, medium) the certainty with which he or she believes a fact has been derived. The mechanism, **fuzzy sets**, is a set of terms which describes the possible values of belief. The expert can select one of the set terms to reflect certainty in the fact. The system can then combine these values during inferencing. Conflict resolution is accomplished through comparison of the fuzzy set values.[10]

Uncertainties

Several numerical **uncertainty** methods are available for use in resolving conflicts. Many of these have origins in probability and statistics. Methods such as Bayesian probability and Dempster-Shafer (Kanal & Lemmer, 1986) have been used extensively in decision analysis and psychology.

The acquisition of the numeric values associated with knowledge can be a tedious process unless the information can be extracted from data available to the expert. The advantage of using uncertainty methods is the established calculations for combining the certainty values. The comparison of the certainty values for conflict resolution is fairly straightforward numerically; the problem is in determining contextual meaning of the numbers.

In resolving conflicts with numeric methods, the values of competing information are compared to select the path with the highest degree of certainty. This process is simple if the selections involve measures of uncertainty of the same type (e.g., all probabilistic values). If the selections have differing measures of uncertainty, the resolution involves a procedure or set of meta rules. For example, selection is complicated when a conflict has one path that is tagged a Bayesian uncertainty measure *and* one path that is tagged with a fuzzy set value. In this case, the expert must have provided information on how to resolve the conflict or will be required to do so during knowledge-base refinement.

ENDNOTES

[1] The authors gratefully acknowledge the assistance of Major Steve LeClair in his review of this chapter. Additionally, many of these ideas reflect the contributions of Mary R. Seale (McGraw & Seale, 1987b, 1988).

[2] This use of multiple experts is described in Bylander, Mittal, and Chandrasekaran (1983) in their explanation of segmenting a knowledge base so that each segment represents a different expert's input.

[3] FRESH was developed under DARPA ARAP #5211, Contract Number N00039-85-C-0001.

[4] See Chapters 4 and 5 for more details.

[5] See Chapters 4 and 7 for more information on the knowledge engineer's leadership style.

[6] Chapter 4 provides more information on the selection of individual experts.

[7] Chapter 7 provides more detail on debriefing a domain expert.

[8] What You See Is What I See, which is pronounced, "Whizzy-whiz."

[9] For a more in-depth description of Colab and its numerous tools, see M. Stefik, G. Foster, D. Bobrow, K. Kahn, S. Lanning, and L. Suchman, "Beyond the chalkboard: Computer support for collaboration and problem solving in meetings," Communications of the ACM 30:1 (1987), 32-47.

[10] For more information on fuzzy sets, see C.V. Negoita, Expert Systems and Fuzzy Systems (Menlo Park, CA: Benjamin/Cummings Publishing Co., 1985) or G. Klir and T. Folger, Fuzzy Sets, Uncertaintly and Information (Englewood Cliffs, NJ: Prentice-Hall, 1988).

SUGGESTED READINGS

The information within this chapter represents research from multiple fields. Considerable research continues concerning methodologies to integrate or accommodate multiple expert knowledge. Material from multiple fields is suggested for further reading on the subjects relating to the use of multiple domain experts.

Multiple Experts
Mittal & Dym, "Knowledge acquisition from multiple experts." The AI Magazine, Summer, 1985.

Group Problem Solving

Huseman, R.. "The role of the nominal group in small group communication." In R. C. Huseman, D. M. Logue, and D. L. Freshley, <u>Readings in Interpersonal and Organization Communication</u> (2nd ed.), Boston: Hollbrook, 1973.

Linstone, H. and M. Turoff. <u>The Delphi Method: Techniques and Applications</u>, Reading, MA: Addison-Wesley, 1975.

Uncertainty and Knowledge Acquisition

Gale, W. <u>Artificial Intelligence & Statistics.</u> Reading, MA: Addison-Wesley, 1986.

Hink, R. F., and D. L. Woods, "How humans process uncertain knowledge: An introduction for knowledge engineers" <u>AI MAGAZINE</u>, 8:3, (Fall 1987), 41-53.

Kanal, L., and J. Lemmer. <u>Uncertainty in Artificial Intelligence</u>. Amsterdam: North-Holland, 1986.

Klir, G., and T. Folger. <u>Fuzzy Sets, Uncertainty and Information</u>. Englewood Cliffs, NJ: Prentice Hall, 1988.

Negoita, C. V. <u>Expert Systems and Fuzzy Systems</u>. Menlo Park, CA: Benjamin/Cummings Publishing Co., 1985.

APPLICATION

Using brainstorming, consensus decision making, and the nominal-group technique with a small group of multiple experts is not difficult if the knowledge engineer is prepared and has practiced the technique. The application exercise that follows provides an environment for practicing each technique before using it in an actual knowledge acquisition session.

Brainstorming

Directions: Divide into small groups of 5 to 7 persons. Select a group discussion leader and a person to record responses. Use the brainstorming guidelines to conduct a 5-minute brainstorming session on the topic that follows. Your goal is to identify creative solutions to the problem:

> Employees in large companies often complain that personal worth perception is low. They feel that the company does not overtly reward them for their contributions and set procedures that allow them to be most productive and creative. Brainstorm ways a company can reward efforts and increase the perception of personal worth other than issuing pay increases.

Nominal Group Technique

Directions: Divide into small groups of 5 to 7 persons. Select a group discussion leader and a person to record responses. Use the nominal-group technique guidelines in this chapter to complete a 5 minute session. Your goal is to find the best solution to the employee personal-worth perception problem (above). Consider the solutions from the brainstorming activity and select the "best" solution from that set.

Consensus Decision Making

Directions: Divide into small groups of 5 to 7 persons. Select a group discussion leader and a person to record responses. Use the consensus decision-making guidelines in this chapter to conduct a 5-minute session whose goal is to select a solution to the employee personal-worth-perception problem (above) to which all members of the group can commit.

10

Aids and Tools for Knowledge Acquisition

The Lure of Automation

> **Weaknesses of Manual Approaches**
> **Domain Expert as Knowledge Engineer**

Automating Knowledge Acquisition--A Continuum

> **Using Simulations for Knowledge Acquisition**
> **Using Prototypes of the System for Knowledge Acquisition**
> **Using Computer-Based Knowledge Acquisition Tools**

Types of Knowledge Acquisition Programs

> **Expert System Shells as Knowledge Acquisition Tools**
> **Tools Designed for Knowledge Acquisition**
> **Knowledge Acquisition Workbenches and Environments**

Problems to be Resolved

INTRODUCTION

Each profession has its own methodologies, techniques, and tools/aids. This chapter discusses some of the tools and aids that make knowledge acquisition more efficient. Moore and Agogino (1987, p. 214) draw a distinction between tools and aids. *Tools* provide software support for application of knowledge engineering techniques; however, they do not typically provide guidance. *Aids* are specific types of tools that provide guidance in the development process. For example, procedures, templates, and forms discussed in Chapter 3 are knowledge acquisition aids. Tools that will be considered in this chapter include expert system prototypes, simulation programs that help expose and extract expert knowledge, and software that allows the expert to encode his or her own expertise.

This chapter first explains why expert system developers looked to automation of the knowledge acquisition process. Some of the frustrations that motivated them included weaknesses of some manual approaches, domain experts' problems in the expression of expertise, access problems, and the desire to be able to acquire knowledge from examples.

Next, we present a continuum approach to the automation of knowledge acquisition. We discuss the use of simulations, prototypes, and automated aids and programs for knowledge acquisition. Next, we introduce different types of knowledge acquisition programs, including those that exist as components of expert system shells, those based on repertory grids, and those that serve to interview experts and build domain models. The chapter concludes with a presentation of selected examples of existing knowledge acquisition programs and a brief discussion of problems persisting in their development and use.

Objectives

This chapter presents information on knowledge acquisition aids and tools. Specifically, it enables readers to accomplish the following:

- Identify benefits of using automated knowledge acquisition aids and tools
- Recognize constraints and problems related to the use of knowledge acquisition tools
- Identify applications for the use of knowledge acquisition tools and aids that reflect varying levels of automation
- Determine the role of simulation tools and prototypes in a knowledge acquisition program
- Identify the types of assistance that knowledge acquisition programs most often provide
- Contrast the benefits and limitations of a variety of knowledge acquisition tools.

Key Terms

knowledge acquisition tool	qualitative model	machine learning
example-based systems	simulation program	hybrid tool
intelligent editing program	hierarchical representation	

THE LURE OF AUTOMATION

Knowledge acquisition is a time consuming and thus, an expensive component of expert system development. Boose (1984) estimates the time required to extract expert-level knowledge, translate it into code, and complete a prototype to be from six to 24 months. Similar stories are derived from other expert system development efforts. Knowledge acquisition difficulties stem from an inability to access the expert and problems associated with expressing expertise, to the application of knowledge acquisition techniques and the inability to map a domain expert's knowledge into an appropriate representation scheme.

To alleviate some of these problems, developers have suggested that the elicitation, acquisition, and in some cases the representation of domain knowledge be automated. The idea of developing tools and other aids to enable more efficient knowledge acquisition is not by any means new. McCarthy's Advice Taker was an early effort to develop a program that could accept advice similar to that presented to a human novice (1968). Attempts since that time have included tools that acquired knowledge via an **intelligent editing program**, those that acquired knowledge by extrapolating from given knowledge and "learning," and those based on psychological interviewing methods, to name a few. Researchers continue to investigate the use of natural language in an automated acquisition program so that the expert can communicate directly with the system (i.e., ROSIE, Fain, et al., 1981a, 1981b). Other research efforts have investigated applications of **machine learning** to assist in solving problems associated with representation of knowledge and expressing expertise (Hayes-Roth, Klahr, Mostow, 1980a, 1980b). Machine-learning efforts are exemplified by META-DENDRAL (Buchanan & Feigenbaum, 1978), a program that learns rules that predict how classes of compounds break up in a mass spectrometer.

Successes in research and development efforts such as these have spurred researchers to develop knowledge acquisition systems or "workbenches." These systems seek to manipulate the process of conceptualization, knowledge "mapping," elicitation, or representation (or a combination of these) in the development of an expert system. They typically promote interaction between a domain expert and the computer system itself, such that the knowledge engineer acts primarily as a facilitator (Figure 10-1).

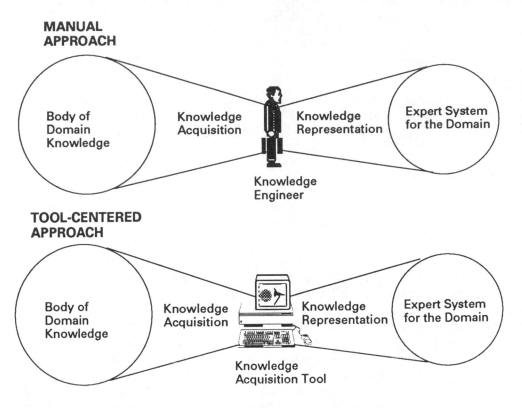

MANUAL APPROACH

Body of Domain Knowledge

Knowledge Acquisition

Knowledge Representation

Expert System for the Domain

Knowledge Engineer

TOOL-CENTERED APPROACH

Body of Domain Knowledge

Knowledge Acquisition

Knowledge Representation

Expert System for the Domain

Knowledge Acquisition Tool

Figure 10-1. Eliciting and Representing Domain Knowledge: Two Approaches

Buchanan (1983) identifies the possible benefits of automating (at least part of) the knowledge acquisition process as including:

- Automated tools might prove to be more competent than humans in acquiring or refining specific types of knowledge

- Automated methods might significantly reduce the costs (time and money) of human resources involved in expert system development.

Additionally, automated methods can help standardize the knowledge acquisition process, the use of specific techniques for certain types of knowledge, and methodologies in general. The sections that follow explore some of the issues that have helped to stimulate the quest for automating the knowledge acquisition process.

Weaknesses of Manual Approaches

Although manual approaches to the elicitation of domain knowledge are currently more common, they are not without disadvantages. Not the least among these is the time and cost required for a knowledge engineer to become familiar enough with the domain to elicit knowledge from a domain expert in an efficient manner. An added factor is the variety of skills that a knowledge engineer may be called on to use during the knowledge acquisition process. The next section explores these issues in more depth to help explain the lure of automated knowledge acquisition.

Translating Expertise into Code

As noted by Moore and Agogino (1987, p. 214), "The thought of having experts encode their expertise is compelling." Most **knowledge acquisition tools** have been developed to expand the bottleneck in the process of building expert systems, regardless of whether they were designed for research or retail distribution. Most developers would agree that the primary cause of this bottleneck is the difficulty of retrieving the appropriate problem-solving knowledge from a human expert and appropriately translating or representing that expertise. If tools could be developed such that a domain expert could sit at the workstation and encode his or her own expertise, the bottleneck might be loosened.

Researchers and practitioners who support the use of knowledge acquisition tools argue that aprogram that acquires knowledge can have the following positive benefits:

- Enhanced quality of the knowledge base
- A knowledge base that is more reflective of the domain expert's model
- Reduction in the domain-familiarization period for knowledge engineers.

Friedland (1981) summarizes the temptations to use knowledge acquisition tools, noting that without an intermediary between the expert and the system there is less "noise" introduced to the encoded knowledge. Manago and Kodratoff (1987) define noise as being: erroneous information, mission information, poor description language, or unreliable data.

Using a knowledge acquisition tool, the knowledge engineer expends less time learning the domain, its language, and concepts. Additionally, the expert system reflects the domain expert's view of the domain rather than an intermediary's view. Finally, because the domain expert interacts directly with the tool that translates his or her knowledge into code, the quality of the problem-solving knowledge that is captured may be enhanced.

Requirements for Diverse Techniques, Approaches, and Skills

There is a general lack of standardization in the field of knowledge acquisition methodologies, approaches, and techniques. Even when techniques are very similar, authors ascribe new terms to them. Knowledge acquisition is a multidisciplinary field in which computer scientists, psychologists, and communication specialists (among others) contribute their own particular sets of expertise. The result is a rich array of techniques and viewpoints that are, unfortunately, difficult to compare because they are based on diverse backgrounds and experiences. This general lack of standardization in the field of knowledge acquisition has helped fuel the quest for knowledge acquisition tools. Their developers often contend that such tools provide expert system designers with a common base for development.

Related to the numerous techniques and methodologies are the various sets of skills that knowledge engineers require. For example, the development of expert systems may require that the knowledge engineer exhibit the skills of a cognitive psychologist, a communications expert, a programmer, and a domain expert. In some cases the knowledge engineer may be required to play more than one of these roles concurrently.

Domain Expert as Knowledge Engineer

While few developers wish to rid themselves of the role of "knowledge engineer," most of them recognize the complications brought on by the issues previously presented. In some cases, developers seek out domain experts to train as knowledge engineers. In others, they attempt to acquire or build a system that would allow the expert to input his or her knowledge directly, leaving the knowledge engineer free to focus on knowledge refinement and implementation issues.

Going from Knowledge to Code

Expert systems were based on the idea that it would be useful to capture a domain expert's problem-solving expertise in a computer system. To do so, researchers have developed a number of techniques that knowledge engineers can use. In some cases, however, expert system developers may confront "translation" problems that can be eased by tools that allow domain experts to input their expertise. For example, Moore and Agogino (1987) note that structured knowledge acquisition approaches encourage developers to build a conceptual or knowledge-level structure of the domain before programming efforts begin. However, developers may not understand the domain or may not know how to explicitly map an expert's knowledge. First, they must tap the knowledge, then elicit or extract it, and finally translate or reformulate it for representation in the knowledge base. This process is arduous if the domain expert is not trained to express a "model" of his or her knowledge. (See Chapters 5 and 7 and Appendix B for information on related issues, such as a domain expert's inability to be introspective and difficulties experts have verbalizing knowledge.)

Allowing domain experts to at least partially direct knowledge acquisition efforts by encoding their own knowledge via a knowledge acquisition aid or tool may be either an alternative or an adjunct to a structured knowledge acquisition program. In many cases the domain expert may be intrigued by using such a tool and may be more willing to investigate, input, and correct pieces of knowledge that comprise domain expertise. As domain experts become interested in conceptualizing, they may develop a better understanding of the type of knowledge that is required. Anxiety may be bridled by some degree of enthusiasm. When this occurs, Boose notes that the expert "tends to look on the knowledge engineer as an assistant rather than as an encroacher in his private domain" (1985, p. 515). The knowledge engineer, instead of functioning as an active "eliciter," functions as a facilitator who handles special situations and coding and refinement issues. This additional distancing reduces the tendency of the knowledge engineer to confine the expert by the knowledge engineer's focus on implementation and representation issues during knowledge acquisition.

Should the development program elect to build or modify a knowledge acquisition tool, certain issues should be considered, including

- The extent of the tools used and their role in the total knowledge acquisition program
- Specific goals for the use of the tool
- The way in which knowledge engineers and domain experts will be trained to use the tool.

Figure 10-2 summarizes ways to reduce the risks involved in allowing a domain expert to encode his or her knowledge.

The domain expert should be cognizant of the problem and the way in which he/she would approach its solution.

The domain expert should be able to conceptualize about the domain.

The domain expert should be able to analyze his or her own knowledge.

The domain expert must be motivated to use the tool in a conscientious manner (Moore & Agogino, 1987).

The domain expert should be able to assure the performance of the model that he or she encodes (Moore & Agogino, 1987).

Figure 10-2. Using Expert-Encoding Tools: Suggestions for Risk Reduction

Alleviating Access Problems

Access to domain experts for knowledge acquisition sessions is often cited as a primary development constraint. This access problem may be triggered by geographic distances or physical locations, time demands, or costs, to mention a few. It is not uncommon for domain experts to request the use of a computer so that they can simply input the information as it occurs to them.

For example, during development on a complex naval resource management expert system (FRESH), knowledge acquisition efforts were aggravated by both physical location and demands on the experts' time. The domain experts were practicing experts in their fields and their work location was outside of the continental United States. The development team was based in the southern United States. Knowledge acquisition trips to the experts' location were expensive. To be cost-effective and worthwhile, they needed to be scheduled and planned in advance. Even when planned in advance, the knowledge engineer's physical presence at the domain expert's site did not guarantee that the target knowledge could be acquired. The nature of the experts' job assignments necessitated that the job come first and, especially in the case of emergencies, it superseded the need for knowledge acquisition sessions. After several attempts to meet the goals for a knowledge acquisition session, one of the primary domain experts suggested that the development team simply "put a computer on my desk" so that he could type in the important information when he thought of it.

Example-Based Acquisition

How do interns learn to be expert physicians? How do student teachers become master teachers? In both of these cases, the master-apprentice approach to learning is used. That is, given a foundation or background in the domain, an individual works with an expert in the domain to learn by watching and participating in problem solving. As the apprentice watches the master, he or she observes examples of commonly occurring problems, as well as "hard cases" and notes the master's responses in each case. While the master may not directly or explicitly instruct the apprentice in all of the heuristics that are applied during the problem-solving activities, the apprentice begins to learn by induction.

Induction is the process that allows us to infer a "law" or develop theories by observing and analyzing events or cases in which that law is applied. Thus, after observing a "master" claims adjuster working a homeowner's claim, we begin to infer which questions to ask first, which answers trigger alternate paths through the questioning, and which variables (e.g., type of damage, type of coverage) and their associated values are pivotal. This type of learning, while it is intense and requires commitment on the part of the apprentice, is often preferred by learners because it is active. Just as apprentices can extract and generate heuristics in this manner, so too can knowledge engineers acquire important domain knowledge using this approach.

Machine-learning research has focused on learning (inducing rules) by the input of the domain expert's examples. For example, AQ11 (Michalski, 1980) was used to formulate factual knowledge as rules that diagnose plant diseases. In some cases, its rules were more effective than the rules that were generated manually by a domain expert.

It is possible that theories can also be generated from incomplete example sets. The generation of knowledge from such incomplete cases or examples makes induction an excellent means of knowledge acquisition. Experts in many domains may not be able to explain the theories from which they work but can explicate a number of case studies or examples. In fact, domain experts have a natural tendency to provide *examples* of problems, critical questions to ask, and sample solutions during knowledge acquisition sessions. Thus, it is reasonable to automate the induction process. Induction-based knowledge acquisition requires the domain expert to provide the examples and critical information by typing them into a computer program which builds an induction table for the analysis of the information.

A number of automated knowledge acquisition tools have been developed based on induction theory. Most of them use induction either at the module level of a large problem or as the major method for acquiring knowledge for the solution of a small, bounded problem. However, the mere fact that we can infer theories from examples does not guarantee the acquisition of knowledge that is of high quality. The extent to which the theories are representative of the complete solution depends on the goodness and completeness of the training set of examples which form the theory. Thus, induced descriptions are guaranteed valid only for the facts from which the induction is made (Shapiro 1987).

AUTOMATING KNOWLEDGE ACQUISITION--A CONTINUUM

Attempts to improve knowledge acquisition by having the domain expert transfer his or her knowledge directly to the expert system knowledge base via an intelligent editing program "replaces one set of communication problems with another" (Buchanan, et al., 1983, p. 130). Even without the knowledge engineer as the central point in the process, the "bottleneck" may still exist. Depending on the scope, complexity, and type of application, knowledge acquisition tools may be appropriate. However, the following constraints hinder their widespread use:

- Requirements that the domain expert be an experienced user of the knowledge acquisition tool selected for development

- The difficult nature of being aware of one's own reasoning processes

- The need for a knowledge acquisition tool to conduct intelligent dialogue with an expert to help focus the expert, identify critical variables, and refine elicited information to the required level of detail.

In spite of the above deficiencies, we believe that knowledge acquisition tools can be useful as one component of a knowledge acquisition methodology like that proposed in Chapter 2. Knowledge acquisition tools may fall along many points on a continuum of automation, such as that depicted in Figure 10-3. The sections that follow discuss applications of each type of automation.

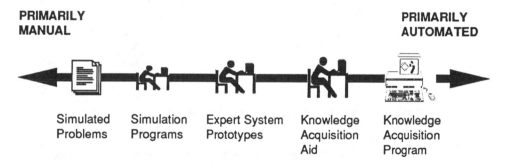

PRIMARILY MANUAL				PRIMARILY AUTOMATED
Simulated Problems	Simulation Programs	Expert System Prototypes	Knowledge Acquisition Aid	Knowledge Acquisition Program

Figure 10-3. A Continuum of Automation for Knowledge Acquisition

Using Simulations for Knowledge Acquisition

A **simulation program** provides a means of developing a global description of a set of domain tasks (Dallman & Pieper, 1983). An adequate simulation program or activity

- Emulates task performance in the domain

- Provides an environment in which knowledge engineers can observe an expert's hands-on manipulative interaction with typical domain problems

- Provides opportunities to clarify and refine domain conceptualizations or models.

One example is OpusII, a simulation workstation for the development of intelligent vehicle systems (McGraw & Seale, 1987). Adopting the paradigm of crew members operating a platform (i.e., type of aircraft) in a user-determined "world," OpusII provides the user with a simulated world, platforms, simulation facilities, and display facilities (Texas Instruments, 1986). The interactive design and graphics (e.g., dials, gauges, terrain, platforms) used by OpusII makes it a valuable knowledge acquisition aid in many areas of the avionics domain (e.g., mission planning, tactical planning).

Computer-based simulations can also be used for on-going testing, refinement, and validation of the knowledge base and inference techniques. For example, General Electric's LOTTA, a symbolic simulator, generates time-varying scenarios used to test and validate various battlefield management strategies that require decision making capabilities under uncertain and incomplete information (Bonissone & Brown, 1986).

Before using simulation for knowledge acquisition, the domain expert should be oriented to the specific tool in a separate session (McGraw & Seale, 1987). This session should include information on how to operate the equipment and run the simulation software. Additionally, the expert and the knowledge engineer should have clear expectations for one another's role and the session's objectives. The similarities and differences between the simulation being used and the expert system being developed need to be reviewed. The expert also needs to know how long the simulation will run, what information will be gathered (e.g., decisions made, physiological measurements), and how the specified information will be recorded.

The use of simulations for both knowledge acquisition/refinement and validation/testing makes it an important component of the structured knowledge acquisition methodology we propose. In addition to computer simulations and tools, a variety of simulation aids can be used. While these tools vary with the domain (for example, models of aircraft may be of use when discussing fighter tactics), in each case they provide the domain expert with a focus for knowledge acquisition that allows him or her to *demonstrate* expertise, rather than being required to explain it.

Using Prototypes of the System for Knowledge Acquisition

Requesting that the expert periodically review the rules that have become a part of the knowledge base will not ensure proper functionality. In a review of singular rules, the expert is able to observe only the content of one rule at any given time. Reviewing the results of the inferencing process during the execution of the prototype and observing the interaction among rules can be more useful in identifying future knowledge needs. Thus, prototypes of the developing expert system are valuable tools for both knowledge acquisition and knowledge-base refinement. Buchanan and others (1983) describe the use of expert system prototypes for testing the suitability of the selected expert system development tool and later, the implementation of the rules and concepts that the knowledge engineer has acquired. In the latter use of prototypes, the goal is to validate assumptions that "the rules reflect associations and methods that either are used by the expert when solving the problem or are understandable rationalizations of such methods" (Buchanan, 1983, p. 137). In a review of baseline prototypes, the expert is able to view the interaction of existing rules and the result of executing the current prototype and then suggest refinements. This interaction can be especially useful in identifying areas in which inference procedures need to be modified, discovering potential conflicts among rules, or identifying holes in the knowledge base.

Some expert system shells (e.g., Personal Consultant Plus™, KEE™) provide the knowledge engineer with the ability to create knowledge-based applications that incorporate graphical "active images."[1] These images are termed active in that they may be selected and modified during knowledge acquisition sessions. User-interactive dials, gauges, forms, and selection images provide visual data input and enable the use of the prototype as a knowledge acquisition tool. Modifying the graphic (which is easy for a domain expert to do) in turn modifies the code that supports the graphic (which would be a prohibitive task for an expert). Thus, rules concerning the values of certain graphics or images can be tested visually, which may stimulate the acquisition of more knowledge or the refinement of existing knowledge.

Using Computer-Based Knowledge Acquisition Tools

Finally, knowledge engineers who choose to automate at least part of the knowledge acquisition process may select or develop an appropriate knowledge acquisition program. Opinions as to the usefulness and thoroughness of these programs vary from

"with this tool we can *totally* automate the problematic knowledge acquisition process"

to

"although this tool meets a specific knowledge acquisition need, a knowledge engineer is still required to guide the expert, help refine knowledge, and clarify knowledge base content through the use of manual knowledge acquisition techniques."

Considerable research is being conducted in the development of knowledge acquisition programs; their numbers and efficiency continue to increase as developers integrate techniques and methodologies and enhance applicability. Existing knowledge acquisition tools typically attempt to provide the following two kinds of assistance (Marcus, McDermott, and Wang, 1985):

- Increase the ease with which a domain expert can communicate his or her expertise

- Organize or "proceduralize" the knowledge that is communicated so that all relevant knowledge for a situation is exposed.

The next section explores the ways in which this assistance has been incorporated in a selected set of knowledge acquisition tools.

TYPES OF KNOWLEDGE ACQUISITION PROGRAMS

The diversity in the focus of existing knowledge acquisition tools, the manner in which they have been implemented, and the domains in which they have been tested render simple comparison of their features ineffective. Furthermore, the continual increase in the number of tools designed to automate some portion of the knowledge acquisition process prohibits our mentioning each tool.[2] However, it is reasonable to introduce the reader to examples of the different types of existing knowledge acquisition tools. The next section describes a selected set of programs in an effort to present examples of how they currently are used. While these examples are not intended to be all-inclusive or product endorsements, they help the reader develop (1) an appreciation for the type of development that has occurred and is underway and (2) a realization of the types of problems that must be solved before tools become mainstays in expert system development.

Programs that automate the knowledge acquisition process range from those that support the knowledge engineer in conceptualizing or developing a model of the domain to those that purport to automate the interviewing, domain modeling, and refinement processes. Some tools have been developed for the purpose of researching the knowledge acquisition process to identify a more efficient approach; others have been developed as front ends to commercial expert system building tools or as commercially available stand-alone tools (i.e., not a component of an expert system shell).

The tools discussed in this section were selected based on the nature of their design and intent, their representation of a specific type of tool, or the type of hardware on which they run. The reader is advised to review this section to ascertain the major goals, intent, structure, and constraints of each tool mentioned and to contrast one tool to another. While none of these tools has solved completely the knowledge acquisition process by automation, each development signals important efforts and trends.[3]

Expert System Shells as Knowledge Acquisition Tools

Commercially available expert system tools themselves are useful in implementing expert systems, but offer little relief from the knowledge acquisition bottleneck (Miller, 1986, p. 36). The majority of these expert system tools or shells were developed to support the rapid prototyping approach to expert system development. Additionally, many of them require sophisticated symbolic computing hardware to run. Thus, they were designed with the seasoned programmer or artificial intelligence expert in mind. Domain experts without comparable technical skills may be alienated by the user interface, terminology, and the hardware on which these tools run. While it can be argued that the knowledge engineer can use these shells to develop prototypes that the domain expert can then review, few knowledge engineers would encourage "expert to expert-system-shell" input for knowledge acquisition.

Powerful shells, developed for specific applications, are exceptions. For example, Kahn (1987) describes the Trouble Shooting Expert System Tool (TEST), an application shell for troubleshooting systems. Similarly, as more easy-to-use shells are developed, they will be able to provide more knowledge acquisition assistance or support.[4] For example, Expert Ease for the personal computer (PC) accepts examples from a domain expert and the PC-based Expert Systems Toolkit[5] provides templates for rule entry and a component to assist in knowledge acquisition. The next section provides the reader with an example of one expert system development tool that may be of assistance during the knowledge acquisition process.

MacSMARTS

MacSMARTS™ is an expert system building tool that was developed by Cognition Technology[6] for the Macintosh™ family of computers.[7] MacSMARTS combines the ability to design rule-based and **example-based systems** with a user-friendly interface and the ability to link rules and advice to other elements (e.g., graphics, text, spreadsheets, databases, knowledge bases). It is mentioned here as an example of a tool that enables example-based or rule-based input by a domain expert who may not be a trained programmer. MacSMARTS is a production rule-driven system. Rules are constructed on a "spreadsheet" with columns for Facts, Rules, and Advice. By double-clicking on an entry field, the associated entry window appears, allowing easy entering or editing of rules (Rasmus, 1988).

While some domain experts may be able to input knowledge using the rule-based component, the factor that makes MacSMARTS attractive as a knowledge acquisition tool is its example-based knowledge-base development component. The domain expert can create a knowledge base by typing in the

- Primary factors involved
- Questions that the system should ask the user at specific points
- Choices that the user has for each factor
- Advice that the system can offer based on the user's response.

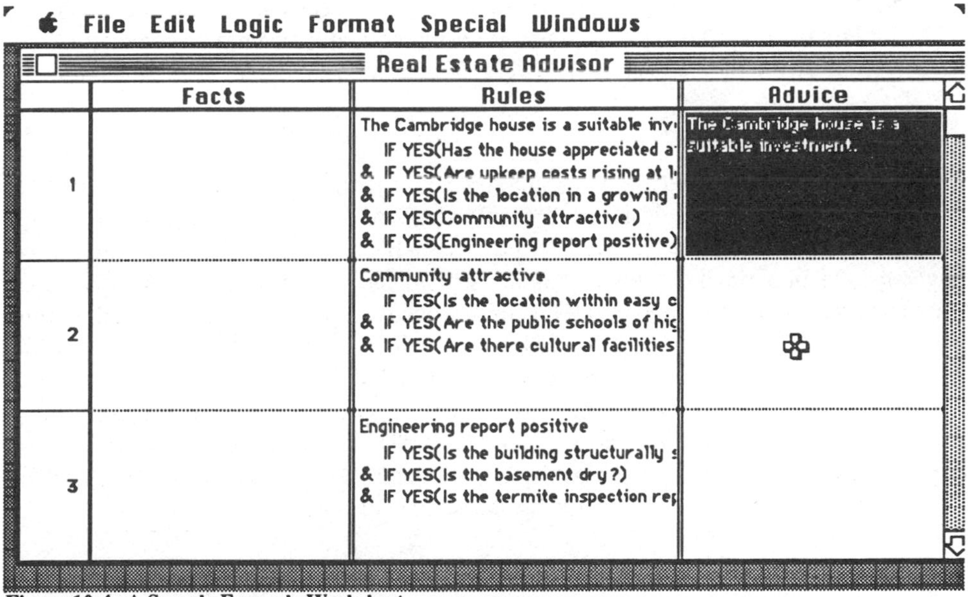

Figure 10-4. A Sample Example Worksheet
(Reprinted with permission from the MacSMARTS Instruction Manual, Version. 2.0. Copyright © 1987, Cognition Technology, Cambridge, MA.)

Highlighting is used to cue the user to active "buttons" and to prompt the user for the next type of input. On-line help provides information when requested by the user.

After the domain expert has provided information on factors, choices, and advice (and user questions, if desired), he or she can review existing knowledge by viewing an Example Worksheet of input for the current knowledge base (Figure 10-4). The Example Worksheet displays the information that has been input in a tabular fashion, allowing the domain expert to review the material for correctness and completeness. The ID3 algorithm (Quinlan, 1982) is used to translate the examples (factors, choices, advice) into the expert system knowledge base.

Tools Designed for Knowledge Acquisition

A number of tools have been designed for the specific goal of automating all, or a portion of, the knowledge acquisition process. As described earlier, most of these tools attempt either to make it easier for a domain expert to communicate knowledge or to provide a means to organize and conceptualize a domain. In fact, a majority of the tools presented in this section exist specifically for the purpose of building a domain model. Clancey (1986) demonstrated that domain problems may be solved by abstracting data, heuristically mapping higher-level problem descriptions onto solution models, and refining these models until specific solutions are found.

As decision making in modern environments becomes more difficult for humans owing to time constraints, numerous alternatives, uncertainty, and information overload, the task of building expert systems will become more complex. Because decision making in complex environments is so complicated, some tools have been developed to assist specifically in helping define or extract a model for decision making in the domain. Other tools have been designed to assist in retrieving and then refining a model of the domain itself or in eliciting examples and inducing heuristics.

TEIRESIAS

One of the earliest attempts to automate knowledge acquisition is TEIRESIAS (Davis, 1977b), which was designed to enable automated acquisition of new knowledge for MYCIN (Shortliffe, 1976). MYCIN provides advice of a consultative nature on the diagnosis and prescribed therapy of a number of infectious diseases. TEIRESIAS uses MYCIN's backward-chaining rules as a framework for acquiring, refining, and adding new knowledge. The focus of these acquisition efforts is on metaknowledge about the representation and use of the rules within MYCIN. Metaknowledge might cue TEIRESIAS, for example, that a new rule about an infectious organism must have a specific structure and content (Hayes-Roth, 1983). This information is used not only to identify rules that are in error, but also as a trigger mechanism for TEIRESIAS to complete critical portions of a new rule for the domain expert.

Tools Based on Repertory Grids

A number of knowledge acquisition tools have been based on George Kelly's Personal Construct Theory (Kelly, 1955; Gaines & Shaw, 1981).[8] Knowledge acquisition tools that are based on repertory grid theory can help a knowledge engineer determine the domain expert's expressed conceptualization of his or her field. The ability to conceptualize the domain is an important precursor to subsequent efforts in organizing and developing a knowledge base. These tools are useful in working with analysis problems (Boose, 1987), which involve classifying, interpreting, or diagnosing problem solutions. In each case, these tasks can be enumerated using a grid.

Researchers and developers have used repertory-grid methods to extract expertise from domain experts. Tapping the experts' tendency to function as scientists in their domains, knowledge engineers can elicit an expert's conceptualization of the domain and its major constructs. Figure 10-5 represents some of the knowledge acquisition tools that have attempted to apply this theory.

TOOL	SOURCE
Expertise Transfer System	Boose, 1984, 1985, 1986
PLANET	Gaines and Shaw, 1986
AQUINAS	Boose and Bradshaw, 1987a, 1987b;
	Kitto and Boose, 1987
FMS Aid	Garg-Janardan and Slavendy, 1987
Kitten	Shaw and Gaines, 1987
Kriton	Diederich, Ruhmann, and May, 1987
	Diederich, Linster, Ruhmann, and Uthmann, 1987
KSSO	Gaines, 1987a, 1987b

Figure 10-5. Repertory-Grid Based Tools

Each of these tools attempts to represent the domain expert's problem-solving knowledge in repertory grids, which allow experts to rate, or judge a solution according to a problem-solving trait. Most of these tools interact directly with the expert to stimulate him or her to refine, expand, analyze, and test problem-solving knowledge (Boose, 1987). A domain expert uses repertory grids to enter knowledge via a rating grid. This grid displays problem solutions that have been elicited from the domain expert, which serve as column headings within the grid. Constructs (e.g., solution traits) are placed beside the grid's rows. The system elicits constructs by presenting the domain expert with sets of solutions and requesting that the expert discriminate among them. The domain expert then provides each problem solution with a rating (e.g., ordinal or nonordinal) that represents how it relates to each trait. In some tools the domain expert associates a value (that reflects "importance") with each trait. Once these initial grids have been constructed, some of the tools in Figure 10-5 assist the domain expert in refining the knowledge base. Figure 10-6 depicts a sample rating grid for expert system shells that a domain expert constructed while interacting with a knowledge acquisition tool.

1 2 3 4 5 6 7 8 9 10	EXPERT SYSTEM SHELLS (1-10)
1 1 1 5 5 1 1 5 1 5	Runs on PCs / Not Run on PCs
2 4 1 3 2 4 2 3 5 1	KA Component / Not KA Component
2 4 1 3 2 4 2 3 5 1	Easy-to-use Interface / Not easy interface
5 4 2 1 1 4 3 1 5 1	Handles Uncertainty / No Uncertainty
1 1 5 5 1 5 1 1 5 1	Frames / Not Frames
5 5 1 1 1 1 5 1 5 5	Prod. Rules / Not Prod. Rules
3 1 4 5 1 5 2 5 2 5	Representation Templates / No Templates
3 5 5 1 1 5 5 1 4 1	HIgh Cost ($400+) / Low Cost (-$400)
1 1 2 4 5 4 5 1 3 1	Handle Hypertext / No Hypertext
2 3 4 5 4 2 3 3 5 2	Good Documentation / No Documentation

5= Important, 1=Less Important

Note: Each number in the first row (1-10) represents a different expert system shell.

Figure 10-6. Partial Rating Grid for the Evaluation of Expert System Shells
(The numbers 1-10 represent specific shells.)

Boose (1987) and others report applications of repertory grid-based knowledge acquisition tools, including those depicted in Figure 10-7.

Personnel Selection	Resource Management
Counseling Aids	Plant Location Selection
Product Marketing	Questionnaire Development
Curriculum Advisor	Wine Advisor
Task Priority Management	Training Evaluator
Personnel Resource Management	Business Development

Figure 10-7. A Sampling of Applications for Repertory-Grid-Based Tools

Expertise Transfer System (ETS). ETS, developed in Interlisp-D, is one of the more commonly cited knowledge acquisition tools that is based on repertory grids. Kitto and Boose (1987) report that ETS has been used to generate numerous prototypes for knowledge-based systems at the Boeing Company. ETS was designed to "interactively" interview a domain expert, analyze the elicited information, assist the expert in verifying the information, and generate a production rule knowledge base (Boose, 1984; Boose & Kitto, 1987). ETS is able to elicit vocabulary, conclusions, problem-solving traits, trait structures, trait weights, and inconsistencies. The problem-solving expertise is then stored in a bipolar rating grid such that probable solutions or elements are displayed across the top of the grid and constructs, or solution traits, are displayed vertically. [9] Following a session, ETS is capable of printing out listings and reports that can then be used in manual interviewing or in verification sessions.

BDM-KAT

Knowledge acquisition research and development efforts at the BDM Corporation have resulted in the design and implementation (in KEE™) of BDM-KAT, a knowledge acquisition tool (Blaxton, Geesey, & Reeker, 1987).[10] Developed to assist in the knowledge acquisition process within the materials processing domain, BDM-KAT provides knowledge engineers with tools that enable them to work with domain experts in an incremental fashion to build an initial knowledge base.[11]

BDM-KAT consists of three modes: Clarification, Prediction, and Diagnosis. In the *Clarification* mode, BDM-KAT provides a framework that encourages the identification of domain concepts and categories and the decomposition of domain processes into subprocesses. The expert responds by specifying the process and related subprocesses in terms of an AND/OR graph (Blaxton & Westphal, 1988). As BDM-KAT manages this decomposition, it can query for information about the subprocesses that have been identified. The end product of this mode is a model of the expert's conceptualization of the process, complete with graphically-depicted interrelationships and composite subprocesses.

Once the model developed during the Clarification mode has been completed, the domain expert-knowledge engineer team may enter the *Prediction* mode. The purpose of the Prediction mode is to expose gaps and fill holes that remain in the knowledge base. Presenting the expert with a flowchart-type representation, the system facilitates the extension of the processes identified to this point. Extensions include specifying the temporal flow of the process, setting parameters for gauges associated with each subprocess, and refinements to the model itself. To attain this information, BDM-KAT uses KEE active images as it (1) prompts the expert to build gauges and dials associated with subprocesses and (2) queries for explicit definitions for inputs, outputs, ranges, and responses to out-of-range settings for each subprocesses.

The domain expert-knowledge engineer team work through the first two modes until an acceptable model has been developed. At this point, the knowledge structure can be refined in the *Diagnosis* mode. In the Diagnosis mode, the expert views the current state of the knowledge base in the form of a flowchart in which each major node represents a process. The domain expert can "step-through" the model to view the interaction of subprocesses dynamically. As the model is activated, appropriate points in the flowchart become highlighted. In addition, gauges for relevant sensors come into view, and the expert can continually access explanation information. The values associated with the parameters, gauges, and dials can be altered to test the model's limits. Combined with explicit queries to the domain expert, these perambulations enable the expert to spot deficiencies in the model and enter other modes to make adjustments.

The current BDM-KAT system functions in the domain of materials processing (specifically, chemical vapor infiltration). The end goals of the system are to accelerate the knowledge acquisition process, enhance the use of an expert's time, increase knowledge base validity, and provide a facility that can help represent difficult portions of the knowledge acquisition process.

KNACK

KNACK is a knowledge acquisition tool that assists in developing expert systems to evaluate designs of electromechanical systems (Klinker, Bentolila, Genetet, Grimes, & McDermott, 1987a; Klinker, Boyd, Genetet, & McDermott, 1987b).[12] Using knowledge acquired from domain experts, this tool "interviews" the expert to build a conceptual model of the domain. To use KNACK, the expert must be able to express knowledge in the form of a report. Thus, he or she must be able to recognize task-relevant information, identify the appropriate way to evaluate how the information is used, and outline the way in which an electromechanical designer typically presents the information.

Based on sessions with the expert, KNACK first requires that general knowledge about design evaluation be incorporated into the system. Later, information from a sample report, in which the expert describes and evaluates an ordinary electromechanical system, is incorporated. Through successive sessions with the expert, KNACK abstracts critical information from report fragments and queries the expert when incomplete information is identified. This information is then used to integrate the sample report with a conceptual model of the domain. As the conceptual model is developed, the initial report is generalized so that it is appropriate to other systems. The expert works with KNACK to correct its generalizations as it "instantiates the generalized report with representatives of the concepts it detected" (Klinker et al., 1987).

After it has demonstrated an initial understanding of the sample report, KNACK queries for information concerning how to customize the generalized report for a specific use. During this process the expert provides strategies (e.g., questions, formulas, inferences, forms) that will be used to acquire values instantiating the identified concepts. KNACK then generalizes the strategies and prompts the expert to review and refine them. Finally, KNACK compares the developing knowledge base with the generalized report or strategies to help detect holes or conflicts in the knowledge base.

MORE

MORE has been used to support MUD (Kahn, 1985), a drilling-fluids consultant, and to build systems to diagnose computer disk faults, computer network problems, and circuit-board manufacturing problems. Based on a model-theoretic approach to the acquisition of diagnostic knowledge, MORE enables enhanced interviewing of domain experts. Its primary purpose is to increase the efficiency of the way in which domain experts contribute their time and knowledge. This goal is accomplished by applying a **qualitative model** of causal relations and a theory of how causal knowledge can be used to achieve more accurate diagnostic conclusions that, in turn, guide the interview process (Kahn, Nowlan, & McDermott, 1985). As MORE interviews experts, it develops a domain model that is a representation of their responses. MORE's domain model consists of the following: hypotheses, symptoms, conditions, links, and paths. Within the model, MORE can represent five types of conditions, frequency-conditions, tests, test-conditions, symptom-conditions, and symptom-attributes. Figure 10-8 depicts a partial MORE model with links.

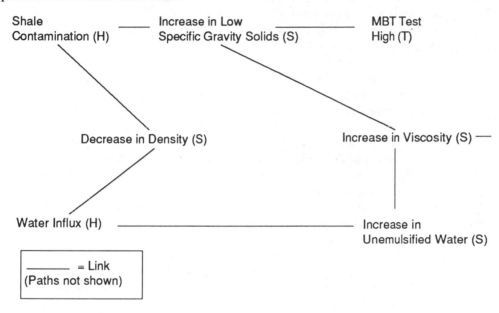

Figure 10-8. Partial MORE Model
Used by permission of the International Joint Conferences on Artificial Intelligence, Inc.; copies of the Proceedings are available from Morgan Kaufmann Publishers, Inc., 95 First Street, Los Altos, CA 94022, USA.

A useful aspect of MORE is its ability to identify areas of the knowledge base that need improvement to increase the accuracy of diagnostic conclusions. To do so, MORE makes use of eight different strategies.[13] The appropriateness of any given strategy is determined by an internal set of heuristics (Kahn, 1984). Selected strategies are used to derive queries such as: "What distinguishing features of DECREASE-IN-DENSITY would make it more likely to be caused by WATER-INFLUX?" As the user responds, he or she provides more diagnostic knowledge, which MORE then incorporates into the underlying domain model.

Auto-Intelligence

A knowledge acquisition productivity tool developed by IntelligenceWare, Auto-Intelligence™ is intended to "enable experts to transfer their expertise easily and quickly to a computer program" (Auto-Intelligence User's Manual, 1987, p. 5).[14] Additionally, the tool could be used to assist knowledge engineers in complex knowledge acquisition applications and to provide automatic induction methods. Designed for the IBM PC™ this tool is most suitable for analysis-type problems that involve structured selection or heuristic decision-making tasks (e.g., diagnosis, investment selection).[15] These types of tasks require that the user make decisions and select from a set of choices.

Auto-Intelligence is composed of the following modules:

- **Interview Manager**--interacts with the expert to elicit knowledge
- **Structure Discovery System**--captures knowledge structure and primary decision making factors
- **Example Manager**--handles bookkeeping of data and examples
- **Induction System**--classifies and generalizes information provided by the expert
- **Expert System Generator**--generates the expert system.

When a domain expert uses Auto-Intelligence, the interaction represents a "self analysis" of his or her decision-making processes in a specific domain. First, the system attempts to discover the overall structure of the key decision-making criteria by using question generation techniques (e.g., how items are similar or different). Auto-Intelligence prompts domain experts to identify traits (basic properties of objects) by the comparison of selections (i.e., Real Estate, Stocks, CDs) and the comparison of examples. Traits, selections, and examples are graphically matched on a horizontal scale by prompting the expert to place a marker at the point that represents how closely related a selection is to a set of bipolar constructs. Auto-Intelligence analyzes the input the expert provides to match selections and traits with the examples to produce a confidence factor for each selection (Auto-Intelligence User's Manual, 1987).

Once these traits have been identified by comparisons, the information (traits, opposites) may be edited or refined. Then the expert may add attributes (either numeric or symbolic) for some traits. Later, the expert provides examples and case histories that are used for the discovery or induction of rules. During this process the expert is prompted to provide a confidence factor (between 0 and 100) to note how confident he or she is in each selection. Confidence factors are determined by the expert's placement of a marker on a horizontal scale between "No confidence" and "Total confidence." Upon completion of this process, Auto-Intelligence generates prototypical rules for an expert system.

Knowledge Acquisition Workbenches and Environments

A manual approach to knowledge acquisition may require that the knowledge engineer use a variety of techniques or methods to elicit, translate, and refine domain knowledge. Similarly, knowledge acquisition tools and aids that are based on a single methodology and reflect the primary use of a single technique may not be the most prudent approach. Additionally, while some of the knowledge acquisition tools may assist in creating a domain model or conceptualization, they may not provide a means to translate knowledge that has been captured into a representation scheme that can be used by the expert system under development. Attempts to alleviate these weaknesses have resulted in the research and continuing development of "workbenches" or knowledge acquisition environments. The next section provides the reader with some examples of these efforts.[16]

AQUINAS

An extension of ETS, Aquinas was originally written in Interlisp (now also available in C/UNIX version) to run on the Xerox family of LISP machines (Boose & Bradshaw, 1987a). Boose (1987) describes AQUINAS as a knowledge acquisition workbench, whose internal reasoning engine is based on repertory grids. AQUINAS provides support for the following knowledge acquisition tasks:
- Eliciting distinctions from experts
- Decomposing problems
- Combining uncertain information
- Incremental testing
- Integrating data types
- Automatic expansion and refinement of the knowledge base
- Accommodating multiple knowledge sources
- Providing process guidance.

In addition to repertory grids, AQUINAS offers **hierarchical representations** organized into cases, knowledge sources, solutions, and traits (Boose, 1987). These hierarchies enable experts to decompose problems into subsets that are manageable in size and equivalent in levels of abstractions. AQUINAS combines several strategies to assist the expert in developing these hierarchies. Primary strategies include laddering (Hinkle, 1965; Stewart & Stewart, 1981; Boose, 1986), cluster analysis, and trait value examination. A second major extension to AQUINAS is the ability to represent nonordinal traits (e.g., nominal, interval, ratio) in the rating grid. AQUINAS allows experts to ascribe arbitrary scales to ordered traits. These values then appear in the grid, replacing numerical ratings.

KRITON

KRITON is described as a **hybrid knowledge acquisition tool** that uses a variety of knowledge acquisition methods to elicit and capture knowledge from a domain expert (Diederich, Ruhmann, & May, 1987). KRITON makes use of the domain expert's declarative and procedural knowledge as well as more static, text-based knowledge. Its developers note that the KRITON architecture supports the use of three knowledge elicitation methods, including automated interviewing, text analysis, and protocol analysis.

Interview methods (e.g., forward scenario simulation and laddering) within KRITON are automated, enabling the domain expert to interact with the system. A combination of these methods and the repertory-grid technique is used to elicit expert knowledge. Protocol analysis is then used to elicit procedural knowledge. The transcribed protocol is broken up into segments based on pauses during production, and these are analyzed semantically such that each segment reflects a proposition. After KRITON checks the operators and arguments that were selected, the system attempts a knowledge-based matching to instantiate variables inside the propositions (Diederich, Ruhmann, & May, 1987).

KRITON also provides the knowledge engineer with incremental text analysis for the elicitation phase. For example, the knowledge engineer may query the system for statistics on key words within the text. If the knowledge engineer determines that the text is appropriate for knowledge acquisition, he or she can set the size of the text in which the key words occur. KRITON generates basic propositions from the text (in a process similar to that used for protocols). The propositional structures that are defined are then presented to the user for refinement. KRITON uses the knowledge that has already been captured to construct what its designers call acquisition knowledge bases (AKB). AKBs are made up of structured objects that define pivotal domain concepts. This knowledge is used to provide guidance during subsequent knowledge acquisition efforts (i.e., identifying incompleteness). Knowledge elicited by KRITON is translated into an intermediate knowledge representation system which allows the integration of knowledge that initially was captured from diverse sources.

TDE

TEST Development Environment (TDE) is a high-productivity workbench that knowledge engineers and trained domain experts can use to build knowledge bases that are used by the Troubleshooting Expert System Tool (Kahn, 1987; Kahn, Breaux, DeKlerk, & Joseph, 1987). TDE knowledge bases represent the "causal consequences of component and functional failures" (p. 355). Using a mixed initiative workbench, TDE acquires knowledge from domain experts through a series of automated interviews. Developers provide guidance, direction, and information as it is needed.

TDE has several features that enhance its usefulness for knowledge acquisition. First, its problem solving strategy is compatible with that of troubleshooting technicians in the domains of manufacturing and customer service. Thus, while it features automated interviewing, it also allows the ad hoc provision of vital information as the expert recalls it. Second, TDE interrogation focuses the first set of questions at a level that enables the system to develop an overall structure for the knowledge base. Third, detailed questions are asked to flesh out the structure at each level. Knowledge acquisition is further facilitated by TDE's graphic representation of information provided in response to prompts. Finally, TDE provides for knowledge base modification through features such as debugging facilities, browsing, and error warnings.

PROBLEMS TO BE RESOLVED

Each tool mentioned in the previous section represents an attempt to enhance the knowledge engineer's ability to acquire knowledge from a domain expert. Some of them are more research-oriented, some are used internally in a company, and others are available for purchase. Some are based on a specific technique (e.g., automated interviewing, repertory grid), while others represent attempts to provide an integrated environment for knowledge acquisition.

In spite of continuing research and development efforts, automated knowledge acquisition tools have not replaced the knowledge engineer, nor do we consider complete replacement desirable. However, knowledge acquisition tools and aids do provide a means to support the knowledge engineer in accomplishing some of the tedious work associated with

- Conceptualizing a domain
- Creating a domain model
- Eliciting domain concepts
- Eliciting decision-making heuristics
- Translating domain knowledge to code

For the potential benefits of automating portions of the knowledge acquisition process to be realized on a more full-scale basis, persistent hurdles must be cleared, including:

- **Limited Application**--Because many of the tools under development are research-oriented, their application is aimed at a specific, manageable domain or knowledge type. Their use is, in principle, applicable in other areas, but wider applicability may require modifications. Continued work in this area should result in more widespread applicability.

- **Cost**--Developing knowledge acquisition programs and environments is an expensive endeavor. Many of the tools mentioned reflect internal research efforts of the corporations in which they were developed. If they are designed for research in a limited area and cannot be easily expanded to accommodate other applications, they become even more costly. As research efforts mature in this area and more of the tools become commercially available, developers hopefully can recover some of these costs.

- **Transportability**--Some of the tools mentioned in this section represent efforts not only to capture domain knowledge from an expert, but also to translate that knowledge into a representation scheme that can be used by the domain expert and the expert system. The form in which this knowledge is presented to the domain expert for review and refinement may be vastly different from the form in which it is represented in the knowledge base. Even when the system accommodates both representations, there is often a transportability problem in the representation of captured knowledge within one system in a manner that can be transported to other systems or expert system shells. Current research (e.g., BBN's KREME) in this area continues to seek a solution to this issue (Abrett & Burstein, 1986).

Until research and development efforts provide tools which reflect solutions to these problems, most knowledge engineers will rely on a manual or hybrid (i.e., part manual, part automated) approach to knowledge acquisition. Software aids or tools may be used even with manual approaches to help organize the process or submerge the domain expert in the domain. For example, hypertext technology such as HyperCard™ can enable knowledge engineer to develop a knowledge management aid that provides[17]

- On-line access to program wide knowledge management templates (e.g., rule headers)

• Expedient access to knowledge acquisition plans, recording forms, and rule logs based on the input of key words

• The integration of knowledge acquisition recording forms with expert-drawn figures, supporting graphics, or other information that is scanned into the computer.

ENDNOTES

[1] Personal Consultant Plus is a trademark of Texas Instruments Incorporated.

[2] The increasing interest in, and effort to develop these tools, is evidenced by the increasing proportion of papers presented about them at AAAI-sponsored functions, among others.

[3] The mention of selected tools within the sections that follow should not be construed as an endorsement. Tools and research that were reviewed for this chapter were selected on the basis of how they would help the reader understand past, current, and continuing efforts in the automation of knowledge acquisition.

[4] For information on a comparison of expert system shells, the reader is referred to R. Freedman, "Evaluting shells," AI EXPERT September 1987, pp. 70-74.

[5] The Expert Systems Toolkit (EST™) is produced by Mind Path Technologies, Inc., Dallas, TX.

[6] Produced by Cognition Technology Corporation, 55 Wheeler St., Cambridge, MA 02138.

[7] Macintosh is a trademark of Apple Computer, Inc.

[8] See Chapter 8 for an explanation of this theory and of repertory grids.

[9] ETS also uses other methods, such as laddering.

[10] KEE is a trademark of IntelliCorp.

[11] This research was partially supported by the US Defense Advanced Research Projects Agency and the Army Research Office under contract Number DAAL03-87-C0019.

[12] This tool has since been applied in the areas of software requirements analysis and business proposal analysis.

[13] See Kahn, Nowlan, and McDermott (1985) for specific details on each of these strategies.

[14] Auto-Intelligence is produced by IntelligenceWare, Inc., 9800 Sepulveda Blvd., Suite 700, Los Angeles, CA 90045.

[15] The *IBM-PC* is a trademark of the International Business Machines Corporation.

[16] Research in this area is currently quite prolific, however, the systems resulting from this research are still prototypical in nature. For further information the reader is advised to investigate tools such as BBN's KREME, a knowledge editing environment.

[17] *HyperCard* is a trademark of Apple Computer.

SUGGESTED READINGS

Few books have been written specifically on the topic of knowledge acquisition tools. Readers are advised to consult the proceedings of various artificial intelligence or expert systems conferences and workshops, as well as professional journals. Examples of these include, but are not limited to the following:

Proceedings of the American Association for Artificial Intelligence (AAAI). The proceedings are copyrighted by the AAAI, Inc. and are distributed by William Kaufmann, Inc., 95 First Street, Los Altos, CA 94022.

Proceedings of the International Joint Conference on Artificial Intelligence (IJCAI). The proceedings are copyrighted by the IJCAI, Inc. and are distributed by William Kaufmann, Inc., 95 First Street, Los Altos, CA 94022.

AAAI-sponsored Workshop on Knowledge Acquisition for Knowledge-Based Systems. Proceedings from the workshop are available only at the workshop, but presentations are published in the International Journal of Man-Machine Studies.

European Knowledge Acquisition for Knowledge-Based Systems Workshop (EKAW). The purpose of EKAW is to assemble theoreticians and practitioners of AI who recognize the need for developing methods and systems to assist the process of acquiring and modeling knowledge for knowledge-based systems.

IEEE Expert Systems in Government Symposiums. Proceedings from these symposiums are available through the IEEE Computer Science Press (Washington, DC).

AI Magazine. Published by the American Association for Artificial Intelligence (AAAI), 445 Burgess Dr., Menlo Park, CA 94025-3496.

IEEE EXPERT. Published by the Computer Society of the IEEE, 345 E. 47th St., New York, NY 10017 (IEEE Headquarters) or 10662 Los Vaqueros Circle, Los Alamitos, CA 90720.

APPLICATION

A. Break up into small groups or teams to analyze and evaluate aids and tools that might be used in any component of the knowledge acquisition process (e.g., conceptualization, elicitation, refinement).

1. Devise a rating mechanism similar to the repertory grids discussed in Chapters 8 and 10. Decide as a group on the constructs that you deem important in a knowledge acquisition tool. Examples include those presented in Figure 10-7, such as cost and hypertext integration. Others might include the ability to handle active graphic images.

2. Next, pick a group of tools (at least 3) against which to apply this evaluation. Tools you select should be available to you for evaluation, if possible. If you do not have access to these shells or tools, secure literature on them from the manufacturer or researcher or visit the library for articles that may have been written about them. For example, you might want to analyze/evaluate some of the following:

TOOL/SHELL	MANUFACTURER/DEVELOPER
KEE	IntelliCorp
ART	Inference Corporation
Expertise Transfer System	J. Boose, Boeing Computer Services
Expert Systems Toolkit	Mind Path Technologies, Inc.
MacSMARTS	Cognition Technology Corporation
PC Easy, PC Plus	Texas Instruments, Inc.
GURU	Micro Data Base Systems Inc.

3. Analyze each tool you selected according to the constructs you chose. To rate a tool based on a construct, for example, you might score the tool from 1 to 5 according to how well it meets the specification in the construct or 1 to 5 according to how important that construct is.

4. Use the ratings ascribed to each tool to decide on an overall evaluation. As you do so, discuss features that make the tool useful or problematic for knowledge acquisition.

B. Break up into groups as in A and select a set of tools/shells to contrast with each other. Analyze each tool in terms of factors that you determine. Compile a report that summarizes the contrast among the tools you selected.

11

Evaluating Knowledge-Base Development Efforts

The Issue of Knowledge-Based System Evaluation

> **Verification and Validation**
> **Difficulties of V&V in Knowledge-Based Systems**
> **Attaining Verification of Knowledge-Based Systems**
> **Attaining Validation of Knowledge-Based Systems**

Evaluating Knowledge Acquisition Sessions
> **The Need for Ongoing Evaluation**
> **A Tool for Appraising Knowledge Acquisition Session Effectiveness**

INTRODUCTION

Usually one of the last questions asked in the development of a knowledge-based system is "Does the system perform as required?" If the answer is "No," then the positive action a developer takes is to continue the software engineering process. An affirmative answer to this question enables the system to enter production. If developers are unable to answer this question, then the value of their existing work is greatly reduced. Users will have difficulty accepting the system, and proponents of the system will be unable make any guarantees regarding its functionality.

The criticality of this evaluative question demands that it be addressed, or at least anticipated, much earlier in the expert system development process. Prior to knowledge acquisition efforts, developers should consider, "Will my knowledge acquisition methodology contribute to validation and verification efforts?" and "What procedures and techniques can I establish to provide ongoing efforts to help ensure that the system will perform as required?" The evaluation methodology selected should be an integral part of the process so that (1) the requirements can be linked effectively to performance and (2) knowledge-base content can be traced, evaluated, and verified.

In Chapter 2 we discussed software engineering methodologies designed to compensate for the complexities of developing expert systems and presented a systems-based knowledge acquisition methodology (depicted in Figure 2-10). In Chapter 3 we described procedures and guidelines that contribute to an organized, auditable approach to knowledge acquisition. This chapter builds on Chapters 2 and 3 as we consider the evaluation of knowledge-base development efforts, specifically in regard to knowledge acquisition. Initially, we review the evaluation phase of software engineering and some of the methodologies that have been applied during this phase. Included in this section is background information on verification and validation (V&V) as it has been defined and applied. Next, we consider approaches to verification and validation within the context of knowledge-based systems. Included in this discussion is a presentation of some of the difficulties associated with V&V for knowledge-based systems and a description of some techniques and methodologies that have been applied.

In the final section of this chapter we consider the issue of measuring the effectiveness of knowledge acquisition sessions as it relates to ongoing validation of the knowledge within an expert system. We briefly present some notions on what others have said constitutes "effective" knowledge acquisition sessions. Finally, we investigate the idea of using a formal survey or questionnaire procedure to evaluate and improve the effectiveness of individual knowledge acquisition sessions.[1]

Objectives

This chapter provides the reader with information relating to the evaluation of expert systems and knowledge acquisition efforts. Specifically, it enables readers to accomplish the following:
- Understand the goal of the evaluative stage of software development in general, and knowledge-based systems in particular

- Recognize the difficulty of knowledge-based system verification and validation
- Become acquainted with some of the more commonly used techniques for attaining verification and validation of a knowledge-based system
- Consider the usefulness of informal measurement tools in monitoring the effectiveness of an ongoing knowledge acquisition program.

Key Terms

evaluation	proof-of-correctness	walk-throughs
static analysis tools	interaction analysis	uncertainty analysis
truth analysis	Likert scale	software reliability
certification	attitudinal measurement	

THE ISSUE OF KNOWLEDGE-BASED SYSTEM EVALUATION

Within the knowledge acquisition and development methodology we have proposed, knowledge-based system development begins with some type and level of specifications, iterates through knowledge acquisition, design, implementation, and test cycles, and ends with "formal" **evaluation**. In an ideal development process, the problem is completely and precisely specified in the initial specifications, prior to knowledge acquisition, design, or implementation. Then the evaluation process is imposed on the system to measure the ability of the system to meet the specifications. Unfortunately, there are many problems worth solving that are difficult to define precisely. The vagueness in specifications for these problems creates complexities for the evaluation process. This is certainly the case in many knowledge-based system applications. In conventional software, builders estimate that the intellectual effort involved in evaluation is equal to that involved in design. There is also evidence that the cost of fixing an error increases by an order of magnitude for each phase of the development process. Given the additional difficulties in the development of expert systems, similar or more drastic consequences ensue.

Within this section we describe evaluation in terms of verification and validation and link its origins to conventional software engineering. Next, we discuss the features of knowledge-based systems which make them different (in terms of evaluation) from conventional systems. Finally, we consider some of the approaches to expert system evaluation that originate from university research efforts and industrial experience or have been proposed by researchers within these environments.

Verification and Validation

The evaluation phase is normally titled verification and validation (V&V) of the system (Figure 11-1). Martin (1986) describes verification as "building the product correctly" and validation as "building the right product." A cursory survey of the literature reveals a number of other semiconsistent definitions and discussions.[2].

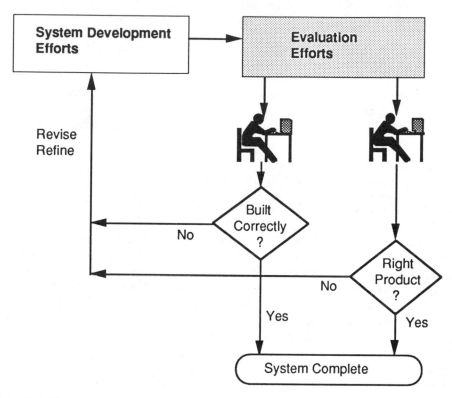

Figure 11-1. The Verification and Validation Process

Defining V&V

Perhaps the basic measure of software quality is that the system performs its functions in the manner intended by its specifiers. This implies not only that the software contain a minimum of mistakes introduced during the implementation of these intentions, but also that it be free of misconstruction of the intentions themselves. As the problems become more complex and include such processes as reasoning and learning, the mistakes can increase in number and severity. The process of verification and validation is the major means of providing software quality assurance and confidence in the system. The need for verification and validation is established readily by considering the numerous ways that the software development process can misconstrue intentions in the requirements specification, design, and implementation phases.

Although testing of the software product is the best understood aspect of verification and validation, correct requirements analysis and specification are the necessary preconditions for software quality. The basic measure of software quality is the reliability of the software product. A reasonable definition of **software reliability** is provided by Shooman as retold by Yourdon (1979):

> . . .the probability that a given software program operates for some given time period, without software error, on the machine for which it was designed, given that it is used within design limits.

A fuller definition of verification and validation is found in Jensen and Tonies (1979):

> **Validation** -- This activity assures that each end item product functions and contains the features as prescribed by its requirements and specifications at the corresponding level.

> **Verification** -- This activity assures that each level of requirements or specification correctly echoes the intentions of the immediately superior level of requirements.

> **Certification** -- This activity assures that the data processing system (hardware and software) properly interacts within the total system and performs its specified function within the total system concept.

Glenford and Myers (1976) give a somewhat different viewpoint:

> **Verification** is an attempt to find errors by executing a program in a test or simulated environment.

> **Validation** is an attempt to find errors by executing a program in a given real environment.

> **Certification** is an authoritative endorsement of the correctness of a program.

Each of these perspectives presumes a well-defined set of requirements and specifications. Developing an adequate AI implementation is a process of intelligently searching an analytically intractable space. In this class of problems, attempts are made to define the search strategy, the inferencing process, the search space, and the contextual associations. The ability to describe the system's complete behavior with these four components is limited severely, since much of the data is incomplete and dynamic. Thus, the verification and validation processes must assist in incrementally refining the behavior and characteristics of the components as part of the software engineering process.

The verification and validation approaches described in the next section exemplify the current attempts at evaluating system performance. They are aimed at satisfying the critics of systems--the domain expert, the ultimate user, the production team, the quality assurance team, and management (Figure 11-2). Evidence from past projects shows that those methods that include many small tests and reviews find more errors and result in better products than those methods that do not (Martin, 1986). This incremental approach fits well with the model and process recommended in Chapter 2.

EVALUATION

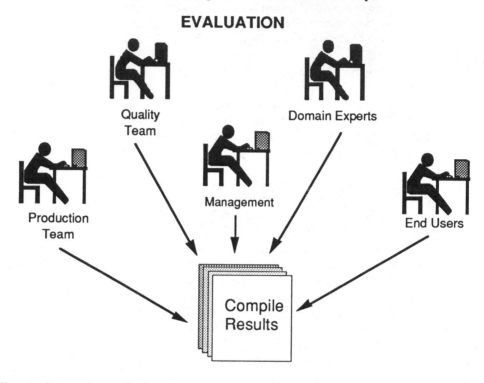

Figure 11-2. Satisfying the Critics--Multi-pronged Evaluation

Techniques for Verification and Validation

While verification and validation are accepted terms in the software engineering community, the processes to accomplish them vary widely. Techniques for conventional software verification should be initiated early in the development process. We propose that verification techniques for AI software also should begin as soon as initial requirements definition ends.[3] Figure 11-3 illustrates some of the techniques that are used for verification.

• Specification standards	• Language checkers
• Consistency checkers	• Inspections
• Simulations	

Figure 11-3. Verification Techniques

Formal **proof-of-correctness** has been advanced as a means of both verification and validation. As a verification method, formal proof strives to ensure that the translation from one level of requirements or specification (considering code as the lowest level of specification) to the next lowest is complete and consistent. As a validation method, formal proof is viewed as a non-executable test of the code. Formal proof does not yet appear to be feasible for verification *or* validation of extensive knowledge-based systems.

Although simulation definitely has a place in validation, testing is by far the dominant aspect. Here, the close linkage of verification and validation becomes apparent. Verification must assure that the requirements definition process yields directly testable specifications. Test specification, test generation, and test case selection are key elements of the testing aspect of validation.

Other evaluation techniques that are accepted in conventional software engineering include reading reviews to uncover errors and style, inspections to facilitate multiple points of view, and on-line testing for scenarios. Additionally, **walk-throughs**, one of the most common evaluation techniques, are especially suitable for management reviews.[4]

Although some of these established practices can be adapted for use with knowledge-based systems, these systems have special characteristics that increase the already-difficult nature of the evaluative process. The next section outlines some of these complexities.

Difficulties of V&V in Knowledge-Based Systems

Since expert or knowledge-based systems (KBS) are a class of software system, it is reasonable to ask how their verification and validation requirements differ from those of conventional software. Knowledge-based systems require verification and validation to ensure user acceptance as much as any other software system. However, differences in the specification and construction of KBS mitigate against the uncritical use of generally accepted verification and validation techniques (Figure 11-4).

- Described in terms of functions or behaviors

- Requirements specifications evolve through development

- Inability to define requirements of knowledge base content a priori

- Incremental development

- Typical construction methods

Figure 11-4. KBS Characteristics That Impact V&V

Given previous discussions of the central role of requirements definition (Chapter 2), it is easy to understand the difficulty currently experienced in defining verification and validation techniques for knowledge-based systems. Partridge (1986) discusses the nature of knowledge-based systems (KBS) as incompletely specified functions (ISF). Summarizing, Partridge notes that AI problems are typically described in terms of behavior (a form of functional description), leading to a characterization that is inherently incomplete and typically context-sensitive. (hence, an incompletely specified function). Requirements specifications for KBS, therefore, evolve through rapid prototyping or incremental development methodologies. While such incremental requirements-specification techniques may lead to a more useful end product, they require substantial modification of existing verification techniques.

Current procurement practice also tends to work against verification of knowledge-based systems. Problems for which reasonably complete requirements specifications exist are usually amenable to solution by conventional techniques. Almost by definition, a problem requiring a knowledge-based systems as a solution will be incompletely specified. The usual result is that verification (and validation) are omitted from the program, leaving resolution of questions as to the "correctness" of the knowledge-based system to be resolved by ad hoc techniques. Other problems with knowledge-based systems verification arise from our current inability to specify, a priori, all of the requirements for knowledge-base content necessary to solve a given problem.[5]

Other issues in verification arise from the methods used to construct knowledge-based systems. It is much more difficult to determine the execution course of systems written in declarative, rather than procedural, programming languages. Even with properly specified requirements and design, it is difficult to ascertain by inspection that the code correctly implements the design. Given that one of the strengths of the knowledge-based systems approach is the clear separation of domain problem-solving knowledge from the execution and control strategy, it is almost impossible to determine if a knowledge-based system will yield correct results by inspection alone. The production of desired outputs is often an emergent property of the interaction of the knowledge base and the inference engine.

The application of current software engineering techniques for test planning, test procedure development, test-case selection, and test execution is meaningless or impossible in the absence of reasonably precise requirements and design specifications. Even modified conventional practices are difficult to apply with the level of specification most often encountered. For the most part, validation of knowledge-based systems has been limited to exercise of the system and human evaluation of the output. In the worst case, the human has been the principal developer of the system, and the test cases have been drawn only from the "training data" used to construct the knowledge base. While such a validation test may be useful as a consistency check (it will provide some level of assurance that construction of the knowledge-based system has correctly captured the intended knowledge), it is totally inadequate as the only validation of the system.

Attaining Verification of Knowledge-Based Systems

Although conventional techniques are not satisfactory for reasonable verification and validation of knowledge-based systems, there are techniques that are currently tractable. In the next two sections we present some of the more promising approaches. Certainly we cannot say that these techniques are foolproof (a statement that is not surprising, since conventional evaluation techniques continue to be refined). While no one has developed a method that has the acceptance of the entire community in the same vein as has the waterfall model in conventional software, we present some of the techniques developers have used and discuss their attainability (Figure 11-5).

- Code-Readings
- Code Walk-throughs
- Documentation, Audit Trails
- Analysis Tools
- Analysis Techniques--Interaction, Uncertainty, Truth

Figure 11-5. A Sampling of Verification Techniques for Knowledge Based Systems

Incremental Verification

A number of steps in the software engineering process render verification useful. First and foremost, requirements and design specifications, no matter how incomplete, must be captured in writing and controlled. Whether a prototyping or incremental development construction methodology is followed, test plans and procedures for each increment must be developed and followed. At the end of each increment, (1) the written requirements and design specifications must be updated to reflect current understanding of the problem solution, and (2) incremental verification must be performed.

The modified waterfall model and other similar methods contain a means for successive refinement. This refinement process enables a metamorphosis from the initial incompletely specified function to an adequately specified function capable of validation against the original real-world problem. While this is not the only technique, it is clear that the starting point of verification and validation is an orderly method of evoking and documenting (reasonably) precise requirements and designs from ill-specified problems.

At any state of specification, the importance of specification standards and inspection techniques such as code-reading and walk-throughs cannot be downplayed. In a like manner, the daily maintenance of module notebooks, knowledge acquisition databases, or similar low-level documentation is important for adequate verification in this environment.

Maintaining Audit Trails for Knowledge-Base Contents

An important consideration for the verification of knowledge-based systems is the verification of knowledge-base contents. This starts with an adequate knowledge acquisition plan for the system and is followed by detailed planning of knowledge acquisition sessions, conducting the session, and using appropriate post session procedures (Figure 11-6). As presented in Chapters 2 and 3, the overall knowledge acquisition plan for the system is determined from the initial requirements and specifications and is updated as these change. At a finer level, goals to meet those requirements help to identify the areas for knowledge acquisition focus which knowledge engineers can use to estimate goals and topics for upcoming knowledge acquisition sessions.

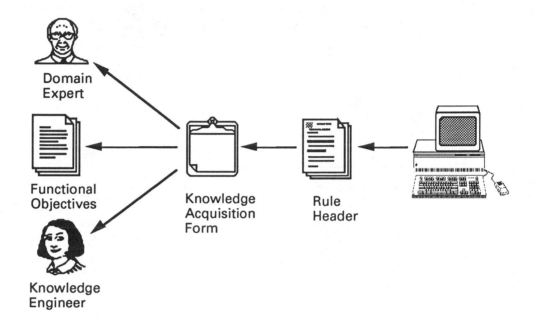

Figure 11-6. Knowledge Acquisition Procedures Enhance Auditability

Verifying that the right knowledge is being acquired can proceed from this type of planning to a quarterly review of the knowledge acquisition plan by a panel of domain experts, the customer, or the primary domain expert. Refinements to the plan can help identify oversights, avoid the omission of important information early in the process, and help determine the proper sequence for the acquisition of specific information. As knowledge acquisition sessions begin, the plan that is in place can be further modified and its usefulness extended. As more is learned about the domain and the expert's conceptualizations and heuristics, knowledge acquisition sessions can be estimated and scheduled more efficiently.

After a session has been held, the knowledge engineer analyzes the notes (i.e., manual notes, videotape, etc.) to extract rules that seem pertinent to the current stage of system development. This information can be summarized on something akin to the knowledge acquisition form or template described in Chapter 3. After it has been compiled, the extracted information should be sent back to the original domain expert for review and sign-off. This aids in certifying and verifying that the correct deductions or extractions have been made and that the information is an accurate representation of the domain expert's behavior during the knowledge acquisition session. If a rule has been incorrectly stated or extracted, the domain expert can initiate corrections prior to its implementation in code. If the information is accurate given the context, the domain expert's sign-off helps contribute to ongoing verification and validation efforts.

Using some type of template or knowledge acquisition planning form can further assist in knowledge-base verification efforts. As described in Chapter 3, such a tool can be designed to include information such as a form number, knowledge-engineer identification, domain-expert identification, planned topic and outline, and date of session. This information is critical to providing a foundation for the "audit trail" of knowledge-base contents. Auditability, in the sense that it is used here, refers to the process of being able to ascertain the source and context of content within the knowledge base. Each of these issues can contribute to the verification and validation process. For example, if the source is not an "authorized" domain expert or if the context (e.g., protocol) from which the rule was acquired limits its accuracy, the resulting accuracy of the rule or fact may be questionable. To enable auditability, a "paper trail" (either printed or electronic) from each item (fact, rule, etc.) in the knowledge base back to the original knowledge acquisition session(s) where it was obtained must be maintained. The use of rule header templates, (also described in Chapter 3), provides a place in which identifying information may be stored and easily printed out for review and the development of knowledge-base documents.

A crucial aspect of knowledge-base verification is determining that the transformation of the knowledge from its source form through one or more intermediate representations to the final machine (computable) representation is accurate. Unfortunately, there is no generally accepted technique for guaranteeing the correctness of this transformation. Techniques that currently seem useful include inspections/walk-throughs with other knowledge engineers and "limited" execution to allow the original expert to see the result of employing the knowledge. These checks require a somewhat different format than those which match to a set of specifications rather than a human expert. Additionally, research into the development of current knowledge acquisition tools is addressing this issue.

Analysis Tools and Techniques
Static analysis tools have been proposed to assist in assuring that the knowledge-base as built is consistent with the domain and design. Such tools include
- Syntactic error checkers
- Cross-reference generators
- Standards auditors
- Structure checkers
- Type analyzers
- Rule consistency checkers.

As the tool user adds new knowledge structures (e.g., rules and their associated certainty factors) to a knowledge base, the system checks the rules and alerts the user to potential problems. The more powerful commercially available tools or shells for developing knowledge-based systems generally include some subset of the above list. However, the construction and use of such tools seems to be done presently on a project-by-project basis. No authoritative ranking of the relative utility of each class of these tools to the verification process has been produced yet, so little guidance is available to the new project manager or knowledge engineer.

Green and Keyes (1986) suggest the importance of engineering analyses to the verification of knowledge-based systems. In addition to analyses common to the software engineering discipline and systems approach (i.e., criticality, sensitivity, stability, efficiency, maintainability), they suggest several that seem more suitable to knowledge-based systems. These include interaction analysis, uncertainty analysis, and truth analysis.

Interaction analysis in this context attempts to deal with the complexity introduced by (quasi-) independent modules and their interaction under the control of an inference engine. Systems using the blackboard model of control probably require the most detailed interaction analysis.

Uncertainty analysis attempts to ensure that the representation and manipulation of uncertainty in the system is consistent with the nature of uncertainty in the domain. This analysis helps ensure that the means of combining uncertainty give "reasonable" results when reasonable uncertainties are assigned to facts and assertions.

Truth analysis is a subset of the techniques used to ensure the integrity of the knowledge base. One special case deserves attention. If the knowledge-based system supports multiple worlds for hypothesis testing and "what if" analysis, it must be able to detect and correct an internally inconsistent world. A powerful means of doing this is the implementation of an automated truth maintenance system. Knowledge-based system verifiers employing such techniques must determine that the truth maintenance system is correct, appropriate, and robust.

Attaining Validation of Knowledge-Based Systems

Validation of knowledge-based systems is possibly more straight-forward than verification, but still requires special attention. Given that suitable requirements specifications can be established, either initially or through a controlled incremental requirements evolution, validation testing of knowledge-based systems can proceed in much the same fashion as for more conventional systems.[6]

However, it is often impossible to validate completely a knowledge-based system because the prerequisite requirements and design specifications do not exist. In fact, this is by far the most common case today. There are still useful things to be done, however, including the notion of adequacy by Partridge (1986), who notes that: "AI programs are not correct or incorrect: they are, at best, adequate. Adequacy is a complex, context-dependent quality. . ." He then defines final validation testing as: "The ultimate test for an adequate approximation is that it displays *no major inadequacies* within its *intended application environment*."

This leads directly to the notion of evaluation rather than strict validation. Hayes-Roth, Waterman, and Lenat (1983) devote an entire chapter to evaluation of expert systems. Within this chapter the authors develop several important themes, including a good discussion of formal versus informal testing and the use of competency criteria for human practitioners as a basis for acceptance testing of knowledge-based systems. Some specific techniques for using human competency to evaluate expert systems are summarized in the sections that follow.

Even if the knowledge of processes and data has been confirmed in the system, the developer must pay special attention to validating the reasoning processes employed by the system. In conventional systems, the sequentiality of the computer processing is a given. In knowledge-based systems, the additional layer of the reasoning process must be considered. Validation of the reasoning processes is essential to establish a minimal baseline of performance for the system. Given the high level of interaction between the knowledge and the reasoning processes, validation of the entire system is more than compounded if the reasoning process is not validated. At present there are few standardized methods to accomplish this task. If development efforts involve the use of a knowledge acquisition tool or expert system shell, it is usually possible to request a description of how a specific conclusion was reached. For example, the inference engine may provide a detailed description of which rules were used, and the sequence of their use during processing. Otherwise, the validation of the system's reasoning usually involves reviews by human experts.

Validation by "Simulation"

Simulation methods can be used to assist in knowledge base system validation. For example, some authors (Westphal, 1988) suggest that sensitivity analysis (Yourdon, 1979) be applied to the system as a whole after confirmation in each stage. For example, sensitivity analysis of a domain model developed with BDM-KAT, a knowledge acquisition tool (Reeker, Blaxton, and Geesey, 1987) consists of structured observations of an event-driven step-through to assist in validating acquired rules that govern its conduct. In this case, sensitivity analysis is applied to test variations of causal input parameters in the process model. As these parameters are manipulated, the KEE SIMKIT™ environment provides facilities to display the results (e.g., clock, pressure gauge, temperature gauge).[7] These tools provide the opportunity to (1) observe changes in relative output variables and (2) establish an acceptance of the model.

Validation by Turing Test

According to Banning (1984), "System validation is ideally accomplished by means of a Turing test" (p. 283). For example, an expert is shown two sets of conclusions from the same problem (or set of problems). One conclusion represents the efforts of another expert in the domain, and the other conclusion can be attributed to the expert system, however, the evaluating expert is not told how the conclusions were obtained. The expert is then asked to evaluate the conclusions. If the expert shows no preference for one of the two sources, it is assumed that the expert system adequately models the human decision process (Figure 11-7).

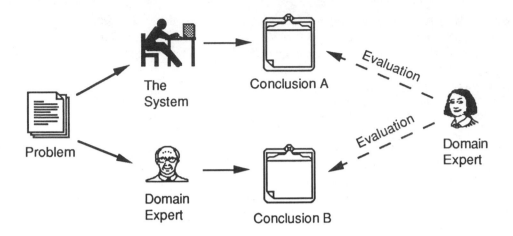

Figure 11-7. The Turing Test as a Validation Technique

In a review of expert systems for managers (ESM), Banning examined the knowledge acquisition and system validation procedures that were most often used and most appropriate for ESMs. In a majority of the cases he examined, knowledge acquisition was accomplished by eliciting protocols from several domain experts as they performed their tasks. From these protocols, rules were extracted. Validation of the resulting systems was accomplished by pitting a human expert against the system in a 'blind Turing test' similar to that described above. If review by human experts is the only method available to developers, this process typically occurs in one of the following two manners: review by single expert or review by panel of experts.

Review by Single Expert. Validation of the system's rules and reasoning processes often occurs by requesting that the original or primary domain expert review the results of system processing. Such a review entails using the expert system to solve domain problems or scenarios that an expert helps identify as typical. Frequently, scenarios are established such that they represent progressively more difficult problems. A typical review process involves testing the system using these sets of novel scenarios until the system consistently behaves (1) within the established domain and (2) in a manner approved by the original expert (Grover, 1982).

Review by Panel of Experts. At some point in the validation process, an expert system may be evaluated by a panel of experts. In fact, extensive behavior checks of a system may occur with both the original expert and a panel of experts. This process was used in the development and validation of INTERNIST (Miller, 1982). For example, the panel may be asked to review the expert system's conclusions in solving the same problem scenarios that the primary expert has already reviewed. Or, the panel may participate in the blind Turing tests previously described to discern whether or not they can differentiate the system's behavior from that of a human expert. Panel review may be particularly necessary if the expert system represents diverse subdomains of knowledge.

Consideration for the Use of Experts in Validation. There are multiple issues involved with using experts to evaluate or validate knowledge-based systems. Experts frequently disagree with other experts, given the same set of initial assumptions. An expert panel is also prone to the same problems as those of a multiple-expert knowledge acquisition session (e.g., equality). Additionally, it is not clear whether experts should evaluate the results of knowledge-based systems execution, the reasoning invoked during the execution, or both. Finally, all experts are subject to biases, including biases against the accuracy of humans. St. Johenser (1986) has constructed the equivalent of a double-blind test to remove some of these biases. His method is worthy of consideration if evaluation by human experts is the only option for validation.

Review by End Users. Gaschnig and others (1983) note that "the ultimate criterion of success is whether an expert system is actually used for expert consultation by individuals other than the system developers" (p. 245). Even after experts in the domain have evaluated the performance of an expert system, developers may wish to consult end users. Expert systems are rarely designed for use by experts in the domain. More often, they are designed as a job aid or tool for a novice or intermediate in the domain. These individuals may be as interested in how the expert system reached its conclusion as in the conclusion itself. Involving end users in the review process can help ensure that the system is being designed to meet the needs of the people for whom it is being developed. These needs include not only what information is provided, but at what level, the adequacy of explanation facilities, the ease of use of the interface (both input and output), and processing needs (e.g., speed).

In summary, to accomplish adequate evaluation in an expert system usually implies that

- A link must be provided from the evaluation processes to the specifications
- A method for evaluation be established.

Since many of the problems are incompletely specified, documentation provided by the knowledge acquisition sessions may provide the only link. The problem then becomes one of determining if the knowledge that has been acquired is valid and verifiable. One method to substantiate that the acquired knowledge is valid and verifiable is by associating it with a domain expert who has been customer-authorized or certified. Another method of addressing this issue is the periodic review of knowledge-base content and system functionality.

The validity and verifiability of elicited knowledge may also be a function of the effectiveness of the knowledge acquisition session in which it was obtained. The next section looks into one method that has been used to evaluate the effectiveness of knowledge acquisition sessions.

EVALUATING KNOWLEDGE ACQUISITION SESSIONS

When does an expert system developer know that a knowledge acquisition session has been effective? The answer is important in determining whether the knowledge acquired is valid and verifiable. Inability to answer may result in inadequate or inaccurate knowledge-base content, poor expert system performance, disgruntled domain experts, extended development time, and unhappy customers. Recognizing any inadequacies of knowledge acquisition (i.e., methodology, selected techniques, knowledge-engineer ability) and progress *early* in the process can allow the developer to make changes that increase the efficiency of knowledge acquisition and the validity of the knowledge base.

Informal discussions of this topic with a number of developers suggest several ways of determining whether knowledge acquisition has been effective:

- A knowledge engineer's verbal report of knowledge acquisition progress and plans.
- The ratio of rules extracted to knowledge acquisition time (i.e., number of rules per minute)
- The successful performance of an expert system in system test procedures.

Informal, verbal self-reports by the knowledge engineer who conducted the knowledge acquisition session can be dismissed as practically useless. These self-reports are usually provided in passing, in response to an open-ended verbal question from management (e.g., "How'd the session go?"). The knowledge engineer's reply to this question is determined by his or her perception of the event, what he or she thinks is important, and a fear of reproach should the answer be negative. Thus, the responses are extremely subjective and cannot be compared to a standard.

The number of rules per knowledge acquisition session can also be questioned as a determinant of effectiveness. While quantity is certainly important (and a measure of efficiency, perhaps), rule quality is an even more critical and a much more elusive metric. To date, we know of no research that has attempted to correlate ratio of rules per session to rule *quality*. Thus, its usefulness as a method to measure knowledge acquisition session effectiveness is debatable.

Finally, the performance of an expert system in formal test procedures *can* be termed a measure of knowledge acquisition effectiveness. These tests, as discussed earlier, provide an indication of whether or not the knowledge-base content is adequate and how it is used to reason through domain problems. This evaluation of knowledge acquisition effectiveness is not without problems, however, in that it occurs "after the fact." Knowledge acquisition-related problems that may have detracted from system performance, verification, and validation perceivably could have been alleviated had the developer recognized their existence during development efforts.

The Need for Ongoing Evaluation

To date, most evaluative efforts, such as verification and validation, occur near the end of prototype cycles. Even ongoing, iterative V&V efforts fail to address some problems that can greatly hinder the quality of acquired knowledge. Ongoing evaluation may include

- Examining knowledge engineer effectiveness
- Monitoring the working relationship between knowledge engineer(s) and domain expert(s)
- Reviewing a domain expert's participation in knowledge acquisition sessions
- Monitoring knowledge acquisition sessions to identify and attack problems.

A Tool for Appraising Knowledge Acquisition Session Effectiveness

Researchers continue to develop and systematize elicitation techniques and tools to prepare and conduct knowledge acquisition sessions. Consistent progress is reported in the ability to work with domain experts, extract necessary knowledge, manipulate knowledge acquisition tools, and represent specific types of acquired knowledge. However, no formal attempt has been reported to evaluate the "effectiveness" of a knowledge acquisition session. Little research has been conducted to identify the issues that contribute to the effectiveness of a traditional knowledge acquisition session. For example, can effectiveness be measured by issues other than the number, type, and complexity of rules a session generated? Even if one suspected that factors enhancing a knowledge acquisition session's effectiveness could be identified, could they be termed "hearsay," or would they be measurable? For example, desired characteristics for knowledge engineers have been suggested, but little data is available to support these descriptions. In addition, domain experts, who play key roles in sessions, are not always made aware of their impact on the process and their contribution to an effective knowledge acquisition session.

This paucity of research has left developers without tools to identify problems in the knowledge acquisition session that may impact later V&V efforts. If developed, these tools could be used in planning knowledge engineer training to strengthen areas of weakness. Documented responses concerning the effectiveness of knowledge acquisition sessions may be analyzed to note trends. Overall assessment of "effectiveness" can be used with customers if knowledge acquisition methods are questioned. The range of uses of such a tool includes the following:

- Identify what knowledge engineers and domain experts consider to be significant contributions to session effectiveness

- Quickly identify specific problems

- Allow knowledge engineering coordinators to work with knowledge engineers to enhance areas in which their skills are not as strong as desired

- Gather inter-rater reliability information and compare rankings among raters on key points

- Validate knowledge acquisition methods or techniques for a specific domain problem.

The manner in which a tool identified problems or isolated areas for improvement would be critical to its interpretation and use. Because knowledge acquisition "effectiveness" is difficult to define, tool make-up must take into account that different respondents may have different definitions of effectiveness. In addition, tool construction must structure the process so that the end result yields data that (1) can be subjected to statistical analysis and (2) is not entirely subjective in nature. Results must be such that analysis will yield data on trends. Finally, personnel with varying backgrounds (e.g., domain expert, knowledge engineer) should be able to use the tool quickly and easily and in a number of settings (i.e., it must be transportable).

A number of techniques have been used in other fields to elicit and compare numerous responses to well-designed items. Questionnaires, survey instruments, and **attitudinal measurement** devices (e.g., Likert, Thurstone scale) have long provided researchers with information on respondent perceptions, opinions, and attitudes. For example, the questionnaire survey requires respondents to read the questions themselves and provide written answers (Jacoby, 1980). When using such a tool, the researcher carefully designs questions that will elicit the attitudes, beliefs, and self-reports of the respondent (Wrightsman & Deaux, 1981).

Questionnaires, Surveys, and Scales: Background and Considerations

Until knowledge acquisition effectiveness can be linked more directly to quantifiable evidence, it is largely a measure of a participant's attitude, belief, or self-report of the process. Researchers have defined these entities differently, depending on their background and expertise. For the purpose of eliciting an appraisal of the effectiveness of a knowledge acquisition session from a domain expert or knowledge engineer, the definitions in Figure 11-8 may be useful.

Attitude -- An evaluation that indicates a "like" or "dislike" toward an object (Fishbein & Ajzen, 1972).

Beliefs -- Probabilistic judgment about whether a particular object has a particular characteristic.

Self Reports -- Verbalization of an individual's own, unstructured perception of an object or

Figure 11-8. Definitions for Appraising Knowledge Acquisition Session Effectiveness

The measurement of attitudes, beliefs, and opinions has a long history. Some of the techniques for tool development in this field may be adapted for use in developing a tool to help evaluate the effectiveness of knowledge acquisition sessions. It is impossible to describe all the applicable methods (e.g., questionnaires, surveys, and scales) that have been developed as measurement devices. Specific tools include Thustone's Equal-Appearing Intervals (Thurstone & Chave, 1929), the Semantic Differential (Osgood, Suci, & Tannenbaum, 1957), and the Likert method of summated ratings (1932). Each of these methods is comprised of a set of directions, a list of statements or items to which the rater responds, and a response set (i.e., placing a number in a blank, marking the point on a horizontal scale).

Measurement-tool structure ranges from open-ended questions, which allow the respondent to expound upon the topic to the level of detail desired, to closed questions, which limit the type of response elicited. Tools based on open-ended questions have two primary difficulties in relation to their use in appraising knowledge acquisition session effectiveness. First, they have low reliability. Second, the answers are extremely difficult to compare and analyze, which limits the usefulness of the data for validating knowledge acquisition session content and structure. Tools structured around closed-questions can be designed such that they are much more reliable and, because the answers are structured within a specific format, the answers are comparable and the data can be analyzed statistically. However, they typically limit the respondent to predesigned responses and risk the loss of important attitudinal information or suggestions for improvement.

To provide the reader with some sense of the type of closed-question tools that may be adapted for use in the measurement of perceived knowledge acquisition session effectiveness, we will briefly detail the design of a **Likert scale**. This tool not only reflects the most often used format, but also has characteristics that may be easily adapted for use in the design of a tool to measure perceived knowledge acquisition effectiveness. Likert (1932) designed his method of "measuring" attitudes to be easy to understand, use, and score. The Likert scale consists of a series of statements that the researcher compiles. Each is either clearly favorable or clearly unfavorable to a specified object. The rater is asked to indicate his or her degree of agreement or disagreement with each statement. Likert described a 5-point scale to provide gradations within the response alternatives. The rater responds by selecting the most appropriate gradation (Figure 11-9). A series of these types of item comprises a Likert scale. The respondent's "score" on the scale is a sum of the responses to all of the items. Although Likert originally used a 5-point scale, it is common to see 6- or even 7-point scales which attempt to tap attitudes or perceptions with even more precision.

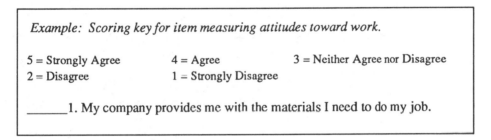

Example: Scoring key for item measuring attitudes toward work.

5 = Strongly Agree   4 = Agree   3 = Neither Agree nor Disagree
2 = Disagree   1 = Strongly Disagree

_____1. My company provides me with the materials I need to do my job.

Figure 11-9. Likert's 5-Point Rating Scale

Constructing a Likert scale involves generating concise statements to which individuals respond. For the purposes of tabulation and scoring, a numerical value is assigned to each of the possible responses (i.e., "1 = Strongly Disagree"). If the scale is used for research purposes, the designer must determine the reliability of the scale using either the split-half (correlating the sum of the odd statements for each individual against the sum of the even statements) or test-retest. Reviews should also be conducted to identify items with good discrimination and the proper assignment of numerical values. Developers may wish to subject the battery to item analysis to determine internal consistency and to refine the statements.

Designing Questionnaires and Scales

Each type of scale will have its own specific directions for constructing it for research purposes. However, a tool to determine the effectiveness of a knowledge acquisition session is less formal and is intended for more pragmatic use. While it need not reflect the highest reliability, it must be designed such that it can meet validation-related needs. The following presents a synthesis of directions for the construction of scales that might be used as knowledge acquisition session appraisal tools (Adapted from Likert, 1932; Koballa, 1984; Andrich, 1978).

1. Request that qualified "judges" assemble a large (e.g., 50 to 60) pool of items that address elements of knowledge acquisition effectiveness. Judges might include potential respondents (i.e., domain expert, knowledge engineer) as well as those with vast experience in knowledge acquisition and AI program management.

2. Eliminate obviously redundant items.

3. Restructure the remaining items according to the following criteria:
   (a) Each proposition should be stated in a clear, concise, straight-forward manner.
   (b) Each statement should be in the simplest possible vocabulary, devoid of acronyms or highly technical terms.
   (c) No statement should involve double negatives or other structures that make it confusing.
   (d) Refrain from using "double-barreled" statements, which should always be broken apart.
   (e) Avoid ambiguity.
   (f) If you are concerned about a stereotyped response, word the statements so that about one-half of them fall at one end of the continuum and the other toward the opposite end.

4. Select the alternatives and numbering scheme the scale will use. It is not important what the terms associated with each response are called, as long as they are reasonable and the intervals between them are constant.

5. Pilot-test the statements with a group of judges and/or potential respondents (or both). If the tool is to be used for research purposes, respondents rate each as the actual subject would. If used informally, judges might be asked to select the response that indicates how important each item is to knowledge acquisition session effectiveness.

6. Compute a score for each respondent by totaling the points corresponding to his or her responses.

7. If you wish to perform an item analysis, identify high scorers (top 25%) and low scorers (lowest 25%) and perform the statistical analysis to identify items that discriminate between respondent groups. To analyze the scale more informally, run descriptive statistics that reveal the most often selected score (mode) and the average score (mean) per item.

8. Retain items that provided good discrimination between high and low scorers (if using the tool for research purposes). Or if the tool is to be used informally, retain items that were rated consistently as being "important" or better.

9. Refine the items; select final statements.

10. Provide an open-ended "Comments" section to allow respondents to offer unsolicited or clarifying information.

11. Use the tool, collect reliability and validity measures over time, and refine the tool as needed.

A Case Study: Developing a Tool for Rating Knowledge Acquisition Session Effectiveness

During efforts on a large-scale, highly visible expert system development project with multiple knowledge engineers and domain experts, we recognized a need to monitor the "effectiveness" of our knowledge acquisition sessions. Prior to use of the tool, this evaluation occurred after each knowledge acquisition session, as the knowledge engineering coordinator followed up with session participants. Informal discussions and brief observations failed to provide information of a historical nature that could be used to spot trends in our ability to set up sessions, deliver knowledge acquisition techniques, or work effectively with domain experts. Additionally, it left us vulnerable regarding the domain expert's or customer's *perception* of the effectiveness of our knowledge acquisition program and its effect on the validity of the acquired knowledge.

To enhance the effectiveness of our ability to conduct knowledge acquisition sessions and to provide documentation of the perceived effectiveness (as rated by domain expert, knowledge engineer, or others), we decided to construct an informal adaptation of a Likert scale. This tool could be applied following randomly selected sessions to allow us to spot problem situations quickly, plan training sessions for knowledge engineers, if necessary, and maintain positive working relations with our domain experts. Developmental goals for such a session effectiveness tool include (1) identifying factors that contribute to session effectiveness and (2) providing ongoing session evaluation.

What Contributes to Session Effectiveness? To meet the first goal for developing our tool, we had to isolate the factors that seemed to contribute to the effectiveness of a knowledge acquisition session. Combing current research provided few clues. Basing effectiveness on a measurement like "number of rules per session" might help us see how precise we were with the use of our techniques, but did not allow us to monitor the domain expert's perception or to track problems. Because of the lack of existing data, we chose to establish a pool of "expert judges" who would help generate and evaluate statements that reflected their identification of important components for effective knowledge acquisition sessions.

Using an electronic mail facility, we sent a request for assistance in isolating these factors to 20 individuals, each of whom was experienced in some facet of knowledge acquisition and expert system development. Our proposed pool of judges included active knowledge engineers, experienced knowledge engineers, current domain experts, managers from expert system development projects, and persons actively involved in training knowledge engineers.

After soliciting and securing their support, we oriented our judges to our goal and provided background information on the development of scales and questionnaires, concentrating on item-development issues in particular. For example, few of our judges understood the development and use of these measurement devices or had experience constructing interpretable items. We then requested that each judge provide us with items that represented concepts or behavior he or she felt contributed to session effectiveness. (We did not limit the number of items contributed by each judge.) Items were submitted by electronic mail, making it possible for us to compile all of the items submitted. Our initial pool of items numbered over 80.

Next, we eliminated redundant items and restructured the statements. Restructuring allowed us to mold the statements into the format that would meet guidelines for questionnaire construction (i.e., the content of each statement is measurable, each item contains only one main clause/idea, etc.). This refinement process yielded 29 items that were recognizably distinguishable from one another. These 29 items were then resubmitted to our judges. They were asked to rate each item (using a Likert scale where 7 = very important and 1 = very unimportant) according to its contribution or affect on a knowledge acquisition session's overall effectiveness.

Using descriptive statistics (e.g., specifically mode, mean), we analyzed the results of this rating. Items that our judges consistently scored low ("neither important nor unimportant, somewhat unimportant, unimportant, very unimportant") were eliminated from the pool of items. Working from the pool of 15 items that resulted, we refined the structure and content based on edits from our judges.

Our next task was to structure the form of the tool itself. We wanted items that measured similar concepts to be grouped together to enable faster response, so we requested that our judges help sort the items into recognizable "sets" or categories sharing an important characteristic. The fifteen items could be sorted into three stacks on the basis of content. A review of the items in each stack allowed us to isolate the thread running through each item in the group. The three areas that emerged from this process were tagged with the following descriptors:

- Session Organization
- Communication/Cooperation
- Facilities.

Figure 11-10 reflects the contents of the tool in its final form. It consists of 15 items presented in three groups. The sixteenth item requests an overall rating of the knowledge acquisition session. Besides the obvious use of an overall session rating, this score allowed us to examine the possible correlation of individual item scores with the score for overall session effectiveness. Thus, we hoped we would be better equipped to isolate factors that consistently seemed to correlate with (and thus contribute to) session effectiveness.

Knowledge Acquisition Session Appraisal Tool

Directions: Using the scale below, place the number that best describes your degree of agreement or disagreement in the blank beside the item. Please include comments and specific suggestions for improving future sessions in the spaces provided.

7 = Strongly Agree	3 = Tend to Disagree
6 = Agree	2 = Disagree
5 = Tend to Agree	1 = Strongly Disagree

4 = Neither Agree or Disagree

Session Organization
___1. The purpose of the session was clearly stated.
___2. The session began at the scheduled time.
___3. The session reflected the proposed agenda.
___4. Important items outside of the agenda were recorded for later
      investigation.
___5. The session's main points were summarized at the close of the session.
___6. Action items were identified at the close of the session.

Comments:

Communication / Cooperation
___7. The knowledge engineer and domain expert worked together to meet
      session objectives
___8. Responsibilities of each session member were made clear.
___9. The knowledge engineer's communication techniques contributed to session
      effectiveness.
__10. Session format or techniques were appropriate for session goals.
__11. Questions asked were pertinent to session goals.

Comments:

Facilities
__12. The area was prepared for the session.
__13. Supplies (e.g., markers, models) were adequate to support the session.
__14. The area was free from distraction.
__15. Interference from the use of recording equipment was minimized.

Comments:

General
__16. Overall, this knowledge acquisition session was productive.

KA Session #_____   Session Date: _____
Knowledge Engineer:_____   DomainExpert:_____
Evaluator:_____   Evaluation Date:_____

Figure 11-10. Knowledge Acquisition Session Effectiveness Appraisal Tool

Because we realized that closed, structured questions have a limitation in that they "cut off" the free flow of information that might help us in enhancing session effectiveness, each item set is followed by a "Comments" area. Respondents were encouraged to use this space to be more specific about their response to an item in the set. The bottom portion of the form is documentation to establish a historical record for the rating. Thus, all rating forms for a particular knowledge engineer, domain expert, or knowledge acquisition session may be analyzed statistically.

Applying the Tool

Upon completion of the tool, the resulting 16-item questionnaire was distributed to the expert system teams and its use was explained. Specifically, we briefed the domain experts and knowledge engineers on its purpose, as we did not want either group to feel reluctant to rate a knowledge acquisition session honestly. In addition, we wanted them to understand upfront that some of the items alluded to their performance, either directly or indirectly. The tool was introduced as a vehicle to accomplish the following:

- Provide documentation on the domain expert's response to a knowledge acquisition session

- Allow trainers, peers, and management to rate knowledge-engineer performance

- Develop plans to enhance performance in an area with consistently low ratings

- Allow a knowledge engineer to review and rate his or her own performance

- Provide ongoing informal evaluation of overall knowledge acquisition effectiveness.

On a random basis, the knowledge engineering coordinator gave a copy of the tool to the knowledge engineer in charge of an upcoming session and to the domain expert who was scheduled to participate in the session. Upon conclusion of the session, the knowledge engineer and the domain expert separately rated the session's effectiveness and provided appropriate comments on the form. Concurrently, the knowledge engineering coordinator completed a form while reviewing a videotape of the knowledge acquisition session.

When completed, the forms were given to the knowledge engineering coordinator, who prepared them for processing. She compiled the results of the tools to review trends and continuously analyze the data acquired. The use of descriptive statistics allowed the coordinator to identify trends and the most commonly selected response (e.g., mode) or the average response (e.g., mean). At no time did the knowledge engineer and domain expert see each other's forms and comments. However, informal conferences with individual knowledge engineers provided a forum during which trends spotted in the forms could be discussed. During the conference, the forms served as a useful mechanism to stimulate feedback and discussion related to strengths, note areas for improvement, and make plans for growth.

The tool provided us with information relevant to the most often selected response for an item across ratings for a given session, score ranges, and the number of external comments a given item generated. We have been able to analyze trends to determine patterns for a specific knowledge engineer, or the manner in which a particular domain expert rates sessions. We have also been able to compare the ratings of groups. For example, domain experts rating a session in which they participated tend to rate the knowledge engineer's behavior *better* than does the knowledge engineer. Additionally, the items that domain experts consider most important in the knowledge acquisition session tend to be those that could be termed "procedural" or "organizational."

The tool has assisted us in several ways. First, it has enabled us to understand how best to meet the needs of specific domain experts during a knowledge acquisition session, regardless of the type of session or technique we used. Second, the tool has helped us rate our own performance as knowledge engineers, either after an actual session or while viewing a videotape of a session. Responding to specific, standard items forces us to view ourselves in a less subjective light and at a finer level than if we simply responded to "How did the session go?" Finally, the use of the tool and the data it has generated provides us with material that we can use to determine the ongoing effectiveness of our knowledge acquisition program.

ENDNOTES

[1] Some of the ideas presented within this chapter were stimulated by several papers presented in workshops and/or from interactions with colleagues building large knowledge-based systems. Particular mention should be made of:
- "Verification and validation of expert systems," a white paper by Shikli, Green & Keyes (1986)
- A training seminar presented by Dr. Nancy Martin of Softpert Systems, (1986)
- Discussions with Dr. Bud Hammons (Texas Instruments, 1987)
- Chapters 7 and 8 of Hayes-Roth (et al.), Building Expert Systems
- Conversations and writings with Artie Briggs (1987).

[2] While many of the sources mentioned in the bibliography would be most adequate, the discussion in this section is indebted to the chapter by Michael S. Deutsch on verification and validation in Software Engineering (Jensen & Tonies, 1979).

[3] We should note that most verification activities are "paper" activities, while validation is focused on computer-based activities.

[4] More information on these methodologies is available in software engineering texts referenced in Chapter 2.

[5] If work currently in progress by Doug Lenat and others on the amount of knowledge required for common-sense reasoning is correct, it may be a decade before it will be possible to specify requirements of knowledge-base content with any hope of accuracy.

[6] The merits and demerits of various test philosophies and strategies to accomplish validation testing are well documented in the literature and will not be discussed here.

[7] *KEE* and *SIMKIT* are trademarks of IntelliCorp.

SUGGESTED READINGS

Proceedings of the Workshop on Verification and Validation of Knowledge-based Systems at the Conference on Aerospace Applications of Artificial Intelligence (1987).

Partridge, D. Artificial Intelligence: Applications in the Future of Software Engineering, New York: Ellis Horwood Limited, 1986.

Gashnig, J., P. Klahr, H. Pople, E. Shortliffe, and E. Terry, "Evaluation of expert systems: Issues and case studies." In F. Hayes-Roth, D. Waterman, and D. Lenat, Building Expert Systems, Reading, MA: Addison-Wesley, 1983.

Lancaster, J. "Expert system evaluation: An experimental perspective," BDM Technical Report, August, 1988.

Liebowitz, J. "A useful approach for evaluating expert systems," Expert Systems, 3:2 (1986), pp. 86-92.

Adelman, L. "On the basis of what criteria should decision support systems be evaluated?" Proceedings of the Second Expert Systems in Government Conference, 1986. Washington, DC: IEEE Computer Society Press.

Buchanan, B. G. and E. H. Shortliffe, "The problem of evaluation." In B. G. Buchanan and E. H. Shortliffe, eds. Rule-Based Expert systems: They MYCIN Experiments of the Stanford Heuristic Programming Project. Reading, MA: Addison-Wesley.

APPLICATION

Research the existing, documented efforts in the development of knowledge-based systems in a domain or application of your choice (e.g., diagnosis). Compile a report that summarizes the knowledge acquisition and V&V methodology for existing expert systems in the field you chose. During the development of the report, analyze any apparent correlation between the two sets of methodologies (KA & VV). To complete this task, ask yourself the following questions:

- In the field you chose, does knowledge acquisition seem to be related to verification and validation?

- How does one (KA or V&V) "feed" the other?

- Did (or how did) the knowledge acquisition approach and methodology selected impact the validation and verification of the systems?

- Does a specific KA methodology or V&V methodology emerge as being dominant in the field you chose? If so, what is the reason?

- Can you hypothesize how KA and V&V methodologies might change if applied in a domain other than the one you chose?

- Can you identify any problems with the approaches applied in the field you chose, and, if so, can you provide ideas for solutions to these problems?

Appendix

Key Terms

short-term memory	cognitive models	semantic nets
long-term memory	problem space	teleologic behavior
knowledge compilation	sensory register	algorithms
production system	information processing theory	

APPENDIX A: HUMAN KNOWLEDGE, MEMORY, AND PROBLEM SOLVING

This appendix contains background information concerning human knowledge, memory, and problem solving. Although its contents should not be considered to be a complete coverage of the field, it presents research summaries and provides information on sources for more in-depth information.

Storing and Accessing Knowledge

Human memory impacts the storage and retrieval of knowledge. Figure A-1 illustrates a view of human memory known as the **information-processing theory** (Atkinson & Shiffrin, 1968; Waugh & Norman, 1965). As depicted here, memory is a system of separate, but interwoven storage receptacles or components. According to the theory, each receptacle (e.g., bins) is able to process certain types of cognitive codes (e.g., visual, acoustic, verbal, linguistic, semantic), which can be transferred from bin to bin. The individual storage bins are the sensory register, short-term memory, and long-term memory, each of which differs in its organization and capacity. Each of these theoretical mechanisms is described in more detail in subsequent sections.

The Sensory Register

The information-processing theory implies that the raw data that your senses perceive is transferred into the **sensory register**. This large-capacity storage bin temporarily holds a copy of all raw sensory images. The raw data is unorganized and unprocessed. If left in the sensory register, the information disintegrates or decays in less than one or two seconds (Bourne, 1979). Specific techniques (e.g., rehearsal) must be used to transfer this data to short term memory or to more permanent status.

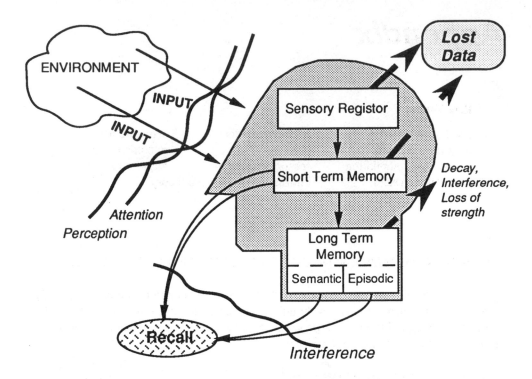

Figure A-1. Memory and the Information Processing Theory

Short Term Memory

Short-term memory is the "working" memory, where conscious mental processes are performed (Bourne, 1979). Information is held briefly in the short-term memory, then is either coded into long-term memory or forgotten. Short-term memory facilitates cognitive organization as information is coded for later use. Klatzky (1980) likens short-term memory to a "mental workbench." Material here can be worked, or transformed, to enable organization.

Short-term memory also has capacity limits and requires some type of active concentration. While we do not know its actual capacity, Miller (1956) proposed that short-term memory could hold or process seven, plus or minus two items. Although the definition of "items" has been debated, most of us can attest that, for unorganized information (e.g., new telephone numbers), our memory span approximates seven. To increase this span, we chunk or organize pieces of information according to a rule or pattern. In fact, Zechmeister and Nyberg (1982) suggest that the short-term memory is comprised of chunks. The human tendency to recall recently-acquired post office box numbers, student or employee ID numbers, and telephone numbers in smaller sub-groups seems to support the use of chunking.

Although more permanent than information in the sensory register, information in the short-term memory also has a tendency to deteriorate. Miller (1964) has referred to short-term memory as a "leaky bucket." Bourne (1979) reports that information in the short-term memory decays in about fifteen seconds unless we take active action (e.g., rehearsal) to retain it. Psychologists (Wickelgren, 1965; Conrad, 1964; Hintzman, 1965, 1967; Atkinson & Shiffrin, 1968) have investigated the types of code that seem common in short-term memory and theorize that the code is primarily acoustic, verbal, or linguistic. Unrehearsed code in the short-term memory disappears. As we rehearse or use some new fact, it becomes transferred to long-term memory.

Long-Term Memory

Long-term memory serves as the "permanent" storehouse for information. Cognitive psychologists theorize that there are two "types" of long-term memory: semantic memory and episodic memory (Bourne, 1979). While forgetting still occurs in this memory system, its cause is due not to deterioration but to retrieval problems (Shiffrin, 1970).

The long-term memory holds not only the vast amounts of information we have learned, but also rules for processing that information. The capacity for holding information in long-term memory is immense, owing to the fact that information there is thought to be highly organized. Apparently, unless it is affected by disease or injury, long-term memory holds material indefinitely. Retrieval failures, or situations in which we cannot access information that is stored in long-term memory, are most often due to interference.

Although information in long-term memory is transferred from short-term memory, the cognitive code in which the information is organized and represented probably differs. Code in the long-term memory bin appears to be semantic, or meaning-oriented as opposed to the acoustic, verbal, or linguistic code. Baddely and Dale (1966) demonstrate this by examining "intrusion errors" of subjects who had been asked to recall a list of words several hours after a single viewing of the words. The most common errors were the recall of words *not* on the list. The interesting point is that the incorrect words that were recalled were almost always semantically equal to the corresponding omitted word. Thus, subjects seemed to have stored the meaning or deep structure of the word as opposed to the actual word itself.

Impact on Knowledge Acquisition

The information-processing theory, as we have seen, holds that human memory is comprised of the three major systems: the sensory register, short-term memory, and long-term memory. Cognitive psychologists argue as to the explicit boundaries and code organization techniques within these systems. However, most agree that we tend to progress through similar sequences in translating information from its initial form to long term storage. Initially, we are inclined to practice the material, transferring it to what was described as acoustic code. Using the material seems to alter its organization or code to be more semantic, or meaning-oriented in nature.

Whether or not the material is actually "transferred" elsewhere during this process is not critical to knowledge acquisition. What *is* important is that knowledge engineers approach knowledge acquisition sessions realizing the limits, storage capacities, and organization mechanisms available to domain experts. For example, if knowledge engineers realize that "forgetting" long-term memory code is most often due to a retrieval problem brought on by interference, they can attempt to alleviate the source of the interference. Interference can be caused by a domain expert's anxiety, concurrent processing tasks, and stress. Effectively setting the stage for knowledge acquisition, then, must include attention to orienting the expert to the task and reducing anxiety. Providing experts with pre-questions that they can review prior to the session can help reduce the stress that can cause interference and give them lead time in which to recall the necessary information.

Using Knowledge to Solve Problems

At the most general level, problem solving can be defined as the process of combining existing ideas to form a new combination of ideas. As commonplace as it is, Bailey (1982) contends that problem solving and expert judgment are among the most complex forms of human mental processing. Since expert systems are designed to serve as decision aids, it is reasonable to examine the notion of how human experts solve domain-specific problems.

Problem Solving: A Historical Perspective

Many theories have been proposed to explain human problem solving. Current problem-solving theories emphasize the "cumulative" nature of problem solving (Best, 1986). For example, Greeno (1976; 1978) argued that problem solving behavior is determined by the type of problem, rather than by a series of stages (e.g., Gestalt theory, Wallas, 1926). The types of cognitive skills people used in each of these problem types often overlapped. This conclusion led to research that emphasized what went on in the mind of a problem solver and resulted in the identification of two general problem strategies.

Problem Solving Strategies. Problem-solving methods range from the very general (e.g., applicable to almost any problem) to the very specialized (Newell, 1969; Polya, 1973). Best (1986) reports that cognitive psychologists typically describe two broad categories of problem solving strategies, (1) algorithms and (2) heuristics. **Algorithms**, procedures that will produce an answer to a problem, are most appropriate for well-defined problems. These types of problems typically begin with a definitive start state and have clearly defined goals (Reitman, 1964). If the problem is well defined, possible solutions can be evaluated against the criteria established by the goal to determine whether or not they meet the requirements

Algorithms are not as effective with ill-defined problems, in which, for example, some data is missing or uncertain. With these types of problems it is more difficult to specify the actions to be taken to reach the solution (Chi & Glaser, 1985). When humans are confronted by ill-defined problems, we typically attempt to solve the problem by relying on heuristics. These "rules of thumb" can be described as all-purpose strategies for solving problems. While they do not always allow us to be successful, they are fast to use and easy to apply in different situations.

Information-Processing Theory. Newell & Simon's (1961, 1972) research in human problem solving expanded the notion of heuristics to include some of the more general strategies that humans use to solve problems. They proposed that humans use a procedure such as the one that follows:

1. Map out the problem's task environment to build an objective problem representation.

2. Encode relevant features of the problem to develop an internal representation, or **"problem space."**

3. Identify points or nodes in the problem space, each of which represents a specific state of knowledge.

4. Link problem space nodes by "operators," which represent cognitive processes that are used to convert one node to another.

In the information-processing theory, a problem solver moves through the nodes in a problem space. As he or she does so, different knowledge states are entered. As Newell and Simon studied and interviewed subjects in their research, they isolated the heuristics or search modes that the subjects seemed to use most frequently. They also identified factors that seem to determine the success of a problem solver and the variables that seem to affect the quality of a solution.

Two variables seem to impact the effectiveness of a problem solver. First, the quality of the problem space sets limits on the problem solver's ability to solve the problem. Quality of the problem space concerns the thoroughness and correctness of elements within the problem space. For example, if the correct solution is not a part of the problem space owing to inadequate knowledge or oversight on the part of the solver), the selected solution will not be the best. Second, the type of search the problem solver uses determines whether or not he or she attains the limits established by the problem space quality. If the problem solver uses a search method that takes more time than another, even though the quality of the solution is equal, problem solving effectiveness is hindered.

Solving Real-World Problems

Regardless of the domain in question, solving complex problems involves the following nondiscrete, nonsequential steps (Shulman, Loupe, and Piper, 1968):

1. Problem sensing (becoming aware of the problem's existence)
2. Problem formulating (defining the problem and anticipating the solution)
3. Searching (asking questions, gathering information)
4. Problem resolution (resolving the problem to a satisfactory level).

Although most problem solvers work through these iteratively, their problem-solving behavior will differ, depending on whether they are attempting to solve familiar or unusual problems. When solving familiar problems, most of us tend to be goal-oriented. We select or set initial goals and gather information that seems to be relevant to meeting our goals. As we work through the problem, we modify our behavior based on signals from the goal (i.e., **teleologic behavior**). Thus, our problem-solving behavior is dependent both on previous experience and on feedback from the current solution trial.

When we attempt to solve *new* problems, our behavior is also focused on the goal but is controlled by heuristics with which we have previously been successful. We try to understand new situations in terms of previous judgments and experiences. If we are solving new problems for which proven rules are *not* available, we may make attempts to reach the goal until we select a successful sequence. Fortunately, these attempts to reach the goal are most often performed internally as "What If (I did this. . .) ?" activity. Based on these internal trials, we select and apply what we hope will be a successful solution.

Selecting Solutions. Exactly how a rule or successful sequence of activities is selected is important, but elusive. A number of theories concerning selection strategies exist. Possibly, we recognize an applicable rule set or solution based on previous experience in similar situations. Humans typically use a number of problem solving strategies. Rich (1983) discusses the application of some of these strategies to expert system reasoning and representation. Expert systems developers have implemented numerous human problem-solving techniques in an attempt to more accurately reflect expert thought processes (Eberts, 1984). Knowledge engineers are encouraged to become familiar with them to help in the identification of those that the domain expert seems to be using.

Shulman (1968) identified two major barriers that knowledge engineers should consider when working with domain experts: habit and pressure to conform. In the knowledge acquisition session these may manifest themselves by the behaviors that follow:

- Fixating on a solution prior to investigating other possible solutions
- Using a mindset that is common, but outdated
- Being predisposed to a solution.

Cognitive Models and Semantic Memory

At the surface level it is very difficult to identify what an expert actually "knows." The propensity for experts to be unable to verbalize metaknowledge (i.e., knowledge about knowledge) is well documented (Nesbitt, 1977; Dixon, 1981; Bainbridge, 1979). However, to be able to acquire enough appropriate knowledge to develop an expert system that emulates expert behavior, knowledge engineers must be able to examine expert knowledge and identify the concepts and principles the expert uses.

Cognitive models represent theories of how humans organize and process knowledge. They were derived from analogies between human and computer memory (Best, 1986) The goal of cognitive modeling is to construct a process explanation of human behavior (Langley & Ohlsson, 1984). Two broad categories of cognitive modeling techniques are semantic nets and production systems.

Semantic Nets

The **semantic network** was one of the earliest techniques to model or represent knowledge (Quillian, 1968). Initially used as a tool to represent word meanings, semantic networks can denote relations between sets of nodes.

Semantic nets have been used to identify relationships among a set of objects (Rich, 1983). Quillian's work with the Teachable Language Comprehender (1968) represented one of the first models of semantic memory. It assumed that each node or concept could have two kinds of relations, (1) a subordinate relationship to another node (i.e., the "is-a" relation) and (2) one or more property characteristics (e.g. the "has" relation). Additionally, TLC assumed that semantic knowledge could be depicted through hierarchical representations (i.e., a robin is a kind of bird).

Collins and Loftus (1975) used semantic nets to depict the concept of semantic interrelations. Figure A-2 shows one way this model could be used to illustrate a semantic memory network. The lines connecting the nodes represent associations between these concepts. The shorter the line connecting two concepts, the more closely the concepts are related.

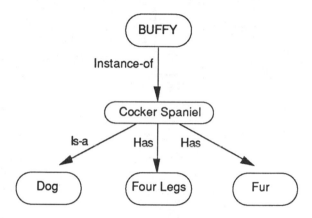

Figure A-2 Semantic Memory Network

Production Systems

Anderson (1976, 1980, 1986) and others have attempted to extend the use of models for representing higher-level cognitive skills. Researchers have attempted to represent these skills in production system models, such as Anderson's ACT cognition architecture (1976). A **production system** consists of three distinct components (Figure A-3).

The data, or primitive symbols, reside in the database. Production rules enable assertions to be made about the data in the database. These assertions are most often in the format "if-then." Thus, the conditions stated in left-hand side of a rule (the "if" component) are compared with available data in the database. If the conditions are met, the action or actions stated in the right-hand side of the rule (the "then" component) are activated. An interpreter, or control strategy, manages the interaction between the data base and production rules. This type of management might include actions such as determining the order in which rules will be applied to search for a solution.

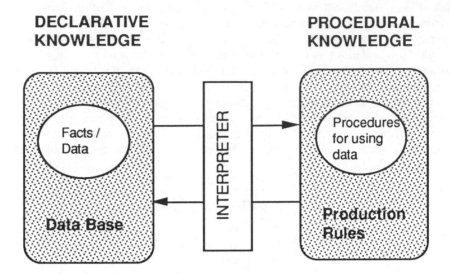

DECLARATIVE KNOWLEDGE

PROCEDURAL KNOWLEDGE

Facts / Data

INTERPRETER

Procedures for using data

Data Base

Production Rules

Figure A-3 Production System Components

A major use of production systems has been modeling human cognition. Specifically, production systems have been used to model a variety of problem-solving techniques, most of which involve the search process (Rich, 1983). Young (1979) suggests three levels at which a production-system architecture could represent human cognition. First, production systems allow researchers to present a theory, such as word comprehension, more concretely. Second, production rules can represent important cognitive processes. Third, some researchers (Newell & Simon, 1972; Young, 1978) believe that they can represent entire human cognitive structures using production systems. For example, Newell, Simon, and Shaw (1958) developed an information-processing framework in an attempt to develop a model of the human control structure that could adequately describe an expert's information processes during the performance of a task.

APPENDIX B: DISADVANTAGES OF VERBAL REPORTING

Verbal reports produced by a knowledge acquisition technique may provide useful data, but they are not without problems. The section that follows explores background research that suggests when verbal self-reports on decision making and problem solving may be inadequate and how knowledge engineers can use them more effectively.

Problems with Verbal Reports

Knowledge engineers should (1) be aware of some of the potential problems associated with the use of verbal reports and (2) be familiar with the literature that defends them. Although problem-solving protocols can be a valuable source of knowledge-base content, their interpretation is often problematic (Wielinga and Breuker, 1985). Deficiencies that may be associated with the use of verbal reports include
- The effect of requesting verbal reports on cognitive processing
- The completeness of resulting verbal reports
- The interpretation of verbal data
- The consistency of verbal reports with other data.

Verbal Reports and Cognitive Processing

When one mentions the use of verbal reporting measures, the most common negative response generally is, "But won't the act of talking about the task interfere with the very cognitive processing you are trying to identify?" Certainly this concern is a valid one. Recall circumstances from your experience in which you were asked to demonstrate *and* explain a task to a less experienced person, only to find how difficult the explanation component made the task-completion component. This is especially true of tasks that are highly procedural in nature. Even supporters of verbal reporting measures acknowledge that if respondents are told that they will be questioned about either general or specific components of their behavior, these instructions may affect their cognitive processes. As could be expected, the potential for this requirement to affect cognitive processing is increased when respondents are asked to report periodically during task completion.

In response to this charge, Ericcson and Simon (1980) argue that the activation of this negative effect depends on (1) the level of automation of the task and (2) the type of information the respondent was required to give. For example, if a domain expert is asked to report information that is available in the short-term memory, describing the task aloud while completing it should not modify the underlying structure of the cognitive processes that are used. However, if the task is highly automated, the domain expert who follows the instructions to "think aloud" may take more time to complete the task, owing to verbalization. In these cases it seems that it is not actually the task of talking that reduces the task completion speed, but the fact that the respondent is taking time to translate his or her knowledge into a verbal form.

In reviewing a number of studies in this area, Ericsson and Simon (1980) concluded that the discriminating factor seemed to be the relation between the main task and the reporting task. For example, if the instructions require the respondent to report the considerations and steps during task completion, less interference is expected than if the instructions require the respondent to explain reasons (Gagne' & Smith, 1962; Wilder

& Harvey, 1971) for actions. Probes such as the latter should not be used as they require the respondent to theorize about conceptual information that may not be accessible. Not only may this reduce the speed of task completion, but it may also result in the production of a "theory" that may not be complete or valid.

Completeness of Verbal Reports

Before the domain expert can report the information, it must be present in the short-term memory, must be attended to, and must be interpreted. If these requirements are not met, the result can be the reporting of incomplete information.

Specifically, a number of factors threaten the completeness of verbal self report data. First, the task of reporting one's own "knowledge" is extremely difficult. Most domain experts have not had previous experience providing self-reports of their decision making; thus, they do not know what or *how much* to express. As a result, they may omit important information or ineffectively report critical information.

Second, important knowledge that at one time was used in reasoning may have been "compiled" (Neves & Anderson, 1981) and no longer be accessible in the short-term memory. This **knowledge compilation** may result in the expert's omission of key factors or a failure to mention special conditions, constraints, or considerations. Many experts may falsely assume that if a consideration, issue, or piece of data was relevant or important, they would remember it. Conversely, if they can *not* recall something, they assume that it must not be important. However, the reason for not remembering something may be that they have chunked or compiled the information (which may be stored in the long-term memory and is not immediately accessible).

Third, experts would like others to believe that they make rational decisions, when actually some decisions may be irrational. In the real world, decisions may be more affected by practical concerns (e.g., time and cost constraints, resources) than by the need to "do it right." In keeping with this need to appear rational, domain experts may offer explanations of the way something should be done (because it is correct) rather than admitting the way they really do it. More rarely, incomplete data may result from an expert's reluctance to share inner thoughts, including any uncertainty concerning the use of specific factors or conclusions. While this protects the expert's ego, it negatively affects knowledge-base validity.

Interpretation of Verbal Reports

Protocols are a record of the domain expert's self-report. Many factors will impact the interpretation of a resulting protocol. For example, a great disparity between the experiential background and domain knowledge of the knowledge engineer and expert may result in the knowledge engineer's "missing" an important point during protocol analysis. This problem can be especially severe if the domain expert falsely assumed during the self report that the knowledge engineer would "know what was meant" by special terminology, situations, or examples. Second, similar words, phrases, and intonation patterns may mean different things to the knowledge engineer and domain expert. Finally, the knowledge states that a domain expert moves through toward a solution may be difficult or impossible to verbalize adequately. The reason could be that the knowledge states are semantically rich or that they require translations from one type of code to another. For example, the domain expert may feel a need to convey an important concept by describing an episode in which it was employed, rather than trying to translate it into everyday language.

Consistency of Verbal Reports

Numerous research has investigated the consistency of verbal reports. Results indicate that consistency is linked to type of verbalization.

Concurrent Verbalization. An oft-cited study claiming the inconsistency of concurrent verbalization was conducted by Verplanck and Oskamp (1962), in which subjects were asked to verbalize the rules they used in sorting a stack of cards. Ericsson and Simon (1980) report that in a later replication and analysis of this study, inconsistencies could at least partially be attributed to other variables. In fact, Dulany and O'Connell (1963) determined that in only 11 out of 34,308 trials did the subjects in the original study actually place the card in a manner that was inconsistent with their verbalizations.

Retrospective Verbalization. Nesbitt and Wilson (1977) conducted a review of studies to compare retrospective verbalization with behavioral reports and concluded that inconsistency was common. The article they produced based on this review is often cited as evidence that verbal reports are inconsistent with behavior and that subjects cannot report accurately on cognitive processes. Their main conclusion was that when asked questions about their cognitive processes, subjects frequently do not base their answers on memory of specifics, but may *theorize* about their processes (p. 233). When subjects are asked for information that may not be immediately accessible (such as reasoning, theories, etc.), they are inclined to guess and may appear to offer responses that are inconsistent with previous behavior. Unless the knowledge engineer makes it clear that the domain expert should go beyond an initial, "top of the head" response, the expert may not engage in the cognitive search that is necessary to retrieve information from long-term memory.

SUGGESTED READINGS

Years of research and experience have provided a wealth of information on the subjects of knowledge, memory, problem-solving behavior, cognitive models, and verbal reporting. Although they are critical to the knowledge acquisition process, it is impossible to provide extensive coverage of any one of these in an appendix. The following materials provide more in-depth information for knowledge engineers who wish to explore these topics further.

Anderson, J. R. Cognitive Psychology and Its Implications. San Francisco: Freeman, 1980.

Anderson, J. R. "On the merits of ACT and information-processing psychology: A response to Wexler's review." Cognition, 8 (1980b), 73-88.

Anderson, J.R. (Ed.). Cognitive Skills and Their Acquisition. Hillsdale, NJ: Erlbaum, 1981.

Kolodner, J. "Organizing memory and keeping it organized." <u>Proceedings of AAAI</u> 1 (1980), pp. 331-333.

Nisbett, R. and T. Wilson. "Telling more than we can know: Verbal reports on mental processes." <u>Psychological Review.</u> 84 (1977), pp.231-259.

Newell, A. and Simon, H. <u>Human Problem Solving</u>. Englewood Cliffs, NJ: Prentice-Hall, 1972.

Polya, G. <u>How to solve it: A new aspect of mathematical method,</u> 2nd edition, Princeton University Press, 1973.

Simon, H. A. "Information processing theory of human problem solving." In W.K. Estes, ed. <u>Handbook of Learning and Cognitive Processes</u> 5 (1978), 271-295.

Sternberg, R., ed. <u>Human Abilities: An Information-Processing Approach</u>. San Francisco: Freeman, 1985.

Glossary

acquisition expert
> One who specializes in the acquisition, elicitation, and capture of domain information from a knowledge source.

algorithms
> Procedures or "formulas" that consistently produce an answer and are effective with well-defined problems.

alternatives
> In protocol analysis, the choices the individual considers when solving a domain problem or completing a domain task.

artificial intelligence
> A branch of computer science that deals with heuristic methods of processing information to design computer systems that exhibit characteristics associated with human intelligence.

aspects
> Values that can be assigned to a specific attribute.

attending skills
> Behaviors that help listeners attend to verbal communication, such as concentration, eye contact, and body language.

attitudinal measurement
> The process of assessing the presence and strength of an individual's attitude toward a particular issue.

attractiveness
> The psychological value, weight, or strength of an aspect, represented with a single value.

attributes
> A characteristic (e.g., color) of a concept or element.

audit trail
> Documented history of a piece of information (e.g., rule) in the knowledge base, from knowledge acquisition source to implementation in code.

baseline
> A version of the software that serves as a reference (sometimes referred to as "configuration baseline"), providing a basis of understanding across the development team.

brainstorming

A commonly used group problem-solving technique whose goal is to generate as many solutions to a problem as is possible.

breadth first

Heuristic search that involves examining all possible paths at one level before progressing down any one solution path.

brittle

A term used to describe expert systems that are not flexible or easily modified.

certification

An endorsement of the correctness of a program that assures that the system performs its specified function.

chunking

The cognitive task of organizing or grouping items that are stored and recalled together.

closed questions

Questions that set limits on the type, level, and amount of information a respondent provides.

clumping techniques

A type of conceptual clustering technique that produces an organizational structure that reflects less distinct or less disjointed groupings of clusters.

cluster analysis

A generic term for a set of techniques that elicits or produces classifications from seemingly unclassified data.

cognitive maps

Conceptual analysis tools that represent a domain expert's ideas concerning primary concepts and interrelationships in a domain.

cognitive models

Theoretical representations of how humans organize and process some type of knowledge.

computer-facilitated session

Using computers as dynamic communication tools in group-oriented multiple expert knowledge acquisition sessions.

communicator style

Signals that are provided to help process, interpret, filter, or understand literal meaning.

concept

A symbol or abstract representation for a common characteristic or relationship that is shared by objects, elements, or events that are otherwise different.

concept clustering/conceptual clustering

A methodology for organizing and summarizing domain data by producing an abstraction of the domain based on the analysis of clusters.

concept dictionary

A conceptual analysis technique that provides a mechanism to visualize an abstraction of the primary concepts in a domain and the terminology used to label them.

concept hierarchy

A structural taxonomy or arrangement of the associations that make up a concept.

concept sorting

A psychological paradigm that can be used to tap the way in which a domain expert has organized key concepts.

conceptual framework

A conceptual analysis technique that provides the knowledge engineer with a structure to depict categories of information or elements a domain expert monitors when drawing conclusions.

conceptual graph

Any of a set of graphs that depicts a conceptualization of a particular domain of knowledge.

concurrent verbalization

A variation of process tracing in which the expert verbalizes his or her reasoning process while completing the task being investigated.

configuration management

The control of requirements definitions, designs, computer programs, test results, and documentation.

consensus decision making

A set of techniques for a group-oriented multiple-expert knowledge acquisition session, whose goal is to identify the best solution to a specific problem.

construct

A bipolar characteristic that is used to analyze the way in which a domain expert has structured his or her domain.

control strategies

Techniques (e.g., meta rules) an expert system uses to control which rules are selected and processed.

decision/action analysis

A variation of operational sequence analysis that produces a diagram portraying major tasks, cues, alternatives, and decisions within a selected scenario.

decision rules

The formalisms an individual seems to be using in making solutions or solving problems.

declarative knowledge

Knowledge that can be verbalized or expressed; "knowing that."

density search

A conceptual clustering technique that is used to discover natural clusters or subgroups by observing high (many related concepts) and low (few related concepts) conceptual density within a domain.

discrimination tree

A technique for organizing domain knowledge that divides sets of elements into subsets (such that each node has only one "parent") based on discriminating evidence provided by attributes and their values.

directional control

Control an interviewer uses to maintain the focus and structure of an interview.

domain expert

An individual who has considerable expertise in the domain in which the expert system is being developed and has the communication skills necessary to relay that information.

domain familiarization

An extension of the Identification stage of expert system development, in which the knowledge engineer becomes acquainted with key vocabulary, terminology, and concepts of the domain.

episodic knowledge

Autobiographical, experiential information that has been chunked or compiled episodically or temporally.

evaluation

The process of verifying and validating the software.

example-based systems

Expert system development tools or shells that handle the creation of rules from the input of examples.

experienced experts

Individuals who have domain expertise but who are not currently practicing in that domain.

expert systems

AI programs, consisting of a knowledge base, inference engine, and user interface, that are designed to emulate the reasoning processes of human experts in a particular domain.

functional analysis

An analysis technique that yields flow diagrams depicting a structure of the primary functions of a system.

funnel

A connective interview technique in which open questions are followed by probing questions and later, closed questions.

goal analysis

An analysis technique that entails discerning the primary goals for the completion of a task and performing a decomposition to identify subgoals toward the completion of each goal.

heuristics

General "rules of thumb" or strategies for solving problems.

hierarchical representation

A display of information (e.g., concepts, elements, etc.) as a series of systematic groups such that parent and child nodes are accommodated.

hybrid (knowledge acquisition) tool

A knowledge acquisition/engineering tool that combines the application of a variety of methods to elicit and capture knowledge from a domain expert.

implementation expert

The individual responsible for translating domain-related information into code.

incremental development

The software development process in which each iteration of developmental effort is geared to the fulfillment of successively more specific requirement specifications.

induction

The process that allows us to infer a law of causation by observing and analyzing particular instances of that law.

inference engine

Expert system component that controls the order in which rules in the knowledge base fire.

information flow analysis

An analysis technique that entails diagramming the operations and binary decisions that may be required to complete major system functions.

information processing theory

A theory proposed by Newell and Simon that describes the procedures and mechanisms that humans use to process information and solve problems.

intelligent editing program

A program that provides editorial assistance (e.g., syntax, templates, checkers) or guidance in the construction of rules.
interaction analysis

interaction analysis

Task analysis procedure that enables knowledge engineers to specify crucial interactions a system requires. The process of investigating or analyzing the independent software modules and their interaction under the control of an inference engine.

inverted funnel

A connective interview technique in which restrictive questions are followed by less restrictive questions, followed by open questions.

job analysis

An analysis procedure that entails structuring the major responsibilities of a job and a gross description of the tasks the job involves.

knowledge acquisition

The process of extracting,transforming, and transferring expertise from a knowledge source to a computer program.

knowledge acquisition database

A database of documentation related to knowledge acquisition, including the knowledge dictionary, knowledge acquisition form, rule contents form, domain expert files, and various templates.

knowledge acquisition tool

Software support for the application of knowledge acquisition or knowledge engineering techniques.

knowledge base

The expert system component that contains facts about the domain and rules for using these facts.

knowledge compilation

The organization, or chunking, of one's knowledge.

knowledge dictionary

A set of domain terms and acronyms that are compiled and updated by knowledge engineers.

knowledge elicitation

The process of interacting with domain experts using techniques to stimulate the expression of "expertise."

knowledge engineer
> The individual responsible for acquiring, structuring, and translating domain knowledge to enable expert system design and development

knowledge engineering
> The discipline that addresses the task of building expert systems; the tools and methods that support expert system development.

knowledge-intensive problems
> Problems that entail the encoding and symbolic manipulation of knowledge that may be in the form of data, information, or processes.

Likert scale
> A scale developed by R. Likert for the purpose of measuring a person's degree of agreement or disagreement with a set of carefully constructed statements.

long-term memory
> The theoretical memory receptacle that is assumed to serve as the permanent storehouse for information.

machine learning
> A field of research that is interested in developing programs that can acquire knowledge; currently the focus of this field is inducing the rules based on the input of an expert's examples.

memory aid
> A tool (e.g., audiotape, videotape) used to record the expert's verbalizations and/or behavior during a process tracing session.

metaknowledge
> Conscious knowledge about what is known.

meta rules
> Control strategies that describe when to apply content or declarative rules.

mission decomposition
> A specific type of timeline analysis that may be useful in depicting major phases, actions, and decision points for a mission or tasks.

model approach
> A development approach in which knowledge engineers use an existing model that is well-suited to the new domain to develop a set of axioms and rules.

multiexpert systems
> An expert system whose knowledge base represents knowledge acquisition from multiple domain experts, each contributing in his/her area of expertise.

multiple-expert team

The domain experts and knowledge engineer who work together in knowledge acquisition sessions to isolate content for the knowledge base.

needs assessment

The process of determining or isolating needs to develop a program that meets specific objectives.

nominal group technique

A group problem-solving technique that reduces the negative effects that may be triggered by face-to-face interaction among members of the multiple-expert team.

nonreflective skills

Behaviors that initiate, guide, or transition communication (e.g., conversation starters, attentive silence).

nonverbal communication

Communication through other than verbal means.

open questions

Broad questions that impose few restrictions on the respondent and encourage free response.

operational sequence analysis

An analysis technique that is used to represent system functionality at a specific level to discern, in detail, the interrelationships between actions and processing tasks in an information system.

participant analysis

The process of analyzing individuals to enable the selection of one who is well suited to the task at hand.

phrasing

The manner in which a question is posed, including terminology, level, and complexity.

practicing experts

Individuals with expert-level skills who are currently active in domain tasks.

primary questions

Questions an interviewer uses to introduce topic areas or transition to other questions.

probability

A numeric rating of how probable it is that a specific event will occur or a specific rule is accurate.

problem space
> An internal representation of a problem, including relevant problem features.

procedural knowledge
> Automatic, skill-based responses to stimuli.

process tracing
> Any of a set of techniques that enables the determination of an individual's train of thought while he or she completes a task or reaches a conclusion.

production systems
> Cognitive models that represent knowledge about high-level cognitive skills through three components: data, production rules, and control structure.

proof-of-correctness
> A conventional software evaluative method that entails a nonexecutable test of the code to insure that the translation from one level of requirements specifications to the next is complete and correct.

protocol analysis
> A method used to discern (1) an individual's general problem-solving approach and (2) the specific operations used to move from one knowledge state to another.

protocols
> Verbal reports that are typically the result of a process-tracing or interview session.

qualitative model
> A representation that describes the conceptual qualities and elements of a domain.

rapid prototyping
> An approach for developing expert systems, in which developers quickly implement a small part of the system to test the efficacy of representation schemes, design, and development approaches.

reflective listening
> Listening behaviors that provide feedback that the message was communicated; techniques including paraphrasing, clarifying, summarizing, and reflecting feelings.

repertory grid
> A psychological technique for eliciting and analyzing a model of the domain expert's world so that similarities and distances among objects can be represented in a grid.

retrospective verbalization
> A variation of process tracing in which the expert verbalizes his or her reasoning process after completing the task being investigated.

salient features

Features that distinguish the objects, events, or ideas that a concept represents.

secondary questions

Questions an interviewer uses to find out more about information offered in response to another question; synonymous with probing questions.

semantic knowledge

Deep-level knowledge that reflects cognitive structure, organization, and representation.

semantic networks

Cognitive models that illustrate associations among elements through the use of links and arrows between them.

sensory register

The large-capacity "storage" tank that is theorized to briefly hold raw sensory images before they are either transferred to memory or lost.

short-term memory

The theoretical memory receptacle that is assumed to house conscious mental processes and facilitate cognitive organization.

simulation program

A program that provides a global description of a set of domain tasks, emulating task performance and providing an environment for interaction with domain problems.

software engineering

The use of sound engineering principles in order to obtain economically software that is reliable and functional.

software reliability

The probability that a software program operates for some time period, without software error, on the machine for which it was designed.

spatial control

Controlling the use of space, including room size, arrangement, temperature, and seating.

static analysis tools

Tools that assist in assuring that the knowledge base as built is consistent with the domain and design (e.g., syntactic error checkers).

structured interview

An interview that is organized, planned, and appropriate for sessions that require specific information.

systems approach

Software development approach that entails requirements analysis and specifications, followed by systematic design methods and techniques, and implementation of the design.

task analysis
The process of determining or describing the nature of a task, job, or procedure by breaking it into its primitive components.

task nature
The original constitution (e.g., discrete, sequential) of a task; a salient feature in determining strategies an expert uses to complete the task.

taxonomies
Basic classification systems that enable designers or knowledge engineers to describe conceptual identifications and dependencies.

team approach
A development approach in which a domain expert and a knowledge engineer work closely together for an extended period of time and produce a model and computer program that is comparable in performance to human specialists.

teleologic behavior
Behavior that is modified during its course by signals from the goal.

temporal control
Controlling the duration and segments of a knowledge acquisition session.

timeline analysis
An analysis technique that is used to determine the influence or relation of time on the completion of a task or sets of tasks.

truth analysis
A subset of the techniques used to insure the integrity of a knowledge base.

uncertainty
A measurement or probability estimation of the degree to which a piece of data can be believed.

uncertainty analysis
A method to insure that the representation and manipulation of uncertainty in the system is consistent with the nature of uncertainty in the domain.

unstructured interview
Interviews that are for the purpose of exploring an issue; used primarily during initial stages of knowledge acquisition.

upward-ripple paranoia
A domain expert's fear of repercussions from supervisors or significant others because of information contributed during the knowledge acquisition sessions.

user interface
Expert system component that handles communications between the system and its user.

validation

An evaluative activity that ensures that the software functions and contains the features prescribed by its requirements and specifications.

verification

An evaluative activity that ensures that the software interacts properly within the system and performs its specified function.

wait time

The period of time directly following a question, which may affect thought processes and response quality.

walk-through

A practice that calls for programmers to critique each other's work for accuracy and consistency with other parts of the system.

waterfall model

A well-accepted conventional software engineering model or method for software development that can be adapted for use in the development of knowledge-based systems.

References

ABRETT, G., AND M. BURSTEIN, "The BBN laboratories knowledge acquisition project: KREME knowledge editing environment," Proceedings from the DARPA-sponsored Expert Systems Workshop, Pacific Grove, CA, April 1986, pp. 1-21.

ADELSON, B. "When novices surpass experts: The difficulty of a task may increase with expertise." Journal of Experimental Psychology: Learning, Memory, and Cognition 10:3 (1984), pp. 483-445.

ANDERSON, J. R., ed., Cognitive Skills and Their Acquisition. Hillsdale, NJ: Erlbaum, 1981.

ANDERSON, J. R., AND B. H. ROSS, "Evidence against a semantic-episodic distinction," Journal of Experimental Psychology: Human Learning and Memory 6, (1980), pp. 441-466.

ANDERSON, J. R. The Architecture of Cognition. Cambridge, MA: Harvard University Press, 1983.

ANDERSON, J. R. "Cognitive skills" (Chapter 8). In J. R. Anderson, Cognitive Psychology and its Implications. San Francisco: W. H. Freeman, 1980a.

ANDRICH, D. "Scaling attitude items constructed and scored in the Likert tradition." Educational and Psychological Measurement 38:3, (Fall 1978), pp. 665-680.

ARBAB, B., AND D. MICHIE. "Generating rules from examples." Proceedings of the Ninth International Joint Conference on Artificial Intelligence (IJCAI, 1985), 1, pp. 631-633.

ATKINSON, R. C., AND R. SHIFFRIN. "Human memory: A proposed system and its control processes." In K. Spence and J. Spence, eds. The Psychology of Learning and Motivation, Vol. II. New York: Academic Press, 1968.

ATWATER, E. I Hear You. How to Use Listening Skills for Profit. Englewood Cliffs, NJ: Prentice-Hall, 1981.

AUGER, B. How to Run Better Business Meetings. St. Paul, MN: 3M Company, 1972.

BADDELY, A. D., AND H. C. DALE. "The effect of semantic similarity on retroactive interference in long-and short-term memory," Journal of Verbal Learning and Verbal Behavior, 5 (1966), pp. 417-420.

BAER, J. "A survey of some theoretical aspects of multiprocessing." Computer Surveys 5:1, (March 1973), 31-80.

BAILEY, R. W. Human Performance Engineering: A Guide for Systems Designers. Englewood Cliffs, NJ: Prentice Hall, 1982.

BAINBRIDGE, L. "Asking questions and accessing knowledge." Future Computing Systems (In press).

BAINBRIDGE, L. "Verbal reports as evidence of the process operator's knowledge." International Journal of Man-Machine Studies, 11:4 (1979), 411-436.

BALL, G. "Classification analysis." Stanford Research Institute, SRI Project 5533, 1971.

BANNING, R. W. "Knowledge acquisition and system validation in expert systems for management," In Human Systems Management, Vol. 4 (1984), pp. 280-285. New York: Elsevier Science Publishers (North-Holland).

BARR, A., AND E. FEIGENBAUM, The Handbook of Artificial Intelligence, Los Altos, CA: Kaufman, 1981.

BARSALOU, L. W. "Ad hoc categories." Memory & Cognition, 11:3 (1983), pp. 211-227.

BASILI, V. R., AND A. TURNER. "Iterative enhancement: A practical technique for software engineering," IEEE Transactions on Software Engineering, (December 1975), pp. 390-396.

BENNETT, J. "ROGET: A knowledge-based consultant for acquiring the conceptual structure of an expert system." Report No. HPP-83-24, Computer Sciences Department, Stanford University, 1983.

BERGER, B., AND H. HAWKINS. "Occupational analysis of an automated approach." In T. Abramson, C. Title, and L. Cohen, eds. Handbook of Vocational Education Evaluation, p. 275. Beverly Hills, CA: Sage Publications, 1979.

BERLINGER, C. "Behaviors, measures, and instruments for performance evaluation in simulated environments," Paper presented at a symposium and workshop on quantification of human performance, Albuquerque, NM, 1964.

BERSOFF, H. E. "Elements of software configuration management." IEEE Transactions on Software Engineering SE-10:1 (January 1984), 79-87.

BEST, J. B. Cognitive Psychology. St. Paul, MN: West Publishing Co., 1986.

BHASKAR, R., AND H. A. SIMON. "Problem solving in semantically-rich domains." Cognitive Science 1 (1977), pp. 193-215.

BLAXTON, T., R. GEESEY, AND L. REEKER,. "A knowledge acquisition tool for process applications." In Proceedings of the 5th Intelligence Community AI Symposium, (1987), Washington, DC.

BLAXTON, T., AND C. WESTPHAL. "Combining explicit queries with simulation techniques during knowledge acquisition," Proceedings of the Eastern Simulation Conference; AI and Simulation Session, (April 1988), pp. 17-22.

BLOSSER, P. Handbook of Effective Questioning Techniques. Worthington, OH: Educational Association, Inc., 1973.

BLOSSER, P. How to Ask the Right Questions. National Science Teacher's Association, 1975.

BOBROW, D., AND M. STEFIK. The LOOPS Manual. Tech. Rep. KB-VLSI-81-13, Knowledge Systems Area, Xerox Palo Alto Research Center, 1981.

BOEHM, B. W. "Seven basic principles of software engineering." Journal of Systems and Software, 1983, no. 3, 3-24.

BOEHM, B. W. "Software and its impact: a quantitative assessment." Datamation, (May 1973), 48-59.

BOEHM, B. W. Software Engineering Economics. Englewood Cliffs, N.J.: Prentice-Hall, 1981.

BONISSONE, P., AND A. BROWN. Expanding the Horizons of Expert Systems. General Electric Corp. Research and Development Report, 1986.

BONNER, R. "On some clustering techniques." IBM Journal of Research and Development , 9 (1964), pp. 22-32.

BOOSE, J. "A knowledge acquisition program for expert systems based on personal construct psychology," International Journal of Man-Machine Studies, 23 (1985), pp. 495-525.

BOOSE, J., AND J. BRADSHAW. "Expertise transfer and complex problems: Using Aquinas as a knowledge acquisition workbench for expert systems." Special issue on the 1st AAAI Knowledge Acquisition for Knowledge-Based Systems Workshop, 1986, Part 1, International Journal of Man-Machine Studies, 26:1, 1987a.

BOOSE, J., AND J. BRADSHAW. "Aquinas: A knowledge acquisition workbench for building knowledge-based systems," Proceedings of the First European Workshop on Knowledge Acquisition for Knowledge-Based Systems, Reading University, September 1987b.

BOOSE, J. Expertise Transfer for Expert System Design, New York: Elsevier, 1986.

BOOSE, J. "Personal Construct Theory and the Transfer of Human Expertise," in the Proceedings of the National Conference on Artificial Intelligence (AAAI-84), Austin, TX, 1984.

BOOSE, J. "Uses of repertory grid-centered knowledge acquisition tools for knowledge-based systems." Proceedings of the 2nd AAAI Knowledge Acquisition for Knowledge-Based Systems Workshop, Banff, Canada, October 1987.

BOURNE, L. E., R. DOMINOWSKI, AND E. LOFTUS. Cognitive Processes. Englewood Cliffs, NJ: Prentice Hall, 1979.

BOUSFIELD, W. A. "The occurrence of clustering in the recall of randomly arranged associates." Journal of General Psychology, 49 (1953), pp. 229-240.

BROWNSTON, L., R. FARRELL, E. KANT, AND N. MARTIN. Programming Expert Systems in OPS5, Reading, MA: Addison-Wesley, 1985.

BRUNER, J. S., R. R.OLIVER, AND P. M. GREENFIELD Studies in Cognitive Growth, New York: John Wiley & Sons, 1966.

BUCHANAN, B. AND E. FEIGENBAUM, "DENDRAL and Meta-DENDRAL: Their applications dimension." Artificial Intelligence, 11 (1978), pp. 5-24.

BUCHANAN, B. "Artificial intelligence: Toward machines that think." Encyclopedia Britannica, Yearbook of Science and the Future, 1985.

BUCHANAN, B., G. SUTHERLAND, AND E. FEIGENBAUM. "Heuristic DENDRAL: A program for generating explanatory hypotheses in organic chemistry." In B. Meltzer and D. Michie, eds., Machine Intelligence, Vol.4, pp. 209-254. Edinburgh: Edinburgh University Press, 1969.

BUCHANAN, B., D. BARSTOW, R. BECHTAL, J. BENNETT, W. CLANCEY, C. KULIKOWSKI, T. MITCHELL, AND D. WATERMAN. "Constructing an expert system." In F. Hayes-Roth, D. Waterman, and D. Lenat, eds. Building Expert Systems, Reading, MA: Addison-Wesley, 1983.

BUCKLEY, F. "A standard for software quality assurance plans," Computer, 12:8 (August 1979).

BUSH, V. "As we may think." Atlantic Monthly, 176:1, (1945), 101-108.

BUSHKE, H. "Learning is organized by chunking." Journal of Verbal Learning and Verbal Behavior, 15 (1976), pp. 313-324.

BUTLER, K., AND J. CARTER. "The use of psychometric tools for knowledge acquisition: a case study." In Gale, W., ed. Artificial Intelligence and Statistics. Reading, MA: Addison-Wesley, 1986.

BYLANDER, T., S. MITTAL, AND B. CHADRASEKARAN, CSRL: A Language for Expert System Diagnosis. National Technical Information Service AD-A-131403, 1983.

CARD, S., T. MORAN, AND A. NEWELL. The Psychology of Human-Computer Interaction. Hillsdale, NJ: Erlbaum, 1983.

CARMICHAEL, J. AND P. H.A. SNEATH, Taxometric maps. Systematic Zoology, 18 (1969), pp. 402-415.

CARMICHAEL, J., J. GEORGE, AND R. JULIUS. "Finding natural clusters." Systematic Zoology, 17 (1968), pp. 144-150.

CARNEY, T. Content Analysis. A Technique for Systematic Inference from Communications. Winnepeg, Canada: University of Manitoba Press, 1972.

CARROLL, J. M., AND J. C. THOMAS, "Metaphor and the cognitive representation of computing systems." IEEE Transactions on Systems, Man, and Cybernetics. SMC-12:2, (Mar/Apr 1982), pp. 107-116.

CHAPIN, N. "Flowcharting with the ANSI Standard: A tutorial." Computing Surveys, 2:2 (June 1970), pp. 89-110.

CHARNESS, N. "Memory for chess positions: Resistance to interference." Journal of Experimental Psychology: Human Learning and Memory, 2 (1976), pp. 641-653.

CHASE, W. G. ,AND H. A. SIMON. "Perception in chess." Cognitive Psychology, 4 (1973a), pp. 55-81.

CHASE, W. G., AND H. A. SIMON. "The mind's eye in chess." In W.G.Chase, ed. Visual Information Processing. New York: Academic Press, 1973b.

CHENG, Y., AND KING-SUN FU. "Conceptual clustering in knowledge organization." IEEE Transactions on Pattern Analysis and Machine Intelligence, 7 (1985), 592-598.

CHI, M. AND R. GLASER, "Problem-solving ability." In R. J. Sternberg, ed. Human Abilities: An Information Processing Approach. New York: Freeman, 1985.

CHI, M., P. FELTOVICH, AND R. GLASER. "Categorization and representation of physics problems by experts and novices." Cognitive Science, 5 (1981), 121-152.

CHI, M. T., R. GLASER, AND E. REES. "Expertise in problem solving." In R. J. Sternberg, ed. Advances in the Psychology of Human Intelligence, Vol. 1, pp. 7-76. Hillsdale, NJ: Erlbaum, 1982.

CLANCEY, W. "Heuristic classification." In J. Kowalik, ed. Knowledge-Based Problem Solving. Englewood Cliffs, NJ: Prentice-Hall, 1986.

CLANCEY, W. "The advantages of abstract control knowledge in expert system design." Proceedings of the National Conference on Artificial Intelligence, 1983, pp. 74-78.

COHEN, B. H. "Some-or-none characterization of coding behavior." Journal of Verbal Learning and Verbal Behavior, 5 (1966), pp. 182-187.

COLLINS, A. M., AND E. F. LOFTUS. "A spreading activation theory of semantic processing," Psychological Review, 82 (1975), pp. 407-428.

CONRAD, C. Strategic Organizational Communication: Cultures, Situations, and Adaptation. New York: Holt, Rinehart, and Winston, 1985.

CONRAD, R. "Acoustic confusions in immediate memory." British Journal of Psychology, 55 (1964), 75-84.

CONTE, S. D., H. E. DUNSMORE, AND V. Y. SHEN. Software Engineering Metrics and Models. Menlo Park, CA: Benjamin-Cummings Publishing Co., 1986.

COOKE, N. "Modeling human expertise in expert systems," Technical Report, MCCS-85-12, Computing Research Laboratory, New Mexico State University, 1985.

COOKE, N., F. DURSO, AND R. SCHVANEVELDT. "Recall and measures of memory organization." Journal of Experimental Psychology: Learning, Memory and Cognition, 12 (1986), pp. 538-549.

COOKE, N., AND J. MCDONALD. "The application of psychological scaling techniques to knowledge elicitation for knowledge-based systems." International Journal of Man Machine Studies, 26 (1987), 81-92.

COOKE, N., AND J. MCDONALD. "A formal methodology for acquiring and representing expert knowledge," Proceedings of the IEEE, 74:10 (1986), 1422-1430.

COOKSON, M., J. HOLMAN, AND D. THOMPSON. "Knowledge acquisition for medical expert systems: A system for eliciting diagnostic decision making histories." In M.A. Bramer, ed. Research and Development in Expert Systems, London: Cambridge University Press, 1985.

COOMBS, C. A Theory of Data. New York: Wiley, 1964.

CORMACK, R. "A review of classification." Journal of Research in Statistics-Social Services, Series A, 134:3 (1971), pp. 321-367.

CRAGAN, J., AND D. WRIGHT. Communication in Small Group Discussions: A Case Study Approach. New York: West Publishing Co., 1980.

DALLMAN, B., W. PIEPER, AND J. RICHARDSON. "A graphics simulation system--task emulation, not equipment modeling." Journal of Computer-Based Instruction, 10:3-4 (1983), pp. 70-72.

DAVIS, R. "Interactive transfer of expertise: Acquisition of new inference rules." In Proceedings of the Fifth International Joint Conference on Artificial Intelligence, 1977, pp. 321-328.

DAWES, R. "Social selection based on multidimensional criteria." Journal of Abnormal and Social Psychology, 68 (1964), pp.104-109.

DEGREEF, P., AND J. BREUKER. "A case study in structured knowledge acquisition." Proceedings of the International Joint Conference on Artificial Intelligence, 1985, pp. 390-392.

DERR, W., AND B. BROWN. "Effective interviewing: Tool for the knowledge engineer," Texas Instruments Paper, 1988.

DERR, W. "The interview in knowledge acquisition," Personal notes and diagrams, 1986.

DIEDERICH, J., I. RUHMANN, AND M. MAY. "KRITON: A knowledge acquisition tool for expert systems." Special issue on the 1st AAAI Knowledge Acquisition for Knowledge-Based Systems Workshop, 1986, Part 1, International Journal of Man-Machine Studies, 26:1 (1987).

DIEDERICH, J., L. LINSTER, I. RUHMANN, AND T. UTHMANN. "A methodology for integrating knowledge acquisition techniques." Proceedings of the First European Workshop on Knowledge Acquisition for Knowledge-Based Systems, University of Reading, September 1987.

DIETERICH, T. Chapter 14, "Learning and inductive inference." In P. Cohen and E. Feigenbaum, eds. The Handbook of Artificial Intelligence. Los Altos, CA: William Kaufmann, Inc., 1981.

DIXON, N. Preconscious Processing, Chichester: Wiley, 1981.

DOUGHERTY, J., AND C. KELLER. "Taskonomy: A practical approach to knowledge structures." American Ethnologist, 9 (1982).

DREYFUS, H. AND S. DREYFUS, "Why expert systems do not exhibit expertise" IEEE Expert, Summer 1986, pp. 86-90.

DUDA, R., P. HART, K. KONOLIGE, AND R. REBOH. "A computer-based consultant for mineral exploration." Technical Report, SRI International, September 1979.

DUDA, R., P. HART, N. NILSSON, AND G. SUTHERLAND. "Semantic network representations in rule-based inference systems," pp. 203-221. In D. Waterman and F. Hayes-Roth, eds. Pattern-Directed Inference Systems, New York: Academic Press, 1978.

DULANEY, D. E., AND D. C. O'CONNELL. "Does partial reinforcement dissociate verbal rules and the behavior they might be presumed to control?" Journal of Verbal Learning and Verbal Behavior, 2 (1963), pp. 361-372.

EBERTS, R., AND N. SIMON. "Cognitive requirements and expert systems." In P. Salvendy, ed. Human-computer Interaction, Amsterdam: Elsevier, 1984.

EGAN, D.E., AND B.J. SCHWARTZ. "Chunking in recall of symbolic drawings." <u>Memory and Cognition</u>, 7 (1979), pp. 149-158.

EISENSON, J., J. AUER, AND J. IRWIN. <u>The Psychology of Communication</u>. New York: Appleton-Century-Crofts, 1963.

ENGLE, R. W., AND L. BUSTEL. "Memory processes among bridge players of differing expertise." <u>American Journal of Psychology</u> 91 (1978), pp. 673-689.

ENOS, J., AND R. TILBURG. Chapter 3, "Software design." In R. Jensen and C. Tonies, eds. <u>Software Engineering</u>. Englewood Cliffs: Prentice-Hall, 1979.

ERICCSON, K., AND H. SIMON. "Verbal reports as data." <u>Psychological Review</u>, 87:3 (1980), pp. 215-251.

EVERITT, B. "Cluster analysis in the analysis of survey data." In C.A. O'Murcheartough and C. Payne, eds. <u>Cluster Analysis</u>, Vol II. New York: Wiley & Sons, 1977.

EVERITT, B. <u>Cluster Analysis</u>. New York: Halsted Press, 1980.

FAIN, J., D. GORLIN, F. HAYES-ROTH, S. ROSENSCHEIN, H. SOWIZRAL, AND D. WATERMAN. "The ROSIE language reference manual." Technical Report N-1647-ARPA, Rand Corp., Santa Monica, CA, 1981.

FAIN, J., F. HAYES-ROTH, H. SOWIZRAL, AND D. WATERMAN. "Programming in ROSIE: An introduction by means of examples." Technical Report N-1646-ARPA, Rand Corp., Santa Monica, CA, 1982.

FAIRLEY, R.E. <u>Software Engineering Concepts</u>. New York: McGraw-Hill, 1985.

FEIGENBAUM, E. "The art of AI." In <u>Proceedings</u> of the Fifth International Conference on Artificial Intelligence, 1977.

FEIGENBAUM, E, AND P. MCCORDUCK. <u>The Fifth Generation: Artificial Intelligence and Japan's Computer Challenge to the World</u>, Reading, MA: Addison-Wesley, 1983.

FISCHOFF, B., P. SLOVIC, AND S. LICHTENSTEIN. "Knowing with certainty: The appropriateness of extreme confidence." <u>Journal of Experimental Psychology: Human Perception and Performance</u>, 3 (1977), pp. 552-564.

FISHBEIN, M., AND I. AJZEN. "Attitudes and opinions," <u>Annual Review of Psychology</u>, 23 (1972), p. 487-544.

FISHBURN, P. "Lexicographic order, utilities, and decision rules: A survey." <u>Management Science</u>, 20 (1974), pp.1442-1471.

FISHER, D. "Improving inference through conceptual clustering." <u>Proceedings</u> of AAAI '87, pp. 461-465. Los Altos, CA: Morgan Kaufmann Publishers, 1987a.

FISHER, D. "Knowledge acquisition via incremental conceptual clustering." <u>Machine Learning</u>, 1987b.

FISHER, D., AND P. LANGLEY. "Approaches to conceptual clustering," <u>Proceedings</u> of the Ninth International Joint Conference on Artificial Intelligence (IJCAI), 1985, pp. 691-697.

FISKE, S. T., AND L. M. DYER. "The development of social knowledge structures: Positive and negative transfer." Unpublished manuscript, Carnegie-Mellon University, 1983.

FISKE, S. T., AND P. W. LINVILLE. "What does the schema concept buy us?" <u>Personality and Social Psychology Bulletin</u>, 6 (1980), pp. 543-400.

FORD, K., PETRY, F., CHANG, P., AND ADAMS-WEBBER, J. "A probabilistic approach to the automated acquisition of production rules from repertory grid data," <u>Proceedings</u> of the Second International Workshop on Artificial Intelligence and Statistics, 1988.

FOX, M. "ISIS: A constraint-directed reasoning approach to job shop scheduling." Technical Report, Robotics Institute, Carnegie-Mellon University, Pittsburgh, PA, June 1983.

FRANK, A. Communicating on the Job. Glenview, IL: Scott, Foresman, 1982.

FREEDMAN, R. "Evaluating shells." AI EXPERT, September 1987, pp. 70-74.

FREILING, M., J. ALEXANDER, S. MESSICK, S. REHFUSS, AND S. SHULMAN. "Starting a knowledge engineering project: a step by step approach." The AI Magazine, 6:3 (Fall 1985), p. 150-163.

FRIEDLAND, P. "Acquisition of procedural knowledge from domain experts." Proceedings of the International Joint Conference on Artificial Intelligence, pp. 856-861, 1981.

FROSCHER, J., AND R. JACOB. "Designing expert systems for ease of change." Kamal Karna, ed. Proceedings of the Expert Systems in Government Symposium, McLean, VA, October 24-25. IEEE Computer Society Press, 1985.

FROST, R. Introduction to Knowledge Base Systems. New York: Macmillan, 1986.

GAGNE', R., AND E. SMITH. "A study of the effects of verbalization on problem solving." Journal of Experimental Psychology, 63 (1962), pp.12-18.

GAGNE', R. The Conditions of Learning. New York: Holt, Rinehart, and Winston, 1975.

GAGNE', R. The Conditions of Learning 3rd ed. New York: Holt Rinehart, and Winston, 1977.

GAINES, B. "An overview of knowledge acquisition and transfer," Special issue on the 1st AAAI Knowledge Acquisition for Knowledge-Based Systems Workshop, 1986, Part 3, International Journal of Man-Machine Studies, 26:4 (1987a).

GAINES, B. "Rapid prototyping for expert systems." In M. Oliff, ed. Proceedings of the International Conference on Expert Systems and the Leading Edge in Production Planning and Control, University of Southern California, 1987b.

GAINES, B., AND M. SHAW. "Interactive elicitation of knowledge from experts," Future Computing Systems, 1:2 (1986).

GAINES, B., AND M. SHAW. "New directions in the analysis and interactive elicitation of personal construct systems." In M. L.G. Shaw, ed. Recent Advances in Personal Construct Technology. New York: Academic Press, 1981.

GALE, W. A. Artificial Intelligence and Statistics, Reading, MA: Addison-Wesley, 1986.

GALLOWAY, T. "TAXI: A taxonomic assistant." Proceedings of AAAI '87, pp. 416-420. Los Altos, CA: Morgan Kaufmann Publishers, 1987.

GAMMACK, J., AND R. YOUNG. "Psychological techniques for eliciting expert knowledge." In M. Bramer, ed. Research and Development in Expert Systems, pp. 105-112. London: Cambridge University Press, 1985.

GARG-JANARDAN, C., AND G. SALVENDY. "A conceptual framework for knowledge elicitation." Special issue on the 1st AAAI Knowledge Acquisition for Knowledge-Based Systems Workshop, 1986, Part 4, International Journal of Man-Machine Studies, 27:1 (1987).

GASCHNIG, J., P. KLAHR, H. POPLE, E. SHORTLIFFE, AND A. TERRY. "Evaluation of expert systems: Issues and case studies," In F. Hayes-Roth, D. A. Waterman,and D. B. Lenat, eds. Building Expert Systems. Reading, MA: Addison-Wesley Publishing Co., Inc., 1983.

GENGERELLI, J. A. "A method for detecting subgroups in a population and specifying their membership." Journal of Psychology, 5 (1963), pp. 456-468.

GENTNER, D., AND A. COLLINS. "Studies of inference from lack of knowledge." Memory and Cognition, 9:4 (1981), pp. 434-443.

GENTNER, D., AND A. STEVENS, eds. Mental Models. Hillsdale, NJ: Lawrence Erlbaum, 1983.

GITMAN, I., AND M. LEVINE. "An algorithm for detecting unimodal fuzzy sets and its application as a clustering technique." IEEE Transactions on Computing, C-19 (1970), pp. 583-593.

GLENFORD, J., AND MYERS. Software Reliability: Principles and Practices. New York: John Wiley & Sons, 1976.

GLUCK, M. AND J. CORTER "Information, uncertainty, and the utility of categories." Proceedings of the Seventh Annual Conference of the Cognitive Science Society, Irvine, CA, pp. 283-287. Hillsdale, NJ: Erlbaum, 1985.

GOWER, J. "A comparison of some methods of cluster analysis." Biometrics, 23 (1967), pp. 623-628.

GOYAL, S., D. PRERAU, A. LEMMON, A. GUNDERSON, AND R. REINKE. "COMPASS: An expert system for telephone switch maintenance." Expert Systems: The International Journal of Knowledge Engineering, 2:3 (1985), pp. 112-126.

GREEN, C., AND M. KEYES. "Verification and validation of expert systems." Technical Report/white paper, 1986.

GREENO, J.G. "Indefinite goals in well-structured problems." Psychological Review, 83 (1976), pp. 479-491.

GREENO, J.G. "Natures of problem-solving abilities." In W.K. Estes, ed. Handbook of Learning and Cognitive Processes Vol. 5, pp. 239-270. Hillsdale, NJ: Erlbaum, 1978.

GRENANDER, S. "Toward the fully capable AI space mission planner," Aerospace America, August 1985, pp. 44-46.

GROVER, M. D. "A pragmatic knowledge acquisition methodology." TRW Research and Development Report, TRW Defense Systems Group, Redondo Beach, CA, 1982.

HAMMONS, C. B. Personal conversation and notes, 1987.

HARMON, P., AND D. KING. Expert Systems, New York: Wiley Press, 1985.

HARBISON-MOSS, K. "Knowledge-based systems for friend-or-foe identification. Final Report. General Dynamics Grant, University of Texas at Arlington, 1985.

HARBISON-BRIGGS, K., AND L. PETERSON. "Survey of research related to knowledge-based systems for cardiac rehabilitation." Proceedings of the First Annual Artificial Intelligence and Advanced Computing Technology Conference/Ease, Atlantic City, NJ, October 29, 1987.

HART, A. "Fact-finding by interviews." In Knowledge Acquisition for Expert Systems. New York: McGraw-Hill, 1986.

HART, A. Knowledge Acquisition for Expert Systems. New York: McGraw-Hill, 1986.

HAYES-ROTH, F., D. WATERMAN, AND D. LENAT. Building Expert Systems. Reading, MA: Addison-Wesley, 1983.

HAYES-ROTH, F., P. KLAHR, AND D. MOSTOW. "Advice-taking and knowledge refinement: An iterative view of skill acquisition." In J. Anderson, ed. Learning and Cognition, Hillsdale, NJ: Erlbaum, 1980.

HAYES-ROTH, F., P. KLAHR, AND D. MOSTOW. "Knowledge acquisition, knowledge programming, and knowledge refinement." Rand paper R-2540-NSF, Rand Corp., Santa Monica, CA, 1980.

HERROD, R., AND M. SMITH. "The Campbell Soup story: An application of AI technology in the food industry." Texas Instruments Engineering Journal, 3:1 (1986), pp. 16-19.

HINK, R. F., AND D. L. WOODS. "How humans process uncertain knowledge," AI Magazine, 8:3 (1987), pp. 41-53.

HINKLE, D. "The change of personal constructs from the viewpoint of a theory of implications," Doctoral Dissertation, Ohio State University, 1965.

HINTZMAN, D. L. "Articulatory coding in short-term memory." Journal of Verbal Learning and Verbal Behavior, 6 (1967), pp. 312-316.

HINTZMAN, D. L. "Classification and aural coding in short-term memory," Psychonomic Science, 3 (1965), pp. 161-162.

HOFFMAN, R. "The problem of extracting the knowledge of experts from the perspective of experimental psychology." AI Magazine, 8:2 (Summer 1987).

HOFFMAN, R. Notes in review of Chapter 9, 1988.

HOFFMAN, R. "Metaphor in science." In R. P. Honeck & R. R. Hoffman, eds. The Psycholinguistics of Figurative Language, (1980), pp. 393-423, Hillsdale, NJ: Erlbaum.

HOGARTH, R. "Process tracing in clinical judgement." Behavioral Science 19 (1974), p. 298-313.

HOPCROCT, J., AND J. ULLMAN. Formal Languages and Their Relation to Automata. Reading, MA: Addison-Wesley, 1969.

HUSEMAN, R. "The role of the nominal group in small group communication." In R. C. Huseman, D. M. Logue, and D. L. Freshley, eds. Readings in Interpersonal and Organizational Communication 2nd ed. Boston, MA: Hollbrook, 1973.

HYMAN, R. T. Strategic Questioning. Englewood Cliffs, NJ: Prentice-Hall, 1979.

JACOBY, J. The Handbook of Questionnaire Construction, Boston, MA: Ballinger, 1980.

JARDINE, N., AND R. SIBSON. "The construction of hierarchic and non-hierarchic classifications." Computing Journal, 11 (1968), pp. 117-184.

JENSEN, R., AND C. TONIES, eds. Software Engineering. Englewood Cliffs, NJ: Prentice Hall, 1979.

JOHNSON, S. Hierarchical clustering schemes. Psychometrika, 32 (1967), 241-254.

JONES, K., AND D. JACKSON. "Current approaches to classification and clump finding at the Cambridge Language Research Unit." Computing Journal, 1967, pp. 29-37.

KAGAN, J. Psychology: An Introduction 2nd ed. New York: Harcourt Brace Jovanovich, 1972.

KAHN, G. S. "From application shell to knowledge acquisition system," Proceedings of the Tenth International Joint Conference on Artificial Intelligence (IJCAI '87), vol. 1, 1987, pp. 355-358.

KAHN, G. S., E. BREAUX, P. DEKLERK, AND R. JOSEPH. "A mixed-initiative workbench for knowledge acquisition." International Journal of Man-Machine Studies, 27 (1987), pp. 167-179.

KAHN, G., S. NOWLAN, AND J. MCDERMOTT. "MORE: An intelligent knowledge acquisition tool." Proceedings of AAAI '85, 1985, pp. 581-584.

KAHN, G., AND J. MCDERMOTT. "MUD, a drilling fluids consultant." Technical Report, Carnegie-Mellon University, Department of Computer Science, 1985.

KAHN, G., S. NOWLAN, AND J. MCDERMOTT. "A foundation for knowledge acquisition." Proceedings of IEEE Workshop on Principles of Knowledge-based Systems. 1984, Denver, Colorado.

KAHN, R., AND C. CANNELL. The Dynamics of Interviewing. New York: John Wiley & Sons, 1982.

KANAL, L. N., AND J. F. LEMMER. Uncertainty in Artificial Intelligence, Amsterdam: North Holland, 1986.

KEDZIERSKI, B. "Communication and management support in system development environments." Proceedings of the Conference on Human Factors in Computer Systems (ACM). Gaithersburg, MD, March 1982.

KEIDER, S. "Why projects fail." Datamation, (December 1974), pp. 53-55.

KELLY, G. The Psychology of Personal Constructs. New York: Norton, 1955.

KIERAS, D., AND P. POLSON. "An approach to the formal analysis of user complexity." International Journal of Man-Machine Studies, 22 (1985), p. 365-394.

KING, B. "Market and industry factors in stock price behavior." Journal of Business, 39 (1966), pp. 139-190.

KINTSCH, W. The Representation of Meaning in Memory. Hillsdale, NJ: Erlbaum, 1974.

KITTO, C., AND J. BOOSE. Heuristics for expertise transfer: The automatic management of complex knowledge acquisition dialogs. Proceedings of the 1st AAAI Knowledge Acquisition for Knowledge-Based Systems Workshop, Part 2, International Journal of Man-Machine Studies, 26, 2, 1987a.

KITTO, C., AND J. BOOSE. "Selecting knowledge acquisition tools and strategies based on application characteristics." Proceedings of the 2nd AAAI Knowledge Acquisition for Knowledge-Based Systems Workshop, Banff, Canada, October 1987b.

KLATZKY, R. L. Human Memory: Structures and Processes 2nd ed. San Francisco: Freeman, 1980.

KLEIN, G. A. "Applications of analogical reasoning." Metaphor and Symbolic Activity, 2:3 (1987), pp. 201-218.

KLEIN, G. A. "Validity of analogical predictions." Technological Forecasting and Social Change, 30:2 (1986), pp.139-148.

KLINE, P., AND S. DOLLINS. "Problem features that influence the design of expert systems." Proceedings of the American Association for Artificial Intelligence, 1986, pp. 956-962.

KLINKER, G., J. BENTOLILA, S. GENETET, M. GRIMES, AND J. MCDERMOTT. "KNACK-Report-driven knowledge acquisition." Proceedings of the 1st AAAI Knowledge Acquisition for Knowledge-Based Systems Workshop, International Journal of Man-Machine Studies, 1987a.

KLINKER, G., C. BOYD, S. GENETET, AND J. MCDERMOTT. "A KNACK for knowledge acquisition." Proceedings of AAAI '87, 1987b, pp. 488-493.

KLIR, G., AND T. FOLGER. Fuzzy Sets, Uncertainty, and Information. Englewood Cliffs, NJ: Prentice-Hall, 1988.

KNAPP, M. Essentials of Nonverbal Communication. Classifying Nonverbal Behavior. New York: Holt, Rinehart, and Winston, 1980.

KNAPP, M. Nonverbal Communication in Human Interaction. New York: Holt, Rinehart, and Winston, 1978.

KOBALLA, T. "Designing a Likert-type scale to assess attitude toward energy conservation: a 9-step process." Journal of Research in Science Teaching, 21:7 (October 1984), pp. 709-723.

KOLODNER, J. L. Retrieval and organizational strategies in conceptual memory: A computer model. Hillsdale, NJ: Erlbaum, 1984.

KOLODNER, J. L. "Maintaining organization in a dynamic long-term memory." Cognitive Science, 7 (1983), pp. 243-280.

KOLODNER, J., AND C. RIESBECK, eds. Experience, Memory, and Reasoning, Hillsdale, NJ: Erlbaum, 1986.

KOWALIK, J. Knowledge-Based Problem-Solving. Englewood Cliffs, NJ: Prentice Hall, 1986.

KRAEMER, K., AND J. KING. "Computer supported conference rooms: Final report of a state of the art study." Department of Information and Computer Science, University of California, Irvine, December 1983.

KRECH, D., R. CRUTCHFIELD, E. BALLACHEY. Individual in Society. New York: McGraw-Hill, 1962.

KRUSKAL, J., AND M. WISH. "Multidimensional scaling." Sage University Paper series on Quantitative Applications in the Social Sciences, No. 07-011. London: Sage Publications, 1978.

KRUSKAL, J. "Multidimensional scaling and other methods for discovering structure." In Enslein, Ralston, and Wilf, eds. Statistical Methods for Digital Computers. New York: Wiley, 1977.

KUNZ, J., R. FALLAT, D. MCCLUNG, J. OLSON, R. VOTTERI, H. NII, J. AIKINS, L. FAGAN, AND E. FEIGENBAUM. "A physiological rule-based system for interpreting pulmonary function test results." Report HPP-78-19, Heuristic Programming Project, Computer Science Department, Stanford University, Stanford, CA, 1978.

LAKOFF, G., AND M. JOHNSON. Metaphors We Live By. Chicago: University of Chicago Press, 1980.

LANCE, G., AND W. WILLIAMS. "Computer programs for hierarchical polythetic classification." Computing Journal, 9 (1966), pp. 60-64.

LANGLEY, P., AND S. OHLSSON. "Automated cognitive modeling." In Proceedings of the 1984 National Conference on Artificial Intelligence (AAAI). August 1984, pp. 193-197.

LARKIN, J., J. MCDERMOTT, D.P. SIMON, AND H.A. SIMON. "Expert performance in solving physics problems." Science, 20:8 (1980), pp. 1335-1342.

LAZARUS, S. Loud & Clear: A Guide to Effective Communication. New York: AMACOM, 1975.

LECLAIR, S.R. "A multiexpert knowledge system architecture for manufacturing decision analysis." Doctoral dissertation, Arizona State University, May 1985.

LEE, W. Decision Theory and Human Behavior. New York: Wiley, 1971.

LENAT, D., M. PRAKASH, M. SHEPHERD. "CYC: Using common sense knowledge to overcome brittleness and knowledge acquisition bottlenecks." The AI Magazine, 7:5 (Winter 1986), pp. 65-85.

LEWIS, C. "Skill in algebra." In J.R. Anderson, ed. Cognitive Skills and Their Acquisition. Hillsdale, NJ: Erlbaum, 1981.

LIKERT, R. "A technique for the measurement of attitudes." Archives of Psychology, 140 (1932a), pp. 44-53, Columbia University Press.

LIKERT, R. "The method of constructing an attitude scale." In M. Fishbein, ed. Readings in Attitude Theory and Measurement. New York: John Wiley, 1932b.

LINSTONE, H., AND M. TUROFF. The Delphi Method: Techniques and Applications, Reading, MA: Addison-Wesley, 1975.

LUCAS, H. C., JR. The Analysis, Design, and Implementation of Information Systems, 2nd ed. New York: McGraw-Hill, 1981.

LUCAS, H. C., JR., AND R. B. KAPLAN. "A structured programming experiment." Computer Journal, 19 (1974), pp. 136-138.

MACSYMA group. "MACSYMA reference manual," Technical Report, MIT, 1977.

MAGER, R. Preparing Instructional Objectives. Palo Alto, CA: Searon Publishers, 1962.

MANAGO, M., AND Y. KODRATOFF. "Noise and knowledge acquisition." Proceedings of the Tenth International Joint Conference on Artificial Intelligence (IJCAI '87). 1 (1987), pp. 348-354.

MANDLER, G. "Organization and memory." In K.W. Spence and J.T. Spence, eds. The Psychology of Learning and Motivation Vol. 1. New York: Academic Press, 1967.

MARCUS, S., J. MCDERMOTT, AND T. WANG. "Knowledge acquisition for constructive systems." Proceedings of the Ninth International Joint Conference on Artificial Intelligence, 1985, pp. 637-639.

MARTIN, J., AND C. MCCLURE. Structured Techniques for Computing. Englewood Cliffs, N.J.: Prentice-Hall, Inc., 1985.

MARTIN, N. "Software engineering issues in expert system development." SoftPert Systems, Ltd., 1987.

MARTIN, N. Personal correspondence, January, 1988.

MARTIN, N. "Software engineering for expert systems." Notes from seminar presented for the Texas Instruments DSEG AI Lab, December, Dallas, TX, 1986.

MATHESON, J., AND R. HOWARD. "Introduction to decision analysis." In Readings in Decision Analysis, Strategic Decisions Group, 1977.

MAYER, A. K. "The integration of multiple knowledge sources for solving user-posed problems." Knowledge-Based Engineering Systems Research Laboratory, University of Illinois at Champaign/Urbana, April 1987.

MCCARTHY, J. "Some expert systems need common sense." Annals of the New York Academy of Sciences, 426 (1983), pp. 129-137.

MCCARTHY, J. "Programs with common sense." In M. Minsky, ed. Semantic Information Processing, Cambridge, MA: MIT Press, 1968.

MCCLOSKY, M., AND J. SANTEE. "Are semantic memory and episodic memory distinct systems?" Journal of Experimental Psychology: Human Learning and Memory, 7 (1981), pp. 66-71.

MCDERMOTT, J. "R1: A rule-based configurer of computer systems." Artificial Intelligence, 19, (September 1982), pp. 39-88.

MCDERMOTT, J. "R1: The formative years." The AI Magazine, (1981), pp. 21-28.

MCGRAW, K. "Artificial intelligence: The competitive edge in integrated systems development." Texas Instruments Engineering Journal, 3:1 (1986a), pp. 12-16.

MCGRAW, K. "Producing user documentation for expert systems." IEEE Transactions on Professional Communications, 29:4 (1986b), pp. 42-47.

MCGRAW, K. "User documentation for expert systems." In J. Liebowitz and D. DeSalvo, eds. Structured Methodologies for Expert Systems Development. Yourdon Press, 1989 (in press).

MCGRAW, K., AND A. RINER. "Task analysis: Structuring the knowledge acquisition process." Texas Instruments Technical Journal, 4:6, (November/December 1987), pp. 16-21.

MCGRAW, K., AND M. SEALE. "Pilot's Associate Program Knowledge Acquisition Guidelines and Procedures." Internal Texas Instruments AI Lab document, January 1986.

MCGRAW, K. AND M. SEALE. "Structured knowledge acquisition techniques for combat aviation." In <u>Proceedings</u> of NAECON '87, Vol. 4, (May 1987a), pp. 1340-1348, Dayton, Ohio.

MCGRAW, K., AND M. SEALE. "Multiple expert knowledge acquisition methodology: MEKAM." <u>Proceedings</u> of the Third Australian Conference on Applications of Expert Systems, The New South Wales Institute of Technology, Sydney, May 1987b, pp.165-197.

MCGRAW, K., AND M. SEALE. "Knowledge elicitation with multiple experts: considerations and techniques." <u>Artificial Intelligence Review</u>, 2:1 (Jan/Feb 1988).

MCKEITHEN, K., J. REITMAN, H. REUTER, AND S. HIRTLE. "Knowledge organization and skill differences in computer programmers." <u>Cognitive Psychology</u>, 13 (1981), pp. 307-325.

MCNAUGHTON-SMITH, P. "Some statistical and other numerical techniques for classifying individuals." Home Office Research Unit Report No. 6. London: H.M.S.O., 1965.

MCNEILL, D., AND E. LEVY. "Conceptual representations in language activity and gesture." In R. Jarvella and W. Klein, eds. <u>Speech, Place, and Action</u>, New York: John Wiley & Sons, 1982.

MICHALSKI, R., AND R. STEEP. "Automated construction of classifications: Conceptual clustering versus numerical taxonomy." <u>IEEE Transactions on Pattern Analysis and Machine Intelligence</u>, 5 (1983), 396-409.

MICHALSKI, R. "Knowledge acquisition through conceptual clustering. A theoretical framework and algorithm for partitioning data into conjunctive concepts." In <u>International Journal of Policy Analysis and Information Systems</u>, 4:3 (1980), pp. 219-243.

MICHALSKI, R. "Pattern recognition as rule-guided inductive inference." <u>IEEE Transactions on Pattern Analysis and Machine Intelligence</u>, 2:4 (1980), pp. 349-361.

MICHALSKI, R. "A theory and methodology of inductive learning." In R.S. Michalski, J.G. Carbonell, and T. Mitchell, eds. <u>Machine Learning</u>. Palo Alto, CA: Tioga Publishing Co., 1983.

MICHIE, D. "The state of the art in machine learning." In D. Michie, ed. <u>Introductory Readings in Expert Systems</u>. pp. 208-228, 1982.

MILLER, G. A. "The magical number seven, plus or minus two: Some limits on our capacity for processing information." <u>Psychological Review</u>, 63 (1956), pp. 81-97.

MILLER, G. A., E. GALANTER, AND K. PRIBRAM. <u>Plans and the Structure of Behavior</u>, New York: Holt, Rinehart, and Winston, 1960.

MILLER, J. R. Human-computer interaction and intelligent tutoring systems. MCC Technical Report #HI-086-XX. MCC Interface Program, 1986.

MILLER, R. "Development of a taxonomy of human performance: A user-oriented approach." AIR, Silver Springs, MD, 1971.

MILLER, R., H. POPLE, AND J. MYERS. "INTERNIST-I, an experimental computer-based diagnostic consultant for general internal medicine." <u>New England Journal of Medicine</u> (August 1982), pp. 468-476.

MISHKOFF, H. <u>Understanding Artificial Intelligence</u>, Dallas, TX: Texas Instruments Inc., 1985.

MITTAL, S., AND C. DYM. "Knowledge acquisition from multiple experts." <u>The AI Magazine</u>, 7:2 (Summer 1985), pp. 32-37.

MODESITT, K. Notes and discussions on <u>Knowledge Acquisition: Principles and Guidelines</u>. Spring, 1988.

MONINGER, W., AND T. STEWART. "A proposed study of human information processing in weather forecasting." <u>Bulletin of the American Meteorological Association</u>, 1987.

MOORE, E., AND A. AGOGINO. "INFORM: an architecture for expert-directed knowledge acquisition." In <u>Proceedings</u> of the AAAI Knowledge Acquisition for Knowledge-Based Systems Workshop, Banff, Canada, 1986.

MORSH, J. "Job analysis in the United States Air Force." <u>Personal Psychology</u>, 7:17 (1964).

NEEDHAM, R. "Automatic classification in linguistics." <u>The Statistician</u> 17 (1967), pp. 45-54.

NEGOITA, C. V. <u>Expert Systems & Fuzzy Systems</u>. Menlo Park, CA: Benjamin/Cummings Publishing Co., 1985.

NEISER, U. <u>Cognitive Psychology</u>. New York: Appleton-Century-Crofts, 1967.

NEVES, D., AND J. R. ANDERSON. "Compilation: A mechanism for the automitization of cognitive skills." In J. R. Anderson, ed. <u>Cognitive Skills and Their Acquisition</u>, Hillsdale, NJ: Erlbaum, 1981.

NEWELL, A., AND H. SIMON. <u>Human Problem Solving</u>. Englewood Cliffs, N.J.: Prentice Hall, 1972.

NEWELL, A., AND H. A. SIMON. "GPS: A program that simulates human thought." In H. Billing, ed. <u>Lernende Automaten</u>. Munich: R. Oldenbourg, 1961.

NEWELL, A., J. C. SHAW, AND H.A. SIMON. "Elements of a theory of human problem solving." <u>Psychological Review</u>, 65 (1958), pp. 151-166.

NISBETT, R., AND T. WILSON. "Telling more than we can know: Verbal reports on mental processes." <u>Psychological Review</u>, 84 (1977), pp.231-259.

NORTON, R. <u>Communicator Style: Theory, Applications, and Measures</u>. Beverly Hills, CA: Sage Publications, 1983.

NOTT, H. R., S. PETERSON, AND F. NOTT. <u>Communication Processes in the Organization</u>, Dubuque, IO: Kendall/Hunt, 1983.

NUNAMAKER, J., L. APPLEGATE, AND B. KONSYNSKI. <u>Journal of Management Information Systems</u>, 3:4 (1987).

OPPENHEIM, A. <u>Questionnaire Design and Attitude Measurement</u>. New York: Basic Books, 1966.

OSBORN, A. <u>Applied Imagination: Principles and Procedures of Creative Thinking</u>. New York: Scribner's, 1953.

OSGOOD, C., G. SUCI, AND P. TANNEBAUM. <u>The Measurement of Meaning</u>. Urbana: University of Illinois Press, 1957.

PARTRIDGE, D. <u>Artificial Intelligence: Applications in the Future of Software Engineering</u>. New York: Ellis Horwood Limited, 1986.

PATTON, C. "Knowledge engineering: Tapping the experts." <u>Electronic Design</u> May 1985, pp. 93-100.

PEARL, J. "Learning hidden causes from empirical data." <u>Proceedings</u> of the Ninth International Joint Conference on Artificial Intelligence, 1985, pp. 567-572. Los Angeles, CA: Morgan Kaufmann, 1985.

PETERSON, J. L. <u>Petri Net Theory and the Modeling of Systems</u>. Englewood Cliffs, N.J.: Prentice-Hall Inc., 1981.

PETERSON, J. L. "Petri nets." <u>Computer Surveys</u>, 9:3 (September 1977), pp. 223-252.

POLYA, G. How to solve it: A new aspect of mathematical method, 2nd ed. Princeton University Press, 1973.

POPLE, H., JR.. "The formation of composite hypotheses in diagnostic problem solving: An exercise in synthetic reasoning." In Proceedings of IJCAI 5, 1977, pp. 1030-1037.

PRERAU, D. "Selection of an appropriate domain for an expert system," AI Magazine, 6:2 (1985), pp. 26-30.

PRERAU, D. "Knowledge acquisition in the development of a large expert system." AI Magazine, 8:2 (1987), pp. 43-52.

QUADE, E. S. "Principles and procedures of systems analysis." In E.S. Quade and W.I. Boucher, eds. Systems Analysis and Policy Planning: Applications in Defense. New York, N.Y.: Elsevier, 1968.

QUILLIAN, R. "Semantic memory." In M. Minsky, ed., Semantic Processing, Cambridge, MA: MIT Press, 1968.

QUINLAN, J. R. "Learning efficient classification procedures and their applications to chess end-games." In Michalski, R., G. Carbonell, and T. Mitchell, eds. Machine Learning: An Artificial Intelligence Approach . Palo Alto, CA, 1982.

RASMUS, D. W. "Expert input." MacUser, (January 1988), 136-150.

RAUCH-HINDIN, W. Artificial Intelligence in Business, Science, and Industry, Vol. 2. Englewood Cliffs: Prentice-Hall, 1985.

REBOH, R. "Extracting useful advice from conflicting expertise." Proceedings of the eighth international joint conference on artificial intelligence, Karlsruhe, West Germany. August 1983, pp.145-150.

REISS, G. "Knowledge acquisition and the oleophilic advisor." Teknowledge Federal Systems, Inc., Thousand Oaks, CA, 1986.

REITMAN, J. "Skilled perception in GO: Deducing memory structures from interresponse times." Cognitive Psychology, 8 (1976), pp. 336-356.

REITMAN, W. "Heuristic decision procedures, open constraints, and the structure of ill-defined problems." In M.W. Shelley and G.L. Bryan, eds. Human Judgements and Optimality, New York: Wiley, 1964.

RICH, E. Artificial Intelligence. New York: McGraw-Hill, 1983.

RINER, R. "The ranking of job incumbents using CODAP overlap values to compare task inventories developed by a modified Delphi technique and a more traditional method." Unpublished doctoral dissertation, Florida State University, 1982.

ROLANDI, W. G. "Knowledge engineering in practice." AI EXPERT, (December 1986), pp. 58-62.

ROSOVE, P.E. Developing Computer-based Information Systems, New York, N.Y.: John Wiley & Sons, 1967.

ROSS, R. Speech Communication. Englewood Cliffs, N.J.: Prentice-Hall, Inc., 1977.

ROWE, M. "Reflections on wait time: Some methodological questions," Journal of Research in Science Teaching, 11:3 (1974), pp. 263-279.

ROYCE, W. W. "Managing the development of large software systems: concepts and techniques." Proceedings of WESCON, August 1970.

SATTLER, W., AND N. MILLER. Discussion and Conference. Englewood Cliffs, N.J.: Prentice-Hall, 1968.

SCHANK, R. C., AND R. P. ABELSON. Scripts, Plans, Goals, and Understanding: An Inquiry into Human Knowledge Structures, Hillsdale, NJ: Lawrence Erlbaum, 1977.

SCHRODERBECK, P. Management Systems, 2nd ed. New York: John Wiley & Sons, 1971.

SCHVANEVELDT, R. AND F. DURSO. "Generalized semantic networks." Presented at the Meetings of the Psychonomic Society, 1981.

SCHVANEVELDT, R., F. DURSO, AND T. DEARHOLT. "Pathfinder: scaling with network structures." Memorandum in Computer and Cognitive Science, MCCS-85-9, Computing Research Laboratory, New Mexico State University, 1985.

SHANNON, R. "Performance evaluation tests for environmental research." Presented at the 28th International Congress of Aviation and Space Medicine, Montreal, Canada, September, 1980a.

SHANNON, R. "The validity of task analytic information to human performance research in unusual environments." Proceedings of the 24th Annual Meeting of the Human Factors Society, Los Angeles, CA, October 1980b.

SHAPIRO, A.D. Structured Induction in Expert Systems, Turing Institute Press, Reading, MA: Addison-Wesley, 1987.

SHAW, M.E., AND B. GAINES. "Techniques for knowledge acquisition and transfer." Special issue on the 1st AAAI Knowledge Acquisition for Knowledge-Based Systems Workshop, 1986, Part 2, International Journal of Man-Machine Studies, 27:1 (1987).

SHAW, M. E. "A comparison of individuals and small groups in the rational solution of complex problems." American Journal of Psychology, 44 (1932), 491-504.

SHAW, M. E. Recent Advances in Personal Construct Technology. New York: Academic Press, 1981a.

SHAW, M. E. Think Again, Englewood Cliffs, NJ: Prentice Hall, 1981b.

SHAW, M.E. Group Dynamics: The Psychology of Small Group Behavior. New York: McGraw-Hill, 1976.

SHIFFRIN, R. M., AND W. SCHNEIDER. "Controlled and automatic human information processing: II. Perceptual learning, automatic attending, and a general theory." Psychological Review, 84 (1977), pp. 127-190.

SHIFFRIN, R. M. "Short-term store: The basis for a memory system." In I. F. Restle, M. Shriffrin, N. Castella, H. Landman, D. Pesoni, eds. Cognitive Theory. Hillsdale, NJ: Erlbaum, 1975.

SHIKLI, P., C. GREEN, AND M. KEYES. "Verification and validation of expert systems." White paper, 1986.

SCHNEIDERMAN, B. AND R. MAYER. "Syntactic/semantic interactions in programmer behavior: a model and experimental results." International Journal of Computer and Information Sciences, 8:3 (1979), 219-239.

SCHNEIDERMAN, B. Software Psychology: Human Factors in Computers and Information Systems. Boston, MA: Little, Brown, and Co., 1980.

SHORTLIFFE, E. Computer-Based Medical Consultations: MYCIN. New York: Elsevier, 1976.

SHORTLIFFE, E., B. BUCHANAN, AND E. FEIGENBAUM. "Knowledge engineering for medical decision making: A review of computer-based clinical decision aids." Proceedings of the IEEE, 67 (1979), 1207-1224.

SHULMAN, L. S., M. J. LOUPE, AND R. M. PIPER. Studies of the Inquiry Process: Inquiry Patterns of Students in Teacher-Training Programs. East Lansing, MI: Michigan State University Educational Publications Services, 1968.

SIMON, H. A. "Information processing theory of human problem solving." In W.K. Estes, ed. Handbook of Learning and Cognitive Processes, 5 (1978), pp. 271-295.

SLATER, P. "Contrasting correlates of group size." Sociometry, 25 (1958), pp. 129-139.

SLOBODA, J. "Visual perception of musical notation: Registering pitch symbols in memory." Quarterly Journal of Psychology, 28 (1976), pp. 1-16.

SNEATH, P., AND R. SOKAL. Numerical Taxonomy. San Francisco: Freeman, 1973.

SOKAL, R., AND C. MICHENER. "A statistical method for evaluating systematic relationships." University of Kansas Scientific Bulletin, 38 (1958), pp. 1409-1438.

SOLOWAY, E., J. BACHANT AND K. JENSEN. "Assessing the maintainability of XCON-in-RIME: Coping with the problems of a VERY large rule-base." Proceedings of AAAI-87, vol. 2, 1987. Sixth National Conference on Artificial Intelligence, pp. 824-829.

SOMMER, R. Personal Space, p. 65. Englewood Cliffs, NJ: Prentice-Hall, 1969.

SOWA, J. Conceptual Structures: Information Processing in Mind and Machine. Reading, MA: Addison-Wesley, 1984.

ST. JOHANSER, J. "Validating expert systems: problems & solutions in practice." Presented at KBS '86: Online Publications, Pinner, UK, 1986.

STEEP, R. E. "Concepts in conceptual clustering." Proceedings of the Tenth International Joint Conference on Artificial Intelligence, IJCAI '87, 1987, Vol. 1, pp. 211-213.

STEFIK, M., G. FOSTER, D. BOBROW, K. KAHN, S. LANNING, AND L. SUCHMAN. "Beyond the chalkboard: Computer support for collaboration and problem solving in meetings." Communications of the ACM, 30:1 (1987), pp. 32-47.

STEFIK, M., J. AIKINS, R. BLAZAR, J. BENOIT, L. BIRNBAUM, F. HAYES-ROTH, AND E. SACERDOTI. "The organization of expert systems - a tutorial." Artificial Intelligence, 18 (1982), 135-173.

STEINER, I. Group Process and Productivity. New York: Academic Press, 1972.

STERNBERG, R., ed. Human Abilities: An Information Processing Approach. San Francisco, CA: Freeman, 1985.

STEWART, C., AND W. CASH. Interviewing: Principles and Practices, 4th ed. Dubuque, IO: Wm Brown Publishers, 1985.

STEWART. V., AND A. STEWART. Business Applications of Repertory Grids, London: McGraw-Hill, 1981.

SVENSON, O. "Process descriptions of decision making." Organizational Behavior and Human Performance, 23 (1979), 86-112.

SWARTOUT, W. "Explaining and justifying expert consulting programs." Proceedings of the International Joint Conference on Artificial Intelligence, 1981.

THURSTONE, L., AND E. CHAVE. "The measurement of attitude: A psychological method and some experiments with a scale for measuring attitude toward church." Chicago, IL: University of Chicago Press, 1929.

TIEMANN, P. W. ,AND S. MARKLE. "On getting expertise into an expert system." Performance and Instruction Journal, (November 1984), pp. 25-29.

TULVING, E. Elements of Episodic Memory. Oxford: Clarendon Press/Oxford University Press, 1983.

TULVING, E. "Episodic and semantic memory." In E. Tulving and W. Donaldson, eds. Organization of Memory. New York: Academic Press, 1972.

TULVING, E. "Subjective organization in free recall of "unrelated" words." Psychological Review, 5 (1962), pp. 381-391.

TURING, A. "Computing machinery and intelligence." In E. Feigenbaum and J. Feldman, eds. Computers and Thought. New York: McGraw-Hill, 1963.

TUROFF, M. "Delphi conferencing: Computer-based conferencing with anonymity." Technology Forecasting Societal Change, 3 (1972), 159-204.

TVERSKY, A. "Elimination by aspects: A theory of choice." Psychological Review, 79 (1972), pp. 281-299.

VERPLANCK, W. S. "Unaware of where's awareness: Some verbal operants - notates, monents, and notants." In C.W. Eriksen, ed. Behavior and Awaremeness - A Symposium of Research and Interpretation. Durham, NC: Duke University Press, 1962.

WALDRON, V. "Interviewing for knowledge." IEEE Transactions on Professional Communications, PC-29:2 (June, 1986).pp. 31-35

WALDRON, V. Knowledge Engineering Guidebook (draft). Texas Instruments DSEG AI Lab, 1985a.

WALDRON, V. "Process tracing as a means of collecting knowledge for expert systems." Texas Instruments Engineering Journal, 2:6 (1985b), pp.90-93.

WALLACE, A. "Driving to work." In M.E. Sprio, ed. Context and Meaning in Cultural Anthropology. New York: McMillan, 1972.

WALLAS, G. The Art of Thought. New York: Harcourt Brace Jovanovich, 1926.

WALTERS, J. R., AND N. R. NIELSEN. Crafting Knowledge-based Systems. New York: John Wiley and Sons, 1988.

WATERMAN, D., AND M. PETERSON. "Models of legal decision-making." Rand Report R-2717-ICJ. Santa Monica, CA: Rand Corp., 1981.

WAUGH, N. C., AND D.A. NORMAN. "Primary memory." Psychological Review, 72 (1965), 89-104.

WESTPHAL, C. "Using simulation-like methodologies for knowledge base validation." Proceedings of the 3rd International Symposium on Knowledge Engineering (1988), Madrid, Spain.

WICKELGREN, W. A. "Size of rehearsal group and short-term memory." Journal of Experimental Psychology, 68 (1965), 413-419.

WIELINGA, B., AND J. BREUKER. "Interpretation of verbal data for knowledge acquisition." In T. O'Shea, ed. Advances in Artificial Intelligence. New York: Elsevier, 1985.

WILDER, L., AND D. HARVEY. "Overt and covert verbalization in problem solving." Speech Monographs, 38 (1971), pp.171-176.

WISHART, D. "Mode analysis." In A. Cole, ed. Numerical Taxonomy, 282-308. New York: Academic Press, 1969.

WOLVIN, A., AND C. COAKLEY. Listening. Dubuque, IO: Wm. C. Brown, 1982.

WOODSON, W. Human Factors Design Handbook. New York, McGraw-Hill, 1981.

WRIGHTSMAN, L. S., AND K. DEAUX. Social Psychology in the 80's, 3rd ed. Monterey, CA: Brooks/Cole, 1981.

YOUNG, R. M. "Production systems for modelling human cognition." In D. Michie, ed. Expert Systems in a Microelectronic Age, pp. 35-45. Edinburgh: Edinburgh University Press, 1979.

YOURDON, E. Techniques of Program Structure and Design. Englewood Cliffs, NJ: Prentice-Hall, Inc., 1979.

ZADEH, L. "Fuzzy sets." Information and Control, 8 (1965), 338-353.

ZECHMEISTER, E. B., AND S. E. NYBERG. Human Memory: An Introduction to Research and Theory. Monterey, CA: Brooks/Cole, 1982.

ZUNIN, L., AND N. ZUNIN. Contact: The First Four Minutes. Los Angeles, CA: Nash Publishing, 1975.

_____. "United drops Univac contract for $56 million data system." Aviation Week, (February 9, 1970), p. 31.

_____. "Is there really a shortage of knowledge engineers." Knowledge Engineering: The management report on expert systems technology and applications. Richmond Publishing Corp, (July 1986), p. 2.

_____. "Knowledge-based systems: A step-by-step guide to getting started." The Second Artificial Intelligence Satellite Symposium Proceedings and Sourcebook. Texas Instruments, 1985.

_____. Strategic Computing. Defense Advanced Research Projects Agency, Engineering Applications Office, 1400 Wilson Blvd., Arlington, VA, 1983.

_____. (MIL-h-468558b). "Human engineering requirements for military systems, equipment, and facilities," April 5, 1984.

_____. "Campbell soup puts an expert system to work in their kitchens." Artificial Intelligence Letter, 1:5 (November 1985), pp. 1-4. Austin, TX: Texas Instruments.

_____. AutoIntelligence User Manual. Los Angeles, CA: IntelligenceWare, Inc., 1987.

_____. MacSMARTS Instruction Manual, Version 2.0. Cambridge, MA: Cognition Technology Corporation, 1987.

_____. "OPUS II: An intelligent vehicle workstation." Computer Science Center AI Lab Staff Report, Texas Instruments, 1986.

Index

A

Acquisition expert, 71
Alternatives, 215, 220, 228, 233, 235, 236, 237
Analysis, 38, 156, 157
    as component in systems approach, 33, 38, 46
    diagrams for, 167
    functional, 166, 168
    historical perspective in, 160
    in knowledge acquisition, 53, 55, 162
    in systems approach, 46
    information flow, 169
    interaction, 170
    job, 174
    of difficult cases task, 228
    operational sequence, 170
    planning knowledge acquisition sessions from, 179
    procedures for, 163
    task, 171, 173
    techniques for, 166, 309
    templates for, 167
    timeline, 176
    tools for, 309
Aquinas, 293
Aspects, 234
Attending skills, 114
Attitudinal measurement, 316
Attractiveness, 235
Attributes, 228, 234
Audit trail, 307
Auto-Intelligence, 292

B

Baseline, 35
BDM-KAT, 289
Brainstorming, 256

C

Certification, 303
Chunk/chunking, 16, 17
Clarifying, 120
Clumping techniques, 147
Cluster analysis, 145
COBWEB, 147
Cognitive maps, 139
Cognitive models, 141, 332
Communicator style, 113
Computer conferencing and collaboration, 263
Computer-facilitated session, 261
Concept, 13, 14
    analysis, 73, 135
    definition generation, 130, 136
    dictionaries, 136
    generalization, 133
    organization and analysis of, 14, 135-150
    salient features of, 14
    sorting, 143
Concept hierarchy, 14
Conceptual analysis, 55
Conceptual clustering, 145, 147
    techniques for, 146, 147
Conceptual framework, 138
Concurrent verbalization, 216, 219, 337
Configuration management, 35
Conflict resolution, 266
Consensus decision making, 258
Constrained information task, 225
Constrained solution task, 226
Constructs, 149, 287
Controlling the acquisition session environment, 107, 108
Cued recall, 221

D

Debriefing experts, 254
Decision making, 215

extracting knowledge from observing,
221, 230, 233
tracing the, 215
Decision/action analysis, 170, 177
Decision rules, 235
Declarative knowledge, 21-23
Density search, 147
Design, 33, 34, 38, 39, 44, 47
as a component in systems approach, 39, 47
techniques for documenting, 48
Diagram, 167
dataflow, 48
decision/action, 170, 177
Petri net, 49
Directional control, 188
Discrimination tree, 149
Discussions, 220
Documentation, 265
of problems, 121
Domain analysis, 55, 74
Domain expert, 6, 72
access to, 250
customer authorization of, 101
desirable attributes of, 99
expertise of, 161
files, 105, 121
internal selection of, 101
orientation and training for, 88, 102
practicing vs. experienced, 7, 98
problems with, 115-119
rapport with, 106
selection of, 97, 100, 104
Domain conceptualization, 127
techniques for evoking, 129
time expenditures in, 19
Domain familiarization, 62
Dynamic communicative devices, 262

E

ESCIE, 44
ETS, 289
Episodic knowledge, 21-23, 28
Environmental observation, 224

Episodic analogy task, 227
Evaluation, 46, 301, 304, 314
of session effectiveness, 315, 319, 321
Example-based system, 280, 285
Experts (See domain expert)
comparisons to novices, 15
Expert system, 3
examples of, 7
components of, 4
Expertise, 15, 16

F

Feedback, 195, 196
matrix for, 113
Funnel interview sequence, 204
Fuzzy sets, 269

H

Heuristics, 3, 214, 217
Hybrid knowledge acquisition tool, 293

I

Implementation expert, 71
Incremental development, 36, 37
Incremental verification, 307
Induction, 9, 10, 280
Inference engine, 4
Information flow analysis, 166, 169
Information processing theory, 327, 331
Intelligent editing program, 275
Interaction analysis, 170, 310
Interview, 23, 54, 55, 184
beginning the, 193
body of the, 194
closing the, 197
feedback during the, 196
in knowledge acquisition, 23, 187
model for, 186
nonverbal communication in the, 194

V

W